Adventures Abroad

Recent Contributions in Women's Studies

African American Women and Social Action: The Clubwomen and Volunteerism from Jim Crow to the New Deal, 1896–1936
Floris Barnett Cash

The Dress of Women: A Critical Introduction to the Symbolism and Sociology of Clothing
Charlotte Perkins Gilman, Michael R. Hill, and Mary Jo Deegan

Frances Trollope and the Novel of Social Change
Brenda Ayres, editor

Women Among the Inklings: Gender, C. S. Lewis, J. R. R. Tolkein, and Charles Williams
Candice Fredrick and Sam McBride

The Female Body: Perspectives of Latin American Artists
Raysa E. Amador Gómez-Quintero and Mireya Pérez Bustillo

Women of Color: Defining the Issues, Hearing the Voices
Diane Long Hoeveler and Janet K. Boles, editors

The Poverty of Life-Affirming Work: Motherwork, Education, and Social Change
Mechthild U. Hart

The Bleeding of America: Menstruation as Symbolic Economy in Pynchon, Faulkner, and Morrison
Dana Medoro

Negotiating Identities in Women's Lives: English Postcolonial and Contemporary British Novels
Christine Wick Sizemore

Women in Iran: Gender Politics in the Islamic Republic
Hammed Shahidian

Women in Iran: Emerging Voices in the Women's Movement
Hammed Shahidian

Rebecca West: Heroism, Rebellion, and the Female Epic
Bernard Schweizer

ADVENTURES ABROAD

North American Women at German-Speaking
Universities, 1868–1915

Sandra L. Singer

Contributions in Women's Studies, Number 201

Westport, Connecticut
London

Library of Congress Cataloging-in-Publication Data

Singer, Sandra L., 1959–
   Adventures abroad : North American women at German-speaking universities,
  1868–1915 / Sandra L. Singer
    p. cm. — (Contributions in women's studies, 0147–104X; no. 201)
   Includes bibliographical references and index.
   ISBN 0–313–32371–2 (alk. paper)
   1. Foreign study—Europe, German-speaking—History. 2. Women college
students—North America—History. 3. Universities and colleges—Europe,
German-speaking—History. I. Title. II. Series.
LB2378.E85S56   2003
378'.016'082—dc21   2002029896

British Library Cataloguing in Publication Data is available.

Library of Congress Catalog Card Number: 2002029896
ISBN: 0–313–32371–2
ISSN: 0147–104X

First published in 2003

Praeger Publishers, 88 Post Road West, Westport, CT 06881
An imprint of Greenwood Publishing Group, Inc.
www.praeger.com

Printed in the United States of America

The paper used in this book complies with the
Permanent Paper Standard issued by the National
Information Standards Organization (Z39.48–1984).

10 9 8 7 6 5 4 3 2 1

Copyright Acknowledgments

The author and publisher gratefully acknowledge permission to use material from the following:

Cone Archives, Baltimore Museum of Art, Claribel and Etta Cone Letters
Goucher College Archives
Mills College Archives
Mississippi University for Women Archives
Smith College Archives and Sophia Smith Collection
Special Collections Research Center, University of Chicago
Syracuse University Archives
Wellesley College Archives

Archive of the Canton of Zurich (Staatsarchiv des Kantons Zürich)
Humboldt University Archives (Humboldt-Universität zu Berlin Universitätsarchiv)
University Archive of the University of Freiburg (Universitätsarchiv Freiburg)
University Archive of the University of Göttingen (Universitätsarchiv Göttingen)
University Archive of the University of Halle (Universitätsarchiv Halle)
University Archive of the University of Heidelberg (Universitätsarchiv Heidelberg)
University Archive of the University of Leipzig (Universitätsarchiv Leipzig)
University of Vienna Archives (Archiv der Universität Wien)
University Archive of the University of Wroclaw (Universitätsarchiv Wroclaw)

This story is dedicated
to
OHM
and to
my parents
Doris F. Singer and Sidney Singer
and to the city of
Baltimore, Maryland
May the love of learning guide
the "City that Reads"
through this new century

Contents

Acknowledgments

This book would never have been completed without the support of Otto Helmuth Muller, my colleague and dear friend at Alfred University. Otto helped me to create and use the database that is the heart of this research. He brought new sources to my attention, taught me how to do web searches, and helped me with the endless formatting and technical problems I encountered. He also reminded me that I could write about the nineteenth century without adopting the language of that period.

This book was created with the generous and loving assistance of Doris Anne Fornaci Singer, my mother, friend and a graduate of Johns Hopkins. Doris traveled to numerous archives and libraries with me in both Europe and the United States. She accompanied me to Washington, DC and showed me how to use the U.S. Census statistics. Doris spent numerous hours taking notes from documents and photocopying. She proofread many drafts of this book and was always looking for new sources. Her enthusiasm gave me the strength to continue with this project and give these women a voice.

My father, Sidney Singer, also a graduate of Johns Hopkins, read through early drafts of the manuscript. His direct and insightful comments were extremely valuable in formulating key arguments.

Other friends and colleagues who proofread drafts of this manuscript deserve mention: Lucy Hoopes, Elizabeth Gulacsy, Melody Rosa Herr, Martha (Matt) Mueller, Luanne Clarke Crosby and Helen Szymkowiak. I also received valuable advice about the structure of this book from Barbara Holland Cunz at the University of Gießen. I would like to thank the staff of Herrick Library at Alfred University for its support of this project. Special thanks go to Gary Roberts and Carol Tenaglia, who helped fill my endless Interlibrary Loan requests. My colleagues Gary Ostrower and Linda Mitchell gave me valuable advice about publishing.

Then there are the archivists, the keepers of the gates. Time and again they brought hidden treasures to my attention. My thanks go to Thomas Neukom and Dr. O. Sigg at the Staatsarchiv in Zurich; to Dr. Franziska Rogger at the

University of Bern, who has since published a remarkable book on the first women students at Bern; to fellow researchers Elke Lehnert and Heide Reinsch at the Humboldt University of Berlin, who gave me invaluable advice. In addition, I am grateful for the assistance of Dr. W. Schultze, Imbritt Wiese, Austé Wolff and Rita Nather. I would also like to thank Ursula Lochner and her assistant, Constanze Huhn, at the University of Munich; Dagmar Kicherer at the University of Freiburg; Dr. Kurt Mühlberger, Ms. Greiner, Ms. Lössl, Ms. Maisel and their assistants Barbara Windisch and Silke Kittelberger at the University of Vienna. Special thanks go to Birgit Formanski at the University of Bonn. My thanks also go to Dr. Gerald Wiemers, Jens Blecher, Petra Hesse and K. Werner at the University of Leipzig; Dr. Ulrich Hunger, Dr. Haenel, Dr. Klaus Sommer, Angelika Handschuk, Martin Fimpel and the delightful Rena Rembielinski at the University of Göttingen; Dr.Teresa Suleja and Wieslawa Glab at the University of Wroclaw; Dr. Ann Barbara Kersting-Meuleman of the Musik-und Theaterabteilung of the Stadt-und Universitätsbibliothek Frankfurt am Main; Dr. Andreas Odenkirchen at the Bibliothek der Hochschule für Musik und Darstellende Kunst Frankfurt am Main; Dr. Hans Ewald Keßler and Dr. Renger at the University of Heidelberg; Dr. Alfred Wendehorst at the University of Erlangen; Dr. Inge Auerbach, Dr. Günter Hollenberg, Erik Dielmann and Hans-Joachim Baier at the University of Marburg; Irmgard Rebel at the Technische Hochschule in Darmstadt; Dr. Klaus-Peter Hoepke at the University of Karlsruhe (TH); Angelika Wagner-Strahm at the Pädagogische Hochschule Karlsruhe; Dr. Gerrit Walther at the University of Frankfurt; Dr. G. A. Nogler at the University of Zurich; Dr. Wischnath at the University of Tübingen; R. Haasenbruch at the University of Halle-Wittenberg; Marcus Sporn at the University of Würzburg; and Jana Ratajova at Charles University in Prague.

In the United States, I received patient and generous assistance from the following archivists: Sydney Roby at Goucher College; Wilma Slaight and Jean N. Berry at Wellesley College; Lorett Treese at Bryn Mawr College; Nanci A. Young, Margery Sly, Barbara Trippel Simmons and Kathleen Banks Nutter at Smith College; Patricia J. Albright, Susan L. Perry, Peter Carini and Juliana M. Kuipers at Mount Holyoke College; Elaine S. Pike, Charles Henry and Julie Kemper at Vassar; Jane S. Knowles and Karen Kraft at Radcliffe; Frieda Patrick Davison and Pat Matthes at the Mississippi University for Women; Phillip W. Rhodes at Jones Memorial Library in Lynchburg, Virginia; Janice Braun at Mills College; Judith Ann Schiff at Yale; Polly P. Armstrong at Stanford; Jeri L. Vargo at Wells College; Mark Woodhouse at Elmira College; Diane Gallagher at Boston University; Judith Nagata at Hanover College; Megan Sniffin-Marinoff at MIT; Mary M. O'Brien at Syracuse University; Amy Douglas and Phyllis Hawk at the University of Missouri-Columbia; Jay Satterfield, Daniel Meyer and Marge Kolwicz at the University of Chicago; and Emily Connell at the Baltimore Museum of Art.

I would also like to thank the numerous town clerks, local historians and librarians, who helped me to track down information about less-known women. In particular, I would like to mention J. Berry of the Town of Springport, New York; the town clerk of Piermont, New Hampshire; Irene Crippen and Martha Deyoe of Nevada, Iowa; and Martha Sparrow of the Columbus-Lowndes Public Library in Columbus, Mississippi.

This research was funded in part through Alfred University NEH and Summer Research grants.

Introduction

Zurich. November 25, 1882. A young university student from Baltimore, Maryland, wrote home to her mother about the travails of the past week:

> I could not sleep or eat during all this past week. If it had not been for Dr. Culbertson's medical assistance I do not know how I could have gotten through it.... I took everything she gave me, *strychnine*, *valerian*, etc. Today before the examination she made me drink two cups of strong tea without milk and herself walked with me to the door of the University.[1]

Thus fortified, and wearing the same dress she had worn to her graduation from Cornell University, the young American entered her doctoral examination. She emerged several hours later as the first woman to earn a doctoral degree *summa cum laude* at Zurich and the first North American woman to earn a Ph.D. at that university.

Savoring her triumph, her thoughts immediately turned to one of her most treasured personal goals, that of "stirring up women to revolt, waking up girls."[2] She found it "delicious to plant theories of independence" in women.[3] As a well-connected member of the Quaker community, she longed to be made president of the new Quaker women's college, Bryn Mawr, that would soon open its doors. She believed her experience in higher education in both the United States and at several European universities made her singularly qualified to help Bryn Mawr grow into the best women's college there ever was:

> I do not believe any other person whom they could get would have the interests of other women so at heart and, at the same time, would have the requisite training to enable her or him to see what was needed. I have an American Univ. education to begin with, two and a half years at Leipzig, one of the first Universities of Germany, six months at Zurich and the highest honor the University could award my scholarship, all the higher because I came to them from another University and could expect no favor.[4]

This young woman would soon have the chance to realize her dream of further-
ing women's independence and education. Within a few years of graduating from
Zurich, M. Carey Thomas became first dean and then president of Bryn Mawr
College.

The life of M. Carey Thomas provides a classic example of the positive
effects of German-speaking universities on higher education for North American
women. Her experiences at the University of Leipzig contributed to her belief
that graduate research was necessary for keeping the best students and teachers at
Bryn Mawr. Bryn Mawr emerged as the only U.S. women's college at the end
of the nineteenth century with a graduate school.[5] Many Bryn Mawr graduate
students conducting research in the 1890s and early 1900s maintained their connection with German-speaking research facilities. A number of these graduate
students made significant contributions to their fields, especially in the natural
sciences.

The following is a record of hundreds of women, who shared the same thirst
for knowledge, prestige and women's advancement as Thomas, but who were not
always as well-connected or affluent. This is a chapter of history that has never
been thoroughly treated in histories of North American or European women's
education. Yet the North American women who traveled to German-speaking
universities after the American Civil War and up until World War I played a remarkable role in higher education and research on both this continent and in
Europe.

In this study of North American women, only women from the United
States and Canada have been included. Most of the original statistics from
European archives combine women from the entire Western Hemisphere, including South America, Mexico, the United States and Canada in the non-European
category of "American." Only by checking individual records is it possible to
tell the exact country of origin of each student. The educational background and
opportunities of women from the United States and Canada were similar enough
to integrate information for both groups of women. Latin American women
have been excluded, as opportunities in higher education for women in Latin
America during the period of this study differed significantly from those for
women in the United States and Canada. Moreover, according to lists of auditors
and matriculated students, it appears as though only a few dozen Mexican women
at most would be included among the North Americans. That, in comparison
with the records for over 1,350 women from the United States and Canada included in this study, seemed too low a number from which to generalize. Therefore, while it might indeed be worthwhile for future scholars to examine the experiences of Latin American women, the focus here is on the contributions of
American and Canadian women.

Among the American and Canadian women, it is startling to discover how
many influential scholars, researchers and physicians are included in their ranks.
They played a key role in opening up German universities to all women. They
played a leadership role in almost every academic discipline. They were some of
the first women in North America to receive graduate degrees, and they used their
unusual status to help create greater research opportunities for women and girls.
In medicine, they applied the advanced, specialized clinical training they received
in European hospitals to the patients they treated in North America.

It is impossible to do justice to the accomplishments of all women who
played a role in this critical phase in women's higher education. This book is an

attempt to find representative figures from most academic disciplines. A great number of women have been mentioned by name and many biographies have been included in the narrative. This still represents a tiny fraction of the women who took part in this great experiment and adventure in higher education. There is a collective significance to the contributions of these women. Sources of information about these women, however, are dispersed in numerous archives and libraries on two continents. In addition to being a social history, this work also serves as a necessary central reference source to assist further research, for example, about individual women, women in a particular discipline or at a single university. Sadly, despite great effort, many women are still missing from its pages.

The division of chapters by disciplines makes some of the shared experiences of women across the disciplines less evident. This division, however, serves better to explain different opportunities abroad and in careers back home for women in the various disciplines. Still, although each chapter can be read separately, an attempt has been made to bring shared experiences across the disciplines to light.

The chapters on disciplines begin with women in medicine, as the first North American woman to study at a German-speaking university studied medicine at the University of Zurich. The year 1868 marks the arrival of that woman. The chapters continue with women in the humanities, as women in these fields were among the next to earn degrees. Further, the majority of women included in this study were doing coursework in the humanities. Chapters on women in mathematics and the natural sciences as well as in the social sciences and psychology follow. The book concludes with a chapter on women in the fine arts. Very few of the women in this final chapter studied at a German-speaking university. Many were enrolled at conservatories, but many just received private instruction. Their stories are included here, as they faced some of the same sex discrimination encountered by women at the universities. They also contributed significantly to the rich cultural exchange documented in this study.

Among the women included here are those who have been lost to history as well as a Nobel laureate. There are women who received the benefits of European fellowships as well as those women who taught for many years before they could afford to study abroad. Few of the women in this study took a conservative stance on social issues, and many were radicals. Some embraced socialism and pacifism, and lost their jobs for their political beliefs. Almost all of these women shared a passionate, unselfish dedication to improving education for other women, so that their struggles would not have to be repeated by later generations. A number of women achieved a comfortable degree of success, but never tired of working to improve the lot of other women.

This study uses archival records from thirteen German-speaking universities: Berlin, Bonn, Freiburg, Göttingen, Halle, Heidelberg, Leipzig, Marburg, and Munich in Germany; Zurich and Bern in Switzerland; Vienna in Austria; Wroclaw in Poland, as well as additional sources of information about women studying in Frankfurt am Main, Jena and Würzburg. Additional relevant biographical information has been incorporated for women not included in the database, which was derived directly from university archival records of auditors and matriculated students. The database includes records from Berlin, Freiburg, Göttingen, Heidelberg, Leipzig, Marburg, Munich, Vienna, Bern and Zurich. By far, the majority of North American women who studied at German-speaking universities during this period were enrolled at Berlin, particularly between 1895 and 1914. In 1911, the year with the highest enrollment, North American women registered over 120 times at the University of Berlin.

As this study focuses on graduate and professional education, most of the women discussed in detail studied beyond an undergraduate education. Hence, women included in this study belonged to a select group within the already select group of nineteenth-century women who pursued and were able to complete an undergraduate education. The following is a partial breakdown of the institutes where many of the women completed their studies before studying abroad. The majority of the records, however, did not list prior studies[6]: University of Chicago (64)[7]; Bryn Mawr (48)[8]; Wellesley (48)[9]; Smith (45)[10]; University of Michigan (35)[11]; Cornell University (32)[12]; Vassar (28)[13]; Harvard/Radcliffe (28)[14]; Mount Holyoke (21)[15]; Columbia/Barnard (19)[16]; Goucher (Woman's College of Baltimore) (18)[17]; Stanford (17)[18]; Oberlin College and Conservatory of Music (17)[19]; University of Wisconsin (17)[20]; Boston University (16)[21]; University of California (13)[22]; Swarthmore (12)[23]; Syracuse (12)[24]; University of Toronto (11)[25]; and the University of Kansas (10).[26]

Some 657 records included specific information on the father's profession. This category clearly situated these women in the upper and middle classes. Their fathers were: businessmen (164); ministers (74); landowners (52); physicians (50); industrialists (44); lawyers (40); professors (35); independently wealthy (34); bankers (31); farmers (29); military officers (24); teachers (16); engineers (10); contractors (9); real estate agents (9); insurance agents (7); civil servants (6); railroad agents (5); and editors (5). Other occupations with fewer than five men included: rabbi, clockmaker, ship builder, accountant, journalist, artist, musician, mine director and hotel operator.

North American women studying abroad tended to be between 21 and 45 years old. For the women for whom it was possible to calculate their age, more than half were between the ages of 24 and 33. Of these women, 42 percent were between 27 and 30 years old at the time they were studying abroad. A breakdown by age groups yields the following percentages: 18-21 (0.29%); 21-24 (5%); 24-27 (16%); 27-30 (23%); 30-33 (15%); 33-36 (12%); 36-39 (9%); 39-42 (7%); 42-45 (5%); 45-48 (3%); and 48-51 (2%). As a group, they were considerably older and better educated than the Russian women, who made up the largest group of foreign women students at German-speaking universities during the period of this study.

Before examining the work of women within specific disciplines, it is important to consider what women in the various fields shared. What attracted North American women to German-speaking universities? What was the effect of their work on those universities? What were their experiences while abroad, and what contributions did they make upon their return to Canada or the United States?

Chapter One
Studying Abroad

Since the second half of the nineteenth century, much has been published in the popular press and as scholarly research comparing German education to American education. The studies, while numerous and diverse, can be divided into two groups: (1) historical studies that examine the relation between these two educational systems; and (2) those focused on educational policy, which promote a practical application of the best aspects of both systems. The second group was more significant before World War I, when German education exerted its greatest influence on American education. Excellent and innovative research in the first group continues to this day, especially on the following topics: German schools in North America, the Kindergarten Movement, comparisons of teacher training and pedagogy in the secondary schools, and the German influence on American higher education. It is research on this last topic that informs the basis of this study.[1]

Until recently, most research on the German influence on American higher education focused on American male students who embraced the type of training they received in Germany. These students attempted to set up a similar system of university training upon their return to America. Research has examined the leadership role played by male professors and students in establishing some of the most prominent universities, graduate departments and medical schools in America. The classic example is The Johns Hopkins University and its medical school, which were intentionally modeled upon German institutions.

The greatest contributions of German higher education to American universities were the emphasis on creative research, the development of systematic training to enable students to conduct independent research and the role of the teacher-scholar. The best teachers were thought to be those who were active researchers. The chance to work with the best graduate students and in the best research facilities was said to attract the finest scholars to an institution.

More recently, research in the history of education has also included studies of the German influence on higher education for American women. These studies have examined opportunities German institutions offered women for professional training, particularly in the fields of medicine and scientific research. Bryn Mawr, under the guidance of M. Carey Thomas, is also mentioned as the rare American women's college that embraced the German model of combining research with teaching and that established some of the first graduate programs for women in the United States. Still, in an article from 1995, James C. Albisetti, one of the few researchers on this topic, laments the lack of further studies and tries to explain it. He argues that one reason the German influence on higher education for American women is rarely mentioned is that German models of education adopted in this country tended to have a very negative effect on women's education.[2]

In her classic study of women scientists in America, American historian Margaret W. Rossiter argues that the German model accepted by important American graduate schools was in part responsible for the reluctance to allow women into graduate programs: "Since most American graduate schools were patterned after the German universities, which had introduced the Doctor of Philosophy degree in the eighteenth century and had never admitted women, American deans also rejected coeducation at the graduate level for several decades."[3] The former glorious flag-bearers of the Prussian university system emerge as misogynist educators. Henry P. Tappan, the head of the University of Michigan from 1852 to 1863, based his model of the "true" university upon the all-male Prussian universities of his day. Although Albisetti allows that Tappan's opposition to coeducation may not have been derived solely from his admiration of the Prussian universities, Albisetti does argue that the model of those universities certainly contributed to Tappan's strong objection to women being admitted to Michigan. Further, Tappan's objection to coeducation played a critical role in delaying women's admission to that university until 1870.[4] In her history of women at the University of Michigan, Dorothy Gies McGuigan includes a quote from Tappan from 1867, when he was living in self-exile in Europe. The quote captures his negative opinion of women students very clearly: "After [the admission of women] no advancement is possible....The standard of education must now be accomodated to the wants of girls who finish their education at 16–20, very properly, in order to get married, at the very age when young men begin their education."[5]

Albisetti also examines the role played by Andrew D. White, whom he describes as "a less devoted advocate of coeducation and a more serious Germanophile than he has sometimes been portrayed."[6] White did help a few women, including M. Carey Thomas, gain admittance to the University of Leipzig in the late 1870s. But in the 1880s, he delivered many speeches in the United States praising the German universities without mentioning that these universities excluded women. Albisetti quotes from one of White's speeches in which he suggests that the United States should concentrate its resources on a limited number of universities for young men.[7] No mention is made of young American women. This portrait of White does, however, stand in sharp contrast to that in Charlotte Williams Conable's history of coeducation at Cornell. Conable consistently portrays White as a supporter of women's higher education and coeducation. White selected the word "person" instead of "man" for the university charter in 1865 to allow for coeducation as soon as it was politically and economically feasible.[8] White along with Henry Sage drafted a report for Cornell's Board of Trustees in 1872 to reassure skeptics that coeducation had been successful at many other institutions.[9]

The sad tale of the German model being used to exclude women unfolds further with The Johns Hopkins University. Albisetti notes that among the university's first trustees, the leader of the opposition to coeducation was the one trustee who had studied in Germany, Reverdy Johnson. The medical school at Johns Hopkins, which was established in 1893, admitted women on the same terms as men only because that was the condition of the primary donors.[10] At Columbia, opposition to coeducation came primarily from advocates of the German system of education, such as John W. Burgess and Nicholas Murray Butler.[11] Albisetti condemns those who praised the German universities yet failed to mention that women had little or no access to those universities. Moreover, the excellence of the German universities was traced in part to this very exclusion of women and was used as an excuse for a similar exclusion of women in America.

But the tale of the German influence on women's higher education in all of North America does have a positive chapter. For a period of time, the educational opportunities available to North American women at German-speaking universities and medical institutions would benefit these women in their subsequent careers. This study begins in 1868, when the first North American woman enrolled at the University of Zurich, and ends in 1915 to include those few women who remained at German universities even after the outbreak of war caused enrollments of North Americans at European universities to drop abruptly.

Records for close to 1,300 North American women exist at the most popular destinations among German-speaking institutions. While many women who were not included in the official records or who studied in other cities were undoubtedly missed, these records provide answers for the following topics: (1) why these women went abroad to study; (2) why they chose German-speaking universities rather than, for example, the French or English ones; (3) what the nature of their experience abroad was; (4) how their work influenced policies toward women at German-speaking universities; (5) how their educational experience at those universities affected their later lives. This chapter deals in a general fashion with the first four questions, while more specific answers to these questions and the final question are found in the chapters on disciplines.

Answering the first question is not simple, unless one considers the great ambition and desire for knowledge of the first North American women to get a higher education. Even before the American Civil War, women had access to a number of private colleges. Oberlin College in Ohio, a nonsectarian coeducational institution, allowed women to enroll when it first opened in 1833. Alfred University, which began as a Seventh-Day Baptist sectarian institution in 1836, was the second coeducational college in the United States and the first in the state of New York. Ohio Wesleyan admitted women in 1845, Earlham College in 1847 and Antioch in 1853. When it opened in 1855, Eureka College was the first college in Illinois to admit men and women on an equal basis. Prominent women's colleges that opened during this period included: Mount Holyoke Seminary (1837); Mills College (1852); the Oxford (Ohio) Female College (1854); and Elmira Female College (1855). A side effect of the American Civil War was an increase in opportunities for women in higher education. With many men off fighting, some schools were willing to accept women who could pay the tuition fees.[12] Social change brought about by the war also contributed to women's entrance into higher education. The war had forced many women outside of their traditional roles. Women had organized politically. They had

been forced to run households, when men left to fight or did not return from battle. The years immediately following the Civil War showed a rapid increase in
both women's enrollment at colleges as well as the number of colleges open to
women. By 1870 women made up 21 percent of the total undergraduate enrollment in the United States. This percentage increased to 32 percent by 1880 and
to almost 40 percent by 1910.[13]

Vassar (1865) opened the year the Civil War ended, and was followed by
Smith (1871); Wellesley (1875); the Harvard Annex, which would later become
Radcliffe (1879); Bryn Mawr College (1885); Evelyn College in Princeton
(1888); and Barnard College (1889). Private coeducational colleges that admitted
women from the time the college first opened include Bates (1863); Boston University and Swarthmore College(1869); Syracuse University (1870) and Cornell
University (1872).[14] A number of state universities began admitting women in
the 1860s and 1870s as well. In 1855 Iowa founded the first state university to
admit women.[15] It would not be until after the Civil War that most other states
followed: University of Kansas in 1866; Indiana University in 1867; the Uni-
versity of Minnesota in 1868; the University of California in 1869; the Univer-
sity of Michigan[16] and the University of Missouri in 1870; the University of
Illinois, the University of Wisconsin and the University of Nebraska in 1871;
Ohio State in 1873; and the University of Colorado in 1877.[17]

There were fewer universities and colleges in Canada than in the United
States, but women were able to enroll in several institutions of higher education
by the late 1870s and early 1880s. Women began to enroll at Queens College
and University in Kingston, Ontario, in 1876. The University of Manitoba in
Winnipeg, founded in 1877, admitted women. A Woman's Medical College
affiliated with the University of Toronto was founded in 1883. Women were
admitted to the following universities by the late 1890s with some restrictions:
the University of New Brunswick, founded in 1800; Dalhousie College and University in Halifax, Nova Scotia, founded in 1821; the University of Bishop's
College in Lennoxville, Quebec, which was founded in 1843 and allowed women
to attend courses in medicine; McGill College and University in Montreal,
which was founded in 1821 and had separate classes for women at McGill College and Royal Victoria College; the University of Toronto, which was founded
in 1827; Victoria University, founded in 1830, and Trinity University, founded
in 1852. Women's colleges included the Wesleyan Ladies' College at Hamilton,
Ontario, and the Ontario Ladies' College at Whitby, both of which were affiliated with Victoria University.[18]

Since this is only a fraction of the list of institutions of higher education
open to women in the mid- to late-nineteenth century, one might reasonably ask
what drove thousands of North Americans to study in Western Europe. The answer does differ slightly for each discipline, but there were commonalities.
Women might have had access to an undergraduate education, but they were
barred from most of the prestigious graduate schools until the early 1890s.
Women seeking teaching or research positions in higher education found it difficult to get the graduate training required to compete with men in increasingly
professionalized fields. Some professional organizations required research by
members in part to exclude all or most women.[19]

Historians describe three general phases for women's entrance into graduate
schools. During the first phase, from 1868 through 1890, women were allowed
to audit classes, but they were usually barred from earning a doctoral degree.

When prestigious universities such as MIT or Johns Hopkins admitted women, they were careful to keep such cases from becoming precedent and often kept the names of women students from any public documents. [20] This phase did, however, include the first doctoral degrees by women. Rossiter argues that less prestigious or newer institutions did admit women into doctoral programs during this phase. In 1877 Boston University granted the first doctoral degree to a woman in the United States. By 1889, 25 doctoral degrees had been granted to women by ten different institutions, including Syracuse University, the University of Wooster, Smith College, the University of Michigan and Cornell University.[21] The second phase, from 1890 through 1892, saw six major American graduate schools admit women: Yale, Pennsylvania, Columbia, Brown, Stanford and Chicago. The last two universities also admitted women undergraduates at the same time. Columbia and Brown admitted women as graduate students but kept undergraduates at a separate coordinate college.[22] The third phase, from 1893 through 1907, was the period in which the battle for women to enter graduate programs at the most resistant, conservative institutions intensified. Rossiter chooses 1907 as the end date for this period, the year The Johns Hopkins University officially opened enrollment in its graduate school to women.[23]

The majority of women included in this study who earned advanced degrees did so during this last phase. Some consciously sought to put pressure on the most conservative American schools by succeeding in graduate programs abroad.[24] Another motivation for studying abroad was to help open German universities to all women by applying to graduate programs there. Until the end of the nineteenth century, North American women had better access to an undergraduate education than did German women. North American women could use this to the advantage of all women, by entering graduate programs barred to less educated women. Once they proved that women could successfully complete graduate programs, institutions were more likely to let other women prepare for such degrees.

In medicine, women traveled to Europe during all three phases seeking postgraduate training in clinics and hospitals that was almost impossible for them to obtain in North America. In the fine arts, a period of study in Europe was a virtual rite of passage to embark on a career as an artist, teacher or performer in North America. But for women in the humanities and sciences, other options in North America were available. The first North American woman to earn a non-medical doctoral degree at a German-speaking university was M. Carey Thomas, who earned her Ph.D. at Zurich in 1882. By that time, women had already earned doctoral degrees at Boston, Cornell, Syracuse University and the University of Pennsylvania. What Europe offered were degrees with greater prestige and, in some fields, graduate programs of a much higher caliber.[25] Although English universities had actually been the most popular destination for graduate studies through the 1880s, the 1890s showed a shift towards the German universities.[26] Although German universities did not allow women to matriculate in the 1890s, the appeal of these universities was that if a woman could get in as an auditor, she had a chance of receiving the same education as a man. She was not offered separate examinations or a different degree. She was not forced to attend a separate college.

German-speaking universities examined in this study include universities in Austria, Switzerland and Germany. In Germany, the focus is on those universities most frequently mentioned as destinations of North American women: Berlin, Freiburg, Göttingen, Heidelberg, Leipzig, and Munich. Also included are records from other universities that drew a fair number of North American women: Bonn, Dresden, Halle, Jena, Marburg, and Würzburg.[27] In Switzerland, the main destination was Zurich, the first German-speaking university to allow women to matriculate. Records are also included from Bern, the third Swiss university to allow women to matriculate. In Austria, most women went to Vienna.[28] Major German-speaking universities that now lie within the borders of Poland, the Czech Republic or Russia were for the most part excluded from this study, as they did not attract large numbers of North American women. Breslau was included, as the Canadian Mary Violette Dover earned her doctoral degree in chemistry there. The American Eva Johnston, who earned a doctoral degree at Königsberg (Kaliningrad), was also included.[29] The German part of Charles University in Prague was not included, as archival records contain no names of North American women for the period of this study.

When considering German-speaking universities, it is also important to note the great disparity in the dates in which they were first opened to women. In 1864, one year after the French universities of Paris, Bordeaux, Lyon, Marseille and Toulouse were opened to women, the Swiss University of Zurich began allowing women to matriculate as regular students. The University of Bern did not follow until almost ten years later, in 1873, and the University of Basel did not allow women to matriculate until 1890. In Austria, the universities of Vienna, Graz and Innsbruck admitted women in 1897 to the College of Liberal Arts and Sciences and in 1900 to the College of Medicine. In 1900 the first two German universities admitted women, the University of Freiburg and the University of Heidelberg, both in the German state of Baden. Over the next nine years, other German states slowly opened their universities to women, with the last state, Mecklenburg-Schwerin, finally opening its universities to women during the Winter Semester of 1909/10.[30]

Enrollments of North American women at Zurich peaked in the mid-1890s, the same time several German universities began to keep records of women auditors. From the mid-1890s until World War I, the combined numbers of women auditors and matriculated students at Berlin surpass the figures for all other German-speaking universities. In 1911 North American women made up 120 of those registered at the University of Berlin. In 1914 North American women still registered over 80 times. With the outbreak of World War I, enrollment at Berlin came to an abrupt end. A few North American women remained until 1915 at Göttingen and Munich. Although there were no North American women at Zurich in 1914, the records for 1915 and 1916 again include a few women. These were perhaps women seeking to finish their studies in a neutral country without having to leave Europe.

The answer as to why these women chose to attend German-speaking universities varies with each field. In medicine, for example, women rarely studied at universities except in Zurich. For this field, it would be more accurate to say that women came to work at German-speaking hospitals, clinics and laboratories with experts in the fields of treatment and medical research. But why did so many North American women choose such facilities over similar facilities, for example, in France? In fact, the first North American women and men to study medicine in Europe in the nineteenth century headed for Paris. Gradually, however, there was a shift from Paris to German-speaking universities and hospitals, especially those of Zurich, Berlin and Vienna, due in part to the new emphasis on experimental laboratory research at those institutions.[31]

In other fields, women chose Zurich because there was no struggle to matriculate and they were able to work in the laboratories of leading researchers. They chose universities in Germany because professors who were experts in their fields allowed women to study with them and supported their efforts to earn doctoral degrees. In mathematics, for example, the efforts of one professor, Felix Klein, were instrumental in bringing North American women to the University of Göttingen. Georg Elias Müller drew other women to Göttingen, first, by welcoming women, and second, by his novel work in experimental psychology.

In the humanities and social sciences, women sought out professors who had gained a reputation not only in their fields but also for welcoming women to their lectures. At all German-speaking universities, women were drawn to the courses of the great philologists. Many of the first doctoral degrees earned by North American women were in philology or literary criticism. In the 1890s and early 1900s, North American women came to Berlin to study with Georg Simmel, who was emerging as a leader in the new field of sociology. Women also came to Berlin to study music at some of the most prominent conservatories in the world and to perform at the numerous concert halls. Munich attracted many painters and students in the field of art history.

The experiences of North American women at German-speaking universities differed, depending on when and where women studied. In Zurich in the 1860s and 1870s, North American women were among the first to take advantage of the opportunity to earn a doctorate or medical degree there. While these women did work to preserve the reputation of women as scholars, they did not have to fight to earn the right to matriculate. In Austria, most of the North American women did not study at the university, but rather worked with teachers or in medical facilities outside of the university. Only in Germany did North American women play a critical role in opening up the universities to all female students. Women who studied at a German university after 1908 no longer had to fight for the right to matriculate. That right had already been won for them through years of struggle by thousands of women, many of them from North America. Before thousands of women were admitted as regular students, thousands of other women had to prove that women were worthy of this privilege. As auditors and graduate students, women had faced humiliation, rejection, prejudice and hostility from male students, faculty members and administrators to earn the right to study. Women had been forced to sit in corners or on the stage or behind curtains to keep them from having direct contact with male students. Women had been denied entrance to laboratories and lectures. Some were barred from campus and had to take private lessons with professors. Women had been subjected to the whims of individual faculty members and administrators for gaining admittance to lectures and laboratories, or for receiving permission to work toward a doctoral degree.

One woman studying in the mid-1890s gave advice to other American women about the universities most likely to admit auditors. She listed the subject areas in which faculty were most receptive to women students. She then elaborated on certain tricks that increased the likelihood of gaining permission from a professor to attend his courses:

> The consent of the professor being the *sine qua non* of her admission, the woman student's first step is to obtain it, and she

> must do this in person. A proxy or even a letter is almost
> sure to be fatal to her hopes, whereas the application in person
> is almost sure to succeed....Alone with the professor, the affair
> is simple enough. She states her errand in the best German
> she can command....[S]he may even add that she has crossed
> the sea for the sole purpose of hearing him.[32]

Of course, she warned, such flattery did not always meet with success. One professor "cannot be brought to anything like a cordial agreement" and only guarantees that if a woman attends his lectures, "'no one will interfere'" with her.

In an article from 1896, another woman was extremely encouraging: "American women are received everywhere in Germany and Switzerland with courtesy and consideration."[33] But she also gave sobering advice. The best way to study at a German university was to have already completed an undergraduate education. Moreover, a woman needed two letters of recommendation. One from someone who had studied at that German university "at some time not too remote," and another for a character reference, "if possible, from her pastor."[34] In addition to the above advice, she gave a detailed account of the doctoral examination and of minimum expenses. She urged women to study at several German universities like the men did: "I would advise a young woman to spend her student life abroad, in *several* universities, hearing the greatest men at each one; this has long been the custom of men students."[35]

A student who studied philosophy at Berlin and Freiburg from 1898 to 1900 was equally encouraging: "the writer of this little article was during the whole of her stay happy – nay, glückselig – and that in the very face of continual illnesses."[36] She delighted in being able to study philosophy at Freiburg in a "quaint old building which had been built for a Jesuit college."[37] She also attributed a good measure of her happiness to studying at a smaller university. Berlin had been too large and impersonal. Students suffered from a sense of isolation. Moreover, there seemed to be more paperwork and more formalities at the bigger universities. The student complained about the registration process at Berlin for auditors: "for how many big books does one have to write one's exact age and most of one's family tree!"[38] She encouraged new students to start off at a smaller university, where there was "the constant opportunity offered for coming into personal touch with the professors."[39] The student made light of the formal visits required to receive permission from each professor to attend lectures: "One has only to acquit oneself of the duty of a formal call upon each professor to attend his lectures, and to make friends with the big, good-humored Pedell, who asks one innumerable kindly, curious questions."[40]

Another American hoping to study philosophy at Freiburg during the same period wrote the following of her first experience asking a professor for permission to study with him:

> On the occasion of my introductory call he was seated in his
> drawing-room with a preternaturally grave expression, almost a
> suspicious one, and he received my explanation of the object
> of my visit in deep and distrustful silence. Only very gradu-
> ally, and not before it had filled me with discomfort and some
> confusion, did this mental attitude give way to a realization on
> his part of the necessity of dealing fairly with a somewhat
> novel situation.[41]

After careful consideration, the professor agreed to take a chance on the "female stranger" and dismissed her with a "hearty human handshake." But this student and the writers of the previous articles were more fortunate than those women dismissed out of hand.

In 1897 a woman from New York seeking to audit classes at Munich was denied admission after she had irritated the vice-chancellor of the university, who attributed her persistence in seeking admission to childish obstinacy rather than a true inner calling. Before seeking admisson to Munich, she had studied literature and art in Dusseldorf, Paris and Florence.[42]

Less than three months earlier, another American woman hoping to study philology had been accepted at Munich as an auditor. This woman, Anna Maude Bowen, had the support of faculty in her field at both Munich and Leipzig, but she had also completed most of the work on her doctoral degree before arriving in Germany and was not attempting to earn a German degree. Bowen attributed her acceptance at Munich to invaluable advice she had received from a professor at Munich, who gave her very specific directions about how to make a successful application. "He sent me an explicit reply, giving me all necessary directions as to how to address myself to the University, even suggesting that I use Latin script instead of German in my application, since I wrote Latin with a firmer hand!"[43] At Leipzig, Bowen had been received with some hesitancy. One professor agreed to allow her to attend his seminar, a rare privilege indeed for women students, but only if all male students in the seminar agreed. The male students welcomed her, and Bowen became the first woman to attend that professor's seminar. With the permission of the professor, Bowen became the first woman to gain admittance to the departmental library. The professor also made arrangements for her to be able to check out books from the university and city libraries. Another professor taught a course just for her, when no other students signed up. At Munich Bowen met with similar generosity. She was allowed to study in a room reserved for the faculty at the university library. One professor assigned two students to escort her to a seat in the lecture hall reserved for her. Other professors escorted her through the hallways. But Bowen found such precautions unnecessary, as she was always treated politely by the German male students. But a male American student attending the University of Leipzig a few years earlier had a different tale to tell.

While the male students were "not often rude" to the women in public, in private the American women "were subject to not a little criticism." One American woman was given the name of "Walküre." Although the women tried to enter the lecture halls a little early or a little late to avoid the crowd of other students, they could not always avoid the taunts whispered at them as they passed, such as, "'Da kommt die Walküre.'" The male student did note, however, that as the year progressed, the women attracted less and less attention. The writer praised the contributions of these first American women to higher education in both America and Germany: "The American lady students deserve great credit for their persistence and courage in this particular work; they are not only 'pioneers' for the cause of higher education of women in this country, but also benefactors of the ever-increasing number of German women who are, as yet modestly, demanding greater advantages for education."[44]

Even after women were allowed to matriculate at a university, a woman's struggles were not necessarily over. As one woman from Grinnell College wrote of her experiences at Heidelberg in 1904 and 1905:

Though the university is open to women, each professor may bar or admit them as he chooses, and they tell the true story of one woman, who sat in the lecture room awaiting the professor's arrival. He finally came, greeted with the usual tramping of the students, and began his lecture. Catching sight of the woman he stopped short in the middle of a sentence, walked down to her, offered his arm and escorted her down the aisle to the door amid the cheers of the young men. Another professor on entering a room filled with men and woman [sic] addressed his audience as, "Ladies and Gentlemen," but was prevented from saying more by the hissing and the scraping of feet until he changed his recognition to "Gentlemen and Ladies."[45]

In Bern, where women had been allowed to matriculate since 1873, a woman described a class in 1900, where the professor made the six women in the lecture hall get up and sit on the right side of the room with an aisle between them and the male students. The story ends with a moving demonstration of solidarity between the male and female students. Immediately, a male student got up and sat down between two of the women. He explained that he preferred it much better on that side. The professor laughed and allowed the male student to remain where he was.[46]

A professor in a subject area critical to her studies might refuse to allow a student to take exams or might refuse to admit her to his lectures or laboratories. Sometimes a professor or administrator delayed so long, a woman had to decide whether to forget about a course or risk attending without permission. As one bold, irreverent spirit, May Lansfield Keller, wrote to her father from Heidelberg in May 1901:

Well, to begin that precious old *Dekan* [dean] with the manners of a pig, fooled around over our diplomas until ten days after the opening of the semester, and several days after lectures had begun. On Monday I got desperate, announced my intention of going to lectures the same as if I had permission, and see what would happen. Johnetta was scared to death at this boldness, and wouldn't go, waiting at home anxiously to find out what happened to me. I went to the university at 9 o'clock, was the only woman visible in a perfect swarm of students, attended my class in which there are about 60 men and four women, and returned triumphant. This so encouraged me that I paid a visit to a prof. on my own authority, told my tale of woe about the *Dekan* and received permission to take his seminar, and also his lecture work....Well, after my experiences Johnetta plucked up courage and we went together to see more profs.[47]

On the other hand, a woman might have the full support of the faculty in a certain department, but might face an administration that refused to grant degrees to women. Some women worked months or years for graduate degrees, only to be told in the end that the university would not grant a woman a doctoral degree. Time and again, women had to travel from university to university hoping to find the support needed to complete their studies. The University of Leipzig was one of the first German universities to admit women auditors, but decades would pass before it would grant a degree to a woman. M. Carey Thomas had to leave

Leipzig and complete her degree in Zurich. Twelve years later, Ida Hyde gave up her efforts to earn a medical degree at Strasbourg and completed her doctoral degree at Heidelberg. In 1900, eighteen years after M. Carey Thomas earned her degree, the American Lucinde Pearl Boggs finally abandoned her attempt to become the first woman to earn a doctoral degree at Jena and completed her degree at Halle (1901).[48]

In complete contrast to the difficulties mentioned above, there were also cases of women earning doctoral degrees from universities without ever having attended classes there. In December 1900 Erla Hittle from Richmond, Indiana, completed her doctoral degree at the University of Heidelberg apparently without even auditing a class there.[49] Such cases certainly warrent further attention. There were also cases of women who had their doctoral thesis rejected by one university and accepted by another university. Such was the case of Rowena Morse at Jena.[50] Apparently guidelines were not uniform at all universities.

North Americans were among the first women graduate students and auditors to be admitted to the German universities as exceptions. Professors and administrators were sometimes willing to make exceptions for foreign women that they would not make for European women. Alice Hamilton wrote that she and her sister Edith were told that the only reason women wanted to study was "to prepare themselves for subversive political activity; if foreign governments wished to run that risk, all right, but the German government had too much sense."[51] Foreign women would also not compete in the domestic job market. Moreover, unlike women educated solely in Germany, Austria or Switzerland, women in North America had easier access to institutes for secondary and higher education to prepare for university study.

In Germany, the role North American women played in opening up the universities to all female students was both direct and indirect. Indirectly, they influenced the outcome in German universities by being part of successful models for higher education in North America. For example, the level of scholarship and achievement at the American women's colleges impressed German professors.[52] When Berthold Delbrück (1842-1922), a renowned German philologist, visited the University of Chicago in the early 1900s with four other German educators to closely study the life of women there, he supposedly took in the spectacle of 1,360 women and said: "'I have found these American women wonderfully brilliant and as wonderfully beautiful.'"[53]

North American women played a direct role in opening German universities to the women of Western Europe by being part of the opening wedge, that is, the exceptional cases that eventually became the rule. Albisetti describes the case of one American woman, the mathematician Ruth Gentry, who had a significant impact on university policies toward women in Germany. Gentry applied to audit courses and pursue a graduate degree at the University of Heidelberg in 1891. A German student, Marie Gernet (1860-1925), had also applied for that semester. According to Albisetti, a few days after the applications of both women were rejected, members of the mathematics and sciences faculty proposed that women should be allowed to study with the approval of individual professors. After the university senate rejected the proposal, the Ministry of Education for the state of Baden supported the initial proposal and agreed to allow women to audit courses in the mathematics and sciences faculty.[54] Although Gentry did not end up studying at Heidelberg, Marie Gernet did and in 1895 became the second woman to complete a doctoral degree from Heidelberg.[55] The American student Ida Hyde would also benefit from the proposal inspired by the applications of Gentry and Gernet. In 1894, after Hyde was refused permission to pursue a degree at the University of Strasbourg, she applied to Heidelberg, where Otto Bütschli, a supporter of the proposal of 1891, agreed to direct her doctorate.[56] Hyde's own application in 1894 sparked another round of debate between the regional parliament of Baden and the university faculty about higher education for women. The debate resulted in the Department of Justice, Culture, and Education for Baden ruling in favor of the request of the faculty fighting to let women pursue doctoral degrees.[57]

Ruth Gentry was also in part responsible for a survey conducted in the spring of 1892 by the Prussian Minister of Education asking all Prussian university faculties about the appropriateness of changing matriculation policies for women. This was the first such survey conducted by the Prussian government. While the response was overwhelmingly against allowing women to matriculate, there were some positive responses.[58] A few years later in Prussia, the success of two women, one British and one American, at the University of Göttingen was the direct cause of a new regulation in March 1895, liberalizing admission policies for all women. The new regulation stated that if the government found the credentials of any student recommended by the faculty of a university satisfactory, the matter of sex should not debar her from the privilege of study, or from receiving the degree for which she was qualified.[59]

In an 1899 handbook for American women listing the entrance requirements at numerous foreign universities, the section on the German universities noted that the positive example of the first women at those universities had already done much to destroy the prejudice against women. American women were cautioned not to harm that reputation of seriousness of purpose and ability by their behavior. Every individual woman was warned that her behavior could affect how all women were received at those universities:

> The seriousness of purpose and the ability of individual women who have studied in Germany has, it is believed, done much toward destroying the prejudice against women students in the minds of the professors under whom they have worked. Each woman who applies for permission to attend lectures should bear in mind the great responsibility she incurs in thus becoming, as it were, a test case, by which other similar cases in the future will be judged. If she is insufficiently prepared or lacking in seriousness of purpose in her work she cannot fail to do harm to the cause of women's education in Germany. Women students should also bear in mind that the conditions of German life are very different from the conditions of American life, and that any failure to observe the established customs of the people among whom they are living and whose hospitality they are enjoying, is likely to bring women students as a class into discredit.[60]

In 1896 the Association of Collegiate Alumnae (ACA) established a Council for Foreign University Work to screen American women applying to German universities and make recommendations directly to the German universities. The Council was established to keep out those women "thoroughly unfitted to profit by the difficult lectures given at the German universities" but who still wished to listen to such lectures "for some freakish reason or other." If a woman could demonstrate that she had adequate training to study in Germany, she received an official letter of recommendation from the Council. It was thought this service would be welcomed by German professors, who often did not know the difference between "Walla Walla University and a university of a more recognized standing." But instead, few women used the service and the German government improved the application process through its consular offices.[61]

The American Anna Maude Bowen, studying at Munich in 1897, was adamant about recommending study in Germany only to those women who had already completed a doctoral degree in the United States. She thought "[e]very girl who comes to the university out of mere curiosity injures the real woman student just so much." The ill-prepared student did serious harm to the case of all women students. German study was best suited for the "earnest and mature woman student, who comes not to flirt and not merely to learn the language."[62]

While doing a grave injustice to the achievements of German women, a 1902 article in *The Nation,* describing positive changes for women in German higher education since the 1880s, reminded the reader that "[i]t must not be forgotten that the presence of hundreds, if not thousands, of cultured and attractive American women has helped to instill into German minds a higher ideal for womankind than that typified by the Hausfrau."[63] Two years later an article on the same topic in the *New York Times* noted that male students at German universities had become more civil to the female students due "in large measure to the influence of American women students."[64]

In a 1906 lecture at Wellesley College, the German psychologist Hugo Münsterberg praised American women for helping to open German universities for German women. The college reporter quotes him as follows:

> As to the admission of German women into the German Universities, he said that this has been largely effected through American women. Until rather recent years, women in Germany have not shared equal university privileges with men, but since the American women have studied in German Universities, and shown the ability of women to do graduate work, the conditions have been materially altered.[65]

A 1915 article in *The Nation* celebrating the fiftieth anniversary of Vassar argued that one of the most important accomplishments of the women's colleges had been their effect on German universities:

> Not the least important aspect of the influence which has come from the founding of Vassar College, and its successors at Northampton, Wellesley, Bryn Mawr, and elsewhere, is that which has been exercised on the other side of the Atlantic....the opening of the German universities to women was largely the result of the desire of American women to avail themselves of the opportunities of those great institutions. The kindness, the liberalism, or the appreciation of special worth, shown by one or another of the great German professors, was, as a rule, the entering wedge; later what had been a special exception became the rule.[66]

While a relatively small number of North Americans did indeed play a significant part in opening German universities to all women, there were a number of other key players in this struggle, including progressive women and girls of Germany and other foreign students. The support of government and university administration officials as well as the advocacy of university faculty members also played key roles.

In 1891 the Ministry of Education for Baden decreed that girls who had prepared privately could take the *Abitur*, the German university entrance examination. At that time, Germany had no private or public schools to prepare girls for this examination. In the next two years, however, private courses were established in Berlin, Leipzig and Karlsruhe, which enabled girls to prepare for the *Abitur*. When the first girls in Prussia and Saxony passed the *Abitur*, those states continued to bar women from matriculating at the universities. But when the first girls from the school in Karlsruhe passed the *Abitur* in 1899, they had the support of Wilhelm Nokk, minister of education for Baden. As early as 1897, he had supported the right of women who passed the *Abitur* to matriculate at the universities of Baden with the same rights as men. Under Nokk's leadership, Baden, home to the University of Heidelberg and University of Freiburg, became the first German state to rule in favor of a woman's right to matriculate.[67] Moreover, once Baden ruled in favor of women, there was more pressure on other German states to admit women to their universities. The other German states acted out of a combination of fear of losing their competitive edge to more progressive universities and a sense of fairness.[68] Other German states, in particular Prussia, did not bow easily to this pressure, and the process of opening up all German universities extended over the next nine years.

The process of having females be allowed to take the *Abitur* and then to matriculate involved years of struggle on the part of German women's organizations, such as the German Women's Association, the Women's Welfare Association, the Women's Reform Association and the Women Teachers' Association. These organizations supported women's secondary and higher education through petition campaigns, appeals to legislators, scholarships and by establishing schools. German women also served as pioneers in the cause by studying abroad and then returning home to establish careers. The classic example is that of the first two German women to open a medical practice in Germany, Emilie Lehmus (1841-1932) and Franziska Tiburtius (1843-1927). Both women had received their medical degrees from the University of Zurich, Lehmus in 1875 and Tiburtius in 1876. Although they were denied certification in Germany, they were still able to practice medicine and opened a clinic for women in a working-class neighborhood of Berlin.[69]

German women were also among the first women to receive permission to audit classes and earn doctoral degrees at German universities. The first woman to earn a doctoral degree at the University of Heidelberg was Käthe Windscheid, who earned her degree in 1894. Marie Gernet followed her in 1895. In 1898 Hildegard Ziegler (Wegscheider) became the first woman to earn a doctoral degree at the University of Halle. In 1899 Else Neumann, a physics student, became the first woman to earn a doctoral degree at the University of Berlin. In 1900 Clara Immerwahr, a student in chemistry, became the first woman to earn a doctoral degree at the University of Breslau. In 1901 Mathilde Wagner became the first woman in Germany to pass the state medical board and the first woman to earn a medical degree at the University of Freiburg. That same year Marie Gleiss became the first woman to earn a medical degree at the University of Strasbourg. In 1903 Hermine Edenhuizen and Frida Busch became the first women to earn doctoral degrees (in medicine) at the University of Bonn. That same year, Margarete Schüler became the first woman to earn a doctoral degree (in medicine) at the

University of Munich. The first woman in Germany to earn a doctoral degree in law was Edith Schmitt, who earned her degree in 1908 at the University of Heidelberg.[70]

In addition to the significant accomplishments of German women, breakthroughs at German universities were due in part to the efforts of the largest group of foreign women at these universities, the Russian women. At Heidelberg, two Russians, the mathematician Sofia Kovalevskaia and the chemist Iulia Lermontova, became the first women to audit classes in 1869. Both women also managed to obtain private instruction at the University of Berlin with leading scholars in their fields. In 1874 both women earned doctoral degrees at Göttingen. Kovalevskaia became the first woman in modern times to earn a doctoral degree in mathematics, and Lermontova became the first woman in the world to earn a doctoral degree in chemistry. The first generation of auditors at Leipzig (1873-1880) also included ten Russians. In 1873 the Russian Johanna Evreinova earned a law degree at Leipzig.[71] The Russian Nadezhda Suslova was the first woman to be an officially matriculated student at Zurich. In 1867 she became the first woman to earn a medical degree at Zurich.[72]

There are relatively few firsts that can be attributed to North American women. There was M. Carey Thomas's triumph at Zurich. In 1895 the American Elizabeth E. Bickford and the Dutch student Constance Gelderblom became the first women to earn doctoral degrees at the University of Freiburg.[73] In 1904 Dixie Lee Bryant became the first woman to earn a doctoral degree from the University of Erlangen.[74] That same year Rowena Morse became the first woman to earn a doctoral degree from the University of Jena.[75] Their real firsts were in relationship to other North American women. For example, in 1887 Rachel Lloyd apparently became the first American woman to earn a doctoral degree in chemistry. In 1895 Margaret Maltby became the first American woman to earn a doctoral degree from a German university. One year later Mary Frances Winston became the first American woman to earn a doctoral degree in mathematics from a foreign university.[76]

The accomplishments of North American women who studied at German-speaking institutes of higher education were remarkable and significant. To some degree, however, these accomplishments are praised at the expense of those of the Russians. For during much of the period of this study, North Americans were the "good foreigners" and Russians were not so welcome. The accomplishments of North Americans supported efforts to open universities to women. In contrast, the amazing accomplishments of Russians, despite political turmoil at home and hostility abroad served frequently to inspire threats to close German-speaking universities to all women. Why was there this difference in attitude towards the two groups of students?

There were three basic reasons for the different reception of these two groups of students. First, there never were very many North Americans. In contrast, enrollments of Russian women exceeded those of German, Swiss and Austrian women at times. Second, anti-Semitism played a part in the hostility towards the Russians, and very few of the North Americans were Jewish. Even at Berlin, where the population of Jewish students of all nationalities was relatively high, there were few North American Jews. Although the percentage of Jews among the Russian students fluctuated with time, it was always higher than the percentage among the North Americans. The third charge against the Russians was their political radicalism. North Americans tended not to be politically active, at least while studying abroad. Although the same could be said for the majority of Russian students, a highly visible minority reinforced the stereotype of the dangerous Russian anarchist.

To address the first issue, at Berlin, where most of the women in this study were enrolled, the percentage of North American women among all women auditors was strikingly high the first four semesters for which there are records for auditors: Winter Semester 1895/96 (46.8%); Summer Semester 1896 (40%); Winter Semester 1896/97 (36.7%); and Summer Semester 1897 (21.6%).   By Winter Semester 1897/98, however, the percentage of North American auditors dropped to 12.4. From that semester until Summer Semester of 1914, the percentage of North Americans of all women auditors and matriculated students never exceeded 14 percent and remained below 10 percent for twenty-seven out of the thirty-three semesters.

At Munich, North American women did make up 28 percent of the auditors during Winter Semester 1900/01, but that figure was an anomaly. In fact, from Summer Semester 1906 through Summer Semester 1914, North Americans never made up more than 1 percent of the total women enrolled as both auditors and matriculated students.

Enrollment percentages were significantly higher at Göttingen. As in Berlin, North Americans made up a large percentage of the first women auditors. In Göttingen, however, the higher percentages continued for the first twelve semesters for which there are records for auditors (Winter Semester 1895/96 to Summer Semester 1901) and ranged between 47.6 and 21.6 percent. From Summer Semester 1901 to Winter Semester 1901/02, the percentage of North American auditors dropped from 23 to 6.3 percent and never rose again above 10 percent.

While North Americans did make up a high percentage of the first women auditors, the percentage of North Americans dropped off fairly rapidly and after 1901 remained fairly consistently below 10 percent. In contrast, enrollment percentages for Russian women continued to grow through the first decade of the twentieth century. Between the Winter Semester of 1864/65 and the Summer Semester of 1872, there were 203 women enrolled at Zurich either as auditors or matriculated students. Of those students, 148 were Russian and only six were Americans.[77] In 1873, the height of the first wave of Russian students at Zurich, Russian women made up about 85 percent of the women studying at the university and the technical college.[78] By 1883 there had been 169 Russian women at Zurich and only thirty-four women from the United States; 119 of the Russian women had studied medicine, the field in which there was the most competition for laboratory space among students. During the same period, only twenty-eight American women had studied medicine.[79] Between 1882 and 1913, Russian women made up 75 percent of all foreign women studying at Swiss universities. During that same period of time, they comprised 62 percent of all women studying at Swiss universities. German women made up only 9 percent of the female student body, and Swiss women only 5 percent.[80]

Russian women tended to study medicine. Between 1882 and 1913, 74 percent of Russian women at Swiss universities studied medicine. This is in contrast to 36 percent of the rest of the women students. The majority of the other women, 60 percent, were studying in the humanities and sciences.[81] During the Summer Semester of 1906, Russian women made up 75.7 percent of the women studying medicine in Berlin.[82] Of the 191 women who earned medical degrees in

Berlin before 1918, 60 percent were Russian.[83] During that same period of time, it appears that no North American woman earned a medical degree in Berlin.

These few statistics help to illustrate the huge discrepancy between the numbers of Russian and North American women at German-speaking universities with some of the largest populations of foreign students. But differences in attitudes towards the North Americans and Russians are not explained by enrollment figures alone. An important key to understanding these differences lies in the reasons that drove so many Russian women to come to Western Europe in the first place and the role played by anti-Semitism.

Secondary schools for girls were established in Russia in 1858. Most of the students belonged to wealthy families and trained to become teachers. Some 77 percent of these students were Russian Orthodox, and only 13 percent were Jewish. Sometime between 1858 and 1860, the first women began to audit courses at the universities. Most of these first auditors came for medical classes.[84] Starting in 1861, the year of the emancipation of the serfs, there was an increasing number of student protests. Finally, in 1863, the universities were closed. Although few women had actually been involved in the protests, all women were temporarily barred from the universities. In 1868 a limited number of higher education courses was again available to women. But the years between 1863 and 1868 brought the first Russian women to Zurich. Even when courses for midwives became available to women in Russia, large numbers of women continued to seek opportunities abroad to be able to receive the same medical training as men.

Enrollment numbers for Russian women at Zurich continued to increase until 1873. Then, in June 1873, the Russian government published a ban, or *ukase,* ordering Russian women studying at Zurich to return home. If a student did not return, she risked being barred from any examination, educational institution or job controlled by the government should she ever decide to go back to Russia.[85] Further, any degree earned by a Russian woman after January 1, 1874, would not be recognized in Russia. The ban was an attempt to break up organizing among anarchists and socialists, but it singled out women. At Zurich, Russian women had enjoyed unusual social and educational freedom. The Russian government claimed this freedom had been abused. Russian women were even accused of studying medicine so that they could give each other abortions. This was unlikely, as most of the students affected had not yet had training in gynecology.[86]

The ban forced many women to abandon rare educational opportunities. According to historian Thomas Neville Bonner, about one-fourth of the Russian women enrolled in the medical school at Zurich at the time of the *ukase* completed their medical degrees. The majority of women returned to Russia to practice medicine in some capacity. After serving as physicians in the Russo-Turkish War, these women were allowed to give themselves the title of "doctor." A number of these students came into direct conflict with the Russian government and met a less happy end. Bonner writes, that "[a]t least 22 of the former Zurich students were arrested and sentenced to prison, while others remained under close state supervision. Three died in prison, 4 committed suicide."[87] But some of the Russian women chose not to return to Russia. For example, some transferred to the University of Bern, which began to admit women that year in part because of the numerous applications from Russian women.

Back in the United States, progressive thinkers condemned the *ukase* as a great injustice. In her history of American women, Phebe A. Hanaford,[88] a liberal minister, concluded her book with praise of the maligned Russian women at Zurich: "These quick-minded girls get their eyes open to the enormities of Russian despotism, and their generous impulses are stirred in opposition. As to the charges of immorality, we do not believe a word of them. There never was an opponent of slavery or of tyranny who did not have to bear such odium."[89]

But those North American women studying side by side with Russian women were less generous and worked with other students to limit the enrollment of Russian women. Administrations hoping to limit the number of foreign students tried several tactics, such as raising tuition for foreign students or allowing natives to register before foreigners. A more successful method for reducing the number of foreign students proved to be the adoption of more stringent entrance requirements. But very often the faculties, senates and rectors of universities and technical colleges were opposed to limitations or quotas for foreign students. The demand for policies regulating foreign students, in particular Russian students, frequently came from the students, and it was the government that imposed such policies on the academic institutions.[90] At Zurich, non-Russian women, including Germans and the first American medical student, signed a petition urging the university to adopt stricter admission requirements. By this measure, non-Russian women hoped to limit the enrollment of less qualified Russian women.[91] Non-Russian women wanted to eliminate the possibility that the bad reputation the Russian women were gaining at the university and in the town of Zurich might cause all women to be barred from the university.[92] German and even German Jewish women students took similar actions against Russian women at Berlin (1900-1902), Halle (1901) and other German universities where there were large numbers of Russians studying medicine.[93]

Even M. Carey Thomas, one of the strongest advocates for women's education in the nineteenth century, felt that Russian women threatened her position at the University of Leipzig, where Thomas was enrolled from 1879 to 1882. She believed that the Saxon government was afraid to continue to admit women for fear that a wave of Russian women would descend upon its universities as it had in Zurich. Since the *ukase*, Russian women had either returned home or sought refuge at other Western European universities, in particular, the University of Bern. German universities did not wish to offer Russian women such a refuge. Thomas believed that if one Russian woman applied to the University of Leipzig, that university would close its doors to all women.[94] Thomas's fear was indirectly confirmed by the action taken by the Saxon Ministry of Culture in December of 1879.

On December 4, 1879, the rector of the university, L. Lange, tried to reassure the government that the women students were no threat by stating explicitly that there were no Russians among the ten women auditing classes. Perhaps precisely to keep it that way, the Ministry of Culture issued an order on December 12 declaring the university incompetent on matters concerning the admission of women auditors.[95] Auditors already at the university were allowed to stay, but no new auditors were admitted. Women were not officially allowed to audit classes again or earn doctoral degrees until June 1900, although individual women, including several mentioned in this study, did audit classes before then.[96] Once women were allowed to audit classes again, measures were sought to limit the enrollment of the Russians. Officials were able to limit enrollment by determining what level of prior study was necessary for admission. While officials were quickly able to determine criteria that eased the admission of Americans, time and again objections were made about the qualifications of the Russians.[97] As soon as auditors were admitted, 22 Russian women enrolled in medical courses. The medical faculty complained that these women did not have the proper background; the women did not have sufficient knowledge of Latin. Unless strict standards were enforced, the faculty feared that Leipzig would soon be flooded with these "undesirable Russian women," who were almost all Jewish.[98]

There was a constant struggle at Bern to limit the number of Russian women students, who started to arrive in increasing numbers in 1873. Other women at the university complained about how the Russians were crowding the classrooms. They complained that the Russian women were not required to have the same level of prior education. The protected status of the Russians was due primarily to the efforts of Director of Education (Erziehungsdirektor) Albert Gobat. When he retired in 1908, more restrictive admission requirements for Russians were enforced.[99]

Evidence of the continued fear that Russian women would turn the German universities into another Zurich is found in a document from October 1908, declaring the unanimous intention of the Prussian Committee for Admissions (Immatrikulations-Kommission) to allow women to matriculate at the universities. The document distinguished between the admission requirements for German women and for all foreign women. Among the foreign women, it specifically mentioned two groups of women: the Russians, and a second group including American and British women. The lack of language skills had obviously been a problem for the second group. For this group, a Bachelor's or a Master's degree was considered sufficient, but only if the woman had been examined in two languages. For the Russian women, in addition to similar requirements, the document explicitly stated that it was not sufficient for a woman to have passed the entrance exam at a Swiss university. She must have already been accepted at some non-Prussian German university or a university modeled after the German system.[100]

In the 1890s and early 1900s, students at German technical colleges claimed they were so overwhelmed by the number of foreign students, in particular the Russians, that all foreign students should be banned. While very few North American women were ever enrolled at German-speaking technical colleges, the antiforeigner campaign that started in 1891 at the technical college at Charlottenburg in Berlin soon spread to other technical colleges and universities, thus directly or indirectly affecting all foreign students.[101] Among women students, the large number of Russian women in medical courses were most directly affected by the campaign.

In 1905 a new student movement protested against the privileges enjoyed by foreign students at the technical colleges in Braunschweig, Darmstadt, Karlsruhe and Freiberg. In 1912 medical students at Halle went on strike to demand the same entrance requirements to clinics for German and foreign students. Constant themes emerge in these protests and seemingly legitimate concerns were raised. Students complained of overcrowding, especially in the technical colleges and medical schools.[102] But was there really overcrowding, or was there simply too much competition for space with foreigners, especially Russians and Russian

Jews? In a 1901 article, Germans complain that "the foreigners crowd them out of the laboratories and lecture rooms and that the foreigners are admitted without any documentary evidence of previous education."[103] A 1907 article in *The Nation* mocked such German fears by pointing out that the German students actually resented foreign students who attended lectures with "really censurable regularity," or who remained in residence during vacations to continue their studies, or who "show[ed] as regrettable a purpose to get ahead of their German fellow-students as that displayed by the women in our coeducational institutions to outdo their men rivals."[104]

German professors also claimed that German students were jealous of the more diligent Russians.[105] In an article on Russian-Jewish students in Germany, the American historian Jack Wertheimer cites Abraham Flexner's 1911 study on medical education in Europe, in which Flexner observed that there was a high rate of absenteeism among medical students as the semester progressed and at clinical demonstrations. By the end of the semester, there was plenty of room on the benches.[106] Wertheimer cites further examples where professors of medicine at Heidelberg, Leipzig and Halle wrote letters in support of the Russian students, and where faculty in engineering at the technical college in Karlsruhe protested against a quota system to limit the Russians.[107]

In addition to the complaint about overcrowding, there was also resentment that German taxes were being used to educate future foreign competitors.[108] Supposedly foreigners educated in Germany were responsible for threats to German industry in the world market. An article from 1898 quoted a government official who claimed:

> There is no question that the German technological schools and industrial and scientific institutions will soon be forced to adopt a less liberal policy with foreigners. The tricks of trade we have been teaching them so long are now being used against us to the great injury of our industry. This is especially the case with students of such countries as Japan, Russia, and East Europe; but also, in a lesser degree, with the students of England, America, France, and Belgium.[109]

A 1908 article dealing with efforts to end the free and unlimited admission of foreigners to the German technical colleges specifically mentioned the hostility directed not only at the Russians, but also the Americans. The journalist quoted a professor from the technical college at Charlottenburg in Berlin who advised the graduating class of Germans as follows:

> My parting advice to you is to make a trip to the United States at the earliest opportunity. Go into all the factories you can while you are there. You will find much to instruct you, but when you come home and have become factory managers yourselves here in Germany, don't you ever admit a Yankee to your plant. For an American needs only see a machine to go home and make a better one.[110]

An editorial from 1913 sympathetic to the plight of the Germans argued that the Germans were justified in limiting foreign enrollment, since German taxes supported the universities and colleges. It voiced the continuing German fear that Germany was actually paying for and supporting the education of its future foreign competitors: "[I]t teaches the foreigner at Germany's expense – for none of these schools is self-supporting – to become a successful rival of the German

in commerce, the trades, and the arts."[111] The fear of foreign competition, especially from the Americans, was based upon some fact. Americans were spending
far more than the Germans could on universities and students. They had also
developed graduate programs that compared with the best German universities.
Further, at the beginning of the 1900s, important private foundations had been
established to fund research. America was indeed emerging as Germany's biggest
rival in technological advances and scientific research.[112] But the German government did not impose quotas on American students as it did on the Russians.
Further, when restrictions were imposed on all foreign students, these restrictions were formulated to limit in particular the enrollment of Russian Jews. The
antagonism against foreign students was far more than the fear of competition.[113]

This leads to the second reason for the difference in attitude towards the
North Americans and the Russians: anti-Semitism. Very few of the North
Americans who studied at German-speaking universities during the period of this
study were Jewish. For the 1,266 North American women included in the original database, only 658 records listed the woman's religion. From those records
with the religion included, the majority, 608, were Protestant, and only fifteen
women were Jewish.[114]

The hostility toward Russian-Jewish students dated back at least to the second wave of Russian students at German-speaking universities that began in the
early 1880s. The first wave of Russians had a relatively low percentage of Jewish students. Only about 10 percent of the Russian women at Zurich during the
1870s were Jewish. In contrast, this percentage grew to as high as 80 percent at
some Swiss universities in the period between 1880 and 1914.[115] Between 1900
and 1908, 60 percent of the Russian women studying at Zurich were Jewish.[116]
During the Winter Semester of 1908/09, 17.6 percent of the women matriculated
at German universities were Jewish, although Jews made up only 1 percent of
the general population.[117] Of the Russian women who made up 60 percent of
the women earning medical degrees at Berlin before 1918, the majority were Jewish.[118]

Why did enrollments for Jewish students increase so dramatically starting in
the 1880s? In 1881, after the assassination of Tsar Alexander II, the medical
courses available to Russian women were gradually closed. While the majority
of all Russian women studying abroad chose to study medicine or in the sciences, Russian-Jewish women were especially limited in their career options.
The teaching profession chosen by many Russian women was barred to them.
Therefore, many Russian-Jewish women looked to medicine for a career, or, to a
lesser degree, to mathematics or the sciences.[119] It would not be until 1895 that
women could again study medicine in Russia.[120] Even then, quotas limiting the
number of medical students and political turbulence in the early 1900s made
study at the Russian universities an unpredictable process. Many preferred the
more stable foreign universities. In addition to such limitations for all women,
Jewish students were subjected to further enrollment caps. Two policy changes
in 1886 affected foreign enrollments. The *ukase* of 1873 was finally lifted. That
same year, enrollment limits for all Jewish students were imposed on institutions for secondary and higher education. These ranged from 10 percent in the
Pale of Settlement to only 3 percent in Moscow and St. Petersburg. The result
of these policy changes was an exodus of Jewish students to Europe. Most of
the women went to Switzerland.[121]

A 1907 article in *The Nation* still spoke of the "serious problem" of so many Russian students, "particularly Jewesses," crowding into Swiss universities. The article specifically mentioned the University of Bern, which had the most severe problem because it had been "especially liberal in admitting foreigners." At that point the administration at Bern, like the administration at Zurich the previous year, had just adopted more stringent entrance requirements, which immediately decreased the number of Russian students.[122]

The third strike against the Russian women was their reputation for political radicalism. The first American women who came to Zurich tended to avoid political activism. The labor activist Florence Kelley, who studied in Zurich during the 1880s and became active in the community of socialists there, described most Swiss and American students as lacking any interest in politics: "Barring the absence of athletics, they [the Swiss students] more than any of the others were like American students. Having no political or social grievances, and the most nearly universal educational system the world had yet seen, they shared in no political interest."[123]

The Russians, both men and women, on the other hand, were condemned for their supposed political activism. A highly visible minority of Russian women in Zurich had been involved in anarchist or socialist movements to overthrow the Russian government. But most of the women were dedicated to their studies and hoped to serve society through their medical education. In one study, Bonner quotes Vera Figner, a revolutionary, who despite her political agenda was completely devoted to her medical studies.[124]

The early 1900s saw growing cooperation between the Tsarist government and university and police authorities in Germany in monitoring the activities of Russian students. The surveillance, which grew out of a "desire to please Tsarist officials, fear of subversives, distrust of Slavs, and xenophobia" was heightened even further in 1904 after Germany signed a treaty with Russia and other European countries promising to fight against "anarchists."[125] After the Russian Revolution of 1905, Russian-Jewish students became linked with "bomb-throwing and subversion" and were even less welcome.[126] Yet Russian Jews were even more desperate to find a stable place to study after 1905 and continued to flood the German universities and technical colleges. This influx of students sparked off another round of protests among German students asking for restrictions on Russian or Russian-Jewish students.[127]

For the most part, North American women were spared the blatant hostility directed at Russian students. Back in North America they were able to acquire the prior education required of them at German-speaking universities. At German-speaking universities they were confronted with the same prejudices and barriers encountered by most of the first women students. They were not, however, singled out for additional hostility because of their nationality, religion or political convictions.

It is ironic, as Margaret Rossiter noted in her history of women scientists in the United States, that by the time all German universities finally allowed women to matriculate in 1908, those universities had already lost their competitive edge over the American ones, at least in the sciences.[128] As early as 1904, an article by one of the earliest, most dedicated advocates of women's higher education, Christine Ladd-Franklin, stated that at that time it was "no longer necessary to cross the ocean in order to become a scholar of distinction."[129]

The prestige of German degrees also diminished as these became more numerous. A degree from a German-speaking university had represented mastery of the skills and intellectual training necessary to conduct original research. This was one of the gifts of German-speaking universities to North American higher education. Both men and women with degrees or training at such universities had helped to promote research and graduate training. But a 1907 article in *The Nation* quoted a German professor who was concerned that German universities had made it so easy for foreigners to earn doctoral degrees that the German doctor of philosophy was no longer respected. He mentioned specifically the numerous degrees that had been granted foreigners from America and Holland.[130]   Shortly before World War I, when criticism of degrees from German-speaking universities could also be explained in part by nationalist prejudice or fear of competition from the many women who had earned such degrees, training at German-speaking universities was again being discredited. A 1914 editorial in *The Nation* cited a German report from 1913 estimating that over 5,500 doctoral dissertations had been issued in 1910 by universities of the German Empire alone.[131] The author expressed dismay not only at the large number of dissertations being issued, but also at the flood of students being allowed into German-speaking universities when "many German professors have expressed the opinion that at least 40 percent of their students ought not to be in a university at all."[132]   A professor from Munich was quoted as declaring that "in foreign countries German doctors have come to be regarded as a fit subject for merriment, and that even at home they are not taken very seriously."[133]   The likelihood of so many theses containing valuable, original research was also questioned, for "no one believes it is possible for several thousand persons to prepare as many documents that by any stretch of language could be said to contain anything original. Search is not research."[134]

In fact, the trip abroad was not always as important for the technical and research skills gained as for the ticket it gave the student to membership among the professional elite. As Alice Hamilton wrote of her studies in Leipzig in 1895: "[M]y professors had told me that if I hoped to devote myself to bacteriology and pathology I must study in Germany, otherwise I should never be accepted as an expert." Hamilton claimed that she did not learn anything in Leipzig that she had not already learned in the United States, but that "neither Germans nor Americans would have believed it." In Munich, she found herself doing "purely routine work in bacteriology," just as she had done in Ann Arbor.[135]

In 1897 Anna Maude Bowen wrote while studying at Munich: "It seems to me an advantage for every American student, man or woman, to make his doctor's examination in America. It is true that a doctor's degree from here is apt to weigh more in the eyes of the world than one from America; but from what I know of the work of students here, I judge that the requirements in a first-class American university are decidedly more stringent than here."[136]   Jane B. Sherzer wrote that for a woman "the fact of having studied in Germany enhances – often quite disproportionately – her intellectual value in the estimation of those who have not done so."[137]   In 1888, when Mary Whiton Calkins decided to earn a graduate degree so that she could teach psychology and philosophy at Wellesley, she thought of studying abroad but was discouraged from doing so by her friends. Her colleague, Mary S. Case, wrote of her decision: "She first thought of studying in Europe, but those whom she consulted were unanimous in declaring that this country offered opportunities fully as good, both in psychology and in philosophy, and that, since she had already been abroad and had a good command of both French and German, foreign study would hardly be worth while."[138]

Such accounts, however, must be balanced with those of other women who gained genuine knowledge and significant practical experience while abroad. For example, precisely in psychology, the field mentioned in the previous quote, significant contributions were made by women who worked with the great German experimental psychologists, such as Georg Elias Müller and Oswald Külpe. For the American Lillien J. Martin, her work with these two men between 1894 and 1914 would prove invaluable in her work at Stanford. North American women clearly thought German-speaking universities continued to offer them significant and unique opportunities, for enrollment numbers for these women rose until 1912 and only dropped off sharply in 1914 with the outbreak of World War I. The true significance of Rossiter's comment is that by the time 1908 rolled around, very few North American women were still traveling to German-speaking universities to earn doctoral or medical degrees. Women came primarily for postgraduate study or to supplement an undergraduate education.

The first North American women to graduate from German-speaking universities were aware of their privileged status and worked hard to transmit the lessons they had learned in Europe. They were responsible for establishing some of the first classroom and research laboratories at women's colleges as well as some of the first graduate programs for women in the sciences and the humanities in the 1890s and early 1900s. Realizing the importance of research for teaching, personal growth and academic advancement, they helped establish European fellowships for women pursuing graduate studies. Some of the first graduates in the sciences helped found permanent positions for women to do research at prominent facilities such as the marine biological laboratories in Naples, Italy, and Woods Hole, Massachusetts.

Professional women's organizations were an additional source of funding. Members of the Association of Collegiate Alumnae (ACA), established in 1882, and the Women's Educational Association (WEA) were quick to realize the need for supporting opportunities in graduate studies for women. In 1888, the ACA was able to start funding a series of fellowships to enable the most gifted women to pursue graduate studies in America or to study abroad. Hundreds of women would eventually benefit from these scholarships. The ACA would later become the American Association of University Women (AAUW).[139]

On behalf of the AAUW, Margaret Maltby, the first American woman to receive a doctoral degree from a German university, published a history of the fellowships that had been awarded by the ACA (AAUW) between 1888 and 1929.[140] Half of the thirty recipients of the ACA's European Fellowship between 1890 and 1915 used their fellowship to study at German-speaking universities. Two more of those women studied at German-speaking universities without the help of a fellowship. Of the 17 women who studied at German-speaking universities, seven were in the humanities; five in mathematics or physics; three in the social sciences, education or psychology; and two in the natural sciences.

Two of the six recipients of the Alice Freeman Palmer Memorial Fellowship for research between 1908 and 1915 used the fellowship to conduct research at German-speaking universities. One more woman had studied at a German university before receiving the fellowship. These three women studied in diverse fields: biology, Semitic languages and economics. One of the two Boston Alumnae Fellowship recipients between 1912 and 1915 used the fellowship to study biology in Germany. Two of the five Sarah Berliner Research and Lecture Fellowships awarded between 1909 and 1915 went to women who conducted research at German universities. Both recipients were in physics. Numerous other women, who audited or enrolled in courses at German-speaking universities, were the recipients of undergraduate fellowships from their home university, almost always a women's college. Bryn Mawr College, for example, established a competitive European Fellowship in 1889.

For many women, the return to North America did bring greater professional opportunities. But the successes of certain outstanding women should not blind one to the lot of women who returned from Europe to begin or continue jobs that paid little, that demanded long hours and that offered little or no opportunity for scholarly or artistic development. Few of the women artists and musicians traveling to Europe gained international fame or even launched successful professional careers. In teaching, even those women who were fortunate enough to find a position in higher education, rarely had access to the facilities or time to continue their research. Christine Ladd-Franklin, in a 1904 article advocating endowed professorships for women, described the abysmal job prospects for women with doctoral degrees. She contrasted the opportunities that awaited a young man returning with a degree from Europe to those awaiting a woman:

> For the young man who returns from Europe with his doctor's degree, and with the abstruse thesis which every one, clever or stupid, who studies at a German university is supposed to be able to turn out, the case is very different. Occasionally, it is true, by ill luck, he fails to find at once the opening that he is adapted to fitting into, but for the most part the colleges stand ready to seize upon these gifted beings the moment that they become full fledged (provided only they are of the right sex) and to put them into the first stage of that career which is to end, in the course of time, in the full professorship. But for the women, the teaching positions that are at all worthy of their powers are few in number. The proportion of those who, after their brilliant preparation for the highest work, find that there is nothing in the world for them to do save the drudgery of teaching in the public schools is large, and is constantly becoming larger. Some, of course, find openings in the women's colleges, but the women's colleges are few in number, and it is not even desirable that all of the teachers in them should be women. For most, as far as consequences are concerned, the certificate of their doctorate is but an empty honor.[141]

Those women who did manage to transmit the lessons from abroad to successful careers used several strategies. They made use of and supported organizations that encouraged graduate and research opportunities for women through fellowships and scholarships. Some wealthier women worked without a salary simply to have the chance to teach in higher education and to build up a department. In the sciences, women's greatest opportunities were in newly emerging fields as opposed to well-established research areas. For example, in chemistry a woman had a better chance of obtaining a research position in crystallography or

biochemistry than in organic or physical chemistry. The women's colleges
played a key role in offering employment to many of the first Ph.D.s returning
from Europe, although, as Ladd-Franklin noted, these colleges were few in number. With such highly trained teachers, the women's colleges were able to establish quality research facilities for faculty and students.[142]

With the outbreak of World War I, the value of a degree from a German-
speaking university became irrelevant for a period of time. The adventures of the
first generations of North American women to study at German-speaking universities came quickly to an end, although a few women, such as the physician and
art collector Claribel Cone, did remain in Germany throughout the war. The
famous Miss Willard's American Home School for Girls, which had opened in
Berlin in 1886, closed down. Most students enrolled at the universities returned
home or tranferred to a neutral country or England. Professors cancelled their
sabbatical plans for study in Europe. Tours for North American students in
Europe were cancelled. One American woman, Carolyn Wilson, from the class
of 1910 at Wellesley, was arrested by the German government in February 1915,
on charges of espionage. Wilson had studied at the University of Berlin from
1910 through 1911. She then worked for two years in Paris as a correspondent
for the *Chicago Tribune*. She was later transferred to Berlin because of her
knowledge of German. There she was arrested for showing an "'indiscreet curiosity concerning naval affairs.'"[143] Wilson was freed only through the intervention
of the American ambassador on the condition that she leave the country at once.

By the time the war had ended, graduate and professional opportunities for
women in North America were well established, even if many barriers for
women in higher education still existed, as they do today. North American
music and art had come into their own. The need for study in Europe was no
longer necessary for professional advancement except in certain fields within the
humanities. Moreover, the close bond between many North Americans and
Germans had been severed, at least temporarily. Thus ended this era, which
began with the first North American woman traveling to Zurich in 1868 to
study medicine, and which had brought invaluable opportunities to so many
women.

Chapter Two
Women in Medicine

Although the Geneva Medical College again closed its doors to women after the graduation of Elizabeth Blackwell in 1849, by the time the first North American woman came to the University of Zurich to study medicine in 1868, women had access to a few women's medical schools in North America, such as the Boston Female Medical College established in 1848 (renamed the New England Female Medical College in 1851) and the Female Medical College of Pennsylvania in Philadelphia established in 1850 (renamed the Woman's Medical College of Pennsylvania in 1867). In 1868 Elizabeth Blackwell (1821-1910) founded the Women's Medical College of the New York Infirmary. In 1870 the surgeon, Mary Harris Thompson (1829-1895), helped to establish the Women's Hospital Medical College in Chicago. Other women's medical colleges would be established in the following years, such as the Women's Medical College in San Francisco (1881), the Women's Medical College of Baltimore (1882), and the Ontario Medical College for Women (1883). A few regular schools of medicine began to admit women as early as 1870s. For example, in 1870 the University of Michigan began to admit women to its prestigious medical school. Cooper Medical College in San Francisco, which opened in 1875, admitted women. Until the mid-1890s, however, most women studying medicine were enrolled at women's medical colleges.[1]

By 1868 four women's hospitals where women could receive clinical experience had also opened: the New York Infirmary in 1857, the Woman's Hospital in Philadelphia in 1862, the New England Hospital for Women and Children in 1862, and the Chicago Hospital for Women and Children in 1865. The Hospital for Sick Children and Women opened in San Francisco in 1875, and Northwestern Hospital opened in Minneapolis in 1882.

By the time the first American woman began to study medicine at the University of Zurich, women also had access to a number of women's or coeducational schools of sectarian medicine in America. In her history of women physicians, Regina Markell Morantz-Sanchez defines sectarians as a diverse group of new medical systems that competed with the regular or allopathic medical schools. Among the sectarian systems included are those that were opposed to traditional heroic methods of medical intervention, that is, bleeding, purging and vomiting. Sectarian systems might also oppose the use of drugs or surgery. Homeopaths, hydropaths and those practicing eclectic medicine are included among sectarian systems. Sectarian schools of medicine flourished in the mid-nineteenth century during a period when restrictive licensing legislation had been abolished in most states. Women were particularly welcome at such institutions:

> Favoring the popular diffusion of professional knowledge, and respecting women's enhanced responsibilities in the family, their schools often welcomed women students, and conse-quently middle-class women initially gravitated to sectarian medicine. Many of the first generation of women doctors re-ceived their degrees from sectarian institutions. The challenge posed by sectarian medicine to older concepts of professional-ism worked in favor of women. Paradoxically, in the mid-nineteenth century the abandonment of licensing legislation and the ease of access to a medical degree actually served to maintain a professional identity for all medical practitioners by conferring the title of doctor on a large proportion of them. This temporary fluidity allowed women who wished to achieve professional status to do so before definitions of professional-ism crystallized once more.[2]

Two of the earliest sectarian schools to admit women were Penn Medical Col-lege, which admitted women in 1853, and the New York Woman's Medical Col-lege, established in 1863. In an article about medical women abroad, Bonner notes that the sectarian schools of medicine and the woman's medical colleges were responsible for the large number of women physicians educated in America in the last half of the nineteenth century.[3] But women educated at those institu-tions had a difficult time being accepted by male practitioners educated at regular schools of medicine, who, with some justification, accused both men and women educated at such institutions of lacking sufficient clinical experience and a thorough understanding of all fields of medicine.

Leading women physicians of the time were aware of the inadequacy of their training. Unlike men educated at sectarian schools of medicine, however, women had no access to regular medical schools in the mid-nineteenth century. Their pleas in the 1850s and 1860s to be accepted at regular American medical schools were denied. Mary Putnam-Jacobi (1842-1906), a physician from New York who became a leading advocate for coeducational medical study, wrote that from the very beginning The New England Female Medical College was doomed, for "[t]here was no one connected with it who either knew or cared what a medical education should be."[4] Of the period between 1850 and 1870, Putnam-Jacobi wrote that the poor quality of education at the New England Female Medical College was typical for the early Women's medical colleges: "And still more unfortunately, the same inadequacy, naively or deliberately unconscious of itself, continued in greater or less degree, to characterize all efforts for the iso-lated medical education of women for the next twenty years."[5] Putnam-Jacobi was also well aware that as long as women were able to do internships and resi-dencies only at the smaller hospitals that specialized primarily in obstetrics and gynecology, women would never receive the broad medical training necessary to become even adequate physicians.

Early women leaders in the field of medicine were frustrated in their attempts to have women admitted to regular medical institutions. Elizabeth and Emily Blackwell founded the Women's Medical College of the New York Infirmary only after their efforts to have a limited number of women admitted to the College of Physicians and Surgeons in New York City were rejected in 1865. For a critical period of time in the second half of the nineteenth century, supplementing the education available in America with study in Europe was the only chance some of the first women physicians had to receive a thorough education. "The women physicians who stand at the head of their sex in the profession have acquired it chiefly on the European continent," stated an 1874 article in the *New York Times* sympathetic to women doctors.[6] Putnam-Jacobi claimed that the first adequate teacher at the Woman's Medical College of Pennsylvania was Emmeline Cleveland, who, like Putnam-Jacobi and Elizabeth Blackwell, had studied extensively and intensively in Europe.[7] The physician Kate Campbell Hurd, hired as the medical director of the Bryn Mawr School of Baltimore, was required by the board of that school to "make special preparation for this position by study and observation in the United States and Europe."[8]

The large number of American women studying medicine at German-speaking universities during the last three decades of the nineteenth century corresponds to a similar but much larger wave of American men attending those universities for the same purpose. Both men and women wrote of the frustration of returning to the inadequate system of medical education in America after extensive work in laboratories and clinics in Europe. Putnam-Jacobi wrote of American clinical work: "To students habituated to the daily visits in the wards of the vast European hospitals, this form of clinical instruction, where the patient studied is seen but once, and then at a distance, must seem ludicrously inadequate."[9] The male student returning to America could remedy this inadequacy in part through internships and residencies at general hospitals, where there would be ample opportunities to work with a large number of patients with a variety of complaints. But for the women returning from Europe, such opportunities did not usually exist. During the late nineteenth and early twentieth centuries, a stay in Europe was deemed necessary for either a man or a woman to truly be considered an expert in a particular medical field. But women with training in Europe were still not hired as faculty members of regular medical schools, and had difficulty finding staff positions at general hospitals. Women with such extensive medical training were even rejected as medical students by regular medical colleges. Upon her return from Zurich, the physician Mary Sherwood applied to the College of Physicians and Surgeons in New York City and had her application rejected. This was twenty-five years after Elizabeth and Emily Blackwell had failed to get that same college to admit even a few women. The college would eventually admit women, but not until 1920.

Later in the nineteenth century and even into the early twentieth century, when women had gained access to most of the finest medical schools, women still had difficulties gaining necessary postgraduate clinical experience in hospitals. Despite competitive grades and examination scores, women were denied internships and residencies at general hospitals. They found themselves competing for the few internships and staff positions that opened at women's hospitals. Particularly moving is the struggle of Emily Dunning Barringer (1876-1961), who became the first woman ambulance surgeon in New York City and later studied in Vienna. Barringer twice won first place in competitive Medical Board examinations, but because she was a woman was twice denied the staff position at the general hospital that should have been her reward.[10] Sometimes there were encouraging exceptions. In 1890 two graduates of the Women's Medical College of Baltimore, Claribel Cone and Flora Pollack, were given internships in Blockley Hospital in Philadelphia "after a competitive examination which would have been glad to disqualify them...because they were women, and...because they were neither residents of the State of Pennsylvania nor had they received their medical training in Philadelphia."[11]

It was almost impossible for a woman to find a faculty position except at a women's medical college. As late as 1912, in a speech held on the Bryn Mawr College campus, Alice Hamilton (1869-1970), one of the leading women physicians in industrial medicine, warned women students that they would still have difficulties obtaining staff positions at hospitals. Her recommendation to young women interested in a career in medicine was to start their own practice in a small town "where personality counts." As alternatives, she suggested positions as medical inspectors of public schools, or jobs in research laboratories, police courts, prisons, asylums and reformatories.[12]

In the face of such limitations, the main way in which women used the skills they had acquired in Europe was to establish a private practice or to train and educate other women at colleges, hospitals and dispensaries established primarily by women for women. Institutions such as the Women's Medical College of the New York Infirmary and the New England Hospital for Women and Children provided women with a chance to teach or acquire clinical experience that was unavailable to them elsewhere. When the physician Lilian Welsh returned from Zurich, she was able to find a position as assistant resident physician in the State Hospital for the Insane at Norristown, Pennsylvania. As Welsh wrote, this was "the first hospital for the insane where women patients were entirely under the medical care of women."[13] When the physician Susan Dimock returned from Zurich, she went back to work as a surgeon at the New England Hospital. Eventually, some of the women's medical colleges and hospitals offered women an education and training that was equal to or superior to that available to men at the best medical schools. That did not, however, convince conservative members of the regular medical community that women trained at such facilities were capable of teaching male medical students. For example, in 1900 the Cornell University Medical School in New York City was opened. Until that time, the Women's Medical College of the New York Infirmary had been operating fairly successfully. It faced, however, high costs to repair extensive damage from a fire. Rather than rebuild and attempt to compete with Cornell, the New York Infirmary negotiated a merger with Cornell. Students from the New York Infirmary transferred to Cornell. But while women students could enroll at Cornell, none of the female faculty members from the New York Infirmary were hired to teach at Cornell.

The first American women to travel to Europe to study medicine in the nineteenth century headed for Paris and the École de Médecine, the medical college, or the Paris Maternité, the school for midwifery. The French universities were opened to women in 1863, a year before the first German-speaking university, the University of Zurich, was opened to women. As Zurich and then Bern allowed women to enroll and earn a medical degree, many American women went to Switzerland instead. Women were also drawn to Vienna and Berlin, as both cities had become major centers of medical research in the late nineteenth century. Even before women could earn medical degrees at the universities of Vienna and Berlin, women traveled to those cities seeking clinical and hospital experience or a chance to work in the medical research laboratories. Between 1870 and 1914, approximately 15,000 male and female practitioners from America spent time in Vienna and Berlin engaged in serious scientific study.[14]

The move from Paris to German-speaking universities was typical for both male and female medical students and physicians from America. Medical historians have described developments in medical research during the mid- to late-nineteenth century that gave German-speaking universities a new dominance in the field of medical science. French medicine, which had dominated the first half of the nineteenth century, had been based upon clinical observation and had not placed enough significance on investigating the causes of disease. The mid-nineteenth century saw a major restructuring of German medical science, as there was a distinct move away from the philosophical approach in the biological sciences of *Naturphilosophie* to experimental laboratory investigation. Experimental research came to dominate German medical science to a far greater degree than it did French medical science. Further, as Kenneth Ludmerer notes in his history of American medical education,[15] German medical research had another advantage over the French in that many of the greatest German medical researchers were also professors at the university or worked in institutions or hospitals closely affiliated with a university. Students pursuing either medical studies or postgraduate work in medical research had easy access to laboratory or clinical work with these leading researchers. American students also appreciated the great freedom of German-speaking universities. Students were free to travel to different universities to work in various laboratories or institutes.

This freedom, while essential for the students, has created some difficulties for historians of this century. In his classic work on male American medical students at German-speaking universities, Bonner notes how it is impossible to get an exact count of all the Americans who pursued medical studies at these universities. First, since many students studied at various universities, records of these students may be duplicated in statistics. Second, American students did not necessarily have to matriculate at a university in order to engage in medical research there. A student intending to earn a medical degree had to enroll. But the majority of men traveling to these universities were not there to earn a medical degree. They went to Europe to do postgraduate work. Some went for a brief stay to enroll in courses that lasted only a few weeks. Others did extensive research in laboratories and stayed in Europe for several years. But in either case, men were free to work with professors in their laboratories, institutes or hospital clinics without enrolling at the university. Certainly, there were financial obligations but not necessarily directly to the university.

Even more difficulties arise in finding records for North American women studying medicine, where the situation was in some ways identical to that of the men. In addition to the above problems in finding records, the earliest date women could officially register at certain Austrian and German universities was 1900. Unfortunately, the records of women who audited courses before that year are incomplete for many universities. In other cases, records for women auditing courses were not kept until the 1890s. Whatever evidence does remain of the work of women doing research in medical science must be considered incomplete.

The freedom enjoyed by medical students, which makes finding their records so difficult, was more limited for women. Women did share some of the joys of the German academic freedom with the men, but also had some measure of this "freedom" forced upon them. Those North American women who attempted to study at a German-speaking university before it was officially opened to them were at the mercy of the university administration and the goodwill of individual professors. There are accounts of women who wished to pursue medical studies at one university and had to start all over again at another university, because one professor refused to admit women to his laboratories or would not examine women in a critical subject. Similarly, the university administration might simply refuse to grant the woman a degree.

For these women, Zurich played a critical role. Some of the American women who came to Zurich to study medicine had been refused the opportunity to earn a degree at another German-speaking university or at certain North American medical institutes. As early as 1864, women were able to pursue a medical degree or doctorate at Zurich in a coeducational environment. At Zurich, women were able to learn the same revolutionary research techniques as the men, and were able to gain the same laboratory and clinical experience. Zurich simply did not have this meaning for North American men, as they had numerous other options for medical training.

Morantz-Sanchez provides a detailed profile of the typical American woman medical student of the late nineteenth century, including standard motives for studying medicine. Both the profile and the motives correspond with information on women who studied medicine at German-speaking universities during the period from 1868 through 1915. Most of these women came from the middle and upper middle class in the Northeast.[16] Between 1890 and 1918, women medical students in America were concentrated in the states which had women's medical colleges or exceptional coeducational opportunities. The seven states which had the most women medical students during this period were California, Illinois, Maryland, Massachusetts, Michigan, New York and Pennsylvania.[17] Many women had already attended college before enrolling in medical school.[18] This was remarkable, as it was not until the 1890s that the regular medical schools began to require an undergraduate degree for medical students. Often there was already a physician in the family to serve as a role model.[19] Some families were able to finance the woman's education, but other women had to support themselves and very often did so through medical work or teaching. The average female medical student was older than the average male medical student. Economic difficulties and social disapproval account in part for women entering medical school at an older age.[20]

Economic difficulties played a role in women's ability to pursue a more thorough education and clinical experience in Europe. The cost alone of a medical education in America forced many women to work as they studied or to work for a period of time before beginning their studies. Women did not receive state financial aid for their medical studies. Mary Putnam-Jacobi provides a moving portrait of both the determination and the miserable financial struggles of the first women medical students:

> They have starved on half rations, shivered in cold rooms, or
> been poisoned in badly ventilated ones; they have often borne a
> triple load of ignorance, poverty, and ill health; when they
> were not permitted to walk, they have crept,– where they could

> not take, they have begged; they have gleaned like Ruth
> among the harvesters for the scantiest crumbs of knowledge,
> and been thankful. To work their way through the prescribed
> term of studies, they have resorted to innumerable devices, –
> taught school, edited newspapers, nursed sick people, given
> massage, worked till they could scrape a few dollars together,
> expended that in study, – then stepped aside for a while to earn
> more. After graduating, the struggle has continued, – but here
> the resource of taking lodgers has often tided over the difficult
> time.[21]

Such financial struggles confronted the earliest students in the mid-nineteenth century. But they were still a problem for women fifty years later at the beginning of the 1900s. Scholarships and fellowships would play a key role in enabling many women to pursue graduate studies in medicine and many other fields in Europe. A key source for such funding would be the woman's own college. Early graduates and administrators of women's colleges were particularly sensitive to the need for such funding for students.

In her autobiography, the physician Lilian Welsh, who studied in Zurich, mentioned the scholarships provided by the Baltimore Association for the Promotion of the University Education of Women. Between 1898 and 1922, the organization awarded a fellowship to a woman from Maryland or the South for graduate study in Europe, and later in Europe or the United States. The Woman's College of Baltimore, later renamed Goucher College, also founded a fellowship in 1898 for one of its graduates to pursue graduate studies in Europe.[22] Some fellowships were later converted to research fellowships after women had gained sufficient access to graduate programs in America.

When examining the reasons that women chose to study medicine despite economic hardships and social disapproval, some common motives emerge. Some of the earliest women to study medicine were motivated by the desire to fight against social ills in a profession that allowed them some independence. Emphasizing service to the community gave legitimacy to women's quest for autonomy. As Morantz-Sanchez writes:

> For many women who pursued medicine in the early period be-
> tween 1840 and 1870, religious perfectionism and reform ide-
> ology meshed into a desire to contribute to the community
> welfare. Of course the notion that women, like men, had a
> moral and religious obligation to society could be relatively
> controversial if interpreted too broadly. Yet historians have
> long noted that religious piety often afforded the only means
> by which women could exercise power and autonomy.[23]

Some women came to medicine specifically to prepare themselves as medical missionaries, others to work in settlement projects with the urban poor and immigrant populations. Still others came to medicine in the hope of finding a cure for an illness that had affected their own life or the life of a close friend or family member.[24] A typical example is Rebecca Lee Dorsey (1859-1954), the first graduate of Wellesley College to earn a medical degree. Dorsey, who became the first woman to earn the title of endocrinologist, brought with her the hope of preventing children from being born with the severe mental retardation she had seen while caring for neighborhood children. She was driven to go to

Europe to seek out a cure for her own tuberculosis and that of her partner and close family members.[25]

THE PATH TO ZURICH AND BEYOND

Before discussing the specific experiences of North American women at Zurich, it is important to answer briefly the question why Zurich was the first German-speaking university to admit women. Compared to many other German and Austrian universities, Zurich was a relatively new university. Women had been allowed to audit classes from the time the university had first opened in 1833. There had been no tradition of banning women. When women were finally admitted as regular students in 1864, they were already a familiar sight at the university. Further, the first female students who applied for regular admission were foreigners, who would leave Zurich at the end of their studies and could be expelled from the country or town as necessary.[26]

The faculty of the university was relatively liberal. Some faculty members were progressives who had fled from Germany after the failed revolution of 1848. They had sympathy for the plight of the first women students, many of whom were Russian Jews agitating against the Russian government.[27] However, although women were allowed to study medicine at the university, there were no jobs for women physicians in the Swiss hospitals of the late nineteenth century. Swiss women physicians were forced to start their own clinics and training centers.[28]

Among the great figures on the medical faculty of Zurich in the second half of the nineteenth century were the surgeons Theodor Billroth and Edmund Rose; the internist Hermann Eichhorst; the pathologists Edwin Klebs and Friedrich Loeffler, who helped isolate the diphtheria bacillus; the histologist Heinrich von Frey; the anatomist Hermann von Meyer; the physiologists Ludimar Hermann and Justus Gaule; the bacteriologist and pathologist Carl Joseph Eberth; the pediatricians Oskar Wyss and Hermann Müller; the gynecologist Ferdinand Frankenhäuser; the ophthamologist Johann Friedrich Horner; and Anton Biermer. In an essay on women's medical education in Swiss universities, Bonner describes the general sympathy for women's education that dominated the medical faculty of Zurich. The dean of the medical faculty, Anton Biermer, is described as an early convert to women's education.[29] Hermann von Meyer, who later became dean and rector of the university, "was highly regarded by the women students for his fairness and friendly attitude."[30] Several of these outspoken advocates of women's education also served on the University Senate, where their position was strengthened by supporters of women's education from other departments.[31]

Between 1868 and 1915, fifty-four North American women were registered at the University of Zurich in the College of Medicine. Nine of these women registered as already having a degree in medicine when they first enrolled at Zurich. Seven of the fifty-four completed their medical degree at Zurich. The United States followed only Russia and Germany in the number of women it sent to study medicine at Zurich.[32] Of all German-speaking universities, Zurich had by far the highest enrollment of American women studying medicine during this period.

The first North American woman to receive a medical degree from Zurich was Susan Dimock (1847-1875). When Dimock arrived at Zurich in 1868, she had already studied and worked at the New England Hospital for Women and Children in Boston. In a letter dated from October 1868, which would have been the start of her first semester, Dimock described both the difficulties of adjusting to a foreign culture and university system as well as the amazing opportunities available to her at Zurich:

> Sunday finds me safely through with last week's herculean labors. You know I had a hundred formalities to go through with, and no German to speak of. Looking back upon it, I do not see how I managed it; however, it is plain sailing now, and I have nothing to do except to listen to lectures, study hard, and learn German, &c. Oh, it is so nice to get here, at a word, what I have been begging for in Boston for three years! I have every medical advantage that I can desire. I told the professor of anatomy, for instance, that I wanted a great deal of dissecting; and he immediately bowed, and said so kindly, "You shall have it; I only desire you shall tell me what you prefer." And so it is with everything. I only have to go through the necessary formalities, and pay the fees, and I find that in every respect I have equal advantages with the young men; and then I find also the warmth and protection and feeling of interest which a young man finds in the university. And it is delightful; the professors are all very kind to me.[33]

In the two years that followed that letter, conditions at the university changed and there was increasing hostility toward female students. North American women never attended the University of Zurich in large enough numbers to attract much negative attention as a group. But the late 1860s and early 1870s saw growing numbers of Russian women at Zurich.[34] Non-Russian female students at Zurich grew increasingly uneasy as antagonism toward Russian women grew. They were afraid that the status of all women at the university would be threatened. As Russian women tended to be younger than the other women and did not necessarily have an adequate educational background, it was easy for non-Russian women students to target the Russian women by arguing that all women students had to have the necessary educational background before being admitted to Zurich. Susan Dimock was among the six advanced women medical students who signed a petition to the University Senate asking that all female students be required to have the necessary educational background before being admitted to Zurich.[35] The petition was seen by the women who signed it as a proactive measure to keep the Senate from barring all women from the university. In 1873 conflicts with the Russian students were simplified when the Russian government issued the ban or *ukase* ordering the Russian women at Zurich to return home. When the ban was reversed in 1886, a large wave of Russian women returned to Zurich.

Susan Dimock graduated from Zurich in October of 1871 with a dissertation on "The Different Forms of Puerperal Fever: According to Observations at the Zurich Maternity Hospital" (Über die verschiedenen Formen des Puerperalfiebers. Nach Beobachtungen in der Züricher Gebäranstalt).[36] She then traveled to Vienna and later to Paris to continue her studies in the hospitals there. Dimock eventually returned to Boston to resume her work at the New England Hospital for Women and Children, where other graduates from Zurich soon joined her.

The six other women to complete their medical degrees at Zurich between 1868 and 1915 were Josephine Kendall (1879), Adeline Whitney (1880), Mary Almira Smith (1880), Ellen Powers (1882), Henriette Lothrop (1890) and Mary

Sherwood (1891). The dissertations of these women are remarkable for the diverse medical fields they represent. Kendall wrote on herpes of the cornea ("Über Herpes corneae"),[37] and Whitney on bacterial inflamation of the brain ("Ein Fall von Pyocephalus").[38] Smith's work focused on research on fetal rickets conducted at the Zurich Children's Hospital ("Beitrag zu der Lehre der foetalen Rachitis").[39] Powers examined psychoses related to menstruation ("Beitrag zur Kenntnis der Menstrualen Psychosen").[40] In her dissertation, Lothrop studied the ovaries ("Über Regenerations-Vorgänge in Eier-Stocke"),[41] while Sherwood wrote about research she had done on nerve lesions in the clinic of internist Hermann Eichhorst ("Aus der Medicinischen Klinik des Herrn Prof. Eichhorst in Zurich. Polyneuritis recurrens").[42]

Of the six women, the most complete information was available for Adeline Whitney, Mary Almira Smith and Mary Sherwood. Adeline Whitney (1852-1891?) of Waltham, Massachusetts, was the younger sister of the famous Vassar professor of astronomy, Mary W. Whitney (1847-1921). After graduating from Vassar in 1873, Adeline, Mary and the rest of their family traveled to Zurich together, so that Adeline could study medicine. Mary remained in Zurich for three years, taking classes in mathematics and astronomy, while Adeline studied medicine there for seven years. There is a brief description of their life in Zurich included in Mary's biography by her colleague, Caroline E. Furness: "Life in Zurich with its simple pleasures and freedom from care proved very fascinating to the Whitney family. Many of their Vassar friends passed through the city on their travels abroad and there were other brilliant women in the medical school from several European countries as well as from America."[43]

In 1876 Mary returned to the United States, where she finally received a full-time professorship at Vassar in 1889. Mary would remain at Vassar until 1912. She would inspire generations of women in her field, just as her predecessor and teacher, the remarkable Maria Mitchell, had done before her. In 1880 Adeline returned to the United States, where she started a successful practice in Boston. Her career ended after just a few years, when her health broke down and she became an invalid for the rest of her life. Furness never states explicitly what caused the breakdown in both Adeline's and Mary's health. Both were complete invalids for several years before their deaths.[44]

Mary Almira Smith (1850-1923) of Westfield, Massachusetts, studied at Mount Holyoke after returning from Zurich. At Mount Holyoke she earned her Master's (1903) and doctoral degree (1912). Smith was a surgeon at the New England Hospital for Women and Children in Boston until 1918. She also worked as a consulting surgeon for the Women's Memorial Hospital.[45]

The career of Mary Sherwood (1856-1935), perhaps the most famous of the above graduates besides Susan Dimock, was fairly typical. Sherwood came to Zurich twenty years after Dimock. Before deciding to study medicine, Sherwood, like many other women medical students, had worked as a teacher. Sherwood taught chemistry, and it was her work in chemistry that awakened in her a desire to study medicine. Sherwood was frustrated with the limited opportunities for her to study medicine in America. She wanted a medical education that was equal to the best medical education available to men, so she explored opportunities available to her in Europe. Her friend, the physician Lilian Welsh, wrote of Sherwood: "After investigating opportunities for study in the United States and finding that the two best schools open to her were exclusively women's schools, in order to be sure that her opportunities were equal to any man's, she decided to pursue her medical studies at the University of Zurich."[46]

Sherwood and Welsh gave up their spring vacations to enroll in the first bacteriology course ever offered at Zurich. A physician who had worked in Robert Koch's laboratory taught the course. After receiving her degree from Zurich, Sherwood returned to America to do graduate studies in medicine at the Johns Hopkins Hospital from 1891 through 1892. Sherwood was not able to obtain a residency at the hospital because she was a woman.[47] She was, however, able to find work as an assistant with another physician, Dr. Howard Kelly, and was able to work in the wards and laboratories of William Osler (1849-1919) and William H. Welch (1850-1934). After her work at Hopkins, Sherwood shared a medical practice with Lilian Welsh. In 1892 Sherwood and Welsh began their work at the Evening Dispensary for Working Women and Girls of Baltimore. Sherwood worked regularly at the Dispensary until it closed in 1910. In 1894 Sherwood became the medical director of the Bryn Mawr School, a preparatory school for girls in Baltimore. At that time, Sherwood also traveled to Philadelphia one day a week as a lecturer in pathology at the Woman's Medical College. In 1894 Sherwood accepted a part-time position as a lecturer on hygiene and college physician at Bryn Mawr College. Like Dimock, Sherwood worked throughout most of her career at institutions dedicated to the education of women. Such girls' schools and women's colleges and hospitals provided some of the only career options besides private practice for women pursuing careers in medicine in the late nineteenth century.

Although women were able to enroll at the University of Zurich at such an early date and apparently with few complications, some women did pursue medical studies at the university without registering. As previously mentioned, this was a typical phenomenon for both men and women from America studying medicine at German-speaking universities. Students doing postgraduate studies tended not to register for the work they did in laboratories and clinics. Sometimes a student paid for private instruction. It is difficult to estimate the numbers of these students, as there are no official enrollment statistics for them. There are indications that some American women must have come to Zurich to study medicine in addition to the fifty-four women who registered between 1868 and 1915. In her autobiography, Franziska Tiburtius, one of the first two German women to earn a medical degree at Zurich, mentions studying medicine in Zurich with two American women in the 1870s. One of these women, Kate C. Woodhull of Brooklyn, a graduate of the Women's Medical College of the New York Infirmary (1873), was registered at the university.[48] Woodhull would later work with Tiburtius at a clinic for obstetrics and gynecology run by Franz von Winckel (1837-1907) in Dresden.[49] Woodhull eventually became a medical missionary in China.

Tiburtius also mentioned a Dr. Elizabeth Cushier, who was doing postgraduate work in the laboratories of Eberth in Zurich.[50] Although Cushier is not found in the matriculation records of the University of Zurich, she does appear in histories of American women in medicine as one of the chief surgeons at the New York Infirmary. Cushier was still working in the pathology-anatomy department of a woman's hospital in New York, when Tiburtius visited the United States in 1909. Cushier is also mentioned in Lilian Welsh's autobiography as one of the pioneer women physicians.[51] Cushier's brief autobiography includes

a description of her very productive period of study in Zurich and her less positive stay in Vienna:

> I had become in the meantime, in addition to my work in ob-
> stetrics and gynecology, much interested in normal and patho-
> logical histology, and as there was at that time no opportunity
> in this country for women to do laboratory work in that branch
> of medicine, I decided to go abroad, and on the advice of Dr.
> Isaac Adler went to Zurich and studied with Professor Ebert
> [sic]. My opportunities in his laboratory were varied, ranging
> from the study of the circulation of the blood in the tail of a
> tadpole and searching for nerve endings on striped muscular fi-
> bre, to the pathological cases which we followed from the
> hospital wards to the post-mortem room and finally to the
> laboratory for microscopic examination of the diseased tissues.
> My work, however, was not limited to this; there were most
> valuable lectures and bedside clinics, especially those of Pro-
> fessor Huguenin, professor of general medicine. Every mo-
> ment one felt in an atmosphere impelling to most earnest
> study. To this was added the pleasure of occasional trips to
> other parts of lovely Switzerland which could be taken without
> interruption to the course of study, as the not infrequent short
> holidays gave the necessary freedom for these little excursions.
> The few months which I later spent in Vienna did not compare
> in value with those that I had passed in Zurich. I returned to
> New York at the end of eighteen profitable months, and again
> entered the Infirmary to remain as resident physician.[52]

WOMEN AT VIENNA AND BERLIN

After the Swiss universities, the next German-speaking universities to allow
women to enroll were the universities of the Austro-Hungarian Empire, where
Vienna was the main destination of North American women. As early as 1870,
an article in the *New York Times* claimed,"Female students will soon visit every
hospital, as they do now in Vienna."[53] There was a great time lapse between the
opening of the University of Zurich to women and that of the University of Vienna, as it was not until the Winter Semester of 1900/01 that women were admitted to the College of Medicine in Vienna. No records exist for women auditing courses in the College of Medicine before this Winter Semester. Existing
university records show that there were no North American women registered
either as auditors or as matriculated students in the College of Medicine between
Winter Semester 1900/01 and Winter Semester 1914/15. There are, however,
records from the period between July 30, 1872, and March 22, 1890, for women
who took the exams for midwives. These records contain the names of three
American women.

The records of the University of Vienna seem to stand in direct contradiction
with autobiographical accounts and medical histories which name numerous
women, some leading figures in medicine, such as Susan Dimock, Elizabeth
Cushier, Rosalie Slaughter Morton and Emily Dunning Barringer, who studied
for a period of time in Vienna.[54] According to Anna M. Fullerton, who was
studying medicine in Vienna from 1883 through 1884, there were eight American women taking medical courses there. Why weren't the names of these

women recorded? Part of the answer is that records for auditors are incomplete. Another part of the explanation for the lack of university records, however, is that Morton, Fullerton and some of these other women were not studying at the university even as auditors. They, like many of the American men, were working with professors or instructors outside of the university, often at a hospital or a research institute. Women were studying in a certain city, but they were not officially associated with the university.

Most of the women studying medicine in Vienna seem to have been working in clinics associated with the General Hospital of Vienna. Fullerton wrote that the "chief attraction for foreign students is the series of private classes for diagnosis and practical work in the hospital wards."[55] Just as in America, Vienna offered few prospects for women with a medical degree to acquire a permanent, high-ranking staff position at a clinic or hospital. But women were allowed to work as unpaid residents or to fill in when male physicians were on vacation.[56]

That Vienna played an exceptionally important role for women in the field of medicine is evident from a handbook from the 1890s advising women about studying in Europe. For all other German-speaking universities, the members of the medical faculty are simply listed together. But for Vienna, as the author notes, the "Medical Faculty is large and important, and for this reason the subjects lectured on by the different professors are stated below."[57] The author, Isabel Maddison, who compiled the guide for Bryn Mawr College, then broke down the entire medical faculty of the university into twenty departments: anatomy, physiology, histology, chemistry, medicine, surgery, obstetrics, pharmacy, pathology, diseases of the ear, diseases of the eye, diseases of children, skin diseases, nervous diseases, diseases of the throat, balneology, hospital practice, medical jurisprudence, history of medicine and hygiene.

Thomas N. Bonner provides a detailed and moving account of the glories of Vienna that drew both male and female American medical students and researchers. Vienna primarily attracted those who were interested in extensive clinical experience or short courses in areas of specialization. The city catered to thousands of foreign students, which meant there were many opportunities to take courses taught in English. Specialties that attracted the most Americans to Vienna during the late nineteenth century were ophthalmology, surgery, obstetrics, gynecology, pediatrics, dermatology, otorhinolaryngology, and hospital practice.[58] Some of the famous researchers and physicians in these fields who attracted many foreign students were Theodor Billroth, Ignaz Philipp Semmelweis, Carl Braun, Gustav Braun, Moritz Kaposi, Ferdinand von Hebra, Clemens von Pirquet, Theodor von Escherich, Carl Rokitansky and Josef Skoda. Billroth (1829-1894) was renowned for his surgical techniques and use of a mixture of ether and chloroform to anesthetize patients. Semmelweis (1818-1865) played a key role in changing birthing practices to protect mothers from puerperal fever. He insisted on greater hygiene on the part of the physician. Not only the instruments but also the physician's hands were to be disinfected.[59] Carl Braun specialized in obstetrics, while Gustav Braun headed the department for training midwives. Kaposi (1837-1902) and von Hebra (1816-1880) were leading experts in dermatology. Von Pirquet (1874-1929) was a pediatrician who was also a specialist in tuberculosis. Escherich, another pediatrician, focused on diseases in infants caused by intestinal bacteria. Rokitansky (1804-1878) was most famous for his work in pathological anatomy. His specialty was the anatomy of goiters, cysts and diseases of the arteries. He also introduced the microscope to Viennese pathology. Rokitansky and his colleague Josef Skoda (1805-1881), whose specialty was stethoscopy and auscultation, also worked at the General Hospital of Vienna.[60]

The General Hospital of Vienna was an invaluable resource for those foreign students wishing to gain extensive clinical experience in a short period of time. The hospital was at that time the largest charity hospital in the world and thus provided an excellent opportunity for researchers to examine the numerous ailments that afflicted the poor. Anna M. Fullerton, who graduated from the Woman's Medical College of Pennsylvania in 1882 and later became a medical missionary in India, studied and worked at the hospital from 1883 through 1884. She gave a positive account of the treatment of women physicians at the hospital. Women had almost the same opportunities as men and were treated with great courtesy by the male professors and assistants. But she also noted that for a woman to be able to work at the hospital, she had to have earned a medical degree. This still appears to be the case for women going to Vienna in the 1890s and early 1900s. Fullerton listed those medical professors who opened their clinics, wards and laboratories to women: Billroth, Hanns Kundrat, Kaposi, Carl Wilhelm Hermann Nothnagel, Leopold von Schrötter, H. von Wiederhofer, Eugen von Bamberger, Adam Politzer and Siegmund Exner-Ewarten.[61]

Several professors had closed their wards to women. In the case of two of these professors, Carl Braun and Josef Späth, this is all the more remarkable since Braun and Späth were running birth clinics and specialized in obstetrics and gynecology. The lack of access to Braun and Späth's wards did not disturb Fullerton, however, for she and the other women were able to gain ample experience by taking private courses in the wards of Gustav Braun, which did not admit men. Fullerton described the extensive course work in these wards:

> These consist in a "touch course" (the examination of pregnant women), an operative course on the phantom, and a series of obstetrical operations, versions, breech deliveries, forceps deliveries, etc., on the living in the lying-in wards. The midwives take charge of normal labors alone, and have special lectures and demonstrations from Prof. Gustav Braun. Any woman-physician desiring to study the phases of labor in a number of cases, and willing to enter upon the drudgery it entails, has the privilege of entering the school for midwives. This does not exclude her, however, from the physician's course.[62]

In a letter confirming Fullerton's account, Carl Breus, an assistant to Gustav Braun, wrote of the great opportunities available to women in Vienna. He noted that the foreign women physicians enjoyed privileges beyond those granted the midwives. Under his supervision, the women physicians were allowed "to perform for themselves the difficult operations on women in labor, which are in no case whatever permitted to the midwives, who are never allowed to make even an episiotomy."[63]

About the same time as Fullerton, Rebecca Lee Dorsey was also studying in Vienna. Dorsey, as already noted, was the first graduate of Wellesley College (1881) to earn a medical degree. Dorsey was interested in a variety of medical fields. Between 1883 and 1885, she traveled through Germany, Switzerland, Austria, France and England to supplement the education and training she had received as a medical student at the Boston University School of Medicine. In Vienna she studied under Rokitansky and Konradt, another leading pathologist at the University of Vienna. She studied skin diseases under the dermatologist Kaposi, pediatrics with Fruhwald and obstetrics with Gustav Braun.[64]

About fifteen years after Fullerton and Dorsey were in Vienna, another American physician, Rosalie Slaughter Morton, studied at the General Hospital in 1900. In her autobiography, Morton described the tempting variety of courses available to students at the hospital at that time: "On a bulletin board at the entrance to the great Kaiserlich und Königlich Algemein [sic] Krankenhaus were posted charts of professors and their classes. Classes of ten studied for two months with the various professors; but the list of a hundred possible instructors was a checkerboard maze."[65] But there was a dark side to this grand, living laboratory. The impoverished patients were not usually treated with respect or great compassion. They were often seen merely as specimens illustrating the progress of a certain disease. The frequent deaths at the hospital were seen as opportunities for medical researchers to perform autopsies. This dark side of the hospital was captured vividly by Morton:

> The only thing which disturbed me in Vienna was the unnecessary exposure of patients in the amphitheater when illnesses or operations were being demonstrated before the classes. Never was I more horrified than when I saw a poor woman in all the suffering of childbirth, lying entirely stripped on a revolving table, while students for an hour and a half noted her writhing agony.
>
> At that time every courtesy was shown to the wealthy, none to the poor. One day I actually saw a young surgeon bear not only his arm's weight but, through it, that of his body as well down on the chest of a child while determining, in consultation with his assistant, how extensive an operation to perform and what the next step should be![66]

Morton had already graduated from the Woman's Medical College of Pennsylvania in 1897, when she went to Vienna and Berlin to study. She was drawn to Vienna, in part, because she wanted to follow in the male tradition of supplementing an American medical degree with European medical research. Her two brothers, who were also physicians, had done postgraduate work in Vienna. In Vienna, Morton had the opportunity to observe the work of numerous specialists, especially in surgery. Morton also convinced Kaposi that he should allow her to attend his classes. Despite harassment from some of the male students, Morton remained in Kaposi's class until she was thoroughly shocked and horrified by a class in which a naked, syphilitic man was examined. Fortunately, Kaposi showed compassion toward Morton, and in lieu of the class allowed her to accompany him on his private rounds in the hospital for the rest of the course. Morton found this far more instructive than the class. Altogether, she was satisfied with the exceptional opportunity at the hospital to observe so many patients and operations.

Other famous physicians who studied in Vienna and for whom no university records exist are Mary Jane Safford, Mary E. Bates, Josephine Walter, Anna Maria Gove, Esther Pohl Lovejoy and Emily Dunning Barringer. Like Fullerton, Dorsey and Morton, these women had already completed their medical studies before they went to Vienna. Mary Jane Safford (1834-1891) appears to have been one of the first American women to study in Vienna. Just a few months after graduating from a homeopathic medical school, the New York Woman's Medical College, in 1869, Safford traveled to Vienna to work at the General Hospital of Vienna.[67] Safford became a leading physician in Boston.

Mary E. Bates (1861-?) graduated from the Woman's Medical College of Northwestern University in 1881 and studied in Vienna in 1883. She returned from Vienna to teach anatomy at Northwestern. In 1891 she settled in Denver, where she continued to practice as a physician and surgeon.[68]

Josephine Walter had graduated from the Women's Medical College of the New York Infirmary (1882) before traveling to Vienna in 1888 to do clinical work in gynecology with Robert von Olshausen. In Europe, Walter also did clinical work in Berlin, Leipzig, Paris and London. Before traveling to Vienna, Walter had earned the distinction of becoming the first woman intern in the United States, when she became part of the house staff of Mount Sinai Hospital in New York.[69] Walter returned to the United States to serve on the staff of the New York Infirmary. She was also the attending gynecologist and physician to two private institutions.[70]

Anna Maria Gove (1867-1952) had already completed her medical degree and worked for four years before traveling to Vienna for postgraduate study. Gove completed a two-years biology course at MIT, before enrolling at the Women's Medical College of the New York Infirmary. After graduating from medical school in 1892, Gove worked for a year at the New York Infant Asylum. In 1893 she relocated to Greensboro, North Carolina. There she served as resident physician, professor of hygiene and director of the Department of Health at the State Normal and Industrial School (University of North Carolina at Greensboro). Three years later she went to Vienna for one year of postgraduate work. Gove returned to her position at Greensboro and remained there until she retired in 1937. In 1913 Gove returned for another year of study in Vienna. Throughout her career, Gove continued to study and do clinical work outside of Greensboro at other institutes in New York, Chicago and Michigan.[71]

Esther Pohl Lovejoy (1869-1967) graduated from the Medical School of the University of Oregon in 1894. She married and practiced medicine in Portland, Oregon. After working as an obstetrician for ten years, Lovejoy went to Vienna in 1904 to attend a clinic for obstetrics and gynecology. In 1910 Lovejoy returned to Europe for further training in Vienna and Berlin.[72]

Emily Dunning Barringer graduated from the Cornell University Medical School in 1901, and was already an experienced physician when she came to Vienna with her husband in 1905.[73]

The three North American women for whom university records do exist were listed in the records of women who took the exams for midwifery: Anna Elizabeth Broomall (1847-1931), Annie Galbraith (1859-?) and Lucy Waite (1860-1943). Broomall passed her exams in 1874, Galbraith in 1885 and Waite in 1886.[74]

The most famous of these three women is Broomall, who would become the chair of obstetrics at the Woman's Medical College of Pennsylvania.[75] In 1882 Broomall established a Maternity Hospital in Philadelphia, which became part of the Woman's Medical College three years later. It was Broomall who started an outpatient department of the College, which was the first facility to offer prenatal care in the United States.[76] For better or for worse, Broomall was also one of the first physicians in the country to recommend routine episiotomies.[77] When

Broomall came to Vienna in 1872, her first course of study was in dermatology and otolaryngology. While still in Vienna, she found out that Emmeline Cleveland hoped she would succeed her as chair of obstetrics at the Woman's Medical College of Pennsylvania. Broomall then changed her field of research and enrolled in the midwifery course with Gustav Braun and Hofrath. In a biographical essay on Broomall, Mary McKibbin-Harper noted that Broomall was accepted into the course even though she had not fulfilled the remarkable requirement "that an entrant should herself have borne a child."[78] Broomall was able to create opportunities for other North American women wishing to study in Vienna. Mary W. Griscom, a physician who worked with Broomall starting in 1888 and studied in Vienna in the 1890s, wrote: "'I spent a year, twenty years later in the same hospitals and with some of the same men, and work opened to me as Dr. Broomall's Assistant, because of the record she had made.'"[79]

The records for Galbraith and Waite do not list the physicians or professors with whom they worked. Galbraith had studied at Vassar (1875-1879) and earned a medical degree at the Woman's Medical College of Pennsylvania (1884), before coming to Europe to continue her studies. In addition to Vienna, Galbraith also went to Munich, where she was supposedly the "first woman admitted as resident physician in the Woman's Hospital of Munich."[80] After completing her studies in Europe, Galbraith returned to Philadelphia in 1886, where she worked for three years as a gynecologist at the Woman's Hospital. From 1889 until 1903 she worked as physician, clinician and instructor in clinical medicine at the New York Infirmary for Women and Children. Galbraith became a fellow in the New York Academy of Medicine and was the author of several medical texts, including *Personal Hygiene and Physical Training for Women* (1911), *The Four Epochs of Woman's Life* (1901), and *Hygiene and Physical Culture for Women* (1895).[81]

Lucy Waite had already completed a medical degree (1883) at Hahnemann Medical College (now Drexel University College of Medicine), a college of homeopathic medicine in Philadelphia, before studying in Vienna. After returning from Vienna, Waite earned a second medical degree, this time from a regular medical school, Harvey Medical College (1895). In a rare article about Waite, medical historian William K. Beatty writes that Waite returned to Europe after earning her second medical degree to further her education as a surgeon: "In Vienna she studied with Karel Pawlik who did the first successful total cystectomy and with Carl Braun who was one of the persecutors of Semmelweis."[82] If Waite did indeed study with Braun, this is remarkable as he was known for refusing to allow women into his clinics. Waite became a successful medical professor and surgeon in the Chicago area. She taught gynecology at Harvey Medical College and the College of Medicine of the University of Illinois and for a period of time ran the Chicago Hospital for Women and Children. Waite presented and published numerous medical papers. In her research she questioned whether much of the gynecological surgery being performed at the time was necessary or safe.[83] In 1894 Waite married F. Byron Robinson, a surgeon. Robinson was extremely supportive of Waite's career and the two shared much of their research. In 1907 she and Robinson donated their libraries to help establish the medical library for the newly founded medical school of the University of Wisconsin-Madison.[84]

Although Broomall, Galbraith and Waite came to Vienna long after Semmelweis was gone, his contributions to safer birthing techniques were still no doubt influencing those studying midwifery in Vienna. These students then brought their knowledge of a more hygienic birthing process back to North America. Accounts of Broomall by her younger colleagues give evidence of this. One physician, Kate Mead, recalled:

> Those were the days of strong antiseptics. Dr. Broomall scorned slovenliness and inattention to the most minute details of antisepsis. Her arms dripped with carbolic solution as she demonstrated the course of labor on the old rubber phantom and flabby doll that served as examples of natural as well as of abnormal labor. Pre-natal and post-natal care were her religion, and this almost created a sixth sense in her students, that of duty to the mother, which was as oppressive as a guilty conscience.[85]

In the 1880s and 1890s, Berlin's faculty included such leading figures as Ernst Viktor von Leyden in internal medicine; Robert von Olshausen, Adolf Gusserow and August Eduard Martin in gynecology; Carl Wernicke in nervous diseases; and Julius Hirschberg in ophthalmology. Other important faculty members were Eduard Heinrich Henoch, Otto Heubner and Heinrich Finkelstein in pediatrics.

There are more complete records in Berlin than in Vienna for the women who studied medicine at the university. Women were not allowed to enroll as regular students at the University of Berlin until the Winter Semester of 1908/09. No North American woman received a medical degree from Berlin before this semester, but women were allowed to study at Berlin before then with some of the leading medical experts of the late nineteenth century. For example, in 1899 Rosalie Slaughter Morton studied gynecology with Olshausen and Martin in Berlin before continuing her medical studies in Vienna.

Berlin university records from 1895/96 through 1914 contain the names of twenty-one North American women who studied medicine in Berlin. Morton's name is not included in these records, which again indicates that there were women pursuing medical studies in Berlin who were not registered at the university. Of these twenty-one women, thirteen had already completed a medical degree in the United States before studying in Berlin. In addition, one woman had already studied medicine in the United States, but there is no indication that she had already completed her medical degree. Of the thirteen women with medical degrees, five had completed their degrees in San Francisco, either at the University of California or at Cooper Medical College. Two of the women had received their degrees from the University of Michigan. The rest are a diverse group, having received their degrees from the following universities and colleges: the New York Woman's Medical College, the University of Illinois, the University of Cleveland (Case Western Reserve University), the State University of New York, the University of St. Louis (St. Louis University) and the University of South Carolina. Despite such diversity, it is evident that the majority of these women were not graduates of women's medical colleges. As noted, enrollment at women's medical colleges started to decline in the mid-1890s as more regular medical institutes became coeducational.[86]

The doctoral records of Lillian Delger Powers[87] indicate the type of opportunities open to the women physicians studying in Berlin. Powers, who had completed her medical degree at Cooper Medical College before beginning her studies in Berlin as an auditor in the Summer Semester of 1906 and then as a matriculated student in the Winter Semester of 1908/09, began her studies in the pharmacology laboratory of Liebreich. Powers then spent a semester as an assistant in the children's ward supervised by Finkelstein.   The following semester she worked in pediatrics as an assistant to Noeggerath, who was working under Heubner.   Powers' case demands a special note, as she became so fascinated with the habits of squirrels while in Berlin, that she eventually abandoned the field of medicine to complete a doctorate in zoology.   Other women's records indicate work in physiology, gynecology, eye diseases, ear diseases and pharmacology.

EXPERIENCES AT THE SMALLER GERMAN UNIVERSITIES

Although most of the women who came to German-speaking universities to study medicine or medical science went to Zurich, Vienna or Berlin, some women also chose to study medicine at the smaller German universities, where one did not find the crowds flooding Vienna and Berlin, but one did find some of the best laboratories and some of the best teachers. These were the universities where students had the time and access to facilities to pursue extensive and long-term studies in the basic medical sciences. Here, the new generation of leaders in North American medical education also learned the importance of the whole structure of medical education in Germany.   Medical students learned the importance of a medical college being associated with a university.   They appreciated the opportunities and facilities that were available to pursue research after earning a medical degree, if they could combine a career of research with teaching.   They appreciated the opportunity for students to have extensive exposure to laboratory and clinical work.   This would be the model for the Johns Hopkins Medical School, which opened in 1893.

But women came to these smaller universities under different conditions than men.   Just like the men, these women were drawn by the expertise of the faculty and the quality of the laboratories.   Unlike the men, however, they had to receive permission from individual professors to attend courses or to work in laboratories.   The professors at the smaller universities were more likely to make an exception and allow a woman to stay long enough to earn a doctoral degree. Sometimes, however, even though a professor allowed a woman to work with him, it was not always on very satisfactory terms.

Bonner claims the number of American women studying medicine at Swiss universities fell sharply after German universities opened their medical colleges to women.[88]   Only one American woman studied medicine at Zurich between 1896 and 1915. But there was no great influx of women studying medicine at smaller German universities during this period. Only Berlin maintained its steady enrollment.   The decrease in enrollment at Zurich was probably also due to increased opportunities for women at regular medical institutes back in North America starting in the mid-1890s. But just as in the larger university towns, women working at clinics or hospitals associated with smaller universities would not necessarily have been registered at the university. Hence, the low enrollment of women medical students at the smaller universities might be misleading.

The first two German universities to allow women to matriculate were the University of Freiburg and the University of Heidelberg. These smaller universities were opened to women in the Summer Semester of 1900. Only one American woman, Marie Layman, studied medicine at Heidelberg during the period between 1900 and 1915.

The records at Freiburg include no North American women in medicine during that period. There is evidence, however, that as late as the summer of 1914, Americans were traveling to the Freiburg Women's Clinic (Frauenklinik) to observe the method of so-called painless childbirth, "twilight sleep," practiced there using scopolamin-morphine. The method had been introduced by the physicians Carl J. Gauss and Bernhardt Krönig, and was modified by P. W. Siegel along with a professor of pharmacology, Walther Straub. In 1914, Hanna Rion was sent to the clinic by the American *Ladies' Home Journal* to investigate painless childbirth. Rion's report mentions an American woman physician who visited the clinic after having studied at clinics in Berlin, Munich, and Vienna. This physician came to Freiburg with twelve years of experience as an obstetrician. Despite an initial reaction against Siegel's work, the American physician left Freiburg convinced that the "twilight sleep" method was safe for both the mother and the child.[89]

The university records of Göttingen, another small German university that had been an important center for North American men studying medical science, list the name of one American woman, Florence Adelaide Dyer, who audited classes in pathology during the Winter Semester of 1895/96. Dyer is registered as having previously attended the Woman's Medical College of Pennsylvania. There are no other American women listed as having audited or registered for courses in medicine at Göttingen between 1896 and 1915. The university records of Marburg mention one American woman, Jessie Hyde Matthews, who audited courses in bacteriology and hygiene during the Winter Semester of 1895/96. Matthews is listed as having previously attended Vassar and the Boston University School of Medicine.

Alice Hamilton studied bacteriology and pathology at Munich during the Summer Semester of 1896. Hamilton came to Munich via Leipzig and was traveling with her sister, Edith, a classics scholar. Alice had earned her medical degree from the University of Michigan (1893),[90] before traveling to the University of Leipzig in 1895 to study bacteriology and pathology. She had hoped to study with Paul Ehrlich (1854-1915) and Robert Koch (1843-1910) in Berlin, but they did not admit her to their laboratories.[91] Although Edith had received permission to audit courses at Berlin, the two sisters wanted to stay together, so they went to Leipzig, where they had both been accepted. Alice's teachers at the University of Michigan had recommended Leipzig for the excellent course in gross anatomy, that is, autopsies. But in Leipzig Alice found that women were not allowed to attend autopsies. She was able to conduct research in the laboratory of the pathologist Felix Viktor Birch-Hirschfeld, who was of no assistance but merely passed through the laboratory once a day while everyone else stood up and bowed. She received little assistance from the other members of the laboratory, who were distant and unwilling to be disturbed. She wrote: "I was shown how to prepare specimens, but that was all; no instruction, no comments. A timid plea for help would be met by 'Do not interrupt me now, Fräulein Doktor; you will ruin my whole day.'"[92] Collegiality only surfaced at the shared mealtimes, when at times "one of the men would play a tune on a comb and the rest would dance to it." At Leipzig, Alice was permitted by a few professors to audit their lectures. The lecturers agreed to ignore her presence, even as they benefited from her tuition fees. Only one kind professor changed his greeting to all the students to a gender-neutral expression that included her. When Alice was told that she would not be able to earn a degree from the university, she decided to try to transfer to Munich.   Edith was disappointed by her lectures and was also eager to leave Leipzig.

At Munich, Hans Buchner (1850-1902), the pathologist who headed the Institute for Hygiene, was impressed by the recommendations Birch-Hirschfeld and Max von Frey had given Alice. He became her advocate at the medical school and Alice's application was accepted.[93] In Munich, besides Alice and her sister Edith, there was only one other foreign female student. Two Russian women seeking admission to study political science had been refused admission. The university had also refused admission to the German Anita Augspurg, who had already made an unfavorable impression on the law faculty by her activism in Munich and Nuremberg on behalf of the women's movement.[94] In Munich, Alice was allowed to work in the laboratories, but not with the same freedom as the men. Buchner assumed that she would not want to work with the laboratory animals and refused to allow her to do so.   Hamilton would have preferred to work on the ongoing experiments to determine the role of white blood cells in fighting infection. But as that would have involved working with the animals, she was assigned instead to work in bacteriology. Buchner did allow her to attend a special lecture on immunology he was giving to the male graduate students, but Hamilton had to follow a special procedure. She had to arrive in the laboratory ten minutes before the lecture. There, the oldest student, a grandfather, escorted her to the empty classroom and directed her to a seat in a corner. When the lecture was over, before the male students left their seats, Buchner escorted her out of the room. Alice noted, with slight amusement, that the dangerous men from whom she was being protected were all middle-aged practicing physicians and research scholars. Most were heads of families. She found herself wondering whether they were a danger to her or she was a danger to them.[95]

University archive records at Munich include only five other women who studied medicine between 1900 and 1915. One woman, Annie Hegeler, audited courses in public health during the Winter Semester of 1900/01. The records do not include her previous educational background. One physican, Mary E. Lapham, audited courses in medicine in the Winter Semester of 1903/04. Lapham had earned her medical degree at the Woman's Medical College of Pennsylvania before coming to Munich. She served as head of the Highlands Camp Sanatorium in Highlands, North Carolina.[96] Three matriculated students registered for courses in medicine between 1904 and 1915.[97]

Despite her frustrating experiences at Munich and Leipzig, Alice Hamilton did return to Germany to work at a research institute in Frankfurt am Main. The city of Frankfurt was home to several important research institutes that played a significant role in medical science. Paul Ehrlich was doing research in Frankfurt and was the director of the Georg-Speyer-Haus from 1906 until his death in 1915. Frankfurt was also home to the great Senckenberg Institute, which would later be subsumed by the university. The Senckenberg Society, founded in 1817, erected a museum of natural history in 1820/21. The building that today houses the museum and a research institute was completed in 1907. The library of the institute had large collections in math, the natural sciences and medicine. In 1885, Carl Weigert (1845-1904), a professor of pathology at the University of Leipzig and Ehrlich's cousin, was appointed director of the Senckenberg Pathology and Anatomy Institute. During the break between studying at Leipzig and the start of the new semester in Munich, Alice began her work in Weigert's laboratory. There, Alice worked with Ludwig Edinger (1855-1918), a leader in the field of comparative neurology, on the olfactory system of bony fish.[98] Alice became a close friend of Edinger, his wife Anna and their daughter Tilly.[99]

On the whole, however, Hamilton was disappointed with her studies in Germany. Hamilton's professors had urged her to study abroad, arguing that she would never be considered an expert in bacteriology and pathology unless she studied in Germany. Although Hamilton described the stay in Germany as a pleasant one, she also noted that she did not learn anything in Leipzig about bacteriology that she had not already learned in America.[100] Hamilton also wrote of the contempt shown her by some teachers and students simply because she was a woman and an American. They assumed she was "uneducated and incapable of real study." This contempt for women was not confined to the university. Everywhere she and her sister traveled in Germany, they found that women were treated as inferiors. Men on the sidewalk felt free to knock women into the gutter or push them aside. Once in a crowded theater at the opera, a "tall, blond Siegfried" simply lifted Alice out of her seat so that he could sit in her place.[101]

Although Hamilton was frustrated with the limited opportunities available to her at German universities, her experiences at the Senckenberg Institute were positive. They correspond to those of the Baltimore physician Claribel Cone (1864-1929), who conducted research from 1903 to 1912 at the same laboratory at the Senckenberg Institute where Hamilton had worked.[102] Like Hamilton, Cone was a friend of the Edingers and worked with Weigert until his death. Her closest research supervisor was Eugen Albrecht. Cone's area of research was the behavior of fatty tissues in normal and pathological conditions.[103] Over the course of a decade, Cone wrote hundreds of pages on the subject. Although she never completed or published her manuscript, she worked closely with Albrecht for several years with the intention of publishing at least some portion of her work. Cone sent several letters to her sister Etta, in which she described Albrecht's support and praise of her work. In a letter from December 2, 1906, she wrote:

> Albrecht says he will abridge it for me and translate the article for the Festschrift [publication celebrating a person or an event]. He is really charming and kind. I take tea with him and his sister often in the afternoons at his "gemütlich" [cozy] little house which is charming.
>
> He says he wants the work very much and that he has more belief in it than I have.
>
> I am most terribly flattered by his praise – especially as he is so awfully critical as a rule, and the men in the laboratory, who say how difficult Albrecht is "zu fassen," [to grasp] look at our daily morning confabs behind closed doors with wonder and awe – then we again read over some of the 300 pages together...in the afternoon.[104]

Albrecht's encouragement and praise were very important for Cone's self-esteem as a scientist. She depended on Albrecht and, to a lesser degree, on other colleagues for guidance. In a letter from June 1910, Cone basked in praise of her work by German scientists, whom she referred to as the "scientific aristocrats." Her work had been recognized at a lecture given at the Senckenberg Institute. Her colleague Dr. Eduard Strauss also assured her that she was well known in the medical world. In a letter to Etta dated July 7, 1910, shortly after Albrecht's death, Cone thirsted even for indirect praise from Albrecht handed on to her by his family and colleagues:

> I cannot hear from too many people of Albrecht's interest in me – for it is one of the most flattering and charming things that has ever happened to me in my life – to be approved of *as woman* and *as worker* [emphasis added] by one of the most talented yet critical and learned men in the world for all acknowledge that Albrecht was truly remarkable.[105]

During that same period of time, the Women's Medical College of Baltimore, where Cone had graduated (1890) and taught as a lecturer on Hygiene (1893-1895) and as a Professor of Pathology (1895-1910), closed forever. The school had been unable to meet standards set by the American Medical Association.[106] Although Cone continued to return to Frankfurt for the next two years and received visits there from faculty (Franklin Mall) and young graduates from the Johns Hopkins Medical School, her association with research laboratories was dissolving. In 1893, after completing postgraduate work at the Woman's Medical College of Pennsylvania and an internship at Blockley Hospital for the Insane in Philadelphia,[107] Cone had attended courses and worked in the laboratories at the newly opened Johns Hopkins Medical School. From 1893 to 1903 she had conducted research in William H. Welch's pathology laboratory. At Hopkins she had also done research in pathology with William Osler from 1903 to 1904, and with Simon Flexner from 1907 to 1910.[108] But now her former teachers, Osler and Welch, were no longer running those laboratories. Albrecht was dead and she no longer had a job at the Women's Medical College of Baltimore. Faced with such a discouraging situation, Cone abandoned her career in medicine and, along with her sister Etta, became one of the greatest art collectors Baltimore has ever seen.[109] In July 1914, Cone traveled to Munich for a short stay. When World War I broke out, however, Cone did not flee. Instead, with financial support from relatives, she remained in Munich until the spring of 1921 learning German, and collecting antiques and art.[110]

If Hamilton, Cone and others thrived at private German research institutions but failed to find satisfactory research conditions at German universities, other women fought against similar obstacles yet persevered and eventually did manage to complete a successful, rewarding course of study at a German university. One such woman was Ida Hyde (1857-1945), who in 1896 became the first North American woman to earn a doctoral degree from the University of Heidelberg. Hyde had not been allowed to earn a medical degree at Heidelberg, but she was able to complete her degree in the College of Natural Sciences and Mathematics.[111]

In the *Journal of the American Association of University Women*, Hyde published an amusing and thoughtful essay about her studies in Germany, "Before Women Were Human Beings: Adventures of an American Fellow in German Universities of the '90s."[112] Hyde, who had taught in the Chicago public schools for two years (1881-1883), was working as an assistant in biology at Bryn Mawr College in 1893, when she was awarded the European Fellowship by the ACA. Hyde's work in embryology had attracted the attention of A. Goette, the director of the Zoology Department at the University of Strasbourg. Strasbourg, then part of Germany, was one of the greatest centers of medical science research in Germany. The university would not allow women to matriculate until the same semester as the Prussian universities, the Winter Semester of 1908/09.

Goette invited Hyde to work in his department, and Hyde used her fellowship to do research at Strasbourg. Her goal was to be admitted to the Physiological Institute there, but this institute was part of the Medical College. Neither the professors nor the students at the Medical College were willing to admit women. Encouraged by a female friend from America, Hyde decided to try to earn a doctoral degree from the University of Heidelberg. Much of Hyde's essay describes the ensuing political maneuverings necessary to gain admittance to the University of Heidelberg and to be granted permission to take examinations there. Hyde was finally granted permission to pursue a doctoral degree at Heidelberg with the proviso that this was not a precedent establishing that women could demand admission to the university.[113] Although the Medical Colleges at both Strasbourg and Heidelberg remained closed to women throughout the 1890s, Hyde's admittance to graduate studies at Heidelberg did make it easier for women who followed her to gain admittance to that university.

Even after Hyde gained admittance to the university, however, her problems were far from over. The path to her doctoral degree required great courage and perseverance. After being admitted to the university, Hyde still needed to receive permission from individual professors to be allowed to study in her chosen field, physiology, and to take examinations. One particular professor, Willy (Wilhelm Friedrich) Kühne (1837-1900), whose physiology laboratory was very popular among the male American medical students, caused Hyde much grief. Kühne had succeeded Hermann von Helmholtz (1821-1894) as the chair of physiology in 1871. When Hyde first approached him about studying physiology, he offered her the use of his personal library. But later he refused to give her the necessary examination in physiology. He admitted to having promised to examine Hyde, but confessed that he had thought she was joking when she asked him to do so. Kühne refused Hyde access to his lectures, which she would have to attend to pass the exams. Further, when Hyde asked if his graduate assistants might not be able to help her, Kühne laughed at her and said that his graduate assistants never attended his lectures. Then a small miracle occurred. Kühne asked his graduate students whether they would attend his lectures to take notes for Hyde to help her prepare for the physiology exam. To the amazement of both Kühne and Hyde, the graduate assistants agreed to help her. Kühne was pleased to see his assistants taking notes in his lectures, but he resented the gossip among his colleagues about the unusual behavior of his graduate assistants.

Unfortunately, Hyde's problems were not confined to physiology. By some misfortune, she arrived late for her first lecture in chemistry. She followed some male students into the classroom only to have the entire class grow silent and stare at her as she stood in the doorway. Hyde had barely made it to her seat, when she heard the voice of an American male student saying, "'We shall next have them in the jury box.'"[114] Hyde was humiliated but felt reassured by the response of the German students, who hissed at the American. Throughout her stay at Heidelberg, Hyde was treated by the German students with great courtesy.

Hyde received her doctoral degree in 1896 with a thesis on "The Developmental History of a few *Scyphomedusen*" (Die Entwicklungsgeschichte einiger Scyphomedusen).[115] After completing her degree, she was surprised by an invitation from Kühne, the professor who had caused her so many problems, to work in his laboratory. Hyde thus became the first woman to do research in the Medical College of the University of Heidelberg. Kühne also recommended Hyde for a scholarship to the prestigious Naples Zoological Station, which had been established in 1872 by the German scientist Anton Dohrn. In Naples, Hyde did research on the physiology of the salivary glands, especially in the octopus. Kühne was so pleased with Hyde's research, that he helped her to obtain a position in the Physiology Department at the University of Bern.

At Bern, Hyde met Henry P. Bowditch (1840-1911), who in 1871 had become the first full-time professor of physiology in the United States. Bowditch's uncle, Henry I. Bowditch (1808-1892), had been an influential member of the Boston medical community and an early supporter of women's medical education. The elder Bowditch did not, however, support coeducation. Only after women had received their medical degrees were they to be allowed to work together with men.[116] The younger Bowditch, then teaching at Harvard Medical School, was impressed by Hyde's work. He argued that if Heidelberg and Bern had allowed a woman in their Medical Colleges, there was no reason for Harvard to bar women. Harvard Medical School would remain closed to women students until 1945, but Bowditch was able to provide Hyde with the opportunity to do research in the Physiology Department of the Harvard Medical School. This was the first time a woman had been allowed to conduct research at the Harvard Medical School. Alice Hamilton would later become the first woman professor at Harvard, when she was appointed to the medical faculty as an assistant professor of industrial medicine in 1919.

From 1897 to 1899 Hyde taught as a professor of histology and anatomy at Ingalls and Dr. Sargent's Preparatory School in Cambridge, Massachusetts. She then began her long career (1899-1925) at the University of Kansas. It was Hyde who established the physiology department there in 1903. In 1905 she was promoted to full professor and became head of the physiology department in the medical school and the college. Hyde was the first woman to become a full professor of physiology at a state university.[117]

Even after her successes at Harvard and abroad, Hyde never forgot the need to help other women in their pursuit of opportunities in higher education. It was mainly through her efforts that a permanent position for an American woman was established at the Naples Zoological Station. It was Hyde who helped found the "Naples Table Association for Promoting Laboratory Research By Women" in 1897. In 1927 she established a scholarship in her name at the University of Kansas to be "awarded annually to an advanced woman student specializing in the sciences, preferably biology."[118]

Chapter Three
Women in the Humanities

By far the largest group of North American women to study at German-speaking universities was those studying in the humanities. Women in this group are included among the first women to study and earn doctoral degrees at the University of Zurich. They were among the women who managed to study at German universities as graduate students or auditors before women were officially allowed to matriculate at those universities. Some of these women went to German-speaking universities for obvious reasons, for example, to improve their language skills as German teachers. Others went with friends for summer courses without pursuing a degree. But a large and diverse group went to earn doctoral degrees. Those women pursuing advanced degrees at German universities before the early 1900s faced the same sort of barriers and humiliation as women in medicine and the sciences. They were placed on the stage before male students or hidden behind curtains in lecture halls. Some were allowed to attend lectures only to be told later that they would never be granted degrees. At times, these women also met with kindness and encouragement beyond their expectations. Some praised the same university that another woman had cursed in desperation a few years before. The influence of a few professors or administrators was sometimes all it took for a woman to pursue her dream of earning a doctoral degree.

In the humanities, the names of a few professors stand out for the encouragement they gave women in their field. Some of these men not only welcomed women to their lectures, but also enabled women to earn graduate degrees or appointed women as their assistants. The following professors at the University of Berlin became known for their support of women students: Adolf von Harnack (1851-1930) in theology; Carl Stumpf (1848-1936) in philosophy, psychology, and musicology; Alois Brandl (1855-1940) in English; and Erich Schmidt (1853-1913) in German and literary history. At Leipzig, there were the philologists Friedrich Zarncke (1825-1891), Georg Ebers (1837-1898), and Georg Curtius (1820-1885). At Göttingen, there was Moriz Heyne (1837-1906) in German, Lorenz Morsbach (1850-1945) in English, and Max Lehmann (1845-1929) in history. At Heidelberg, there were Wilhelm Braune (1850-1926) and Kahele in

Germanic philology and Johannes Hoops (1865-1949) in English.   At Zurich, particular mention is made of Theodor Vetter in English.

Like women in the sciences, women in the humanities traveled to German-speaking universities to earn graduate degrees or pursue research opportunities. Graduate programs in the humanities in North America were closed to those women who studied abroad in the 1870s.   In the 1890s, as more more graduate programs in North America opened to women, some women chose to study in Europe for the unique research opportunities as well as for the prestige still attached to European study.   When these women returned to North America, they encountered the same limited opportunities that faced women in the sciences. Their best chance for employment in higher education was at women's colleges. Many of the women returned to teaching positions where they were underpaid, overworked and lacked the time or resources to pursue further research.   What is striking about so many of these women is their willingness to struggle so that other women might have more opportunities to receive a quality undergraduate or graduate education, or even so that girls might receive a quality secondary education. Many of these women were demanding of themselves and of their students. They pushed themselves and their students to the highest levels of achievement, not only for their own satisfaction but also to prove women could thrive in higher education.   Like the women in the sciences, they recognized the importance of establishing European scholarships and fellowships so students could afford to study abroad. Many of the graduate students mentioned here who studied abroad in the 1890s and the first decades of the twentieth century were the beneficiaries of such funding.

HISTORY

While numerous women traveled to German-speaking universities to study history, very few appear to have stayed to earn a graduate degree.   In 1894 one American woman, Emma Rauschenbusch-Clough, earned a doctoral degree in history at the University of Bern. The title of her thesis was "A study of Mary Wollstonecraft and the rights of woman."[1]

Between 1868 and 1915, the only North American woman to earn a doctoral degree in history at the University of Zurich was Minnie Adell Mason Beebe (1865-1957).[2] Beebe completed her doctoral degree under Professor Knonan in February 1900, with a thesis on the "Beginnings of the Roman Revolution to the Dictatorship of Sulla" (Die Anfänge der römischen Revolution bis auf die Dictatur Sulla's).[3] Before coming to Zurich to study, Beebe had graduated from the State Normal School at Geneseo (SUNY Geneseo) and completed a Bachelor's (1890) at Syracuse University. After graduating from Syracuse, she married a former classmate, the Reverend Theodore Beebe, in August 1890.   The two planned to work together in the ministry of the Methodist Church, but Theodore died six months later.   Minnie Mason Beebe became an English teacher at the Wyoming Seminary in Kingston, Pennsylvania.   While teaching, Beebe completed a Master's degree in history from Syracuse University in 1893.   In 1898 Beebe left the Wyoming Seminary to begin her studies in Zurich.   While in Europe Beebe also studied French in Paris.   In 1900, with her degree from Zurich, Beebe was able to become a full professor of history and French at Syracuse University.   She would remain at Syracuse until she retired in 1937.[4]

Three other women are listed as studying history at Zurich, although none of them stayed to complete a degree. In 1886, when she was almost forty years old, Jane Marie Bancroft studied history at Zurich. Bancroft was a graduate of the Troy Female Seminary founded by Emma Willard. After graduating from the school in 1871, she attended the Albany State Normal School (SUNY Albany) for one year. From 1872 until 1876 she directed the Fort Edward Collegiate Institute in New York. She completed her Bachelor's at Syracuse University in 1877, and took a position as a French professor and dean of the Woman's College at Northwestern University. While still at Northwestern, Bancroft completed both her Master's (1880) and her doctoral degree in history (1884) at Syracuse. Her thesis was on "The Parliament of Paris and other Parliaments of France." While a fellow in history at Bryn Mawr the next year, Bancroft published an article about employment for college women. The following year she spent in Zurich, where she studied political and constitutional history. Bancroft also attended lectures in Paris. After her return from Europe, Bancroft published a book on the work of the Deaconesses in Europe. She later served as the Secretary of the Bureau of Deaconess Work in the Home Missionary Society of the Methodist Church. In 1891 she married George O. Robinson.[5]

In 1895 Luhanna R. Jaggar (1866-?) of Burlington, Iowa, left the University of Halle, where she had been auditing classes, to continue her study of history at Zurich. Jaggar remained for two semesters. In 1900, the same year that Beebe earned her doctoral degree, Emma Brill of Hazleton, Pennsylvania, is listed as studying history. Brill had earned a degree from Vassar, before coming to Zurich. Apparently, Brill left without earning a degree.[6]

The first doctorates at Berlin, Göttingen, Heidelberg, Freiburg and Marburg do not appear to include any historians. On the other hand, women did enroll in history courses at those universities. Between 1895 and 1909 there were at least 106 North American women auditing history courses at Berlin. Between 1909 and 1915 there were twenty matriculated students enrolled in history courses. At Göttingen, there were thirty North American women auditing history courses between 1895 and 1915. One matriculated student enrolled in history courses during the Winter Semester of 1912/13. At least five women audited courses in history at Munich between 1900 and 1906. One matriculated student studied history during the Winter Semester of 1914/15. One auditor at the University of Vienna took history courses during the Summer Semester of 1909.

The lack of degrees at Berlin, where most women studied history, may be due in part to a particularly conservative attitude towards women in that department. For example, Albisetti mentions the difficult time women had gaining permission to audit classes while the historian Heinrich von Treitschke(1835-1896) was dean of the philosophical faculty from 1894-1895.[7] Emily Greene Balch recalled that while she was a student in Berlin, Treitschke "told an acquaintance that a woman should cross the threshold of his classroom only over his dead body."[8] In his article on American perceptions of Imperial Germany, Jörg Nagler discusses a more general negative attitude among American historians towards German historians at the turn of the century. For some, German historians "had come to be identified with the interests of the autocratic German-Prussian state."[9] Academic mentors for women studying history might have discouraged them from working with German historians long enough to earn a doctoral degree. In addition to the above factors, it is important to note that two of the most renowned history departments during this period were in Berlin and Leipzig. Neither of those universities granted women doctoral degrees before 1899.

LANGUAGES AND LITERATURE

The largest group of women in the humanities were those who studied languages, literature and literary history.   This group includes not only those women who studied Germanic languages but also those studying English, French, Hebrew, Latin, Greek and linguistics.   Women who studied philosophy have been included in Chapter Five.   Such a grouping was appropriate based upon the status of these disciplines in the late nineteenth and early twentieth centuries. The field of art history has been included in Chapter Six.

The story of women who traveled to German-speaking universities to study languages and literature begins with one of the most remarkable women in this entire study, M. Carey Thomas. Thomas, who later became dean and then president of Bryn Mawr College and the first woman trustee of Cornell University, was the first American woman to earn a doctoral degree from a European university. When she earned her degree in November of 1882 from the University of Zurich, she became the first woman at that university to have passed a Ph.D. defense *summa cum laude* and the third woman to have earned a Ph.D. from Zurich.[10]

Before traveling to Europe, Thomas had completed her Bachelor's at Cornell University in 1877, the same year that Helen Magill (White) became the first woman to earn a Ph.D. in the United States (Boston University).[11] Women had been admitted to Cornell as early as 1872. After graduating from Cornell, Thomas attempted to begin her doctoral studies at The Johns Hopkins University. When it became apparent that she would have to endure a long struggle to gain permission to complete her studies, Thomas traveled instead to Europe, where she began her graduate studies at the University of Leipzig.[12] Before Thomas successfully defended her thesis in Zurich, she struggled for almost three years to earn her degree at Leipzig.   Thomas chose Leipzig over other German-speaking universities, as she preferred the atmosphere of the big city and larger university. Leipzig had also been recommended by her father's acquaintance, A. D. White, who was then president of Cornell University and U.S. Minister Plenipotentiary to Berlin. White recommended Leipzig for Thomas's subject areas: English literature and Germanic languages. During the 1870s Leipzig had become a center for the study of Indo-European languages.   The faculty included such leading philologists as August Leskien, Ernst Windisch, Karl Brugmann and Georg Ebers.[13] White had warned Thomas that while it would be very difficult for her to gain admittance to the University of Berlin, another American woman, Eva Channing of Boston, had already been given permission to attend lectures by several professors at the University of Leipzig.

Archival records for the University of Leipzig are incomplete.[14]   Records for the first women who audited courses between 1870 and the Summer Semester of 1873 are missing. There are, however, records for auditors from Winter Semester 1873/74 through Winter Semester 1889/90, which includes the period during which Thomas studied in Leipzig.   The records show that Eva Channing from Boston studied from Winter Semester 1878/79 through Winter Semester 1881/82.   Harriet Parker from Iowa also studied during the Winter Semester of 1879/80.   The other two American women registered as auditors before 1890 were M. Carey Thomas and her friend Mary (Mamie) Gwinn, who studied together in Leipzig from Winter Semester 1879/80 through Summer Semester 1882.[15]

Eva Channing came from a wealthy Boston family in Jamaica Plain and was a close friend of Helen Magill White. Both women had attended Boston University in the mid-1870s.[16] Channing graduated from the College of Liberal Arts at Boston University in 1877 with a thesis entitled "Myth-Genesis explained by Comparative Mythology."[17] Channing was also active in the Massachusetts Society of the University Education of Women.[18] Harriet Parker's father was a professor at Grinnell. She had completed her Bachelor's at the University of Iowa in Iowa City, before coming to Leipzig. After studying Greek and political economy at Leipzig for one semester, Parker returned home to Iowa, where she completed her Master's (1882) and taught Greek for one year at the University of Iowa. In 1881 Parker married John Campbell, who later became Chief Justice of the Supreme Court of Colorado. In Colorado, Parker taught German, helped run a small newspaper and did volunteer work.[19]

Thomas mentions both Eva Channing and Harriet Parker in her letters home during her stay in Leipzig. Parker, whose father was a "Professor of Greek in a tiny little Iowa university,"[20] was apparently less happy in Leipzig than Thomas, Channing and Gwinn, which might explain why she left after only one semester. Parker found the male students very rude and, after an extended search for lodging, found a room in a boarding house with disgusting food.[21] Channing, on the other hand, seems to have been quite adventurous and outspoken. It was she who found and introduced Thomas to a swimming club just for women. Channing and her mother offended Thomas by their acceptance of a certain degree of sexual freedom[22] and their disregard of some common courtesies. But, for the most part, Thomas found her a "jolly" enough acquaintance. She even benefited from Channing's greater experience. For example, Channing warned her that students who came late to lectures were subjected to being "shuffled," that is, all the students in the lecture hall shuffled their feet in disapproval.[23]

Thomas's experiences at Leipzig were mostly positive, despite her frustration at not being allowed to earn a degree there. Even before choosing to study at Leipzig, Thomas had known there was a good chance that she might not be allowed to complete a degree. She went, however, because of the reputation of the professors and the chance that she might indeed be allowed to earn a degree. Before traveling to Leipzig, she wrote from Stuttgart: "Leipzig is closed on the matter of degrees, but...it prides itself upon being the most advanced of all the universities, and in three years it may be possible."[24] The professor who influenced her work the most at Leipzig and whom Thomas considered to be the best teacher was Zarncke, the philologist. Thomas studied with other professors who welcomed women students, such as the philologists Georg Ebers, Wilhelm Braune, Richard Wülker and Georg Curtius.[25]

While Thomas considered Wülker to be "abominably stupid," she found Curtius and his wife delightful. "Prof. Curtius mimicked the Latin speeches that were made at a late banquet, etc. Frau Curtius is delightful and indeed they were most interesting and talked freely about the other professors."[26] Curtius is singled out as one of the main reasons to study in Leipzig in an anonymous article from 1879 published in the *Atlantic Monthly* about opportunities for women at the University of Leipzig. From matriculation records, Eva Channing was mostly likely the author of the article. The writer shared Thomas's frustration at not being allowed to matriculate or earn a degree. But she found that professors never refused women permission to attend their lectures. The writer was even optimistic about the university allowing women to matriculate in the near future. But it would be over twenty-five years before women would be allowed to matriculate at the universities of Saxony.

With almost all lectures as well as the university library open to her, the writer of the article found few obstacles to her studies and encouraged other women to join her. The male students treated her with civility, and fees and living expenses were minimal. At the time, the writer was supposedly one of eight women at the university. These eight women had diverse interests. Four were studying linguistics, the field in which Leipzig truly excelled. The others were studying medicine, philosophy and the natural sciences. The writer, herself, was studying linguistics and had taken grammar courses in Greek, Latin and Sanscrit. Of Professor Curtius, she wrote: "The mere *name* of Professor Curtius, for example, is of itself a guaranty to the philological student that he or she will find it worth while to turn his or her steps Leipzig-wards, even if having no suspicion beforehand of the clear and interesting manner in which the lectures of this celebrated scholar are delivered."[27] Despite such positive experiences with the faculty and her fellow students, the fear of not being as good as the male students did prey on the mind of the writer. She was relieved to find that her translations were as good as those of the other students in her Sanscrit class.

The writer compared Leipzig positively to Berlin, where "the conservatism is still so strong that no women are admitted to the regular university lectures."[28] But the conservative elements were about to reclaim power at Leipzig as well. While Thomas was at Leipzig, the Saxon government ruled to allow the ten women already at Leipzig to remain but to refuse all further applications by women. Thomas attributed this ruling to the widespread fear that open admission for women would mean a flood of applications from the "dreaded" Russian women. No German university wanted to be subjected to the "hoardes" of Russian women who had descended upon Zurich in the late 1860s and early 1870s. Thomas wrote: "The Universities live in fear – the great opposition to women consists in the terror inspired by the Russian women and their anarchy inaugurated at Zurich until they were banished. I really think the application of one Russian woman would be sufficient to close Leipzig's doors to women."[29] Thomas does not mention that many of these Russian women were Jewish and that the hostility towards both male and female Russian students was in part a manifestation of anti-Semitism.

Finally, in 1881, Thomas realized that she would not be able to complete her degree at Leipzig and explored the option of continuing at Göttingen. Her attempts to study at Göttingen failed for several reasons. First, when she finally met two of the professors, she was appalled at what they thought would make a suitable dissertation. Both professors that she interviewed had no regard for literary studies and would only accept dissertations in linguistics. Thomas refused to abandon her literary studies completely. Second, there were some miscommunications about the likelihood of her application to Göttingen being accepted. Last, the support of the chair of the philology department at Göttingen was insufficient to convince the necessary number of professors to approve Thomas's petition for study.

Thomas realized that her least favorite option, that of studying at Zurich, was now her only possibility of completing a doctoral degree. She had resisted going to Zurich, because she thought it would add additional time to her studies and because the examination process was more rigorous than in Germany. But with Mamie Gwinn by her side, Thomas moved to Zurich for the Winter Semester of 1882/83.[30] She flourished in Zurich and exceeded all expectations in her oral defense. Her major was Old and New English Language and Literature. Her minors were Gothic, and Old and Middle High German. Her thesis was on "Sir Gawayne and the Green Knight. A Comparison with the French Perceval preceded by an investigation of the author's other works and followed by a characterization of Gawain in English Poems."[31]

She was fortunate that the faculty at Zurich recognized her work at Leipzig. Her exams at Zurich were delayed only because she changed schools in the middle of a semester and had to wait until the next semester for her defense. Her oral exam, which she passed *summa cum laude*, was two and a half hours long. It consisted of forty-five minutes of testing in Old English and thirty minutes in German literature by Ludwig Tobler, forty-five minutes in New English by Heinrich Breitinger, and thirty minutes in Old German and Gothic by Heinrich Schweizer-Sidler.[32]

After graduating from Zurich, Thomas spent time in Stuttgart, Paris and England before returning to America in the fall of 1883. While still in Paris during August 1883, Thomas did her best to be appointed president of Bryn Mawr College, which was still being established. In her letter to Dr. James B. Rhoads, the recently appointed vice-president of the Board of Trustees and chair of the Executive and Building Committees and soon to be president of the college, Thomas stated her qualifications and goals for the college. First, she believed a woman would be the best president, as a man would see only the limitations of the college, whereas a woman would see its unique opportunity.[33] Second, she wanted Bryn Mawr to have the highest standards for its students. It should not be part preparatory school and part college. Bryn Mawr should not be a place for elementary college work. She wanted the college to have clear entrance requirements that would be widely published, so that when the college finally opened in September 1885, students would have had a chance to prepare for the requirements *before* coming to college. Third, she wanted the professors to be competent to teach at both undergraduate and graduate levels. Bryn Mawr was to offer women a chance to pursue graduate research so that these women might eventually replace their male professors. Fourth, Thomas wanted to follow the model of The Johns Hopkins University by providing ample fellowships that would attract postdoctoral students from other colleges or from Bryn Mawr itself. She acknowledged that most Bryn Mawr students would not become professional scholars. The real importance of having such graduate research opportunities was that "it is only from such solid and scientific instruction as is meant to pave the way for prolonged studies that there can possibly be acquired the mental discipline and the intelligent comprehension of things."[34]

While Thomas was not selected as president, she was appointed dean of the college in 1884. In this capacity, she immediately began working to implement the above goals. Bryn Mawr soon had the highest entrance standards of any women's college in the country. Together with her partner, Mary Elizabeth Garrett (1854-1915), Thomas also helped to establish the Bryn Mawr School in Baltimore, the hometown of both Thomas and Garrett, to prepare girls for these rigorous college entrance requirements. The Bryn Mawr College entrance exam became the graduation requirement for the new school. Garrett built the preparatory school with her money, and Thomas acted as the headmistress for the first few years, although she was living at Bryn Mawr College outside of Philadelphia. Thomas finally convinced her friend and graduate of Bryn Mawr College,

Edith Hamilton, to take over the position in 1896. Hamilton would remain headmistress of the school until she retired twenty-six years later.[35] In 1893 Garrett again used her money to benefit Thomas. That year, she offered to pay Bryn Mawr College $10,000 a year as long as she remained alive and Thomas remained president. After months of deliberation, the trustees finally agreed to the arrangement, and Thomas became the second president of Bryn Mawr College, a position she would hold until she retired in 1922.

As president, Thomas remained true to her earliest vision for the college and realized her dreams for the college. In her presidential address in 1908, she proudly noted that of the forty-one universities and colleges in the United States that maintained graduate schools, only one, Bryn Mawr, was a women's college. At that time, Bryn Mawr ranked fifteenth in the nation in number of graduate students and nineteenth in number of degrees conferred. It had twice as many women graduate students as Yale and was the third largest graduate school for women east of Chicago.[36] Two years later, Thomas reiterated her belief in the importance of the graduate school for excellence in undergraduate programs and for retaining the best teachers and scholars on the faculty. Her inspiration for this model of women's higher education had been the excellence of the faculties of both The Johns Hopkins University and the University of Leipzig:

> In my contact with the great scholars and teachers of Johns
> Hopkins and Leipzig I learned what every fact in my adminis-
> trative experience has proved to me over and over again, that a
> man or woman actively engaged in research makes the best
> teacher for freshmen as well as for graduates. I believe that a
> great teacher can be produced in no other way. All research
> workers are not good teachers, nor are all professors who are
> ignorant of research good teachers; but given a great scholar
> with the power to teach, then, and then only, we have a great
> teacher....Without this graduate school...we could not possibly
> have drawn to Bryn Mawr the eminent teachers of our faculty.
> We believe that even the best undergraduate teaching cannot be
> given by a college whose professors do not conduct research
> and investigation courses and that such professors would make
> infinitely better teachers even for children in a primary school
> if they were attainable,.[37]

Although few women even among the pioneers of this study shared Thomas's leadership abilities in women's education, a number of other accomplished scholars followed in her footsteps at both Zurich and German universities. Between 1882, when Thomas received her doctoral degree, and 1900, twelve more North American women completed their doctoral degrees at Zurich in the humanities and a number of other women completed doctoral degrees in the humanities at German universities. In 1897 Alice Luce earned her doctoral degree in philosophy and English literature from the University of Heidelberg, a little over a year after Ida Hyde had completed her doctoral degree in biology at the same university.[38] In 1897 Ellen Hinsdale completed her doctoral studies in German at the University of Göttingen. Before the Prussian universities were officially opened to women for the Winter Semester of 1908/09, five American women earned their doctoral degrees in the humanities or social sciences at the University of Berlin. Many of these women would make important contributions in their field upon returning to America.

For some of the eight American women, who completed their doctoral degrees in languages and literature at the University of Zurich between 1884 and
1900, there is little information available beyond the title of the dissertation and
perhaps a short biography included in the doctoral files. Fortunately, those who
pursued teaching careers at women's colleges left a trail to follow.

The first woman to follow M. Carey Thomas was her friend, Frances H.
Mitchell (1854-?) from Philadelphia, who earned her degree in 1887.[39] Her dissertation, like that of Thomas, was both a literary and philological study: "Alfrics Sigewulfi Interrogationes in Genesin. A Critical Edition of the Text by
MacLean with a Translation and Linguistic Commentary (Alfrics Sigewulfi Interrogationes in Genesin. Kritische Bearbeitung des Textes von MacLean mit
Übersetzung und sprachlichen Bemerkungen).[40]

Before coming to Zurich, Mitchell had studied at Cornell University from
1874 to 1876, where she and Thomas had become friends.[41] Mitchell left Cornell after two years to gain practical teaching experience. From 1876 until 1881
she served as principal at various Quaker high schools in Philadelphia and New
York. Finally, Mitchell decided to become a college professor. After being refused admission to several graduate programs in the United States, she entered
the University of Zurich in 1884. Mitchell came into contact with another
American, Florence Kelley, who would later become a leading labor activist. In
Zurich, Mitchell also met Hans Froelicher, a fellow student, whom she later
married.[42] After completing her doctoral degree, Mitchell returned to the United
States, where she taught Anglo-Saxon for one year at Bryn Mawr College (1887-
1888). Froelicher remained in Zurich that year to complete his doctoral degree.
At the end of the year, Mitchell and Froelicher met in Baltimore, where they
were married. Eight days after the wedding, they both began teaching at the
newly opened Woman's College of Baltimore (Goucher). Their careers at the
college would take very different paths. Froelicher had an uninterrupted career
and later served as president of the college. Mitchell taught as an associate professor of German for two years (1888-1890) and then halted her teaching career to
raise three sons, all of whom later became leaders in the field of education. Even
while not teaching, Mitchell remained active in the Goucher community and the
German department. Mitchell later resumed her teaching career at Goucher,
where she taught German for another seven years before retiring a second time.
In 1922 she returned to teach for one final year.

Mitchell remained an advocate of German studies and women's education
throughout her life. She encouraged other women to follow in her footsteps and
study abroad. In an 1896 lecture given at the Woman's College of Baltimore
(Goucher) as part of a series organized by the Alumnae Association, Mitchell
spoke about "Germanic Philology at Zurich." After describing Zurich's beauty,
Mitchell noted that women could study more freely at Zurich because they didn't
need to ask for special permission for everything. Women at Zurich did not have
to fight the battles of the pioneer: "Everywhere outside of Switzerland a woman
who wishes to study in a university must do some pioneer work before the privilege is accorded her; even then the privileges have been, so far, limited. In Zurich a woman can study without being conspicuous; without being looked upon
as a doubtful and dangerous experiment."[43] Mitchell recommended Zurich over
other universities because women had more privileges as officially matriculated
students. In another essay from that same year, Mitchell argued that American
women would feel more at home in Switzerland than in Germany because Swit-

zerland was a republic like America and because the interactions between women and men were more like those in America.[44]

She also recommended a stay in Germany, particularly in Berlin, Leipzig, Göttingen or Heidelberg, for American women to experience as many of the great professors as possible. Mitchell had studied for a semester at Leipzig while completing her degree at Zurich. She also recommended that after three semesters of work in as wide a variety of German philological courses as possible in Zurich, a student should study for a semester in Berlin. Although women were still not able to matriculate there, the stay was worthwhile, if only to sit in on lectures and to experience the cultural life of that city: "In Berlin she will also have unequalled opportunities of hearing the best music, and of seeing the best dramatic talent."[45] This exposure to the best of German culture was to inspire the student with a desire to work on her dissertation. As a thesis topic, Mitchell recommended tracing changes in German and Old English through modern times. After the delights of Berlin, the student was to return to Zurich for the "final ordeal of examination." Mitchell was optimistic about students' chances of success, and she considered such a degree "well-earned."

The next American woman to earn her doctoral degree in languages and literature at Zurich was Mrs. Mary Noyes Colvin, daughter of a judge in Dansville, New York.[46] She came to Zurich Winter Semester 1884 and completed her degree in 1888. Colvin's dissertation was "A Phonetic Study of the Works of Robert von Blois from Manuscript 24301 in the Paris National Library" (Lautliche Untersuchung der Werke Robert's von Blois nach der Handschrift 24301 der Pariser Nationalbibliothek).[47] Her thesis was a philological investigation of a novel in Old French. Her minor was Old English.[48] After completing her doctoral work, Colvin continued her work in Old French and Old English. In 1893 she published an edition of William Caxton's 1481 translation from a French edition of *Godeffroy of Boloyne, or, The Seige and conquest of Jerusalem*. The book was originally part of a Latin text, *Historia rerum in partibus transmarinisgestarum* (History of Deeds Done Beyond the Sea), written in the twelfth century by William of Tyre. Colvin's edition of Caxton's manuscript was reprinted in 1973 and for over a hundred years remained the only treatment of this manuscript.

After Colvin, came Helen L. Webster[49] of Lynn, Massachusetts, who earned her degree in 1889 with a philological thesis "On the Use of the Guttural in Gothic" (Zur Gutturalfrage im Gotischen).[50] She became the third American woman at Zurich to earn her degree *summa cum laude*. Webster came to Zurich Summer Semester 1886. She majored in Gothic, Anglo-Saxon, Old High German and Middle High German.[51] After earning her degree in Zurich, Webster lectured at Barnard College and was appointed to a chair at Vassar. In 1890 she was appointed as a professor in Comparative Philology at Wellesley. At Wellesley, Webster taught, among other courses, advanced Latin and Anglo-Saxon. Patricia Ann Palmieri notes in her history of Wellesley College that Webster's degree from Zurich impressed the college's trustees: "[T]he trustees considered her a 'teacher of excellent and rare ability and an advanced student of comparative philology.' They were pleased that she held a Ph.D. from Zurich and felt her appointment brought 'honor and strength to the Faculty.' The trustees considered it so important to secure her services that they met her contract demands and made her a full professor at a high salary."[52] Unfortunately, Webster's tenure at Wellesley lasted only eight years. In 1898 she was fired "because of deficiencies in her department." Palmieri writes that she had also earned the disapproval of the trustees by suggesting that Wellesley be used as a summer school for working girls.[53] According to Palmieri, Webster became part of a group of younger faculty members who embraced a more radical form of women's rights activism. In 1893, Webster traveled with her colleague in mathematics, Ellen Amanda Hayes, who was a radical activist for women's rights,[54] to Chicago for the International Congress of Women. There Hayes gave a talk on one of her favorite topics, dress reform. Webster spoke on "America's Debt to Zurich."

In 1895 Webster wrote an article for the *Wellesley Magazine* about "University Education for Women in Germany." The article, which begins with praise for the French and Swiss universities for welcoming women, continues with a summary of the sad state of women's education at German universities. She notes, however, that it is a time of change, for women were auditing courses at Heidelberg, Göttingen and Berlin. Although Leipzig had considered the experiment of allowing women to attend lectures a failure, Webster adds that women had continued to attend lectures there unofficially with the permission of the professor. Her praise for German universities is reserved for their teaching of the scientific method. Their students were taught the limits of what was already known and then were guided in how to proceed with research beyond that point. She ends her lecture by recommending that "[s]ome direct instruction in the principles of scientific method might to good advantage be included among the courses offered in every institution of higher learning."[55]

In 1890 Anne Louise Leonard[56] from Easthampton, Massachusetts, earned her doctoral degree in English with a critical edition of "Two Middle English Stories about Hell" (Zwei Mittelenglische Geschichten aus der Hölle).[57] Leonard's minor was in Old Norse. Leonard had studied at Wesleyan College (Wesleyan University) and Smith, before coming to Zurich Winter Semester 1887.[58] The same year that she completed her doctoral degree, Leonard returned home to marry the physiologist Jacques Loeb. She settled in New York City and raised a family. Leonard's older sister, Alice, came to Zurich to study medicine two years before her in the Winter Semester 1885, but never completed her degree. Alice had graduated from Wellesley in 1881. In 1887, the year Anne arrived in Zurich, Alice married a German physiology professor at the university, Justus Gaule, and remained in Zurich to raise a family. Later Wellesley classes mention visiting her as they passed through Zurich.[59]

There is only the most basic information available about the remaining graduates in languages and literature. After Leonard came Emma A. Yarnell[60] from Baltimore, Maryland, who completed her degree in 1896 with a thesis on "Abraham Cowley." Yarnell came to Zurich Winter Semester 1894 and chose the History of the English Language and Literature as her major. Her minors included German Literary History and the History of Ancient Philosophy.[61] The next American to earn her degree in languages and literature was Sarah May Thomas[62] from Green Bay, Wisconsin, who came to Zurich Winter Semester 1892[63] and completed her degree in 1897 with a philological thesis on the "The Phonetic Structure of the Leyden Manuscript of Williram's 'Hohelied' [Song of Songs]" (Lautstand der Leidener Handschrift von Willirams Hohem Liede).[64]

In 1899, two years after Sarah May Thomas, Virginia Eviline Spencer[65] from Lawrence, Kansas, graduated with a thesis on "The Alliteration in Spenser's Poems." Before coming to Zurich in 1893, Spencer had completed her

Bachelor's at the University of Kansas (1891) and had taught in the public high school in Lawrence, Kansas for two years. She spent the summer of 1893 vacationing in Germany before beginning her studies in Zurich that fall. At Zurich she majored in Philology, English Literature and Anglo-Saxon. Her minors were Old and Middle High German, Gothic and Aesthetics. After one year at Zurich, Spencer returned to Lawrence to complete her Master's. In 1895 she returned to Europe to continue her studies in Zurich and to do research at the British Museum in London.[66]

Mary Vance Young[67] from Washington, Pennsylvania, completed her degree in 1899, the same year as Spencer, with a thesis in French on "Les Enseignements 'Trebor des Rober' de Ho." Before coming to Zurich in 1894, she had studied for two years at Shorter College in Rome, Georgia, for one year at Albert Lea College in Albert Lea, Minnesota, and taught for two years in Georgia. Young majored in French Language and Literature. Her minors were Italian Language and Literature, and Pedagogy. Young frequently interrupted her studies at Zurich with lengthy stays in Italy and France for vacations or study. After completing her degree at Zurich, Young taught for one year at Smith College and then became a professor of Romance Languages at Mount Holyoke College. Young was a gifted linguist and published in German, French and Italian.[68]

While Zurich had been the only German-speaking university willing to grant a doctoral degree to a woman in the humanities in the early 1880s, the 1890s saw a liberalization of admission policies at both the University of Heidelberg and the University of Göttingen. While Berlin continued to bar women from earning doctoral degrees until 1899 and Leipzig waited even longer, fifteen American and Canadian women earned doctoral degrees at Heidelberg and at least four did so at Göttingen before 1915. Of the four women who earned degrees at Göttingen, one studied philology, two mathematics and one physics. At Heidelberg, eight of the dissertations were in philology or literary history, three were in art history, two were in philosophy and two in the natural sciences. The two women who earned degrees in the natural sciences, Ida Hyde (1896) and Janet Russell Perkins (1900) are discussed further in Chapter Four. Helena Adell Snyder (Dickinson) (1902) and Jennie Giehl (1911) are mentioned in Chapter Five. The three women who earned doctoral degrees in art history, Elizabeth H. Denio (1898), Neena Hamilton (1901) and Henrietta Tromanhauser (1912) are included in Chapter Six. The eight women who earned doctoral degrees in philology or literary history were: Alice Luce (1897), Georgiana Lea Morrill (1898), Ellen Clune (Buttenwieser) (1899), Erla Hittle (Rodakiewick) (1900), Louise Pound (1901), May Lansfield Keller (1905), Phoebe Mary Luehrs (1910) and Grace Edith MacLean (1910).

There were certain favorite professors among those women studying languages and literature at Heidelberg. In addition to English with Hoops, who taught at Heidelberg from 1896 to 1934, and German philology with Theodor Wilhelm Braune, who taught from 1888 to 1919, students took German language and literature courses with Max Freiherr von Waldberg (1858-1938), who taught from 1889 to 1935. For Romance languages, there was Friedrich Heinrich Georg Neumann (1854-1934), who taught from 1878 to 1882 and from 1890 to 1923. A favorite for modern history was Karl Hermann Gerhard Oncken (1869-1945), who taught at Heidelberg from 1907 to 1923.[69]

Alice Hanson Luce (1861-1940), the first of the eight women to earn a doctoral degree, was born in Winthrop, Maine, and received her Bachelor's from

Wellesley College in 1883. She was a high school teacher for ten years, including eight teaching English and mathematics at the Girls' Latin School of Boston. From 1893 to 1895 she studied philosophy, English philology and literature at the University of Leipzig. Apparently unable to complete her doctoral degree at Leipzig, Luce transferred to the University of Heidelberg, where she earned her doctoral degree *magna cum laude* two years later. Her dissertation was on "The Countess of Pembroke's *Antonie.*" After returning to the United States, Luce taught for a year at Smith College and then taught English literature at Wellesley for three years. From 1900 to 1904 she was a professor of English and dean of women at Oberlin College. After that, Luce began the career for which she is most famous. From 1904 until the outbreak of World War I, Luce was the principal at Miss Willard's American Home School for Girls (Willard School for American Girls) in Berlin. As principal, she spent half the year at the school and the rest of her time leading her students on tours through Europe. After World War I Luce began a new career on the West Coast as chair of the German Department and English professor at Mills College in Oakland, California. She remained there from 1920 until her retirement in 1928. After her retirement, Luce remained active in the AAUW, the Mills Club, the Women's Faculty Club of Berkeley and Phi Beta Kappa. She also continued her travels around the world.[70]

Georgiana Lea Morrill, an American, wrote her dissertation on "Speculum Gy de Warewyke: an English poem." Her dissertation was the first printed edition of the manuscript and was published for the Early English Text Society in 1898.[71]

In 1899, one year after Morrill, the Canadian Ellen Clune[72] completed her doctoral degree with a thesis on Old English, "Study of the Authorship of the Old English Poem *Andreas*" (Studien zur Verfasserschaft des altenglischen Gedichts *Andreas*).[73] Clune had studied at Queen's University in Kingston, Ontario (1888-1892), before coming to Germany. In Germany Clune followed the same path to Berlin and Leipzig traveled by many others. From the examples of others, it is fair to assume that when it became apparent that she would not be able to earn her degree at either Berlin or Leipzig, Clune came to Heidelberg.[74] Clune married Moses Buttenwieser, a fellow student at Heidelberg, who later became a professor at Hebrew Union College in Cincinnati. She became active in the suffrage movement and was the author of one pedagogical study, *The Obstinate Child* (1911).

Erla Hittle (Rodakiewick) from Richmond, Indiana, received her doctoral degree in December 1900 with a thesis on "The History of the Old English Prepositions 'mid' and 'wid' with Consideration of their two-sided Relationship" (Zur Geschichte der altenglischen Präpositionen 'mid' und 'wid' mit Berücksichtigung ihrer beiderseitigen Beziehungen). Hittle's thesis was published in a 1901 issue of *Anglistische Forschungen*. Hittle would return later to Europe to audit classes in English literature and philology at the University of Vienna.[75]

Louise Pound (1872-1958), who received her degree in May 1901 with a thesis on "The comparison of adjectives in English in the XV and the XVI century,"[76] is perhaps the most famous member of this group of Heidelberg graduates. Pound grew up in a prominent family in Lincoln, Nebraska, and did her undergraduate work at the University of Nebraska. Pound was extremely talented and active. Some of her activities while at the university included editing a literary magazine along with Willa Cather,[77] becoming the university's tennis champion for 1891 and 1892, managing and being captain of the women's basketball team, organizing a women's military company, competing and winning titles in several other sports, and writing a five-act satire which was performed and acting in the drama society. Pound's remarkable career continued as she returned from Heidelberg to become an English professor at the University of Nebraska. At Lincoln, she had "a distinguished career as a philologist and folklorist, managing to write several books, hundreds of articles, and to found and edit the journal *American Speech*, all the while teaching five courses a semester without the benefit of sabbatical."[78] *American Speech* is still published quarterly by the American Dialect Society. But all of this barely touches upon Pound's many accomplishments. At 82, she became the first woman president of the Modern Language Association. She was the first woman inducted into the Nebraska Sports Hall of Fame. Pound was a talented musician and trained generations of folklore scholars. One of her most famous students was Benjamin Botkin (1901-1975).[79]

Although women could officially matriculate at Heidelberg and Freiburg starting in 1900, the change in policy did not mean an end to discrimination against women at those universities. Accounts from North American women attending those universities in the early 1900s describe the red tape and hostility women continued to encounter. Even after women could officially matriculate, they still needed to get permission from individual professors and approval from the dean to attend classes.

A vivid account of this period immediately after women were allowed to matriculate is captured in the published correspondence of the next of the eight women to earn a doctoral degree. The American May Lansfield Keller (1877-1964)[80] came to Heidelberg in 1901 and earned her doctoral degree there in February 1905. Keller wrote of both the hardships and triumphs of her stay. She remained undaunted throughout, facing most obstacles with unusual daring. Almost immediately after her arrival, she was confronted with a dean who kept her documents so long, that she was still waiting for his permission to attend lectures when the new semester began. Keller decided to attend courses without the dean's permission to see what would happen. Her friend, Johnetta Van Meter, a Goucher graduate like Keller, lacked Keller's daring and did not attend lectures. Keller discovered that nothing would happen to her and Van Meter drew courage from her experiences.[81]

A year later, rules got even stricter to exclude more women. Individual professors hoping to exclude women could make up their own rules and new requirements for seminars. Keller was not to be deterred. According to her letters, she was the only woman and the only foreigner to apply for a particularly difficult seminar. In part to exclude women, the professor required that anyone attending the seminar had to submit a thesis on a grammatical subject and pass an oral examination. Ironically, Keller, the only woman to apply, was the only person who passed the qualifying exam unconditionally.[82]

The positive side of such strict measures was that when a woman did pass an exam or get admitted to a class, she knew she had met the same standards applied to men. Keller found this to be an important advantage of the German universities over the English ones. She preferred women's colleges or total equality to half measures for women that existed at Oxford and Cambridge. In 1903, she wrote in praise of the German system: "Take it all in all, I like the German way – disadvantages everywhere for women, but if they are clever enough to get through it, and over it, and around it, no difference between men and women. That suits me, not rose-tinted rooms, a lady principal, and third-rate masters, who don't teach the boys."[83] But such statements seem to contradict her earlier observations. Only three months before writing the letter above, Keller had worked closely with a professor to help another American woman gain admittance to Heidelberg. That woman, a graduate from Mount Holyoke, had been refused admission to the University of Leipzig, because Mount Holyoke was not on Leipzig's list of approved foreign institutions. The administration had kept that woman waiting for two months and then refused to admit her.[84] Cleverness was no help when a woman's credentials were rejected.

Keller had to struggle to hold her own and succeed at the university. She had little compassion for women less stable, less prepared or more easily intimidated. She had survived and even laughed about seminars where she was the only woman and had to read in front of thirty men. She had seen other women leave Heidelberg when their doctoral theses were rejected. Keller's thesis was accepted with no corrections required. The thesis, which combined elements of linguistics with a study of archaeology, had the lengthy title of "The Anglo-Saxon Weapon Names – with an Archaeological Investigation of the Weapons of Attack and Defense in use among the Anglo-Saxons from the 5th century to the time of the Norman Conquest." Keller received her doctoral degree *magna cum laude*, and was praised by professors for her "coolness." She was proud of having earned her degree without "patronage or protection."

Of course, Keller had received financial support for her studies from both her family and Goucher. Without belittling her remarkable accomplishments, it is only fair to recall the extensive support network that had created the opportunity for Keller to succeed. This network surfaced once more during the week following her successful doctoral defense. Her professors from Goucher, including the physicist Fanny Cook Gates, and the Germanists Frances Mitchell Froelicher and Hans Froelicher, immediately sent her written congratulations. Through this network, a job was already waiting for her at Wells College. She also received a visit from another Goucher fellow, Bertha May Clark, who had been studying physics for two years at Göttingen.

After receiving her degree from Heidelberg, Keller devoted the rest of her career to creating opportunities for women in higher education. She served as the head of the German Department at Wells College in Aurora, New York for two years (1904-1906). She then returned to Goucher to teach English for the next eight years. In 1914 the newly created Westhampton College, the women's college affiliated with Richmond College in Virginia, was looking for a Baptist woman with a doctoral degree for its dean. Keller was apparently one of only two women in the United States, at that time, who met those criteria. She served as dean of Westhampton from 1914 until her retirement in 1946.

Keller's training in German influenced many of the curricular decisions she made at Westhampton. As Pauline Turnbull, her biographer, wrote: "Miss Keller, trained in the philology of German universities, was...certain that Latin, Greek and modern languages were important."[85] Keller battled for years to keep languages as part of the general education requirements. She did not want women's education to be reduced to purely professional courses.

In 1910, five years after Keller left Heidelberg, the next two women, Phoebe Mary Luehrs (1878-?) and Grace Edith MacLean (1882-?) completed their doctoral degrees. Luehrs was a native of Cleveland, Ohio, and had earned her Bachelor's (1900) from Western Reserve University College for Women in Cleveland (Case Western Reserve University). Before coming to Heidelberg, Luehrs had studied German literature at Berlin. After beginning her studies at Heidelberg the Winter Semester of 1905/06, Luehrs completed her thesis on "Der nordische Aufseher," a weekly journal that had been edited by Friedrich Gottlieb Klopstock (1724-1803).[86]

Grace Edith MacLean was a native of Vineland, New Jersey. Before coming to Heidelberg, she had completed her Bachelor's (1903) at Temple College (Temple University) in Philadelphia and studied for six semesters at the University of Pennsylvania. Her thesis, "*Uncle Tom's Cabin* in Germany," appeared in a publication by the University of Pennsylvania and was published by D. Appleton in New York City (1910).[87]

Although Keller's letters and similar accounts by others of life at Heidelberg make clear that women faced many obstacles even after they could matriculate, Heidelberg along with Göttingen appear to have had relatively liberal policies towards women. Many of the women included in the sections on mathematics and physics were able to study and earn degrees at Göttingen. In 1895 Margaret Maltby became the first American woman to earn a doctoral degree at a German university by successfully defending her thesis in physics on electrolytic resistance, "Eine Methode zur Bestimmung grosser elektrolytischer Widerstände" at Göttingen. The following year, Mary Frances Winston earned her degree with her thesis on differential equations, "Über den Hermitéschen Fall der Laméschen Differentialgleichung." The next year, in 1897, Ellen Clarinda Hinsdale[88] from Hiram, Ohio, became the first American woman at Göttingen to earn a doctoral degree in philology with her thesis, "On the Rendering of the Latin Future by Old High German Translators from the 8th to the 10th Century" (Über die Wiedergabe des lateinischen Futurums bei den althochdeutschen Übersetzern des 8. bis 10. Jahrhunderts).

Hinsdale earned her Bachelor's from Adelbert College (Case Western Reserve University) in Cleveland in 1885. After teaching for the next two years, she traveled to Europe to study modern languages. Hinsdale then taught for three years at a high school in Joliet, Illinois. From 1892 to 1893 she studied German, French and pedagogy at the University of Michigan, where her father was a professor, and earned her Master's degree. She taught the following year at a high school in Ann Arbor before returning to Europe to continue her studies. She spent the Winter Semester of 1894/95 at the University of Leipzig before transferring to Göttingen the Summer Semester of 1895. In Göttingen, she received permission to attend the lectures of German scholar Moriz Heyne, English scholar Lorenz Morsbach and the philosopher Julius Baumann. In Göttingen Hinsdale majored in German and had minors in English and philosophy. [89]

It was Heyne who used his influence to see that Hinsdale could complete coursework in German that was necessary for her degree, after a junior faculty member refused to allow her to attend his lectures and seminar. The following account of Hinsdale's success was in the *Wellesley Magazine*:

> This is the first time that the authorities at the Göttingen University have allowed a woman to try for the degree in Philology, a department which, in Göttingen, requires an unusually thorough and laborious preparation. The case was, moreover, complicated by the violent resistance offered by one of the professors of Philology, against letting a woman take the Ph.D.

in his sacred department. He tried everything in his power to prevent the catastrophe, but, fortunately, failed in his efforts. Professor Heyne, under whose direction Miss Hinsdale wrote her thesis, expresses the highest regard for her work in his department. Since Miss H. holds one of the intercollegiate fellowships this year, her marked success will be especially gratifying to American college women.[90]

Hinsdale wrote with enthusiasm of the support she received from the German students after passing her doctoral examination *cum laude*. "The climax was reached when one of the German Ph.D.'s came in with a laurel wreath, tied with the colors of the philosophical faculty, which he put on my head to the great glee of the rest. I felt a bit silly, but it made a jolly time and showed the good will of all." While preparing for her examinations, Hinsdale had almost collapsed under the strain of fighting against faculty and administration members who were against women earning degrees. After earning her degree in Göttingen, Hinsdale was satisfied to leave the "pioneer work" to "those who have the philanthropic reformatory temperament." Despite such a resolution, Hinsdale remained an advocate for women in higher education and took a position in the German department at Mount Holyoke. As a professor, Hinsdale returned to Europe to further her education. During the summer of 1903 she enrolled in art history courses at the University of Berlin. As late as 1955 Hinsdale's accomplishments were recounted in the Göttingen daily newspaper. [91]

In contrast to Heidelberg and Göttingen, Leipzig and Berlin remained far more conservative in their policies towards women. Nevertheless, women were still able to take advantage of remarkable opportunities at both of those universities. Women might not have been able to complete doctoral degrees at Leipzig or Berlin, but they were able to study with leading scholars in their field at those universities.

In the 1890s the American Alice Walton studied at the University of Leipzig. She faced none of the conflicts of women like M. Carey Thomas or Alice Luce, who had hoped to earn a doctoral degree there, because she had already completed her Ph.D. before traveling to Germany. In 1897 Anna Maude Bowen would have a similar successful experience in Leipzig, where she went to study with her doctorate almost complete and with no intention of earning a German degree.[92] Walton traveled to Leipzig for the 1892/93 academic year as the recipient of the ACA's European Fellowship. Before studying in Leipzig, Walton had earned her Bachelor's from Smith College in 1887 and her Ph.D. from Cornell in 1892. Walton was a classics scholar and did postgraduate work at Radcliffe. After returning from Germany, she was chosen several times as the American Scholar of Classical Studies to do research in Athens and Rome. Walton spent summers doing research in museums in Paris and London and returned to Germany. For the first two years after earning her Ph.D., Walton taught classics at a private girls' school in New York City. In 1895 she was appointed to the faculty of Wellesley, where she taught archaeology, Greek and Latin. Walton published several articles on archaeology and art.[93]

Mary Inda Hussey studied at the University of Leipzig from 1904 to 1906, right before the universities of Saxony allowed women to matriculate. Hussey may have hoped to break the Leipzig barrier that had thwarted so many women before her and earn her doctoral degree at Leipzig. Her biography simply notes that she earned her Ph.D. at Bryn Mawr the year after returning from Leipzig.

But the case of Walton and others mentioned here makes clear that women no longer needed to travel to Europe to earn their doctoral degrees. In the early 1890s, women could earn doctoral degrees at some of the best institutions in the United States, including Bryn Mawr College, Cornell, Chicago and Yale.

Hussey studied Semitic languages and biblical literature. She received her Bachelor's (1894) and her doctoral degree (1896) from Earlham College in Richmond, Indiana. She studied on a graduate scholarship at Bryn Mawr College from 1897 to 1901. For the next two years, she was a fellow in Semitic Languages at the University of Pennsylvania. In 1910 Hussey received the Baltimore Fellowship, which she used to decipher Sumerian tablets at the Harvard Museum. The following year she continued her research as an Alice Freeman Palmer fellow. Hussey taught for a brief period of time at Wellesley and was an assistant at the Harvard Semitic Museum from 1911 to 1913. She then took a teaching position at Mount Holyoke, where she taught religion.[94]

Like Leipzig, the University of Berlin remained cautious about granting graduate degrees to nonmatriculated women. The first North American women to earn doctoral degrees in the humanities at Berlin did so after 1900. Before 1908, the year all Prussian universities finally allowed women to matriculate, five American women had earned doctoral degrees. By 1914, a total of eight American women had earned doctoral degrees at Berlin. Four of the dissertations were in philology, one in philosophy, one in chemistry, one in economics, and one in zoology. The following is a description of the work of the philologists: Caroline T. Stewart, Mary Williams Montgomery, Jennie Belle Sherzer and Grace Fleming Sweringen. After the German physicist Elsa Neumann completed her doctoral degree in 1899, Stewart, Montgomery and Sherzer were the next three women to earn doctoral degrees at Berlin.

Caroline T. Stewart from Memphis, Tennessee, was the first foreign woman to complete a doctoral degree at the University of Berlin. She successfully defended her thesis on the "A Grammatical Representation of the Language of St. Paul's Glosses to Luke" (Grammatische Darstellung der Sprache des St. Paules Gloassars zu Lukas) in 1901. Mary Montgomery defended on the same day as Stewart, and, along with Jennie Sherzer, attended Stewart's defense. Before coming to Berlin, Stewart had completed a Bachelor's in English at the University of Kansas in Lawrence in 1892. For the next two years she taught in a high school. In 1895 she earned her Master's in German from the University of Michigan, and then studied on a scholarship at Bryn Mawr College. From 1895 to 1896 she was the Bryn Mawr Scholar in Germanic languages and philology. The following year she taught at Washington College in Chestertown, Maryland. For the academic year 1898/99 she was the recipient of the ACA's European Fellowship. Stewart used this fellowship to support her studies in German and French at the University of Berlin. The following year she received the European Fellowship of the Women's Educational Association of Boston, which enabled her to continue her studies at the University of Berlin. In Berlin, Stewart attended lectures by Karl Weinhold, Andreas Heusler and Erich Schmidt in German and by Wilhelm Dilthey in philosophy.[95]

After returning to the United States, Stewart taught at the State Normal School at Plattsburg, New York (SUNY Plattsburg), from 1901 to 1902. She then began a long career as professor of German and French at the University of Missouri. Stewart has a lengthy list of publications on German language and literature as well as on translation and pedagogy.[96]

The same year as Stewart, Mary Williams Montgomery (1874-1955) earned her degree in Semitic philology with a thesis "Letters from the time of the Babylonian King Hammurabi" (Briefe aus der Zeit des Babylonischen Königs Hammurabi). Montgomery was born on November 21, 1874, in Turkey, the daughter of Dr. Giles Montgomery, who was United States Consul in Turkey and a Congregationalist minister. She completed her secondary education at Hillhouse High School in New Haven, Connecticut. Montgomery graduated with a major in German philology and French literature from Wellesley College in 1896. After spending the next two years in Asia, she studied Semitic philology for six semesters at the University of Berlin. She attended lectures, including ones by the leading philologist and cuneiform expert, Friedrich Delitzsch (1850-1922), and the philosopher and pedagogue Friedrich Paulsen.[97] In 1901, after earning her degree in Berlin, Montgomery returned to the United States to teach languages at a private school in New Haven, Connecticut. She also spent time in New York City translating from Hebrew for an encyclopedia. She eventually moved to New York City and established herself as a freelance writer, translator, and editor. She edited the volume on Turkey for the *Encyclopedia Brittanica's Historian's History of the World*. She also wrote articles on Arabic subjects and Jewish scholars of antiquity for the *Jewish Encyclopedia*. In 1905 Montgomery and two friends founded the firm of Daly, Montgomery & Lewis, which "engaged in literary and editorial work, translation, etc."[98] Eventually Montgomery's two partners left the firm to marry, and she continued to run the firm on her own. Montgomery was active in a number of women's organizations, including the AAUW, the DAR, American Penwomen and the Women's University Club of New York. In 1909 Montgomery married Gutzon Borglum (1867-1941), the sculptor of the Mount Rushmore National Memorial. Montgomery remained a member of the Deutsche-Orient-Gesellschaft and was interested in child labor legislation.[99]

The third American philologist to earn her doctoral degree at Berlin was Jennie Belle Sherzer. Sherzer was born on October 23, 1858, in Franklin, Ohio. Sherzer successfully defended her thesis on "'The Ile of Ladies,' as Published According to the Manuscript of the Marquis of Bath at Longleat" ('The Ile of Ladies,' herausgegeben nach einer HS des Marquis von Bath zu Longleat) in 1902. Before coming to Berlin, she worked for many years as a high school teacher and principal. From 1882 to 1885 she was the principal of the high school in Franklin, Ohio. From 1889 to 1891 she taught English at Oxford College in Oxford, Ohio, the oldest women's college in Ohio. From 1891 to 1892 Sherzer interrupted her career to study abroad. She first went to Jena to study German language and literature and then continued her studies at Zurich. After returning from Switzerland she served as the principal of Oxford College from 1892 to 1894. While serving as principal, Sherzer was also earning her Bachelor's at the University of Michigan (1893). In 1894 she returned to Europe to study in Paris. Upon her return, she took a new position as the principal of the Academy for Young Women in Jacksonville, Illinois (1895-1899). Sherzer then returned to Europe once more to earn her doctoral degree. From 1899 to 1902 she studied English philology at Berlin, attending lectures by Alois Brandl in English, Wilhelm Dilthey in philosophy, and Karl Weinhold and Andreas Heusler in German.[100]

Sherzer showed great perseverance in both her studies and career. In Berlin she had difficulties gaining admission to a doctoral program. After a particular professor refused to see her several times, she decided to try a new tactic:

> [S]he wrote him such an appealing, urgent, and earnest note of how she had journeyed all the way from America for the one purpose of seeking the highest degree from the University, he relented and agreed to talk with her. He saw a woman of much capacity, of deep earnestness, of intellectual attainments, of a gracious and winning personality, and his objections waned to the point of agreeing to examine her after due course of work.[101]

Upon her return to the United States, Sherzer was praised in the newspaper for crashing "through doors long closed to her sex to win an education" and was seen as "representing the emancipation of womanhood."[102] Sherzer became a professor of English philology and the dean of women at Illinois College in Jacksonville, Illinois. Her stay at that college, however, was brief. In 1905 she returned to Oxford College to serve as its president, a position she would hold until her forced resignation in 1917.

Upon assuming the presidency, Sherzer immediately worked with the Board of Trustees to establish scholarships to attract better students. She organized a chapter of the ACA, revived two ancient literary societies and revised the catalog and the curriculum. She dropped the preparatory department, established a student government and brought speakers to the college. "She was attentive to any suggestion that might increase the power or efficiency of Oxford College."[103] She also helped in the process of reorganizing the college as a nonprofit corporation. As president, Sherzer was a tireless fundraiser for the college. After years of close work with the trustees, Sherzer felt abandoned when the Board voted against her proposed merger with Western College. The merger was to have alleviated some of Oxford College's financial difficulties. The alumnae and those in power, however, voted to maintain the college's status as a women's college. Sherzer was "allowed" to resign shortly thereafter.[104] After leaving Oxford College Sherzer traveled in Asia. She then took a position at the Veterans' Service Bureau in Washington, D.C., where she remained until shortly before her death in 1930.[105]

In her doctoral file in Berlin, Sherzer gave special thanks to the Shakespeare scholar Alois Brandl for his kindness to her as a foreign woman. Brandl appears again as a supporter of women's education in a 1904 article from the *New York Times* on positive changes in women's education in Germany. The article mentions that the literature department of the University of Berlin, especially Brandl in English and Erich Schmidt in German, had done much to open the way for women.[106] Brandl had even chosen an American woman, Grace Fleming Sweringen[107] from Fetterman, West Virginia, as his assistant. After completing her Bachelor's at Cornell University in 1893, Sweringen came to Berlin the Winter Semester of 1900/01 to study philology and earn a doctoral degree. She remained at Berlin through the Winter Semester of 1903/04, serving as Brandl's assistant, and apparently completed her doctoral degree at Berlin in 1904 on "The English Written Language in Coverdale" (Die englische Schriftsprache bei Coverdale). Sweringen later became a professor of Germanic languages at the University of Colorado in Boulder.[108]

In addition to the numerous women listed above who earned doctorates from Zurich, Heidelberg, Göttingen and Berlin, supposedly one woman, Eva Johnston (1865-?) of Ashland, Missouri,[109] completed her doctoral degree in classical philology at the University of Königsberg (Kaliningrad) in 1905. Before coming to Europe, Johnston had completed her Bachelor's (1892) and Master's (1895) at the University of Missouri-Columbia. Shortly after joining the faculty at the University of Missouri as an Associate Professor of Latin, Johnston traveled to Germany, where she studied at Heidelberg and audited courses in Berlin in classical philology between 1899 and 1902. Although other Americans were earning their doctoral degrees at Berlin and Heidelberg during that period, Johnston chose to complete her degree at Königsberg. After leaving Königsberg, Johnston returned to the University of Missouri, where she taught Latin and served for a period of time as dean of women until her retirement in 1933. Johnston returned to Germany for the 1911/12 academic year to study classical philology at Göttingen. She published two works, *De Sermone Terentiano, Quaestiones duo* (1905) and *Gemination in Latin* (1906). Johnston is still honored at the University of Missouri for her accomplishments and dedication to women's education. A building was renamed in her honor in 1951 and her portrait hangs in the university archives.[110]

MUNICH 1895-1906: A CROSS-SECTION OF STUDENTS

As hundreds of North American women came to German-speaking universities to study in the humanities during the period of this study, only a few representative or remarkable cases could be included in this chapter. Those women who earned doctoral degrees, received fellowships or played a significant role in research or women's education received the most attention. To provide a more vivid account of the many women who came to the universities, this chapter continues with a representative cross-section of women who studied at the University of Munich between 1895/96 and 1905/06.

Records for women auditing courses at the University of Munich begin with the Winter Semester 1897/98 and end with the Winter Semester of 1905/06. Women were officially allowed to matriculate at the University of Munich and the other Bavarian universities in Erlangen and Würzburg starting in Winter Semester 1903/04. Bavaria was the second German state to allow women to matriculate, following only the state of Baden, which had opened the Universities of Freiburg and Heidelberg to women in the Summer Semester of 1900. Even after women were allowed to matriculate at the Bavarian universities, most North American women still chose to register as auditors.

Between 1897/98 and 1905/06 sixty different North American women registered to audit courses at the University of Munich. Two additional women matriculated during this period, bringing the total count to sixty-two. Of these sixty-two women, twenty-three women studied art history and are mentioned in Chapter Six. Five women studied medicine and two studied in the natural sciences. Within the humanities, twenty-nine women studied literature and languages, seven philosophy and three history. The following cross-section of women focuses on seven women who studied in the humanities: Edith Hamilton, Clara Landsberg, Winifred Warren, Belle E. Wright, Pauline Vandegraff Orr, Miriam Pasley and Hope Traver. Two of these women, Edith Hamilton and Winifred Warren, came to Munich before auditor records were kept.

The Hamilton Sisters and a Friend

In 1895 Alice and Edith Hamilton joined some of the first women auditors at the University of Munich. Their adventures in Germany have been well preserved and publicized in Alice's autobiography.[111] The sisters' first destination was the University of Leipzig. Edith had just graduated in classics from Bryn Mawr and was recipient of the Mary E. Garrett European Fellowship. Her sister Alice had recently completed her medical degree at the University of Michigan (1893) and accompanied her to Germany. The Hamiltons were acquainted with M. Carey Thomas and would have been aware of her frustrating experiences in Leipzig in the late 1870s and early 1880s. But this was over a decade later, and a number of women had been permitted to audit classes in the meantime.

When the Hamilton sisters arrived in Leipzig, they found a fair number of foreign women studying at the university. They were told that they could attend lectures but would not be able to participate in discussions. Alice had come to Germany to continue her studies in pathology. She was allowed to work in the laboratories and received permission from two professors to attend their lectures, but she was not allowed to attend autopsies.[112] Edith had come to Germany to study classics, and attended lectures by Brugmann and J. H. Lipsius.[113] According-ing to Alice, Edith was extremely disappointed with the lectures she attended. The lecturers were thorough, but lost sight of the beauty of literature by focusing on obscure grammatical points. "Instead of the grandeur and beauty of Aeschylus and Sophocles, it seemed that the important thing was their use of the second aorist."[114]

When the sisters discovered that women were still not allowed to earn a doctoral degree at Leipzig, they decided to try their luck at the University of Munich. As it turned out, Munich was hardly much of an improvement over Leipzig for Edith. At first it was unclear whether Edith would be able to audit lectures at all. Candidates for the priesthood would have to attend lectures with her and possibly share reading materials with her. She was finally able to attend lectures, because there was tension within the classics department between the Protestants and the Catholics. The Protestants supported Edith and she was allowed to attend classes, albeit under trying conditions. She had been told that a little alcove would be built in the lecture hall where she could sit behind a green curtain. But, as Alice writes in her autobiography, when Edith arrived, she was forced instead to sit on "a chair up on the platform beside the lecturer, facing the audience, so that nobody would be contaminated by contact with her." At Munich, Edith attended the lectures of Wilhelm von Christ and Eduard Wölfflin.[115] Of that period in Munich, Edith is quoted as saying: "The head of the University used to stare at me, then shake his head and say sadly to a colleague, 'There, now you see what's happened? We're right in the midst of the woman question.'"[116]

Edith had intended to stay at Munich and earn a doctoral degree, but her plans changed. M. Carey Thomas persuaded Edith to return to the United States to take over as head of the recently opened Bryn Mawr Preparatory School for Girls in Baltimore, Maryland. Edith never completed a doctoral degree, but she was the inspiring and respected head of the Bryn Mawr School for twenty-six years.[117] After retiring, she published her most famous works in the classics, *The Greek Way* (1930) and *The Roman Way* (1932). Alice went on to become an integral part of Hull House, a pioneer in industrial medicine and a professor at

Northwestern University and Harvard Medical School, where in 1919 she became Harvard's first woman professor.

Their younger sister Margaret studied in Munich for the Summer Semester of 1899 with another sister, Norah, and a close friend, Clara Landsberg. Margaret was studying on a Bryn Mawr European Fellowship and took courses in embryology with Karl Wilhelm Kupffer (1829-1902) and in zoology with Richard Hertwig.[118] Alice described how different she thought Margaret's experiences were from her own. Women were still isolated from the men, but this time for quite a different reason. The men had gotten lazy! Her former laboratory partners might have ignored her, but they had also worked very hard. Now, Margaret "was assigned a separate room where she was to work alone, not because the men resented her presence, but because they were freshmen, and they had been so strictly dominated in high school that the new liberty went to their heads, and instead of working they loafed."[119]

Clara Landsberg (1873-1966), a family friend, was studying in the humanities. At Munich, she took a course in paleography with Eduard Wölfflin, one in German literature with Franz Muncker (1855-1926) and one on Demosthenes with Wilhelm von Christ.[120] Landsberg was from Rochester, New York, where her father was a Reform rabbi.[121] After graduating from Bryn Mawr College in 1897, she returned to Rochester and took a position as a librarian.[122] In 1899 she traveled with Margaret and Norah to Germany. That fall she moved to Chicago to work at Hull House, which would become one of the most famous centers for social reform and assistance.[123] At Hull House she shared a room with Alice Hamilton, who had lived there since 1897. Landsberg remained at Hull House for eighteen years and was in charge of the adult education department. She also taught German at the University School for Girls.[124] Eventually, Landsberg left Hull House to teach Latin at the Bryn Mawr School, where Edith was head of the school, and Margaret taught English and was in charge of the lower grades. When Edith retired, Margaret took over as head of the school. Margaret, Alice and Landsberg later shared a home in Hadlyme, Connecticut. Alice considered Landsberg part of the Hamilton family: "I could not think of a life in which Clara did not have a great part, she has become part of my life almost as if she were one of us."[125]

The Classics Scholar

Shortly after Alice and Edith Hamilton left Munich, another American, Winifred Warren,[126] received permission to audit classes in philology at the university. Warren was a graduate of Boston University (Bachelor's 1891), where her father was president. After completing her Bachelor's, Warren began graduate studies at Bryn Mawr College in classical philology. She held fellowships in Latin from 1893 through 1896. For the 1896/97 academic year, she was the recipient of the Mary E. Garrett European Fellowship, which she used to study philology for one semester in Munich and one semester in Berlin. After studying in Germany Warren taught Latin at Vassar. While at Vassar Warren completed her doctoral degree in Greek at Bryn Mawr in 1898. Warren remained at Vassar until 1902. In 1909, at the age of thirty-nine, Warren returned to Berlin for a semester to study classical philology.[127]

A High School Teacher

During the Summer Semester of 1903, Belle E. Wright of Union Springs, New York, studied at Munich along with nine other North American women. The semester before that, Wright had audited classes at the University of Freiburg. Wright attended Franz Muncker's lecture class on the Storm and Stress period of German literature. She also took courses on German and Dutch painting, German sagas and the "Relationship of these Sagas to Ceramic Art." During the Winter Semester of 1903/04, Wright registered for only one class in German literary history with Muncker. [128]

Wright was born in April 1879, and graduated from Middlebury College in Middlebury, Vermont in 1900. Before going to Munich, Wright studied at the University of Freiburg at least for the Winter Semester of 1902/03. Unfortunately, all records of auditors before that semester have been lost, so it is impossible to know when Wright first came to Freiburg. In a 1961 letter, however, she mentions having spent two years in Germany. Of her career upon returning from Germany, Wright gave the following account: "Then I taught German in a large high school in Rochester, N.Y., until German went out of schools in the world war of 1914. After that, I made up in Spanish, in summer schools at Middlebury College. I taught Spanish in high schools until I stopped teaching in 1935. I came back to Burlington, Vt., and have tutored a lot for the University of Vermont since then."[129] At the time she wrote that letter, Wright was living in an endowed home for retired teachers funded by the Ruggles Foundation. She never married. Wright's story represents that of many German teachers who had to retrain themselves in another language or change their profession, when many school districts eliminated German from the curriculum after World War I and World War II.[130]

Two Professors

During the Winter Semester of 1904/05, three American women, all of them auditors, studied at Munich. One of them was an art history student from Newton, Massachusetts; and the other two were professors from the Mississippi State College for Women (originally the Mississippi Industrial Institute and College, and now the Mississippi University for Women) in Columbus, Mississippi. The professors remained at Munich for two semesters. Pauline V. Orr took courses in philology, German literature and English literature as well as art history. Miriam Pasley took courses in Latin, philology, Roman history, German literature and art history. Before coming to Munich, both Orr and Pasley had studied together for a year at Zurich.

As it turns out, Orr played a major role and Pasley a significant one in the history of the Mississippi State College for Women.[131] Orr came from a prosperous, politically powerful Southern family. Her father, Jehu A. Orr, was a very influential judge, statesman and trustee for the state university. Her uncle, Lawrence Orr, served as governor of South Carolina and then as minister to Russia. Her half-brother, Congressman William Gates Orr, was, however, one of the leading politicians who opposed the establishment of a women's college in Mississippi. Fortunately, his sister proved to be the triumphant one of the siblings, and in 1884 the first women's college in Mississippi opened its doors.[132]

Pauline Orr was born in November 1860. Her mother, Cornelia Vandegraff, was the second wife of Jehu A. Orr. Pauline Orr traveled north for her college education and studied at the Packer Institute in Brooklyn. She earned a Master's from Columbia and also studied at Harvard and Cornell. Orr describes her days in Brooklyn in the early 1880s with great joy: "'We used to ride those old-fashioned tally-ho's from the school on Brooklyn Heights out to Flatbush, which was then a small rural community. It was great fun.'"[133]

Orr was intending to pursue a career in journalism in New York when she heard about the women's college starting in Mississippi. Inspired by the opportunities for women she had seen in the North, Orr decided to return to her hometown to help build up the new women's college. Recalling those early years, she said: "'It wasn't easy. There were always those snobby people who said girls didn't belong in college. And there were those people who thought we shouldn't "go easy" on the girls.'"[134]

A history of the college describes Pauline Orr as "one of the school's strongest intellectual forces."[135] She played an invaluable role in promoting women's higher education in Mississippi: "Miss Orr's career at the college was to be of historic value to Mississippi as she took as her mission the goal of proving to the world that Mississippi's women scholars could be the finest in any setting."[136] Considering the historical period, it is perhaps obvious, but still worth noting that Orr was fighting for the cause of white women. The college was segregated and admitted only white women.

In 1954 a chapel on the campus was dedicated as the Orr Chapel in Pauline Orr's honor. Orr was too ill to attend the dedication ceremony, but sent a speech of appreciation, a tribute to the many women she had helped to educate:

> I spent my whole working life within these walls. Here it was my privilege to instruct thousands of the brightest and best girls of our state. These women, I say without prejudice and with high pride, have no superiors in all the world. And few equals. I cherish them all as friends who have proven their loyalty. Their kindess has warmed me throughout the long, long years. And their influence will bear fruit after I am gone.[137]

On that occasion, the first president of the college was just as generous in his praise of Orr herself: "'Her work has been of historic value to Mississippi. Miss Orr's name should be written in the stars.'" Orr was the head of the English department from 1885 until 1913, when she resigned to protest what she saw as a compromise in academic standards.[138] After resigning, Orr became an active advocate for women's suffrage, traveling across the country for the cause. In 1920 she moved to Manhattan, where she continued to write, lecture and do some teaching. Orr never married and spent the last years of her life on Long Island with her nephew.

Orr's colleague and traveling companion, Miriam Pasley, was born in September 1873 and was a member of the first graduating class of the Mississippi State College for Women in 1889. She remained at the college to teach Latin for almost thirty years. Pasley and Orr appear to have had a close friendship. Not only did they travel to Europe together, but the 1900 U.S. Census lists Pasley as a boarder at Orr's family home. Pasley and several other faculty members resigned when Orr did in 1913 to protest the college's decision to drop Latin and modern languages from the requirements for a B.S. in home economics. Orr and Pasley, along with other faculty members, had long waged a struggle to maintain the highest standards of a liberal arts education at the college. They had resisted reducing the curriculum to the most basic classes for teacher training. After resigning, Pasley, like Orr, eventually moved to Manhattan, where she worked at the Alcuin School.[139]

The Future Professor

During the Summer Semester of 1905, Hope Traver joined Orr and Pasley at Munich and remained there for two semesters. Traver came to Munich to study philology and took courses in Gothic, Old English, Old French, Provençal and phonetics. Hope Traver was born on January 14, 1873. Before coming to Munich, Traver had earned her Bachelor's from Vassar (1896) and done some teaching and graduate research. She interrupted her studies at Vassar to do home mission teaching in Memphis, Tennessee, for a year. After graduating from Vassar, she taught at the Passaic Collegiate Institute in Passaic, New Jersey, for one year and at the Calhoun-Chamberlain School in Red Bank, New Jersey, for the next four years. In 1901 she came to Bryn Mawr, where she was a graduate student and private tutor the first year. Her second year at Bryn Mawr she continued her graduate studies in English and taught at a local private girls' school, Miss Wright's School. She was a resident fellow in English for 1903/04. The following year she was awarded the Mary E. Garrett European Fellowship, which she used to study in Munich and Paris. After returning from Europe, Traver taught English for a year at Huntington Hall, Los Angeles, while finishing her doctoral thesis for Bryn Mawr, which she completed in 1907. Her thesis was on "The Allegory of the Four Daughters of God."[140]

Traver then continued to teach at Huntington Hall for two more years until she found a teaching position at Mills College in Oakland, where she remained until she retired in 1934. While at Mills, Traver remained an active scholar, traveling to Europe to continue her research or teach and publishing numerous articles about English literature.

Her own experiences in graduate school and studying abroad made her strive to create such opportunities for her own students. The history of Mills College notes that she gave her students the "enthusiasm for graduate study and found for them the means to pursue it."[141] She played a key role in helping women at Mills secure fellowships and scholarships. Her experiences abroad also made her realize the importance of establishing close ties and academic exchanges with foreign universities. She was an active supporter of the Institute of International Education. In the 1919 Bulletin of the Class of 1896 from Vassar College, Traver wrote of her efforts at encouraging such international understanding at Mills College:

> For the last ten years I have been at Mills College as Head of the English Department. Part of my war work there, through interest in internationalism, partly induced perhaps by two years' foreign study before taking my Ph.D. at Bryn Mawr, has been a course in War Literature, in which my aim was less historical than philosophical, a search for the underlying spirit of each nation as revealed in its best poetry and prose.[142]

In a similar strain, Traver wrote the following tribute to international education in the *Mills Quarterly*: "No better method for developing international good will exists than the establishment of intimate relations between the universities of different countries by means of the interchange of teachers and especially of students."[143] Hope Traver never married and died in 1963.[144]

FELLOWSHIPS

The women's colleges, and in particular Bryn Mawr, played a key role in encouraging graduate study abroad by establishing a number of European fellowships in addition to their resident fellowships and scholarships. From the 1890s through 1915, the end of the period covered in this study, a large number of graduates from these colleges studied in Europe, many of them at German-speaking universities.

Goucher established a fellowship for its alumnae in 1898. Of the first twenty-five recipients, nine used the award to study at a German university. In this section, Goucher represents typical efforts by women's colleges to encourage European graduate study among its students.

Bryn Mawr was exceptional in having several fellowships for European study. Those hoping to study at a German-speaking university could compete for four different fellowships: the President's European Fellowship, the Bryn Mawr European Fellowship, the Mary E. Garrett European Fellowship and the Anna Ottendorfer Memorial Research Fellowship in Teutonic Philology. The Bryn Mawr European Fellowship was first awarded in 1889. Of the twenty-five students who received the fellowship between 1889 and 1913, there were students enrolled at six different German-speaking universities: four at Berlin, two at Göttingen, one at Heidelberg, four at Leipzig, six at Munich, and two at Zurich.[145]

A 1908 article in the *Bryn Mawr Alumnae Quarterly* described the important benefits other students received from the returning European fellow. The student returning from Europe helped to broaden other students' minds and make them aware of how much more there was to learn. The returning fellow promoted more serious scholarship on campus. The first fellows also returned with encouraging or disheartening accounts of all they faced as some of the first women students at German universities:

> The returned European fellow enlivens many an afternoon walk
> with accounts of the methods and manners of foreign universi-
> ties. She tells how Professor Sievers in Leipsic[sic] kindly
> promised to "overlook her presence" at his lectures - but that
> was some ten years ago; or more recently of how Professor
> von Wölflin [sic], of Munich University, escorted her on his
> arm to the first Greek lecture of the term and gave her a seat of
> perfect security on the platform at a little desk by the side of
> his own desk....But always her influence makes for broadness
> and modesty. She has learned, more surely perhaps than she
> ever could by staying at one institution, how small a thing in
> the world of scholarship her own attainments are, and her com-
> rades clearly perceive how much she in her turn is their supe-
> rior. And the resolutions they mutually form to devote them-
> selves seriously to work in philology, to problems of educa-
> tion and government, to writing poetry or plays or novels, to

scientific investigation and the like, have already born good
fruit. [146]

In addition to these fellowships, there were those granted by national organizations already mentioned, such as the ACA or AAUW European Fellowship or
the Sarah Berliner Research and Lecture Fellowship. The names of most of
those fellows who studied at German-speaking universities and earned doctoral
degrees have been included in other chapters or earlier sections of this chapter.
The following section is an attempt to give some perspective on the quality of
the fellows who did not all complete their doctoral studies. This section includes
three representative fellows each from Goucher and Bryn Mawr. The section
concludes with four women who received national fellowships but did not use
the fellowship to complete a doctoral degree.

Goucher Fellows

Johnetta Van Meter was the fourth recipient of the Goucher Alumnae Fellowship. She grew up in Baltimore and attended the Girls' Latin School before
enrolling at Goucher. After graduating from Goucher in 1894, she remained at
the school as a German instructor for one year. She then returned to the Girls'
Latin School, where she taught Latin for one year and German for four. She
used her fellowship for the 1900/01 academic year to study Germanic languages
and literature at the universities in Berlin and Heidelberg. In Berlin, Van Meter
took phonetics with Brandl and German literature with E. Schmidt. In Heidelberg, she took courses in German philology with Braune, in German literature
with Waldberg and on Ibsen with Kahle. After returning from Germany, Van
Meter once more taught German at Goucher. She eventually did graduate studies
at The Johns Hopkins University (1908/09) and returned to Germany to study at
the University of Munich in 1909. After returning from Munich, Van Meter
was promoted to Associate Professor at Goucher, where she remained until
1915.[147]

Like Van Meter, May Lansfield Keller grew up in Balitmore and attended the
Girls' Latin School before enrolling at Goucher, where she graduated in 1898.
Keller then did graduate work at the University of Chicago. She was the recipient of the Goucher Alumnae Fellowship for the 1901/02 academic year. As her
stay in Europe overlapped that of Van Meter, the two women used the opportunity to travel together in Italy. Keller used the fellowship to study English and
German at the universities of Berlin and Heidelberg. She then remained in Heidelberg, where she completed her doctoral degree in 1905. After returning from
Germany, Keller taught for two years at Wells College in Aurora, New York,
before returning to Goucher to teach English. She eventually left Goucher in
1914 to become dean of women and professor of English at Westhampton College, the women's college affiliated with Richmond College in Virginia. She
also served as the president of the Southern Association of College Women.[148]

Like Keller, Annina Periam (?-1953), the eighth recipient of the Alumnae
Fellowship, also graduated from Goucher in 1898. She did graduate work at
Columbia University, where she was the first woman to be awarded a German
fellowship. After completing her Master's in 1901, she spent the summer of
1902 studying in Marburg. She remained in Germany and used the Goucher
fellowship to study Germanic Languages and Literature at the University of

Leipzig for the 1902/03 academic year. After returning to the United States, she taught German language and literature courses at Barnard College from 1903 to 1905 while completing her Ph.D. at Columbia. After earning her degree in 1905, she continued to teach for two more years at Barnard. In 1906 she published an article on "Hebbel's Nibelungen; Its Sources, Method and Style" (1906).[149] In 1907 Periam married George Henry Danton, a fellow Germanist, and they both began teaching at Stanford University. The following year, Periam stopped teaching until 1915. In 1915 she resumed teaching at Reed College in Portland, Oregon for one year. Then began a particularly adventurous stage of Periam's life. For the next ten years, she was a German professor at the National Tsing Hua University in Beijing. Periam left China in 1925 to study for a year in Leipzig. She then returned to the United States and taught for one year at Hunter College. Periam published numerous reviews and magazine articles, as well as the text, *Wie sagt man das auf Deutsch* (How Do You Say That In German?) (1936), which went through five editions. She was also co-translator with her husband of a work on Grillparzer. Periam and Danton also translated works on Confucius from Chinese into English.[150]

Bryn Mawr Fellows

In 1907 Anna Woerishoffer founded the Anna Ottendorfer Memorial Research Fellowship in Teutonic Philology in honor of her mother.[151] The fellowship was then worth $700. The first recipient of the fellowship, Anna Sophie Weusthoff (1884-1933) of Dayton, Ohio, held the fellowship for two years.[152] She received her Bachelor's from Goucher in 1906 and was a graduate scholar in Teutonic Philology at Bryn Mawr the following year. She spent the next two years on the fellowship studying at the University of Berlin. From 1909 to 1910 she continued her graduate studies at Bryn Mawr. She then took a teaching position as a German instructor at a private girls' school, the Misses Shipley School in Bryn Mawr, Pennsylvania, from 1910 to 1914. In 1914 Weusthoff married Joseph A. Mosher.[153] Weusthoff resumed teaching in 1920 at the Brearley School in New York, where she taught geography for two years and German for another year. In 1927 Weusthoff took a position at Hunter College.[154]

The next recipient of the Anna Ottendorfer Fellowship was Esther Harmon (1876-?).[155] She received her Bachelor's from the University of Michigan in 1906. Like Weusthoff, she was a graduate scholar in Teutonic Philology at Bryn Mawr for the 1906/07 academic year. She traveled to Berlin for the 1907/08 academic year when Weusthoff did, but on the President's European Fellowship from Bryn Mawr. Harmon then returned to Bryn Mawr College as a Resident Fellow in German and Teutonic Philology for the 1908/09 academic year while Weusthoff was still at Berlin. But the following year Harmon received the Ottendorfer fellowship and went to study in Munich. After returning from Munich, Harmon worked as a high school teacher in Toledo for two years while completing her doctoral studies at Bryn Mawr. Her doctoral thesis was on "Johanna Schopenhauer as a Writer" (Johanna Schopenhauer als Schriftstellerin).[156]

Adah Blanche Roe (1884-1964) from Omaha, Nebraska, was the recipient of the Ottendorfer Fellowship for the 1911/12 and 1913/14 academic years. Roe had studied at Goucher, where she graduated in 1909. She did graduate work in

German at Bryn Mawr from 1909 to 1911. She used the Ottendorfer Fellowship to study at the University of Berlin. From 1912 to 1913 she was a resident fellow at Bryn Mawr. Roe then received the Ottendorfer Fellowship a second time and spent the 1913/14 academic year at the University of Leipzig. After returning from Leipzig, Roe completed her doctoral degree in German Philology at Bryn Mawr (1914) and became head of the German department at Simpson College in Indianola, Iowa.[157] Her teaching career, however, was very brief. In 1915 she married Herman Lommel, a professor at the newly founded University of Frankfurt, and spent the rest of her life in Germany.[158]

National Fellows

Adolphine B. Ernst used an ACA European Fellowship to study Germanic languages and comparative literature at the University of Leipzig for the 1908/09 academic year. Ernst had received her Bachelor's (1901) and Master's (1907) from the University of Wisconsin-Madison before studying in Leipzig. From 1901 to 1907 she had also worked as a German instructor at Milwaukee-Downer College. After returning from Leipzig, she continued to teach and work on her Ph.D., which she completed at Madison in 1912. Ernst taught for two years at Kansas State University before returning to Madison in the German Department.[159]

Susan Helen Ballou, a scholar in paleography and Latin, used her ACA European Fellowship to study in Rome. Only later did Ballou take a leave of absence from her position as Latin instructor at the University of Chicago to study at Göttingen and Giessen in 1910 and 1911. Ballou completed her doctoral thesis in classics at the University of Giessen in 1912 on the topic: "On the clauses used by the historian Vopiscus Syracusus in the *Historia Augusta*" (De Clausulis a Vopisco Syracuso scriptore historiae Augustae adhibitis). She would later publish several articles on the *Historia Augusta*. Ballou taught in different capacities at the University of Chicago from 1898 to 1915. In 1915 she left Chicago to head the Latin Department at the Western State Normal School in Kalamazoo (Western Michigan University) for two years. Ballou then taught ancient and medieval history at the University of Wisconsin for three years, before finally becoming a professor of Latin at Bryn Mawr College in 1921.[160]

Susan Braley Franklin took a leave of absence from her position as chair of the Latin Department at the Ethical Culture School in New York City to study classics at the University of Munich for the Winter Semester of 1911/12. Franklin had previously received an ACA fellowship in 1892/93 for research in the United States, but she had also traveled to Athens and studied classics at the University of Berlin during the 1898/99 academic year.

Franklin had earned her Bachelor's (1889) and Ph.D. in Greek (1895) from Bryn Mawr College before traveling to Europe. She taught Latin at Vassar from 1893 to 1897. She then taught Latin for a year at the Baldwin School in Bryn Mawr, Pennsylvania, before studying in Athens and Berlin. After returning from Europe, she taught at the school for four more years, before taking a position at the Ethical Culture School, where she remained from 1903 to 1920. Franklin then left to teach Latin at Rogers High School in Newport, Rhode Island.[161]

Elizabeth A. Herrmann studied German at the University of Munich and the University of Berlin during the academic year of 1912/13. Herrmann would later receive an Anna C. Brackett Memorial Fellowship, which she used to take graduate courses at Radcliffe in Gothic, German literature and history, and comparative literature. Herrmann earned her Bachelor's at the University of California in 1902. She then taught for three years at the high school in Red Bluff, California. Herrmann completed her Master's at the University of California (1910) while working at Mills College, where she taught German from 1905 to 1917. Herrmann married in 1918 and gave up her own career to edit the work of her husband, N. Henry Black, a German scholar.[162]

Chapter Four
Women in Mathematics
and Science

The experiences of women within the different disciplines included in this chapter varied enough so that it was meaningful to separate the chapter into discipline areas. Common to the experiences of women in all of the disciplines was the importance of a mentor, either a man or a woman, who encouraged women students and who actively sought out or created research opportunities for them. Professors such as Charlotte Angas Scott in mathematics and Florence Bascom in geology left a legacy of women professors and researchers in their field. The same would prove true at German-speaking universities. Often the mentor would have a contact at a German-speaking university and would send North American women to study or do research at that particular university. Such was the case with mentors E. B. Wilson and T. H. Morgan in biology, who sent their students to study with Theodor Boveri in Würzburg. In a similar fashion, professors at German-speaking universities eager to encourage women in higher education also used their contacts in North America to recruit students. Such was the case with Felix Klein at the University of Göttingen, who used his contacts at the University of Chicago to recruit women students for his department.

According to American historian James C. Albisetti, the very first American woman to audit courses at a German university appears to have been Rebecca Rice. Rice was studying mathematics at the University of Heidelberg in 1873, when the university senate ruled that no further women would be allowed to audit courses.[1] The eight women auditors, including Rice, who were already attending courses, were allowed to remain, but no more women were accepted as auditors or doctoral candidates. A similar situation arose six years later at the University of Leipzig. The group of women auditors, which included the future president of Bryn Mawr College, M. Carey Thomas, was allowed to remain, but all other applications were rejected. The actions of the administrations of both universities were motivated to a large degree by the fear of being "flooded" by applications from Russian women, the largest group of foreign women enrolled at Swiss universities. The applications of Russian women to the University of Heidelberg in 1873 were the direct result of the Russian *ukase* of June of that year ordering Russian women studying at Zurich to return home or risk not having their degrees recognized. To avoid returning home, Russian women applied to other Western European universities. The University of Bern began to admit women in 1873 because of the applications of Russian women. The month of the *ukase*, two Russian women applied to study medicine at the University of Heidelberg. One month later, Heidelberg banned future applications from women to audit courses or pursue a doctoral degree. By September of that year, permission for the two Russian women to study medicine had been withdrawn.[2] It would not be until the 1890s that women would be allowed to pursue doctoral degrees at German universities. This chapter begins with the work of a small group of mathematicians and physicists, who came in the 1890s to study at the University of Göttingen, which had become part of the Prussian university system in 1866.

MATHEMATICS

Göttingen

By the time the first North American women were admitted to doctoral programs in mathematics at German universities in 1893, prospects for women in graduate programs in mathematics in the United States were actually improving. The first American woman to earn a Ph.D. in mathematics was Winifred Haring Edgerton (1862-1951), who earned her degree at Columbia University in 1886. By 1900 nine more American women had earned Ph.D.s in mathematics. Eight of those women had earned their degrees in America. The ninth woman was Mary Frances Winston, who had earned her Ph.D. in Göttingen in 1896. Winston was the first American woman to earn a Ph.D. in mathematics from a foreign university.[3] Between 1900 and 1939, an additional 216 American women earned Ph.D.s in mathematics. Although only three of these women earned their Ph.D.s at European universities during that period, Göttingen played a significant role in the careers of these early mathematicians.[4]

Of the thirty-three American women who earned doctoral degrees in mathematics between 1886 and 1911, ten studied mathematics at Göttingen.[5] Two of these women, Mary Frances Winston (Newson) (1896) and Anne Lucy Bosworth (Focke) (1900)[6] earned their doctoral degrees at Göttingen. Another, Ruth Goulding Wood, who had earned her Ph.D. at Yale (1901), was promoted to full professor at Smith College after a year of study at Göttingen.[7]

From the late 1880s until 1932, Göttingen was the center of some of the most advanced work in mathematics and physics in the world. In the early nineteenth century, the mathematician and astronomer Carl Friedrich Gauss (1777-1855), along with his friend and colleague, the physicist Wilhelm Weber (1804-1891), had made Göttingen a center for mathematics and physics. This legacy continued in the work of Gauss's immediate successors, Peter Lejeune Dirichlet (1805-1859) and Bernhard Riemann (1826-1866). Later successors included the legendary mathematician, Felix Klein (1849-1925), who came to Göttingen in 1885, and his colleagues, David Hilbert (1862-1943) and Hermann Minkowski (1864-1909), to name only a few of the leading scholars of the Mathematical Institute at Göttingen. Anecdotes from this "golden period" of research are still recounted in current literature, with Klein alternately depicted as an authoritarian or surprisingly tolerant figure.[8]

A link between women in mathematics and Göttingen was established as early as 1804, when the noted French mathematician Sophie Germain (1776-1831) began corresponding with Gauss under a pseudonym. When Gauss discovered Germain's true identity, he was amazed and generous in his praise of her intellect and courage. His praise, however, led to little concrete support of her work. Only shortly before her death did he convince the University of Göttingen to award Germain an honorary degree. Unfortunately, Germain died before receiving the degree.[9] Over forty years later, in 1874, the Russian mathematician Sofia Kovalevskaia (1850-1891) was awarded a doctoral degree in absentia from Göttingen.[10]

In the 1890s the efforts of the mathematician Felix Klein and Friedrich Althoff (1839-1908), director of academic affairs in the Prussian Ministry of Education (1882-1907), resulted in Göttingen becoming the first German university to grant a doctoral degree to a North American woman in 1895.[11] According to German historian Renate Tobies, Klein actively recruited women to study at Göttingen. Klein was motivated in part by the efforts of his friend Althoff. Althoff had convinced Klein to leave his position as a professor of geometry at the University of Leipzig to teach at Göttingen. Althoff's critics accused him of being an autocrat, as he frequently chose and promoted his candidates for academic positions against the will of departments.[12] On the other hand, Klein attributed all of the progressive changes made in the Prussian university system during that period to Althoff's direct or indirect influence.[13] Althoff had gradually become an advocate of women in higher education, and many of the scholars he promoted were those who supported women's education. He was impressed and inspired by the work of Franziska Tiburtius and Emilie Lehmus, the first two German women to open a medical practice in Germany. Tiburtius and Lehmus had been forced to earn their medical degrees at the University of Zurich, because no German university would admit them for medical studies.

Similarly, Althoff was impressed by the numerous state and private institutions in the United States which admitted women.[14] When Klein traveled to Chicago to attend the 1893 Congress of Mathematicians, he was asked by Althoff's Ministry of Education to attend the World's Columbian Exhibition, also being held in Chicago, to gather information on the American experience with women in higher education. The World's Columbian Exhibition included numerous exhibits and special congresses on women's education and women in science.[15]

By the time Felix Klein arrived in Chicago, he already enjoyed the reputation of a highly respected mathematician in North America.[16] Former German and North American students of his had found excellent teaching positions in the United States. One of those students, German scholar Heinrich Maschke (1853-1908), was teaching at the University of Chicago at the time of Klein's visit. The spring before Klein arrived in Chicago, Maschke had written to Klein asking him to use his influence to help a student, Mary Frances Winston, study mathematics at Göttingen.[17] The combined efforts of Althoff, Klein and other supportive administrators and faculty were sufficient to overcome even the opposition of the trustee of the University of Göttingen. In the Winter Semester of 1893/94, three women were allowed to audit courses in mathematics and physical chemistry. One of these women, Grace Emily Chisholm (1868-1944), was English.[18] The other two were Americans, Mary Frances Winston and Margaret Maltby.

Two years before Winston and Maltby came to Göttingen, another American woman, Christine Ladd-Franklin, had attempted to earn her doctorate there. Ladd-Franklin had been admitted as a special student at The Johns Hopkins University but had been denied her doctoral degree there in 1882. When Ladd-Franklin accompanied her husband, the mathematician Fabian Franklin, to Germany for the academic year 1891/92, she hoped to finally be able to earn her doctorate. But while she was permitted to audit courses in Berlin and Göttingen, she was not allowed to earn her doctorate. Felix Klein and Georg Elias Müller, a psychologist, argued on Ladd-Franklin's behalf but failed.[19] Ladd-Franklin returned to the United States without her degree. Two years later, Klein and Althoff had finally consolidated enough power to allow foreign women into the degree program of the Mathematical Institute.

Motivated in part by her own thwarted efforts to earn a doctorate, Ladd-Franklin devoted herself to securing study and research opportunities in higher education for other women. When she heard that Mary Winston might be able to study in Göttingen, she sent Winston $500 of her own money for her studies.[20] Ladd-Franklin's efforts were also instrumental in the establishment of a European Fellowship for graduate studies by the ACA. In 1889 she became chair of the first Committee on Fellowships of the ACA.[21] Winston would remain at Göttingen from Winter Semester 1893/94 until Summer Semester 1896. Maltby would study from Winter Semester 1893/94 until Winter Semester 1895/96. Both Winston and Maltby remained long enough to complete their doctoral degrees. They would be joined and followed by a series of other North Americans, including numerous students of mathematics. The majority of North American women who came to study in Göttingen, either as auditors or as matriculated students, were, however, enrolled in the humanities.

In general, the atmosphere in Göttingen at that time was favorable towards both foreign and German female students. By the time the first American women came to study, Göttingen had long been a popular destination for American male students. Notable American scholars and leading entrepreneurs had been coming to Göttingen to study since the early 1800s. Many Americans preferred the small-town atmosphere of Göttingen to the larger centers of Berlin and Leipzig. The German historian Konrad H. Jarausch claims that Göttingen was especially popular with Americans because of "its long-standing British ties."[22] Women might have had limited opportunities for study at the university itself, but other educational institutions apparently compensated for such barriers. Margarette Muller, a German teacher who emigrated to the United States and taught German at Wellesley, described life at the University of Göttingen in 1895 in the following passage:

> In closing, I want to say a few words about the opportunities for studies here at Göttingen. They are especially favorable for women, as they are allowed not only to attend lectures and recitations and working classes at the university, but also those at the annex arranged for German women teachers. This annex is especially valuable for foreigners, as the classes are small and the work carried on with much more enthusiasm both by professors and students than at the university. All Americans who have graduated from a college, never mind of what grade, can enter the university, as well as the annex, as workers, while among the hearers at the annex are a number

who do not possess a degree. The Göttingen library is one of
the finest in Germany, and can be freely used by all students.[23]

Muller continued by mentioning several professors, including Klein in mathematics, Hermann Walther Nernst (1864-1941) in physical chemistry, Lorenz Morsbach (1850-1945) in English philology, Ulrich von Wilamowitz-Moellendorf (1848-1931) in classical philology and Georg Elias Müller (1850-1934) in psychology, who admitted women to their courses and encouraged women to earn doctoral degrees.

An account written by Virginia Wadlow Kennedy, who spent one semester at Göttingen after completing her Bachelor's at Goucher in 1896, is equally positive about life for American women in Göttingen.[24] Kennedy wrote of having to make "a series of formidable calls on professors and the rector," but found the work manageable despite her poor German language skills. She found comfort and a new patriotism when she joined the American Colony of Göttingen for its traditional Thanksgiving dinner. The Colony had been formed in 1855, as a source of academic support and social activities.[25] About half of the seventy-five people attending the dinner were students. The president of Wesleyan University gave a toast and Kennedy joined in the singing of American songs. Her description is of a quiet and friendly town. The courses were intimidating for one with such a poor knowledge of German, but the lectures were of such quality as to make it worth struggling to understand them.[26]

The career of Mary Frances Winston (1869-1959)[27] shows some of the limitations faced by married women despite the increased opportunities for women in higher education. Winston studied mathematics and graduated with a Bachelor's from the University of Wisconsin in 1889. She then taught for two years as an instructor of mathematics at Downer College in Fox Lake, Wisconsin. She then completed a year of graduate studies at Bryn Mawr College under Professors Charlotte Angas Scott, Harkness and Mackenzie. [28]

It is not by chance that Winston and several other women mentioned in this section were associated with the mathematics program at Bryn Mawr College. Charlotte Angas Scott, who came to Bryn Mawr in 1885, the year the college opened, established the only significant graduate program in mathematics at a women's college at that time.[29] Scott was English and had earned her doctoral degree from the University of London before coming to Bryn Mawr, where she headed the mathematics department until 1924. In 1907 there were only fifteen women with doctorates in mathematics who were members of the American Mathematical Society (AMS). One of those fifteen women was Scott and four others had studied with her.[30]

Financial reasons forced Winston to abandon her work at Bryn Mawr and return to her home in Illinois. Winston was fortunate enough to be able to continue her studies at the newly opened University of Chicago (1892/93). The graduate program in mathematics was not only supportive of women, but also perhaps the best in the country at that time.[31] At the University of Chicago Winston studied with Heinrich Maschke and Eliakim Hastings Moore (1862-1932), both former students of Felix Klein. Her professors encouraged her to finish her degree with them, but they also understood when she was "bitten by the German bug."[32] She used a fellowship from the University of Chicago to fund her extensive studies in Göttingen (1893-1896). For one of those years, 1895/96, her studies were funded by both an ACA European Fellowship and a WEA fellowship. In Göttingen Winston did coursework in mathematics with

Klein, Hilbert and Heinrich Weber. She studied physics with Woldemar Voigt and did coursework in astronomy.[33] When times were difficult in Göttingen, Winston received encouragement from her parents and from fellow students, including Grace Chisholm, her best friend.[34]

After returning from Göttingen, Winston was a high school teacher in Missouri for one year. She then taught at Kansas State Agricultural College (Kansas State University) for three years, until she married Henry Bryon Newson, a mathematics professor from the University of Kansas. For the next thirteen years, Winston taught only part time. Green and Laduke, as well as Winston's son, speculate that nepotism rules were probably responsible for Winston not being offered a position in the same department as her husband at the University of Kansas. But Winston did no original research after her marriage in 1900, and that surely played a role in limiting her career opportunities as well. Winston later found a teaching position at Washburn College in Topeka, Kansas in 1913. She taught there until 1921, when she resigned after disagreeing with the college president about the firing of another faculty member. She then taught from 1921 until 1942 at Eureka College in Eureka, Illinois.[35]

Winston's only contribution to mathematical literature after 1900 was her translation of a speech by David Hilbert on the principal problems facing mathematicians in the new century. Winston's graduate work had focused on a major research area of Klein's: "problems that arise in connection with physical applications of the theory of analytical functions of a complex variable."[36] Winston's doctoral file in the university archives at Göttingen includes a letter from Klein praising the dedication and care with which Winston conducted her work.

From the time Göttingen began to keep records of women students in the Winter Semester 1895/96 until Winter Semester 1913/14, at least one and often two or three North American women studied mathematics at Göttingen each semester. North American women were drawn to Göttingen if only to benefit for a semester or two from the superior opportunities offered by its faculty.

Although Margaret Maltby was also encouraged by Klein to study at Göttingen, she eventually chose to do her doctoral work there in physics. She will thus be included in the next section of this chapter. Other North Americans continued to come to Göttingen to study mathematics. During the 1895/96 academic year, three new women arrived: Annie Louise MacKinnon (Fitch), Fidelia Jewett and Ellen Burrell.

The Canadian MacKinnon was from Woodstock, Ontario, and had earned her Bachelor's (1889) and Master's (1891) from the University of Kansas and her Ph.D. from Cornell (1894) under James E. Oliver and Lucien A. Wait before studying in Göttingen.[37] She had also worked as a mathematics teacher at Lawrence High School in Kansas from 1890 to 1892. MacKinnon came to Göttingen on an ACA European Fellowship the first year, 1894/95 and a WEA Fellowship for the following year. In a letter of introduction to Felix Klein, she described how she had heard from her advisor Oliver and read in *The Nation* about the opportunities Klein had created for women at Göttingen. She expressed her gratitude to him.[38] After returning from Göttingen, MacKinnon taught at Wells College in Aurora, New York from 1896 to 1901. In 1901 MacKinnon married Edward Fitch, whom she had met while both of them were studying at Göttingen. Fitch completed his doctoral degree with the philologist Ulrich von Wilamowitz-Moellendorf in 1896.[39] After Mackinnon married, she continued to study mathematics on her own, but apparently never taught again. MacKinnon published one article on "Concomitant binary forms in terms of the roots."[40]

The second American woman that year was Fidelia Jewett from Weybridge, Vermont. Before coming to Göttingen, Jewett had taught mathematics and botany without a college degree since the 1880s at a girls' high school in San Francisco.[41] At that school, Jewett was a colleague of Lillien Jane Martin, who is discussed in Chapter Five. She and Jewett had been intimate friends almost from the moment their paths crossed in San Francisco in 1889, and they remained friends until Jewett's death in 1933. In 1894 Martin resigned from the girls' high school to earn a doctoral degree in psychology in Göttingen. Apparently, Jewett joined her there the following year. Back in San Francisco, Jewett resumed her teaching at the same high school. When Martin returned to the United States in 1898, she was immediately offered a position teaching psychology at Stanford. But between the time she returned from Germany and her job began at Stanford, Martin had no source of income. Jewett gave Martin half of her salary until Stanford paid Martin. Martin, an equally supportive friend, encouraged Jewett to earn a college degree.[42]

The third woman was Ellen Burrell, who had earned her Bachelor's from Wellesley. Burrell never completed a graduate degree, but did end up teaching mathematics at Wellesley for thirty years.[43]

During the 1897/98 academic year, five more North American women came to Göttingen to study mathematics. For the Winter Semester of 1897/98, Fanny Cook Gates of Waterloo, Iowa, with a Master's from Northwestern University, came to Göttingen to study mathematics and physics. Gates eventually focused on physics and is discussed further in the next section of this chapter. That semester, three other women joined Gates: Katherine Hodgdon of Waltham, Massachusetts, who had studied at Boston University; Emilie Norton-Martin (1869-1936) from Elizabeth, New Jersey, who had received her Bachelor's from Bryn Mawr in 1894; and Virginia Ragsdale (1870-1945) from Jamestown, North Carolina, who had earned a B.S. (1892) from Guilford College in Greensboro, North Carolina and a B.A. (1896) from Bryn Mawr College.[44]

Norton-Martin studied in Göttingen on a Mary E. Garrett Fellowship from Bryn Mawr. After returning from Göttingen, she completed her doctoral degree (1901) at Bryn Mawr under Charlotte Angas Scott. Her dissertation was "On the Imprimitive Substitution Groups of Degree Fifteen and the Primitive Substitution Groups of Degree Eighteen." In 1903 Norton-Martin began teaching at Mount Holyoke College, where she was promoted to associate professor in 1911. In 1904 she completed an index to the first ten volumes of the *Bulletin of the American Mathematical Society*. Norton-Martin remained at Mount Holyoke until she retired in 1935. She was a member of the American Association for the Advancement of Science (AAAS) and the AMS.[45]

During 1896/97 Virginia Ragsdale had worked as an assistant demonstrator in physics at Bryn Mawr College. Like Norton-Martin, she went to Göttingen the following year on a fellowship from Bryn Mawr. Upon her return from Göttingen, she taught math and science at the Bryn Mawr School in Baltimore, Maryland. For the 1901/02 academic year, Ragsdale used a fellowship from the Baltimore Association for the Promotion of the University Education of Women to continue her graduate studies at Bryn Mawr College. Her doctoral thesis, "On the arrangement of the real branches of plane algebraic curves," was published in the *American Journal of Mathematics* in 1906. In 1911 Ragsdale became a professor of mathematics at the Woman's College in Greensboro, North Carolina (University of North Carolina), where she remained until 1928, when she retired to care for her mother. Ragsdale was perhaps best known for the Ragsdale Conjecture, which "provided an upper bound on the number of topological circles of a certain type."[46]

In the Summer Semester of 1898 Anne Lucy Bosworth (Focke) (1868-?) of Woonsocket, Rhode Island, with a Bachelor's from Wellesley (1890) and a Master's from the University of Chicago arrived in Göttingen. At Chicago, Bosworth had studied with Eliakim Hastings Moore. Before coming to Göttingen, Bosworth had also taught for six years as a professor of mathematics at Rhode Island State College in Kingston, Rhode Island (University of Rhode Island). Bosworth studied in Göttingen for three semesters and did her doctoral work under Hilbert. She and Mary Frances Winston were the only two North American women to complete a doctoral degree in mathematics at Göttingen before 1911.[47]

In the fall of 1898, Bosworth was joined by Anna Peckham from Kingston, Rhode Island, and Anna Helene Palmié (1863-1946) from Brooklyn. Peckham was a graduate of Wellesley (1893) and had studied at the University of Chicago and Stanford. She had also taught in the public schools for one year and at Rhode Island State College for three years before coming to Göttingen. After returning from Göttingen, Peckham earned her Master's at Denison University (1900) in Granville, Ohio, where she became a professor of mathematics.[48] Palmié had completed her Bachelor's at Cornell University (1890) and taught at Western Reserve University College for Women in Cleveland (Case Western Reserve University) before studying for two semesters at Göttingen. Palmié continued to teach at Western Reserve until her retirement in 1928. She was a member of Sigma Xi.[49]

The fall of 1899 brought two more American mathematicians to Göttingen. The first, Grave Alden (1874-?) from Waltham, Massachusetts, had previously studied at Radcliffe. The second, Adelaide Smith (1870-?) from Boone, Iowa, had earned her Bachelor's at Wellesley (1893), and studied at Columbia and the University of Chicago. Smith came to Göttingen on an ACA European Fellowship. After Göttingen, she moved to South Africa, where she earned a Bachelor's at the University of Cape of Good Hope (1905). Smith returned to the United States, where she earned her Master's at the University of California and taught mathematics at Rhode Island State College. Her path led her back to South Africa, where she taught mathematics at Huguenot College. Smith eventually settled in California, where she taught at the University of California at Berkeley and at Mills College.[50]

The fall of 1900 brought another two women. Anna Lavinia van Benschofen (1866-?) from Elmira, New York, had previously completed her Bachelor's at Cornell (1894) and her Master's at the University of Chicago (1900). She had also taught mathematics at a high school in Binghamton, New York (1894-1898). After returning from Göttingen, Benschofen took a position teaching mathematics at Wells College and completed her Ph.D. at Cornell in 1908.[51] The second woman, Mary Esther Trueblood (Paine) (1872-1939) from Richmond, Indiana, had completed her Bachelor's at Earlham College (1893) and her Master's at the University of Michigan (1896) before coming to Göttingen. She had also taught at Earlham as an instructor in mathematics (1897-1899). After returning from Göttingen, Trueblood taught at Mount Holyoke until 1911, when she married. In 1914 she began teaching again as head of the Extension Department of Mathematics at the University of California at Berkeley.[52]

The following fall of 1901 saw the arrival of Helen Abbot Merrill (1864-1949)[53] from Orange, New Jersey, who had previously earned her Bachelor's at Wellesley (1886) and studied at the University of Chicago (1896/97). After graduating from Wellesley, Merrill taught for five years at the Classon School for Girls in New York and for two years at the Walnut Lane School in Germantown, Philadelphia. In 1893 she began teaching at Wellesley as an instructor in mathematics. In 1901, the year she traveled to Göttingen, she was promoted to associate professor. After returning from Göttingen, Merrill completed her doctoral studies at Yale University (1903). She then returned to Wellesley, where she remained until her retirement in 1932. Merrill became a fellow of the AAAS and was a member of the AMS and the Mathematical Association of America. She was active in settlement work as well as in the Consumers League.[54] During her career, Merrill published two college textbooks on algebra, which she co-authored with Clara Eliza Smith, who had also earned her Ph.D. at Yale (1904) and studied at Göttingen (1911/12).[55]

The 1903/04 academic year brought two more Americans, Amanda J. Becker (1879-?), from Missouri State University, and Bertha May Clark (1878-1963), from the Woman's College of Baltimore (Goucher).[56] After studying at Göttingen, Clark went on to earn a Ph.D. in physics at the University of Pennsylvania in 1907. She is mentioned further in the next section on physics.

Helen Schaeffer Huff (1883-1913)[57] studied mathematics and physics at Göttingen for the 1905/06 academic year. Her studies were financed by a Mary E. Garrett European Fellowship from Bryn Mawr College. Before traveling to Göttingen, she had already earned her Bachelor's from Dickinson College (1903) in Carlisle, Pennsylvania, and her Master's from Bryn Mawr College (1905). After returning from Göttingen, she taught mathematics at the Baldwin School and earned her doctorate from Bryn Mawr in math and physics (1908). Her thesis, "A Study of the Electric Spark in a Magnetic Field," was published in the *Astro-Physical Journal*. During 1911/12, she again taught at the Baldwin School and was a reader in mathematics at Bryn Mawr College. Schaeffer Huff's career was cut short when she died in 1913 shortly after giving birth to twins. A research fellowship at Bryn Mawr was later established in her name.[58]

Alice M. Gray (1881-?), a graduate of the University of Chicago (B.A., 1903), arrived in Göttingen in the fall of 1906, the same year that brought Anna Johnson (Pell Wheeler) (1883-1966), who would emerge as one of the leading women mathematicians of the twentieth century.[59] Pell Wheeler studied at Göttingen for almost three years. It was there that she developed her interest in the growing field of integral equations through her contact with Hilbert and his colleagues.[60] Pell Wheeler continued to do research throughout her career and was instrumental in bringing national recognition to the mathematics department at Bryn Mawr, where she taught graduate courses. Before coming to Göttingen, Pell Wheeler had earned her Bachelor's from the University of South Dakota, where she studied under her future husband. She had also completed her Master's from Radcliffe. For the 1906/07 academic year she was the recipient of the Alice Freeman Palmer Fellowship, which she used to study in Göttingen. Soon after arriving in Göttingen, Pell Wheeler wrote of her experiences there for the *Wellesley College News*. The following is her first report to Caroline Hazard, then president of Wellesley:

Dear Madam: – I send herewith my report as Alice Freeman
Palmer Fellow for 1906-'07. I came to Göttingen the last of
August. The library and reading room of the university were
open during the vacation and I easily obtained permission to
make use of them. Until the university opened my time was
occupied in learning German and reading mathematics.

The lectures began October 25th and the first two weeks
the students were allowed to hear all the lectures before deciding on the courses which they wished to pursue. I have now
registered for the following lectures in mathematics: "Ellip-
tische Funktion," (four hours) by Professor Klein; "Mechanik
der Continua," (two hours) by Professor Hilbert; "Invarianten-
theorie," (two hours) by Professor Minkowski; "Die Partiellen
Differentialgleichungen der Mathematischen Physik," (four
hours) by Dr. Abraham.

Besides the lectures I am working especially on Integral
Equations, the field in which Professor Hilbert is interested,
and I hope soon to work directly under him on this subject for
my Doctor's thesis.

I am quite well satisfied with the opportunities afforded
women studying mathematics. All the mathematical lectures
and seminars are open to them, subject only to the same restrictions as the men. The mathematical reading room contains all the mathematical books and journals which one ordi-
narily needs, and since they cannot be taken from the room
there is little difficulty in procuring the necessary books.

I am certainly looking forward to a successful year.[61]

Pell Wheeler subsequently changed her plans and earned her Ph.D. from the University of Chicago in 1910. She taught her husband's classes at the Armour Institute of Technology (Illinois Institute of Technology) after he suffered a stroke.
She then went on to teach at Mount Holyoke for seven years. In 1918 she came
to Bryn Mawr College, where she taught for almost thirty years. While teaching
at Bryn Mawr, Pell Wheeler became an active member of a community of
mathematicians in the Philadelphia area. She also had close ties to mathematicians at Princeton University and its Institute for Advanced Study. There is an
account of her meeting with Einstein there:

When Einstein first came to Princeton there was a reception
for him. Mrs. Wheeler, sensing his shyness and problem with
the English language, started talking to him in German. He
looked so pleased she continued by telling him a story about
mutual friends in Germany. He laughed out loud. Everyone
looked – Einstein was laughing! During the remainder of the
evening many people came up to her asking, "How did you
make Einstein laugh?"[62]

Pell Wheeler became a close friend of the renowned mathematician Emmy
Noether (1882-1935), who fled from Germany in 1933 and became a mathematics professors at Bryn Mawr.[63] Pell Wheeler published twelve papers and was a
doctoral advisor at Bryn Mawr. In 1927 she was invited to give a series of Col-
loquium Lectures for the AMS. As of 1978 she was still the only woman to
enjoy that honor. She was a member of the Council of the AMS. Pell Wheeler

received honorary doctoral degrees from Mount Holyoke and the New Jersey College for Women (Douglass College-Rutgers University). She retired in 1948.[64]

In 1908 Ruth Goulding Wood (1875-1939)[65] came to study for a year in Göttingen. Before coming to Göttingen, Wood had earned a Bachelor's at Smith College (1898) and her Ph.D. at Yale (1901). She had taught at Mount Holyoke for one year (1901/02) and six years at Smith as an instructor in mathematics. After returning from Göttingen in 1909, Wood was promoted to full professor at Smith, where she was considered an excellent teacher. Wood was a member of the AMS.[66]

In 1910 Margaret E. Brusstar, another Bryn Mawr alumna, traveled to Göttingen to study mathematics. Brusstar was born in Birdsboro near Reading, Pennsylvania. Her father was a physician in Philadelphia. She graduated from Bryn Mawr in 1903. Before studying in Göttingen, Brusstar had taught Latin and mathematics at Ellen's School in Pittsburgh and mathematics at Miss Shipley's School. Brusstar studied in Göttingen for three semesters, from Winter Semester 1911/12 through Winter Semester 1912/13.[67]

The last mathematics scholar to study at Göttingen before World War I was Eugenie M. Morenus, who came to Göttingen in 1913. Morenus earned her Bachelor's (1904) and her Master's (1905) from Vassar. The following year, she taught mathematics and Latin at Watertown High School. The next year she taught as a substitute at Vassar. From 1908 to 1909 she was a mathematics teacher at Poughkeepsie High School. She then began a long career as an instructor and then professor of mathematics and Latin at Sweet Briar College in Sweet Briar, Virginia. Morenus continued to do research while at Sweet Briar. During the 1918/19 academic year, she was the recipient of a Vassar Alumnae Fellowship, which enabled her to study at Columbia University. In 1922 she finally completed her Ph.D. at Columbia. Five years later, she received the Anna C. Brackett Memorial Fellowship, which enabled her to do research at Cambridge for a year.[68]

Berlin

Although the Mathematical Institute at Göttingen has dominated this section, a few North American women were also drawn to the mathematics lectures of Lazarus Immanuel Fuchs (1833-1902) at the University of Berlin. In an 1895 article for the *Wellesley Magazine*, Helen L. Webster mentions women obtaining permission to attend Fuch's lectures.[69] In the 1880s, Berlin was considered by some to be the "mathematical center of the world."[70] Three brilliant scholars dominated the mathematics department: Ernst Eduard Kummer (1810-1893) and his two students Karl Weierstrass (1815-1897) and Leopold Kronecker (1823-1891). Kummer had come to Berlin in 1855 from Göttingen, where he had studied with Gauss. In the following decades, he managed to promote Weierstrass and Kronecker to professorships. The next generation of Berlin mathematicians, which included Immanuel Fuchs along with Georg Ferdinand Frobenius, Kurt Hensel, Hermann Amandus Schwarz and Friedrich Hermann Schottky, did not enjoy the same reputation as had Kummer, Weierstrass and Kronecker, and Göttingen reemerged as the leader in the field.[71]

In general, however, mathematics does not appear to have been popular among North American women at Berlin. There are no records of a North American woman earning a doctorate in mathematics during the period of this study. Historical accounts and the records of Bryn Mawr do, however, preserve the story of one American woman, Ruth Gentry (1862-1917), who overcame numerous barriers to study mathematics in Berlin.

After Gentry completed her Bachelor's at the University of Michigan in 1890, she received a fellowship in mathematics from Bryn Mawr College for the 1890/91 academic year. Gentry then decided to continue her education in Germany "to acquire a needed ease in the use of the German language, to see something of a German University, and to gain acquaintance with German methods of presenting Mathematics."[72] She eventually was allowed to spend the Winter Semester of 1890/91 in Berlin. Before attempting to study in Berlin, Gentry had been refused admittance to lectures at several other German universities. Leipzig had accepted her, but she preferred the conditions and type of mathematics courses at Berlin. For the 1891/92 academic year Gentry became the second recipient of the ACA European Fellowship, which she used to continue her studies in mathematics at Berlin. At the beginning of that academic year, Gentry applied to and was rejected by the University of Heidelberg.[73] The University Senate of Heidelberg held fast to its ruling of 1873 barring women from auditing courses or pursuing doctoral or medical degrees at the university.

In an 1892 article about her experiences in Berlin, Gentry did not encourage other women to study in Germany. She concluded that it was only through luck and unusual circumstances that she had gained admission to Immanuel Fuchs's lectures. Fuchs was very supportive of her efforts, but his support would have done her little good, if a new rector who was also supportive of her cause had not just been appointed. Fuchs and the new rector, Förster, conveniently "forgot" about an edict that would have prevented Gentry from attending any lectures. According to Rossiter, Gentry was the first woman to attend lectures at Berlin. This is questionable, however, since Gentry does mention an exception for a woman having been made before her in 1884. The edict that almost kept her from the classroom was a reaction to that exception of 1884.

Gentry had nothing but praise for Fuchs, who treated her with the utmost respect from their very first meeting. Gentry wrote:

> Prof. Fuchs did not politely "thank me for the honor, etc., while regretting to be unable to admit a woman to his lectures;" he did not assure me Mathematics was a difficult subject which women, for the most part, could not comprehend (as one Professor had written); he did not, as the Rector of one University did, advise me to apply to the Ministerium, and accompany his advice with the assurance that my request would not be granted; he did not make me feel that a woman possessed of interest in Mathematics was a sort of natural curiosity, whose existence demanded explanation. He asked me in his quiet, restful way, what I had done in Mathematics and under whose instruction, talked a minute or two about Briot and Bouquet's *Fonctions Elliptiques*, and told me to ask the Rector of the University whether a way could not be found to favor my petition.[74]

Gentry spoke with equal praise of the male students, who always treated her as a peer. They quietly attended to their own affairs and allowed her to do the same. Although Gentry was allowed to attend lectures for that semester, she was not allowed to pursue a degree. Gentry continued her studies at the Sorbonne and then returned to the United States, where she received another fellowship in mathematics from Bryn Mawr for the next two years. In 1894 Gentry began teaching as an intructor in mathematics at Vassar College. While teaching, Gentry continued work on her Ph.D., "On the forms of plane quartic curves," which she completed in 1896 at Bryn Mawr under Charlotte Angas Scott. She taught at Vassar (1894 to 1902), where she was the first faculty member with a Ph.D. She was promoted to associate professor in 1900. Gentry left Vassar to become associate principal and head of the Mathematics Department at a private school in Pittsburgh. From 1902 until her death in 1917, Gentry suffered from a chronic illness, which limited her career but did not keep her from leading a fairly active life. From 1910 to 1911 she worked as a volunteer nurse. She traveled extensively in the United States and Europe between 1911 and 1914.[75]

PHYSICS

Closely associated with the renowned Mathematical Institute at Göttingen was the physics department, which included crossover courses like mathematical physics, taught by the famous physicist Woldemar Voigt (1850-1919). In 1897 a department for technical physics was founded, which would later do revolutionary work in aerodynamics. The following year the first institute of geophysics opened at Göttingen. Göttingen was also famous for the early work done in electromagnetism by Wilhelm Weber, Gauss's colleague. The physics department would actually reach its height in the 1920s with the revolutionary work in quantum mechanics by Max Born (1882-1970), James Franck (1882-1964), Robert Wichard Pohl (1884-1976) and Werner Heisenberg (1901-1976).[76]

The first American woman to get a doctoral degree from a German university was Margaret Eliza Maltby (1860-1944),[77] who earned her degree in physics from Göttingen in 1895, *cum laude*. The title of her doctoral thesis was "A Method for the Determination of Great Electrolytic Resistance."

The success of Maltby and her peers at Göttingen proved extremely important in bringing about reforms at German universities that would make it easier for German women to receive a higher education. An editorial from 1895 in the Wellesley newspaper states that the success of Maltby along with that of a British woman [Grace Emily Chisholm] has:

> materially improved the position of women at the universities of Germany, since it was the cause of a new regulation issued from Berlin last March. This document states that if the government finds the credentials of any student recommended by the faculty of a university satisfactory, the matter of sex shall not debar her from the privilege of study, or from receiving the degree for which she is qualified.[78]

Before studying at Göttingen, Maltby had received her Bachelor's (1882) from Oberlin College. She then studied art in New York City and taught high school for four years in Ohio. In 1891 she returned to college to earn another Bachelor's from MIT, where she majored in physics and mathematics, and a Master's from Oberlin. From 1889 through 1893, Maltby also taught physics at Wellesley.

Like Mary Frances Winston, Maltby came to Göttingen in 1893 and remained until 1896. Maltby's first two years of study at Göttingen were funded by a European Fellowship from MIT; her last year was supported by an ACA

Fellowship. In Göttingen, Maltby did coursework in physics with Paul Drude, Eduard Riecke and Woldemar Voigt. She studied chemistry with Walther Nernst and Otto Wallach. She also attended lectures by Richard Abegg and Friedrich Pockels.[79]

After returning to the United States, Maltby taught both physics and mathematics at Lake Erie College in Painesville, Ohio, for one year. She then returned to Germany to work for the following year as a private research assistant to Friedrich Kohlrausch (1840-1910), who had taken over as president of the Imperial Physical and Technical Institute (Physikalische-Technische Reichsanstalt) after the death of Hermann von Helmholtz. In 1901 Maltby began her long career first as a chemistry instructor and then as a physics professor at Barnard College. At Barnard Maltby introduced an intriguing course for music students on "the physical basis of music." She retired in 1931.[80]

Maltby's career, with positions at Wellesley and Barnard, was typical of the first generation of women physicists. In the 1890s and the first two decades of the twentieth century, women were dependent on women's colleges for teaching positions in higher education. In her study of women scientists in America, Margaret W. Rossiter notes that it was not coincidental that the two women present at the founding of the American Physical Society in 1899 were both employed by women's colleges. Using the 1906, 1910 and 1921 editions of *American Men of Science*, Rossiter constructs tables, first for academic institutions employing women scientists and then for employers of women physicists. In both tables for the entire time period, the women's colleges emerge as the main employers of women scientists and, specifically, female physicists. Wellesley emerges as the main employer for the entire period in both tables, employing six female physicists during the period studied. Vassar and Mount Holyoke follow as the second and third employers of women physicists.[81]

Sarah F. Whiting, who was chair of the Departments of Astronomy and Physics at Wellesley, wrote of her experiences as a physicist in a 1913 article in the *Wellesley College News*. Whiting did her undergraduate work at Ingham University in LeRoy, New York, outside of Rochester. She later studied abroad in Berlin and Edinburgh, and earned her Ph.D. in science from Tufts University. At the time she was writing in 1913, women were still a tiny minority among professional physicists. Only seventeen of the 619 members of the American Physical Society were women. Whiting attributes women's failure to make greater progress in the field to two factors: the perception that higher mathematics and certain mechanical skills were unfit for ladies; and women's discomfort at professional gatherings held "in the dense cloud of smoke which envelops scientific and academic banquets."[82]

Whiting played a key role in bringing Wellesley to the cutting edge of physics education in the United States. Influenced by developments in Giessen, Glasgow and MIT, Whiting helped develop the laboratory method of teaching science, which eventually spread throughout the United States. When Wellesley opened its students' laboratory in physics in 1878, it was only the second such laboratory in the United States, with MIT having opened the first.

In the article of 1913, Whiting writes of her own experiences in Heidelberg, Leipzig and Berlin in 1888 and 1889. In Heidelberg, she was allowed to visit laboratories when the male students were not around. There, she was also warned that men would end up having to do the food shopping for the family, if women decided to study. A professor from Heidelberg later apologized to her for his reluctance to allow her more access to university facilities. He was simply afraid that such a deviation from normal behavior "'would be talked about and criticised by everyone.'"[83]

In an earlier article from 1889, written while she was in Heidelberg, Whiting seemed impressed by the research done by such luminaries of the university as the chemist Robert Bunsen (1811-1899), the physicist Georg Hermann Quincke (1834-1924) and the geologist Harry Rosenbusch (1836-1914). But mostly she wrote with dismay that the excellent education German girls received ended abruptly at age seventeen or eighteen. A leader in women's education told her that German women were not interested in higher education. German women supposedly were discouraged by the social disadvantages they would face as students. Whiting was not convinced by such arguments and left a few Wellesley calendars "in judicious places" to help foster liberal ideas.[84]

In Berlin, Whiting was not allowed into the research facilities of Hermann von Helmholtz (1821-1894), then the renowned chair of experimental physics, but was allowed to attend the lectures of the physicist August Adolph Kundt (1839-1894) and the meteorologist Wilhelm von Bezold (1837-1907). Kundt was astounded by Whiting's intelligence. Back in the United States, Whiting had met chemistry professor August Wilhelm von Hofmann (1818-1892), who was then being honored by the American Chemical Society. It was Hofmann who helped her gain access to lectures in Berlin. Hofmann's wife, on the other hand, was afraid that her husband's efforts on behalf of the American would get him into trouble with the ministry.[85]

Despite her seeming isolation, Whiting was part of what seems to have been a merry and supportive Wellesley colony in Berlin. The Wellesley *Courant* of February 1889, mentions her entertaining fourteen Wellesley students and their friends at a reception. Most of these students were studying in the fine arts or the humanities or were simply traveling abroad. Such receptions or informal gatherings of students and faculty from women's colleges seem to have been fairly common, especially from the 1880s through 1914. From Wellesley newsletters, for example, it is evident that even abroad, faculty and students were able to keep their "community" intact.

In 1898 the Canadian Elizabeth R. Laird (1874-1969) followed in Whitings's footsteps and came to Berlin to study physics and mathematics. Laird was the recipient of the President's European Fellowship of Bryn Mawr that year, and used the fellowship to study at Berlin. Before studying in Berlin, Laird had already completed her Bachelor's (1896) at the University of Toronto. After completing her Bachelor's, Laird taught mathematics for one year at the Ontario Ladies College in Whitby, Ontario. The following year she was a fellow in physics at Bryn Mawr. Laird returned to Bryn Mawr after Berlin and completed her doctoral studies there in 1901. She then began a long career in physics and mathematics at Mount Holyoke, where she became a full professor of physics in 1905. While teaching at Mount Holyoke, Laird continued her research on the vibration of solids in liquids, magnetic lag, and spectral analysis.[86] In 1905 and 1909, she left Mount Holyoke to do work as a research assistant to J. J. Thomson at Cavendish Laboratory at Cambridge University. For the 1913/14 academic year, she received a Sarah Berliner Research and Lecture Fellowship, which she used to do research at the University of Würzburg. Laird did research in physics at the University of Chicago in 1919 and at Yale in 1926. She published numerous articles on X-rays, and in 1927 she received an honorary degree from the University of Toronto for her scholarship.[87]

Two other early physicists whose careers were associated with another women's college, the Woman's College of Baltimore (Goucher), turned, like Maltby, Whiting and Laird, to German-speaking universities for their graduate work. The first, Fanny Cook Gates (1872-1931) from Waterloo, Iowa, studied in Göttingen for Winter Semester 1897/98 and then at the Polytechnikum in Zurich for a semester. Although Gates's name is not found in the official records of the Polytechnikum, she was apparently one of five American women who studied there between 1871 and 1913.[88] Before traveling to Europe, Gates had already completed her Bachelor's (1894) and her Master's (1895) at Northwestern University. She had received a scholarship (1895-96) and a fellowship (1896-97) from Bryn Mawr College. From 1898 to 1911, she was head of the Physics Department at Goucher. At Goucher, she did research on radioactivity. A 1904 article on Gates in the Goucher *Kalends* notes that Gates had gained some renown in scientific circles for her publications on radium. Her research contributed to a body of work proving that radioactivity was not a simple chemical or physical process.[89] Gates took several leaves of absence from Goucher to continue her research. She did experimental work with light at the University of Chicago. She took a leave of absence from Goucher in 1902/03 to study at the McDonald Laboratory at McGill University with Ernest Rutherford (1871-1937). She also took leaves to do research with J. J. Thomson at Cavendish Laboratory in Cambridge, England (1904 and 1905). Her studies in Europe were financed by a fellowship from the ACA. She spent most of 1907 and 1908 at the University of Pennsylvania, where she received her doctoral degree in 1909. In 1911 Gates finally left Goucher for the University of Chicago, where she studied psychology and eugenics and conducted research for two years. In 1913 she took a position as Professor of Physics and dean of women at Grinnell College, where in 1914 she was also made a Professor of Mental and Physical Hygiene. From 1916 to 1918 she taught as an Associate Professor of Physics while serving as the dean of women at the University of Illinois, Urbana-Champaign. According to her biographers, Marelene F. and Geoffrey W. Rayner-Canham, Gates was confronted at the University of Illinois with an administration that did not keep its promises to her and was unresponsive to her needs. Her threat of resignation was readily accepted and Gates had to find a new position. For the rest of her career, she had a series of shorter jobs that offered her no chance to continue her research. She served as General Secretary of the YMCA of New York from 1918 to 1919 and from 1921 to 1922. She taught at two private schools, one in New York and one in Bryn Mawr. Her last teaching position (1928-1931) was as a physics teacher at Roycemore School in Evanston, Illinois.[90]

The second physicist, Bertha May Clark (1878-1963), was born in Baltimore, and both studied and taught at Goucher. She received her Bachelor's from Goucher in 1900. She was a scholar of physics at Bryn Mawr College in 1900/01. The following year, she worked at Goucher as a laboratory assistant (1901/02) and then as an instructor in physics (1902/03). Clark received two fellowships, which enabled her to study physics and mathematics in Göttingen. A note in a 1903 issue of the Goucher *Kalends* mentions that Clark intended to study at the University of Berlin, but she evidently changed her plans before even registering as an auditor at Berlin. The first fellowship Clark received was a foreign fellowship offered every year to an alumna of Goucher. The second, awarded for the 1904/05 academic year, was from the Baltimore Association for the Promotion of the University Education of Women. Clark used these fellowships to extend her stay in Göttingen from the Winter Semester 1903/04 through the Winter Semester 1904/05. She then returned to Göttingen for the Summer Semester of 1906. Upon her return to the United States, Clark received a fellowship from the University of Pennsylvania (1905/07), where she completed her Ph.D. in 1907. From 1907 to 1924, Clark served as head of the Science Department at William Penn High School in Philadelphia. Although Clark was working at the high school level, she spoke publicly about the "necessity of a knowledge of the methods and applications of research" for high school teachers.[91] Clark continued to publish. Her textbook *General Science* (1912) was published by the American Book Company, as were her *General Science Laboratory Manual* (1913), her *Introduction to Science* (1917) with its accompanying manual and her *New Introduction to Science* (1927).[92]

On September 19, 1906, after the Bavarian universities had begun to allow women to matriculate, Edna Carter (1875-?) earned her doctoral degree in physics at the University of Würzburg. Her dissertation was on "The Relationship of the Energy of X-Rays to the Energy Created by Cathode Rays" (Über das Verhältnis der Energie der Röntgenstrahlen zur Energie der erzeugenden Kathodenstrahlen). She was one of only fourteen women to earn a doctoral degree at Würzburg before 1914 and one of only three Americans to do so. The other two Americans were Mary J. Hogue, who earned her degree in biology in 1910, and Helen Dodd Cook, who earned her degree in psychology that same year.[93]

Before studying at Würzburg, Carter had completed her Bachelor's (1894) at Vassar, where she took biology from Marcella O'Grady (Boveri), with whom she remained a lifelong friend. She then studied at the State Normal School at Oshkosh, Wisconsin (University of Wisconsin-Oshkosh), in 1894/95. The following year she was an assistant principal at the high school in DePere, Wisconsin. Carter then taught physics for two years at Vassar, before doing a year of graduate study at the University of Chicago. For the next five years, Carter taught physics at the Normal School in Oshkosh. Carter then studied for two years at Würzburg, where she earned her doctoral degree.[94]

Carter chose to study at Würzburg, because of research being conducted there on X-rays. She was also drawn to Würzburg, because her former teacher Marcella O'Grady had married the German biologist Theodor Boveri (1862-1915) and was living there. Carter was a frequent visitor at the Boveri home during her stays in Würzburg. She returned from Würzburg to begin a long career teaching physics at Vassar. In 1911 she received a Sarah Berliner Research and Lecture Fellowship, which enabled her to return to Würzburg for additional research. During that visit to Würzburg, Carter founded a club for physicists, which helped students exchange ideas and socialize together. Carter remained a supportive friend to Marcella O'Grady Boveri. Immediately following World War I, she offered to support the family until Marcella could establish herself again as a teacher in the United States. Marcella rejected this offer, but later did return to the United States to teach. After establishing her own career at Vassar, Carter took subsequent sabbatical leaves in 1917 and 1924 to conduct research at the Mt. Wilson Observatory.[95]

BIOLOGY

Like their fellow women scientists in mathematics and physics, women in the natural sciences were also dependent on women's colleges for employment in higher education and on women's associations for fellowships to study or do research abroad. Women biologists are remarkable, however, among women scientists of the late nineteenth and early twentieth centuries for their great numbers and professional productivity. As G. Kass-Simon writes in her history of women in biology, "[i]n almost every journal in every month since the mid-nineteenth century, the names of women biologists abound."[96] Women were also well represented at the prominent marine biology research center at Woods Hole, although they were excluded from management roles.

Considering the number of women biologists publishing during the late nineteenth and early twentieth centuries, Kass-Simon legitimately asks why modern readers are not more familiar with the names and research of these women. She argues that the work of these women has been incorporated into the basic body of knowledge of the discipline without being attributed to the women responsible for the research. Although the work of male scientists has suffered a similar fate, she argues that women's research becomes disassociated from the researcher earlier and more frequently than men's does.[97] Such is certainly the case with the work of the women discussed in this section.

The paths of all of the women mentioned in this section passed through at least one of three institutions in the United States: Bryn Mawr College, Goucher College or Woods Hole. At Woods Hole, graduate students and faculty were able to conduct research during the summer months. Here, women met future colleagues or research partners. With its strong pre-med undergraduate program, it is hardly surprising that Goucher graduates emerged as leaders in biological research. As for Bryn Mawr, its exceptional faculty and graduate research program became a magnet for women interested in newly emerging fields of biological research.

In the natural sciences, women had the greatest chance of being accepted as researchers in newer, developing fields where the tradition of excluding women was not well established. The 1880s saw the development of the field of experimental embryology, which focused on determining how cells ultimately acquire their identities. Research on sex determination dominated work in this field during the 1890s and early 1900s. Scientists were investigating whether external factors, internal factors or heredity determined the sex of an individual. Two leading male researchers in this field, Edmund Beecher Wilson (1856-1939) and Thomas Hunt Morgan (1866-1945), both taught at Bryn Mawr College for a period of time and influenced the work of several noteworthy women biologists. Women studying with them were thrown into the heart of the debate about sex determination.

E. B. Wilson spent time at both Cambridge and Leipzig after earning his Ph.D. at Johns Hopkins. In 1882 Wilson traveled to Leipzig where he worked in Rudolf Leuckart's zoology laboratory and attended lectures in physiology by Carl Ludwig. Equally important was the time Wilson then spent at the Naples Zoological Station. Wilson was one of the first two Americans to visit the laboratory.[98] Wilson became close friends with Anton Dohrn, the founder of the laboratory, and made contact with other zoologists and embryologists. T. H. Morgan made his first visit to the laboratory eight years later, and like Wilson was inspired by the exchange of ideas and modern research possible there.

From 1885 to 1891 Wilson headed the biology department at Bryn Mawr College. He left Bryn Mawr to take a position at Columbia University, where he remained for the rest of his career. Morgan replaced Wilson at Bryn Mawr and remained there until 1904, when Wilson was able to offer him the chair of experimental zoology at Columbia. The friendship between the two scientists and their association with the biology department at Bryn Mawr would greatly benefit the students. First, they could take part in Wilson's and Morgan's pioneering research. For example, Morgan would assign his students problems in cell regeneration, a particularly popular topic for research and dissertations. Second, these students were encouraged to pursue research opportunities abroad, especially at the University of Würzburg in Germany or at the Naples Zoological Station. In this context, one particular contact of Wilson's in Germany bears mentioning.

Before beginning his position at Columbia, Wilson spent a year abroad in Munich and Naples. He worked with the biologist Theodor Boveri, who was then teaching in Munich. Wilson remained a close friend until Boveri's death in 1915. From Boveri, Wilson learned about cytology, and the importance of chromosomes in determining an organism's heredity. Back in the United States, Wilson gave lectures about Boveri's work and encouraged students to study with Boveri.[99] T. H. Morgan sent several of his best students to study with Boveri, who by that time had become the director of the Zoological-Zootomical Institute and a professor of zoology and comparative anatomy at the University of Würzburg.

A remarkable network emerged of women influenced by Wilson and Hunt to study with Boveri and at the Naples Zoological Station. These women would in turn inspire other students to do graduate research and study abroad. The paths of these women intersected at summer research institutes, at women's colleges and girls' schools. The network began with Marcella O'Grady (1863-1950), the first official female auditor at the University of Würzburg.[100]

O'Grady was born into an affluent Catholic family in Boston. Her father was an architect. Her family was very supportive of her education. In 1885, she became the first woman to earn a degree in biology from MIT.[101] William Thompson Sedgwick supervised her research at MIT, and it was through him that she met E. B. Wilson, then at MIT as a visiting researcher. Wilson and Sedgwick had studied together at Yale and The Johns Hopkins University.

From 1885 through 1887, O'Grady taught at the newly opened Bryn Mawr School for Girls in Baltimore, Maryland. The school had been founded by M. Carey Thomas, then Dean at Bryn Mawr College, and her partner, Mary Garrett. O'Grady was responsible for organizing a science program for the school. In 1887 she won the Fellowship in Biology from Bryn Mawr College and left Baltimore to begin her doctoral research. O'Grady spent the next two years at Bryn Mawr College conducting research with E. B. Wilson and Frederic S. Lee. When the Marine Biological Laboratory opened at Woods Hole, Massachusetts, in 1888, O'Grady was one of the first seven researchers enrolled there.

Although O'Grady's fellowship at Bryn Mawr was renewed, she interrupted her doctoral research to accept a teaching position at Vassar College. The position offered her rare professional opportunities. She was the only member of the newly created Department of Biology and could structure the curriculum as she had done at the Bryn Mawr School. She encouraged her students to do research and received funding for them to attend Woods Hole. Enrollment in her department grew and she was able to hire assistants, including Elizabeth E. Bickford (1861-1939).

Bickford and O'Grady had met at Woods Hole,[102] where Bickford spent six summers. Before coming to Vassar, Bickford had already had an extensive teaching career and had earned degrees from MIT (Bachelor's, 1890) and from the University of Freiburg (Doctorate, 1895). She had taught at a number of secondary schools in New Hampshire as well as at the Bryn Mawr School in Baltimore. While teaching in Baltimore, she also took courses in biology at the Johns Hopkins Laboratory. In 1893 she left for Germany, where she studied at both Leipzig and Freiburg. Two years later, she completed her doctoral thesis, "The Morphology and Physiology of the Ovaries of Worker Ants" (Über die Morphologie und Physiologie der Ovarien der Ameisen-Arbeiterinnen).[103]

When O'Grady took a sabbatical in 1896 to continue her doctoral research with Boveri at Würzburg, she left the biology department in Bickford's capable hands. O'Grady never taught at Vassar again.[104]   Bickford left the department three years later to continue her graduate studies at Radcliffe and to teach for ten years in the secondary schools of Connecticut and Massachusetts. After teaching for one year at the Rhode Island State Normal School of Providence, Bickford moved to California, where she taught biology at South Pasadena High School for more than twenty years. She never married. Eventually Bickford retired to Hermosa Beach where she remained until her death.[105]

O'Grady went to Würzburg with the intention of studying the latest developments in zoology with Boveri. Her application went to the university senate with the support of Boveri and the entire philosophical faculty. The support of the faculty along with O'Grady's extensive training in her field worked in her favor during the senate meeting. Moreover, a number of women had already been allowed to audit courses at Munich. Thus on June 15, 1896, an exception was made for O'Grady, and she was permitted to spend her sabbatical at Würzburg as the first female auditor at that university.[106]   In 1869 another American, Laura Reusch-Formes, had been the first woman to apply for permission to attend courses at Würzburg. She had wanted to audit courses with Friedrich Wilhelm Scanzoni von Lichtenfels (1821-1891) in obstetrics and gynecology, and remain to earn a medical degree. Her application had been approved by the faculty but rejected by the university senate. Now, twenty-seven years later, another American had finally broken the barrier at Würzburg.[107]

O'Grady changed her plans dramatically after she began her research at Würzburg. At Würzburg, both Boveri and Wilhelm Conrad Röntgen (1845-1923), the famous physicist who was also Boveri's closest friend, encouraged O'Grady.[108]   At that time, Boveri was almost completely confined to a wheelchair because of his rheumatism. Boveri and O'Grady soon became engaged. O'Grady realized she would have to give up her career, but, according to her daughter's autobiography, she felt that nursing Boveri back to health and helping him to continue his research was worth the sacrifice. In 1903, O'Grady published her doctoral thesis, but she never took her oral exams and thus never earned her doctoral degree.

Margret, the daughter of Marcella and Theodor Boveri, wrote in her autobiography that Marcella regretted this sacrifice her whole life. She urged Margret to earn the doctoral degree that she herself never completed. Her love of teaching and doing research could not be repressed. Marcella thrived when the family went to Naples to work at the Zoological Station for Theodor's research. There, she was able take a more active part in his research than in Würzburg. Marcella, herself, had once been the recipient of the American Women's Table at Naples.

Throughout this period of her life, Marcella always grasped at opportunities to teach and do research. She gave regular science lessons to her daughter and other children who were privately tutored. She taught English on occasion and advised young scientists at the university. She was also supportive of American women who came to Würzburg to work in Boveri's laboratory. These women included the biologists Nettie Marie Stevens, Florence Peebles, Mary Jane Hogue and Alice Middleton Boring. A former student of hers from Vassar, the physicist Edna Carter, came to Würzburg twice to study and remained in close contact with Marcella. Carter was almost a part of the family, and Margret refers to her in her autobiography as "Tante Carter." The Boveris helped Carter gain entrance into the exclusively male laboratory of the Nobel-prize winning physicist Wilhelm Wien. In 1906, Carter was able to complete her doctorate at Würzburg on the energy of X-rays. For more on Carter, see the section on physics.[109]

As a child, Margret had little compassion for her mother's frustration about leading the life of a German housewife. She compared her mother's generation of women pioneers in science unfavorably with Carter's younger generation, which was more playful and less obsessed with women's equality:

> While my mother belonged to that first generation of women
> students in America who devoted all their time and thought to
> science, Edna was more a college girl of the turn of the cen-
> tury. She was less focused on trying to prove her intellectual
> equality with men. She did sports. She was always ready to
> play and have fun. That was missing in my mother.[110]

Marcella reluctantly relocated to the United States in 1927. She was lured back by an offer to teach science at a women's college and the promise that she would have complete access to resources of nearby Yale University. Back in the United States she quickly took her place again in a social and professional network that included colleagues at Columbia, Bryn Mawr, Vassar and Mount Holyoke.[111] She was hired to build up the biology department of Albertus Magnus College, a women's college in New Haven, Connecticut, which had been founded in 1925. In 1929, with the support of Maynard M. Metcalf from The Johns Hopkins University, she translated Theodor's work on malignant tumors into English.[112] Marcella remained in the United States for the rest of her life, although she vacationed regularly in Europe to spend time with her daughter and friends. In 1939 she reapplied for U.S. citizenship, which she had relinquished when she married Theodor. She died in 1950.

The American biologists Marcella O'Grady Boveri supported while in Würzburg went on to have remarkable careers in teaching and research. Seven of the biologists included in this section earned Ph.D.s, three at Bryn Mawr and four at German-speaking universities: Freiburg (2), Würzburg (1) and Zurich (1). Eight of the scientists studied at Bryn Mawr College, which emerged in the late 1880s as a center for advanced biological research for women. The most famous of these women, Nettie Maria Stevens, was credited along with E. B. Wilson for proving that chromosomes are the basis for sex determination.

Nettie Maria Stevens (1861-1912)[113] graduated from the Normal School in Westfield, Vermont, and then enrolled at Stanford University in physiology. She earned both a Bachelor's (1899) and a Master's (1900) from Stanford. Stevens spent the summers of 1897, 1898 and 1899 studying at Stanford's Hopkins Marine Station in Pacific Grove, California. Immediately after earning her Master's, Stevens enrolled in the doctoral program with T. H. Morgan at Bryn Mawr College, where she did predoctoral work in morphology and embryology. The following year, she received Bryn Mawr's European Fellowship, which enabled her to do research at the Naples Zoological Station and at the Department of Zoology at the University of Würzburg with Theodor Boveri. Stevens returned to Bryn Mawr to complete her doctoral research. In 1903, after earning her Ph.D. from Bryn Mawr, she began a joint study with Morgan on sex determination in aphids. Stevens's work with Morgan and her subsequent independent work on sex determination in the beetle *Tenebrio* proved that the chromosome was the basis of sex determination. Stevens published her findings in 1905, the same year that E. B. Wilson, then at Columbia University, published similar findings from his work on insects. Wilson, along with Morgan and other leading biologists of the day, cited Stevens's work. Wilson considered Stevens's discovery about sex determination to have been made at the same time as his.[114]

Unlike the work of other biologists included in this study, Stevens's research has not been forgotten by modern scientists. Kass-Simon lists many of Stevens's significant contributions to the field of genetics: (1) she was the first person to describe the chromosomes of the European vinegar fly, *Drosophila melanogaster*, which has become the model animal for the study of chromosomal inheritance; (2) she was the first person to establish that chromosomes exist as paired structures in body cells; (3) she was the first person to discover that certain insects have supernumerary chromosomes.[115]

The *Bryn Mawr Alumnae Quarterly* described Stevens as one of the very few women really eminent in science and one who took a foremost rank among biologists of her day. Her name was apparently an "Open Sesame" for her students among biologists.[116] When Stevens died after a brief illness in 1912, she had already received numerous fellowships and had traveled to research facilities in various parts of the United States and Europe.

Stevens was a prolific writer, publishing forty-one research articles during her brief career. In a survey conducted by the Naples Table Association for Promoting Laboratory Research by Women, Stevens headed the list of winners of the Association's prize for number of publications. By the time her Ph.D. thesis on "Ciliate Infusoria, Licnophora and Boveria" was published in 1903, Stevens had already published five articles in major journals, such as the *American Journal of Physiology*, the *Archiv für Entwicklungsmechanik* and the *Zoölogisches Jahrbuch*.[117] Her 1905 article about sex determination in aphids, "Study of the Germ Cells of Aphis Rosea and Aphis Oenotheroe," won the Ellen Richards Research Prize for the best thesis written by a woman on a scientific subject. [118]

After completing her Ph.D., Stevens remained at Bryn Mawr College, first as a reader in biology and then as an associate professor in experimental morphology. Throughout her career, Stevens continued her research. She was the Carnegie Research Assistant in Biology in 1904/06. She received the Alice Freeman Palmer Memorial Fellowship for 1908/09, which she used to return to the Naples Zoological Station for three months and to work in Boveri's laboratory in Würzburg for another semester. During that particular stay in Europe, Stevens also visited the German Marine Station on Helgoland, as well as the zoological laboratories at the German universities of Jena, Halle, Leipzig and Munich.

During that stay, Stevens also traveled to England and Ireland. She visited the marine laboratory of Liverpool University at Point Erin, Isle of Man. At Cambridge, she observed experiments in genetics conducted by William Bateson and a Miss Saunders. Stevens was invited to attend the September 1908 meeting of the British Association at Dublin. She took part in the general discussion about sex determination and reported on recent work in the field by American biologists.[119]

Like Stevens, Florence Peebles (1874-1956) received her doctoral degree, which was in physiology, from Byrn Mawr College (1900).[120] Peebles had hoped to become a physician like her father, but when he objected, she chose to study biology and bacteriology instead. She did her undergraduate work at Goucher, earning her Bachelor's in 1895. That same year, she spent the summer at Woods Hole. She then received several fellowships and scholarships from Bryn Mawr College, including the Mary E. Garrett resident scholarship in biology (1896/7). In 1897/98, Peebles was an instructor in biology at Bryn Mawr. For the 1898/99 academic year, Peebles was the recipient of the Mary E. Garrett European Fellowship, which enabled her to study at the German universities of Munich and Halle. In 1898 Peebles was also chosen to fill the American Women's Table at the Zoological Station at Naples. This was the research position Ida Hyde helped to establish in 1897. Peebles would hold this position for five different summers: 1898, 1901, 1907, 1913 and 1927. In Munich, Peebles studied botany and German. In Halle, she did coursework in botany and entomology.

Peebles spent her vacations conducting research and published extensively.[121] She belonged to numerous professional organizations, including the American Society of Zoologists, the American Society of Naturalists and the National Geographic Society. In 1911 she became a fellow of the AAAS. From 1899 to 1906 Peebles was an instructor and then associate professor of biology at Goucher. During that period Peebles spent the summer of 1902 as an investigator at Woods Hole and the summer of 1905 doing research at the University of Bonn. In 1907 and then from 1912/13, Peebles also worked at the Marine Biological Laboratories in Naples and Monaco. From 1907 to 1910, she was a demonstrator in biology at Bryn Mawr. Peebles then returned to the University of Würzburg in 1911 to continue her research. For the 1912/13 academic year Peebles received a Boston Alumnae fellowship, which enabled her to study in Berlin with Dr. Hartmann and to do research at the Robert Koch Institute. The fellowship also enabled her to spend the summer of 1913 at the University of Freiburg. Peebles was accompanied on that trip to Freiburg as well as on other trips abroad and to Woods Hole by Mary Jeffers, her companion and colleague at Bryn Mawr. Jeffers also enrolled in courses at Freiburg as well as at Munich, Halle, Bonn, Würzburg and in Italy. Jeffers had received her Bachelor's (1895) and Master's (1897) from Bryn Mawr College. She became a lecturer in German and French at Bryn Mawr. Jeffers and Peebles shared a house at Woods Hole and a farm in Pennsylvania.[122]

Peebles returned from the semester at Freiburg to take a position as a lecturer and acting head of the biology department at Bryn Mawr. She was then head of the biology department of the Sophie Newcomb College of Tulane University in New Orleans from 1915 to 1917. After Tulane, Peebles returned to

Bryn Mawr, where she taught for the next two years, before trying some experimental farming. Between 1924 and 1927 she traveled extensively in Europe and along the Pacific Coast. She spent the summer of 1927 at Woods Hole and then taught for a year as a lecturer at the University Extension of the University of California. In 1928 she took a position as professor of Biological Science at Chapman College (Chapman University) in Orange, California, where she remained until 1942. From 1942 until her retirement in 1946, she was a professor of biology at Lewis and Clark College in Portland, Oregon. After retirement, Peebles settled in Pasadena, where she became a leading advocate for senior citizens. She founded the Senior Citizens of San Gabriel, an organization, which offered social, vocational and recreational opportunities to the elderly.[123] A grant from the AAUW was named after her, as were laboratories at both Chapman College and Lewis and Clark. In 1954 she received an honorary doctoral degree in law (LLD) from Goucher.[124]

Kass-Simon's study of women in science includes a brief description of Peebles's research, which was rarely cited by her peers and is hardly known today. Yet it remains relevant as some of Peebles's views are reemerging among developmental biologists. Peebles's key contribution was her observation that external influences, especially those of the immediate environment, can affect cell differentiation.[125]

A third biologist, Mary Jane Hogue (1883-1962), was born into an old Quaker family in West Chester, Pennsylvania. She received her Bachelor's in German and Biology from Goucher in 1905, and immediately began her graduate studies at Bryn Mawr College on a Founders College Scholarship. She received the Dean Van Meter Alumnae Fellowship from Goucher for 1907/08 and 1908/09. Hogue used this fellowship to study biology at the University of Würzburg, where she earned her doctoral degree in 1910 on the effect of centrifugal force on the eggs of the *Ascaris* (Über die Wirkung der Centrifugalkraft auf die Eier von *Ascaris megalocephala*).[126] Stevens's second visit to Würzburg would have overlapped with Hogue's stay there. At Würzburg, Hogue worked with Boveri on a study of blastomere potentiality in *Ascaris* and co-authored an article with him in 1909.[127]

Upon her return to the United States, Hogue took a position as head of the science department at the Pennsylvania College for Women in Pittsburgh in 1909/10. She then moved to New York City, where she worked as an instructor in science at Miss Chapin's School for a year while doing postdoctoral work at Columbia University. Hogue taught as an instructor in zoology at Mount Holyoke College from 1911 to 1914. While at Mount Holyoke, Hogue began her long association with Woods Hole, where she studied protozoan infestation of oyster beds. Hogue taught at Wellesley College from 1914 until 1918 and then spent a year working at the hospital in Fort Sill, Oklahoma.

In 1919 Hogue conducted tissue culture research at the Carnegie Institution. She then continued her research on a fellowship in protozoology at The Johns Hopkins University School of Hygiene and Public Health. In 1921 she was made an instructor in bacteriology at the Johns Hopkins Medical School. The following year Hogue became an associate professor at the North Carolina College for Women, and in 1923 was made full professor. Hogue began her long career at the University of Pennsylvania School of Medicine in 1924, where she taught until her retirement in 1952. At the University of Pennsylvania, Hogue taught as an instructor in anatomy and later as an associate professor. Even after her retirement, Hogue continued her research and was still working in her laboratory until shortly before her death.

Hogue was best known for her research on the effect of the poliomyelitis virus on the brain cells. She was one of the first researchers to make microphotographs of a polio virus attacking a nerve cell. Hogue had more than eighty-one publications. Other research included tissue culture studies of human heart muscle and brain cells. Hogue conducted research in which she supposedly established that brain and nerve cells could outlive the organism by as much as eight days. She was a member of numerous professional organizations and honor societies, including the AAAS, the American Society of Zoologists, the American Association of Anatomists, the Tissue Culture Association and Sigma Xi.[128]

A fourth biologist, Alice Middleton Boring (1883-1955)[129] of the class of 1904 at Bryn Mawr College, continued her graduate studies at Bryn Mawr (1904/05) and at the University of Pennsylvania (1905/06). She returned to Bryn Mawr for another year and then taught zoology at Vassar for one year. She received a Mary E. Garrett European fellowship from Bryn Mawr for the 1908/09 academic year. She spent the year studying biology at the University of Würzburg and at the Naples Zoological Station, where she was the recipient of the American Women's Table. While at Würzburg, she published two articles about her research on the nuclei and chromosomes of the *Ascaris* conducted in Boveri's laboratory.[130]

After returning from Würzburg, Boring completed her Ph.D. at Bryn Mawr College in 1910 and took a teaching position at the University of Maine in Orono (1909-1918). The rest of Boring's career is dramatic and unusual. From 1918 through 1920 she taught in China at Beijing Union Medical College. She returned to the United States to teach at Wellesley for three years, but then took a position at Yenching University in Beijing. She remained there until 1950, despite spending part of World War II interned in Beijing.[131] Boring was a member of numerous professional societies, including the AAAS, the American Society of Naturalists and the Society of American Zoologists.[132]

A fifth Bryn Mawr alumna in biology, Julia B. Platt, completed her graduate work, like Elizabeth E. Bickford, at the University of Freiburg. Women were officially allowed to matriculate at the University of Freiburg starting with the Summer Semester of 1900. Before that semester, as at other German universities, women were allowed to audit courses. Unfortunately, all records of auditors at Freiburg before the Winter Semester of 1902/03 have been lost. The names of three American women who earned their doctoral degrees from Freiburg between 1895 and 1903 have been saved, as they were recorded in the standard reference work about the history of women at the University of Freiburg, Ernst Theodor Nauck's *Das Frauenstudium an der Universität Freiburg* (1953). Key sources for Nauck's work have disappeared and the documentation cannot be confirmed. Two of the American women mentioned in Nauck's work, Platt and Bickford, earned their doctoral degrees in biology. At Freiburg, both women majored in zoology with minors in botany and geology. Bickford completed her defense and thesis on December 13, 1895; Platt completed hers on May 28, 1898.[133]

Platt[134] received her Bachelor's from the University of Vermont in 1882. She later did graduate work at the Harvard Annex (Radcliffe) for four semesters between 1887 and 1889. There she studied zoology, histology and microscopy.

Platt then studied for two semesters at Bryn Mawr College in 1889/90, where she studied biology and physiology, and did laboratory work in neurology with E. B. Wilson and Frederic S. Lee. After two semesters at Bryn Mawr, Platt enrolled at Freiburg for the first time. She remained there for two Winter Semesters, 1890/91 and 1891/92, doing research in comparative anatomy and embryology with Robert Wiedersheim (1848-1923), the director of the Institute of Anatomy and Comparative Anatomy at the University of Freiburg. Platt continued to move between American and German universities for the rest of her graduate studies to work with leading pioneers in the new and growing field of developmental biology. During the Winter Semester of 1892/93 she was at the University of Chicago, studying morphology and osteology with G. Baur, neurology with Henry Herbert Donaldson and zoology with C. O. Whitman.

In 1894 Platt returned to Germany to do research in the laboratory of Karl Wilhelm Kupffer at the University of Munich. After that she spent two semesters at Harvard doing comparative anatomy with G. H. Parker, experimental morphology with C. B. Davenport and botany with William Gilson Farlow. For the Winter Semester of 1896/97, Platt returned to Munich to work with Karl Goebel in botany and with Richard Hertwig in zoology. With a strong recommendation from the faculty in Munich, especially from Hertwig, Platt was accepted as a doctoral candidate at Freiburg, where she spent two semesters completing her doctoral thesis. At Freiburg, she studied zoology, geology, paleontology and botany. She continued her research with Wiedersheim and attended lectures by the anatomist F. Keibel and the zoologist August Weismann (1834-1914), who was famous for his lectures on Darwinian theory and heredity. Platt's doctoral thesis was in developmental biology on "The Development of the Cartilaginous Skull and of the Bronchial and Hypoglossal Musculature in Necturus." Even before Platt completed her doctoral studies, she already had an impressive publishing record. By 1896 she had published eight articles in both German and American journals, including the *Journal of Morphology* and the *Anatomischer Anzeiger*.[135]

A sixth Bryn Mawr alumna in biology, Lillian Vaughan Sampson Morgan (1870-?), earned her Bachelor's at Bryn Mawr in 1891. She continued her graduate studies at Bryn Mawr and used a Bryn Mawr European fellowship to study in Zurich for the 1892/93 academic year. Sampson continued her graduate studies at Bryn Mawr until 1899. In 1904 she married T. H. Morgan, the professor who had inspired the research of numerous graduates in biology at Bryn Mawr. After her marriage, Sampson Morgan continued her work as a cytologist and embryologist and followed Morgan to the laboratories of Columbia University.[136]

In addition to the Goucher and Bryn Mawr alumnae already mentioned, others went to German universities that did not usually attract biologists. These alumnae include those who have been lost to history, such as Clara Langenbeck of Cincinnati, Ohio, who received a degree from the Cincinnati College of Pharmacy in 1890. From 1893 to 1895, Langenbeck worked as an assistant in the biology department of the University of Cincinnati, where she received her Bachelor's in 1895. She was a fellow in biology at Bryn Mawr College in 1895/96. She received Bryn Mawr's European Fellowship the following year and used it to study at the University of Marburg, where she remained from Winter Semester 1896/97 through 1898.[137]

The list also includes a scholar of great renown, Margaret Adaline Reed Lewis (1881-1970), who was most famous for her work with her husband, Warren Harmon Lewis, on tissue culture techniques. Reed Lewis studied at a number of European universities, including Zurich and Berlin, after earning her Bachelor's from Goucher (1901). At Berlin, "she may have conducted the first known successful *in vitro* mammalian tissue culture experiment."[138]   Reed Lewis returned to the United States, where she worked as a laboratory assistant for T. H. Morgan at Bryn Mawr. She later followed him to Columbia University. Reed Lewis worked for over thirty years as a collaborator and research associate at the Carnegie Institution of Washington in Baltimore. In 1946 she was made a member of the Wistar Institute of Anatomy and Biology of Philadelphia. Reed Lewis presented almost 150 scientific papers. In 1938 she and her husband received an honorary degree from Goucher in addition to the William Wood Gerhard Gold Medal of the Pathological Society of Philadelphia.   Reed Lewis was also made an honorary lifetime member of the Tissue Culture Society.[139]

World War I interrupted these valuable research opportunities for women in Germany.   The renowned biologist Ethel Browne (Harvey) (1885-1965), a Goucher graduate from 1906, received her graduate training at Columbia University (1906-1913) with T. H. Morgan and E. B. Wilson.   In 1914 she was going to use a Sarah Berliner Research and Lecture Fellowship to spend that year doing research in zoology at the University of Würzburg and the Naples Zoological Station.[140]   But her plans changed with the outbreak of World War I, and she continued her research instead at Stanford's Hopkins Marine Station.[141]

This section ends with a biologist who was not associated with Bryn Mawr or Goucher but rather with Wellesley.   She did not do research at Woods Hole, but worked at the Agassiz Anderson School of Natural History on Penikese Island.[142]   Wellesley had a strong science program and faculty employing modern research methods.   According to Palmieri, Wellesley had more "distinguished women scientists" on its faculty than all other women's colleges. Wellesley had better laboratory facilities for student research than some prestigious men's colleges in the East.   It was also the first women's college in the world to have a separate chair of botany.[143]

In 1898, the same year that Platt earned her doctoral degree at Freiburg, another biologist, Mary Alice Willcox (1856-1953), earned her doctoral degree at the University of Zurich. Willcox took a leave of absence from her position as a professor of zoology at Wellesley to earn a doctorate. During her five-year tenure as president at Wellesley, Julia Irvine drove out older and less-qualified faculty members. ·Willcox had come to Wellesley in 1883 with a degree from a normal school but no Bachelor's. Realizing that she would have more job security with a doctorate, Willcox left for Zurich in 1896.[144]   She completed her dissertation, "On the Anatomy of Acmaea fragilis Chemnitz,"[145] and was able to return to her old position at Wellesley. Willcox was a demanding teacher, dedicated researcher, and outstanding malacologist.[146]   Before coming to Wellesley, she had attended the Agassiz Anderson School of Natural History on Penikese Island.   She had also studied at Newnham College in England with Michael Foster, a physiologist, and Francis Balfour, a leading embryologist.[147]   Willcox was the recipient of the American Women's Table at the Zoological Station at Naples.[148]   A 1903 article in *The Wellesley College News* described her research on limpits, a type of mollusk, in Bermuda, where Willcox was considering establishing a research station.[149]   Willcox made sure that her zoology courses at Wellesley met the biology requirements of the Johns Hopkins Medical School. At times, her curriculum was more demanding than that at Harvard. She required four hours of lab per week in her physiology course, whereas Harvard only required one. She created labs for her students to be thoroughly trained in dissection, when she saw that such training was limited at two women's medical colleges. Her students also took research trips to the Harvard Medical Museum.[150] Willcox retired early in 1910, apparently for health reasons. Palmieri is skeptical about this claim of poor health, as Willcox lived for another forty-three years. She attributes Willcox's retirement to guilt over having a successful career, while her sister Nellie, who was also on the Wellesley faculty, never really excelled professionally.[151]

CHEMISTRY

In North America, those women seeking to earn a doctoral degree in chemistry before 1900 had limited choices among institutions. Colleges like Mount Holyoke, with a tradition of excellence in chemistry, did not have doctoral programs in the field.[152] Still, thirteen women did earn doctoral degrees at U.S. institutions before 1900.[153] The institutions awarding these degrees included: Yale (4), the University of Pennsylvania (4) and one each at the University of Chicago, Cornell University, the University of Wooster and the University of Illinois. Certain chemistry departments were particularly welcoming to women. Yale was known for its women graduate students, particularly those working with Lafayette B. Mendel (1872-1935) in physiological chemistry.[154]

Even with a doctoral degree, these women had difficulty finding positions as research chemists. The opportunities that did arise were in the new and expanding fields, such as nuclear chemistry, biochemistry, crystallography, chromatography, chemotherapy, agricultural chemistry, home economics and nutrition. Some women did find research positions in the central disciplines of organic, inorganic and physical chemistry, but primarily at women's colleges.

The limited opportunities available in America combined with the excellence of chemical education and research in Germany drew a number of women to the chemistry laboratories of the German universities in the late nineteenth century. As German universities were still closed to women, these women had to receive permission of individual professors and administrators to attend lectures, to work in laboratories or to pursue a degree. But the reputation of Germany in chemistry, especially in the areas of applied chemistry and research, could hardly be matched at that time. Women wanted to take advantage of the opportunity to study with some of the best researchers in chemistry.

Until Justus Liebig (1803-1873) forever changed the study of chemistry and chemical research in Germany, the centers of chemical research in Western Europe had been Paris and Stockholm. With Liebig, who taught at the University of Giessen from 1825 to 1851, and at the University of Munich for the rest of his career, Germany gained worldwide renown in the field of chemistry. Liebig is most famous for his role in the development of organic chemistry, but he also played an important part in systematizing chemical education and in popularizing chemistry. He developed a system for training students to progress from basic experiments to complex independent research. His students became leading faculty members in chemistry at German universities and published what became classic textbooks in chemistry. The second half of the nineteenth century saw a number of other German pioneers in chemistry, such as August Wilhelm von Hofmann, Viktor Meyer and Robert Bunsen. German universities deserved the reputation of excellence they had acquired in this field, and attracted students from all over the world.

Influenced by Liebig, Germany's research in chemistry in the late nineteenth century focused primarily on analytical and synthetic processes for manufacturing products that served the practical needs of the country's growing industries and urban population. Germany had large coal reserves, but needed to find alternative sources of fuel to run gasoline and diesel oil engines, and to provide cleaner, more convenient and more efficient energy. By the beginning of the twentieth century, Germany excelled in metallurgy and in the production of synthetic dyes, fertilizers and petroleum products.[155]

Berlin, along with Giessen, was long the center of advanced chemical research in Germany. Research in Berlin was led by the chair of chemistry, August Wilhelm von Hofmann, a former student of Liebig. But by the time of Hofmann's death in 1892, the chemistry department in Munich, where Adolf von Baeyer (1835-1917) was conducting research on synthetic dyes, was emerging as Berlin's rival. Other important centers of chemical research in the late nineteenth century were Heidelberg with Robert Bunsen and Viktor Meyer (1848-1897), Bonn with Friedrich August Kekulé (1829-1896) and Würzburg with the later Nobel Prize winner, Emil Fischer (1852-1919). Fischer, who gained prominence for his research on sugar beets, was appointed to chair the chemistry department in Berlin after Hofmann's death.[156]

The autobiography of Helen Abbott Michael, published in 1907, provides the best description by an American contemporary of opportunities for women in the world of German chemistry of the late 1800s.[157] In her brief life (1857-1904), Abbott quickly gained an international reputation for her work in plant chemistry. Born into an affluent Philadelphia family, Abbott was able to pursue her incredibly diverse interests ranging from music and art to medicine, botany and chemistry. She received private instruction and took classes at the Woman's Medical College in Philadelphia. Abbott is remarkable for her extensive connections among leading male scientists of her day. When Abbott came to Europe in 1887 to study plant chemistry, her research was already known to leading European scientists in the field. During her tour of laboratories in Sweden and Denmark, Abbott realized that all of the chemists she was meeting had not only received training in Germany or France but also returned regularly to those countries to remain in touch with recent developments in the field. Abbott determined to do the same. Her subsequent travels through Germany and Switzerland brought her in contact with most of the leading German chemists of her day. Her accounts paint a clear picture not only of limitations faced by women but also of the remarkable opportunities available to them if a male professor was willing to make an exception for a woman. While Abbott was barred from lectures and laboratories at German universities, she was welcome at the private laboratories of several leading researchers.

Arriving in Kiel, Abbott was impressed by the laboratory of Albert Ladenburg. She was told that "no lady can enter as a student within the university walls."[158] But Ladenburg was courteous to Abbott and took the time to show her synthetic products from his own work in plant chemistry with coniin.

From Kiel, Abbott traveled to Hamburg, where she visited the private laboratory of Dr. Wiebel. As Abbott waited outside with her maid for admittance to the laboratory, she noticed that the male students within were staring at her and her maid through the windows. She found Wiebel's labs well equipped but too small and inconvenient. Abbott was told that she could study at the private laboratory but she would have to know German.

So Abbott continued her search for more promising research facilities, and made her way to Berlin. There she viewed the extensive chemical collection of Carl Liebermann. Abbott was very impressed with the reception she received. She wrote: "'I have found in all cases the utmost willingness on the part of scientific men to give me all the information possible in the limited time at our disposal.'"[159] Abbott inquired about working in Hofmann's laboratory. She was told that places in the laboratory were so sought after that she would have to apply in advance for a place. She would also have to attend his lectures in secret, as women were not permitted in the auditorium and could not work in the same rooms as the male students. Before leaving Berlin, Abbott did manage to attend one session of the Berlin Chemical Society in the company of Liebermann. Hofmann was the speaker that night. Abbott spent an enjoyable evening speaking with another chemist, Witt, about research in silica and starch.

While in Berlin, Abbott also visited the Agricultural School and the plant physiology laboratory of Leopold Kny. At the Botanical Institute she was able to visit the laboratories of Simon Schwendener, of whom she wrote:

> [He] was rather afraid to say he would admit a lady-student. He was very firm in his opinion that the Minister of Instruction was so much opposed to ladies being admitted that it would be exceedingly rare to have the permission, and to do so without permission, was to lay one's self open to severe reprimand. It is quite opposed to the regulations to have any women present in the lecture auditoriums, and when women attend lectures, they must do so under cover, behind a screen, or back of a window or door. Schwendener said he had been much reprehended for having Miss Gregory as a student, but as he had her in his private room, no one had a right to complain.[160]

As Abbott was on a whirlwind tour of her study opportunities and had only a week to spend in Berlin, she left before being able to make use of her letters of introduction to Robert Koch and his rival, Rudolf Virchow.

Her next stop was in Dresden, where she met Walter Hempel. Hempel was kind to Abbott and spent time showing her his laboratory apparatus for gas analysis. He also introduced her to his colleague, Oskar Drude, who was the director of the botanical garden and had compiled a botanical encyclopedia. Drude's wife welcomed Abbott and explained that she had done many of the drawings for the encyclopedia. After exploring Drude's library and laboratory, Abbott left Dresden promising to send Drude specimens of American plants.

The next stop was Leipzig, where Abbott became aware of the disadvantages of a larger university. Although large universities provided opportunities to work in many specialized fields in a short period of time, the professors were too busy with their own research to help students. Abbott was offended by Johannes Wislicenus, who could not be bothered to show her his laboratories himself and who told her to go to Zurich to study. Abbott found it disgusting "'the way all women are shoved to Zurich.'"[161] Wislicenus told her there was no room for her in his lab, which was already crowded with male students. Moreover, it was against university rules to admit women. But he did at least encourage her to contact another professor at Leipzig, Ernest von Meyer, who might make an exception for her. Meyer, along with Strohmann, an expert in plant chemistry, agreed that Abbott would benefit from a stay in Leipzig. She would be able to work at Wilhelm Pfeffer's botanical garden, which would be ready in about a year, and in Gruber's chemical physiological laboratory. Strohmann agreed to let Abbott work in his private laboratory and even promised to have anything planted at the Agricultural Station that Abbott requested for her research.

In Jena, Abbott was given a warm reception by chemists and botanists. The chemist Anton Geuther showed her his chemical collection and allowed her to attend a lecture. In the botanical garden, she was given a thorough tour of the facilities by Ernst Stahl. Although the faculty welcomed Abbott, she observed that it was just as well that women weren't admitted to that particular university, as the male students were a "rough, brutal set" and dueled too much.[162] North American women did come to Jena to study chemistry. A year after Abbott's visit, the Wellesley *Courant* mentions three women studying chemistry and physics there: Martha Sturgis of Muskegon, Michigan; Gertrude Frommholz of Lowoke, Arkansas, who also studied in Zurich; and Jessa J. Pearson of Xenia, Ohio.[163]

In Würzburg, Emil Fischer showed Abbott the substance from which he had synthetically produced glucose. Fischer was friendly but informed her that women were not permitted to study in his laboratory. From Würzburg, Abbott traveled to Munich to visit Baeyer's laboratory. Unfortunately, that segment of her autobiography has been lost. After Munich, Abbott continued to Zurich, where she was favorably impressed by the facilities for chemistry and botany. The programs were so well funded, that any deficiencies in apparatus she noticed could quickly be corrected. Her guide in Zurich was Georg Lunge, the director of the chemical laboratory at the technical college. Despite her annoyance at being "shoved to Zurich," Abbott was more inclined to return to Zurich than to any of the German facilities. In Zurich, all fields of chemistry were open to her. She was also promised that she would be received as an advanced student and would be able to take whatever courses she wanted.

After Switzerland Abbott returned to Germany where she visited three more universities: Freiburg, Heidelberg and Bonn. In Freiburg she met the chemists Adolf Claus and E. Baumann, as well as the English chemist W. J. Smith. Baumann's laboratory, like that of Emil Fischer, was working on synthetic sugars. Baumann agreed to accept Abbott as a private student. In Heidelberg, she drove to the house of Bunsen, which was adjacent to his laboratory, but Bunsen refused to let her into his laboratory. He explained that women were not admitted to the university and he could only allow her to visit the laboratory on a Sunday, when no male students would be working there. Abbott decided to continue on to Bonn, where she was able to meet with Friedrich August Kekulé, a pioneer in carbon-compound research. Kekulé was friendly but not very encouraging, as he, himself, had not had good experiences with female students. One of his students had committed suicide and another had spent her time reading literature. Another professor, Johannes Justus Rein, proved more adventurous and welcoming. He took her to the professors' table at a local tavern.

Still, after such a thorough testing of the waters, Abbott never did study in Europe. She chose to study chemistry at Tufts College, where she met Arthur Michael, whom she married in 1888. For the next four years, Abbott worked with her husband in his laboratory for organic chemistry on the Isle of Wight in England.[164] After the couple returned to the United States, Abbott continued her research in organic chemistry using the facilities at Tufts and published several papers. In 1887 she became the eighth woman to be elected to the American Philosophical Society.[165] In 1893 she became a corresponding member of the Philadelphia College of Pharmacy and in 1900 she became an honorary member of that college. She was a member of the German Chemical Society of Berlin, a fellow of the AAAS, and a member of the Academy of Natural Sciences as well as the Franklin Institute of Philadelphia. In 1900 Abbott enrolled in Tufts Medical School, where she hoped to realize an old dream of becoming a physician. In 1902 she traveled to London to observe procedures at some of the best hospitals and clinics. After receiving her medical degree in 1903, Abbott turned a private house into a free hospital. Sadly, the following year she contracted the flu while working at the hospital and died.[166]

Although Abbott was reluctant to study at Zurich, several women with successful careers in chemistry did follow that path. This group of women included Rachel Lloyd (1839-1900) of Philadelphia, who became the first American woman to earn a doctoral degree in chemistry at Zurich. Lloyd studied organic chemistry with August Viktor Merz, and completed her thesis "On the conversion of some of the homologues of benzol-phenol into primary and secondary amines" in 1887.[167] She became the second woman to earn a doctorate in chemistry in Europe and may have been the first American woman to earn a doctoral degree in chemistry anywhere.[168]

After Lloyd's husband died in 1865, she taught in a private girls' school in Louisville, Kentucky. Lloyd did research with Charles F. Mabery (1850-1927) on acrylic acid derivatives at the Harvard Summer School from 1876 to 1884.[169] Realizing she would need a doctorate to ever become a university professor, she decided to study at the University of Zurich. Immediately after earning her doctorate in Zurich, Lloyd was hired as an associate professor of analytical chemistry at the University of Nebraska in Lincoln. She was the second woman to join the faculty at Lincoln.[170] She also worked as an assistant chemist at the Nebraska Agricultural Experimental Station, which had been started in 1887 with federal funds from the Hatch Act.[171] In Zurich, Lloyd had become interested in the chemistry of sugar beets. For the next four years, she continued her research on sugar beets at the Nebraska Agricultural Experimental Station with its director, Henry Hudson Nicholson (1850-1940), Lloyd's colleague at the university. Nicholson had also become interested in sugar beet production while in Europe. He had noticed a similarity between the soil used for sugar beets in Germany and that of Western Nebraska. Working together with farmers from thirty counties, Lloyd and Nicholson proved that beets with adequate sugar and a high degree of purity could be grown with satisfactory yields and costs per acre in Nebraska.[172] Their experiments led to two sugar beet factories being built in Nebraska. Lloyd and Nicholson continued their research on sugar beets to produce better seeds, to improve storage, and to find new uses for by-products. Lloyd helped write twelve bulletins for the "Sugar Beet Series."[173] She contributed to the sugar beet legacy of Nebraska, which, as of 2000, was the eighth largest producer of sugar beets in the United States. In 1891 Lloyd became the second woman to become a member of the American Chemical Society.[174] Lloyd retired as a full professor in 1894 because of health reasons.

Fifteen years after Lloyd left Zurich, she was still remembered in the German-speaking community of progressive women. The progressive women's journal, *Dokumente der Frauen*, mentions Lloyd's death in a 1901 issue.[175] The obituary notes that Lloyd was a member of the German Chemical Society in

Frankfurt as well as the American Chemical Society (ACS), the English Chemical Society, the AAAS, the Hayden Art Club, the Browning Club and the Photographic Society of Lincoln, Nebraska. Lloyd was also the first woman to publish in the *American Chemical Journal*.

Other chemists who studied in Zurich include Charlotte Fitch Roberts and Helen S. French, both associated with Wellesley College. In her history of Wellesley College, Patricia Palmieri describes the extremely supportive nature of the chemistry department, where senior faculty mentored junior faculty. Charlotte Almira Bragg, who taught chemistry at Wellesley for thirty-nine years, was not an active researcher, but encouraged colleagues and students to pursue research opportunities. The chemistry department flourished between 1876 through the early 1890s. In the glory days of chemistry at Wellesley, a Wellesley graduate, who would later study at Berlin and Zurich, Charlotte Fitch Roberts, joined the department. Roberts was born on December 13, 1859, in New York. Her father was a police officer. After earning her Bachelor's from Wellesley in 1880, Roberts became an instructor in chemistry and later an associate professor at Wellesley, where she taught for thirty-six years. In 1894 she became one of the first two women to earn a doctoral degree in chemistry at Yale. Five years later, during the Winter Semester of 1899/00, Roberts studied chemistry at the University of Berlin. In 1906 she returned to Europe to study in Zurich.[176]

In 1913 the American Helen S. French earned her doctorate in chemistry at Zurich, where she was the first North American woman after Lloyd to earn a doctorate in chemistry. By the time French came to Zurich, opportunities for women to study chemistry had greatly expanded. In Europe, women were able to enroll at all German-speaking universities. French audited courses at Leipzig, but chose to do her doctoral studies at Zurich. Her research in Europe was funded by a Horsford Fellowship from Wellesley. In Zurich French worked with Professor Wemer.

After returning from Zurich, French spent the rest of her professional career, from 1913 to 1950, at Wellesley, where she became a disciple of Charlotte Almira Bragg. Unfortunately, by the time French came to Wellesley, the chemistry department had fallen far behind similar departments at equivalent colleges, such as Mount Holyoke. The department had failed to modernize and produce sufficient Ph.D.s.[177] French advanced from an instructor to a full professor and then to a research professor, the first ever at Wellesley. French left Wellesley twice during her teaching career to do research at Cambridge (1923/24) and then at the California Institute of Technology (1939). Her research in organic chemistry was widely published. She was a fellow of the AAAS and was very active in the ACS.[178]

At Berlin, five American women in addition to Charlotte Fitch Roberts audited chemistry courses and one of them earned a doctoral degree before women could matriculate at the university. Two of these women, Marcia A. Keith (Winter Semester 1897/98 and Summer Semester 1898) and Mary Alling Hall (Summer Semester 1899), were graduates of the chemistry department of Mount Holyoke. Another woman, Ellen R. Cook (Winter Semester 1896/97 and Summer Semester 1897), was a graduate of Smith College. The two other women were graduates of larger institutions, Annie L. Flanigen (Winter Semester 1899/1900 through the Summer Semester 1901) of the University of Pennsylvania, and Ina A. Milroy of Michigan State Normal College.[179]

Milroy was the only one of these women to earn a doctoral degree at Berlin. She began auditing courses in Winter Semester 1898/99 and completed her doctoral thesis in 1904. Before studying in Berlin, Milroy had attended public schools and earned her teaching degree at Michigan State Normal College in Ypsilanti (Eastern Michigan University) in 1890. The next eight years she taught at the high school in Sedalia, Missouri. She then spent the next five years earning her doctorate in Berlin, where she took courses in chemistry with Emil Fischer and Jacobus Henricus van't Hoff (1852-1911).[180]

Although only six American women were registered as auditors in chemistry at Berlin, other American women were doing research there at private laboratories, such as those mentioned by Helen Abbott. One such case is that of Maude Menten (1879-1960), who studied in Berlin with Leonor Michaelis (1875-1949). With Michaelis, Menten developed the Michaelis-Menten equation, which is used to calculate the rate of an enzyme reaction.[181] Menten and Michaelis published an article together in a German journal for biochemistry in 1913.[182] Menten later returned to the United States to earn her doctorate at the University of Chicago. She taught at the University of Pittsburgh School of Medicine and was the chief pathologist at the Children's Hospital in Pittsburgh.[183] Menten continued to work and publish in the field of histochemistry throughout her career.

Besides Berlin, the University of Breslau was also known for its work in chemistry. Clara Immerwahr, who in 1900 became the first woman to complete a doctorate there, had earned her degree in chemistry. In 1908 the Canadian Mary Violette (Violet) Dover (1874-1934) of Peterborough, Ontario, completed her doctorate in chemistry. Dover's father was part owner of a fire insurance company. She attended private schools and received her Bachelor's at McGill University in 1898. After continuing her studies in chemistry, mineralogy and geology, she completed her Master's in 1900. From 1900 to 1905 she worked as an assistant at McGill and published research with her colleague, Walker. She received a fellowship from Bryn Mawr College for the 1905/06 academic year. An article based upon her research at Bryn Mawr on diphenylcyclohexenone was published in the *American Chemical Journal*.[184] In October 1906 Dover began her studies at Breslau. Dover majored in chemistry and had minors in mineralogy, physics and philosophy. Otto Lummer (1860-1925), who examined Dover in physics, criticized her poor German, but Dover passed the exams and completed her thesis on "The Equilibrium between Ferro-Ferri and Silver Ion and Metallic Silver" (Das Gleichgewicht zwischen Ferro-Ferri-und Silber-Ion und metallischem Silber).[185] After completing her doctoral degree, Dover taught chemistry at Mount Holyoke from 1909 to 1914. Dover then took a position at the University of Missouri-Columbia, where she taught in the chemistry department until her death. During her tenure at Missouri, Dover did research on lubricants.[186]

BOTANY

Of all the disciplines within the natural sciences, botany was most closely associated with women during the nineteenth century. In her study of women scientists, Rossiter includes a brief study of popular literature and textbooks of the early to mid-nineteenth century written to further women's informal science education. These texts typically focused on botany.[187] Using one particularly popular text, Almira Hart Lincoln's *Familiar Lectures on Botany*, Rossiter illustrates how appropriate botany was for both introducing women to science and encouraging feminine behavior. Collecting and identifying plants was to bring women closer to god and nature. This in turn would elevate women's minds, strengthen women's faith and enhance domestic harmony. Botany was so identified with women, that an 1887 article in *Science* actually asked, "Is Botany a Suitable Study for Young Men?"[188] Rossiter sees this close identification of botany with women as the most likely reason so many women were hired as scientific assistants by the U.S. Department of Agriculture's Bureau of Plant Industry, which was started in 1887.[189] Despite such opportunities in the field for women, the highest and most prestigious research positions were still off limits to women until the 1920s. Moreover, as some of the amateur botanical clubs consolidated into professional organizations, female members were not necessarily welcome any longer. When the Botanical Society of America formed in 1893, its membership requirement of publications or other important contributions to the field resulted in the exclusion of all but one woman. In the late nineteenth century women botanists in higher education were mostly employed at women's colleges where they rarely published. The gap between them and their male colleagues only widened as the field was increasingly professionalized.

A similar tale of women botanists' experiences unfolds in Marianne Gosztonyi Ainley's study of Canadian women natural scientists between 1815 and 1965. Women in Canada "indulged in the widespread mania for collecting natural history specimens that formed an integral part of nineteenth-century scientific culture."[190] Canadian women then experienced the same marginalization during the 1890s as botany, along with the other natural sciences, became more institutionalized and professionalized. Like their American counterparts, highly educated Canadian women botanists had a difficult time finding jobs in higher education or doing independent research. Most women in the field found jobs as high school teachers, instructors or research assistants. These were all positions that involved heavy teaching loads, low salaries and little chance for independent research. Some women found jobs with the Canadian Department of Agriculture.[191] Unfortunately, even those women who met with some success in higher education continued to face gender discrimination.

The first Canadian woman to teach botany at a university was Carrie Matilda Derick, the first woman on McGill University's instructional staff. Despite Derick's apparent success, she had to struggle against gender discrimination during her entire career. Margaret Gillett gives a moving account of Derick's struggles at McGill.

Derick was born on January 14, 1862, in Clarenceville, Quebec, the daughter of Edna Colton Derick and Frederick Derick. She was educated at the Clarenceville Academy, where she began to teach at age fifteen. She later trained as a teacher at the McGill Normal School in Montreal. In 1881 she became the principal of the Clarenceville Academy. Two years later she returned to Montreal to teach in a private girls' school. Then in 1887 she enrolled at McGill, where she completed her Bachelor's in 1890 and graduated with the highest grade point average in her class. She won prizes in botany, zoology, natural science and the classics.[192]

Derick continued to teach as she worked on her Master's at McGill. After receiving her Master's in 1896, Derick was promoted to a full-time position, but only through the intervention of a wealthy advocate of women's education, Sir Donald A. Smith.[193] Derick continued to take courses at Harvard, Woods Hole and at the Royal College of Science in London during the summers.   During 1901/02, she used grant money from McGill to study for eighteen months in Germany. She visited laboratories and botanical gardens in Munich and Berlin, and studied for two semesters at the University of Bonn. Gillett writes that Derick completed all the research there for a doctorate, but was not awarded a degree, because Bonn would not grant a doctorate to a woman. Though exceptions for women had already been made at other German universities, it seems that no professor at Bonn was willing to make one for Derick.

Derick published for both lay and scholarly audiences. She was one of the first female members of several professional societies, including the AAAS, the Botanical Society of America, the American Genetics Association and the Canadian Public Health Association. She was also active in women's issues on both the local and national levels.

When her mentor in the botany department, David Penhallow, became ill, Derick took over as chair of the department. She remained in this position after Penhallow died. When the university finally got around to hiring someone for the permanent position, Derick was passed over for a very well qualified male scholar from the outside. To soften the blow, Derick was given the "courtesy title" of Professor of Morphological Botany. The title brought no increase in status or salary. Derick was also outraged when her new colleague tried to assign her work that she felt was below one of her rank and experience. Still, Derick remained at McGill until she retired in 1929 and trained many successful graduate students.

Women's colleges offered a much more supportive atmosphere for women in higher education. Women there did not have to struggle, as Derick did, against such an open bias against women. Yet, as already noted, women's colleges did not necessarily offer their faculty sufficient resources or time for conducting independent research and that often limited a faculty member's chance for professional advancement. Of interest here is the work of five American women botanists who were associated either as a student and/or as a teacher with a women's college. All five women had successful careers as teachers and managed to maintain some level of research and publication after graduate school. All earned their Ph.D.s in botany at the University of Zurich between 1886 and 1894.

The first to earn her doctoral degree in Zurich was Emily L. (Loriva) Gregory (1840-1897) of Buffalo, New York. She was the "Miss Gregory" who was mentioned in passing in Helen Abbott's account of Schwendener, the plant physiologist in Berlin. Gregory apparently had hoped to earn her doctoral degree in Germany, but gave up and went to Zurich, where she studied with one of the most popular professors of botany, Arnold Dodel (1843–1908). Dodel was famous for his controversial support of Darwin. He also gave numerous lectures in popular science.[194]

Gregory's dissertation, completed in 1886, was on "Comparative Anatomy of the Filz-like Hair-covering of leaf-organs."[195]   Before studying at Zurich, Gregory had taught botany at Bryn Mawr College. Even after earning a doctoral degree, Gregory had difficulty finding a suitable academic position. She took a position for the 1888/89 academic year at the University of Pennsylvania, where she was the first woman to teach on the faculty. Being independently wealthy, she was able to accept an unpaid position the following year as a professor of botany at Barnard College. Rossiter notes that this was not uncommon for wealthy women scholars. Such women spent their money and careers building up an academic department.[196]

While teaching at Barnard, Gregory published a textbook, *Elements of Plant Anatomy*. She became the first woman admitted to the American Society of Naturalists. Apparently, her foreign doctoral degree carried some prestige with it, as Gregory and the botanist, Ida Augusta Keller, were admitted to the society after earning degrees from Zurich, whereas two American women with Ph.D.s from Syracuse University were not invited to join. The Botanical Society of America did not, however, ask Gregory to join.[197]

Like Gregory, Ida Augusta Keller (1866-?)[198] worked for a period of time at Bryn Mawr College. After completing her teaching exams in 1884, Keller studied the natural sciences at the University of Pennsylvania from 1884 to 1886. She became the first woman to complete the two-year biology course there. Keller then went to Germany to study botany and chemistry at the University of Leipzig. In Leipzig she worked with Pfeffer, who ran the botanical garden. Keller then apparently realized she would have to leave Leipzig to earn a doctoral degree, and went to Zurich. Like Gregory, she did her research at the University of Zurich with Dodel in botany. Her minors were chemistry and zoology, for which she did coursework in organic chemistry with Haruthiun Abeljanz (1849-?) and August Viktor Merz. Her dissertation "On Protoplasmic Flow in the Plant Kingdom" (Über Protoplasma-Strömung im Pflanzenreich) was completed in 1890.[199]

Keller returned to Leipzig for an additional year of study before taking a position in botany at Bryn Mawr College. After one year, Keller left Bryn Mawr to become head of the Department of Chemistry and Botany at the Philadelphia High School for Girls. Keller published several scientific articles and co-authored the *Handbook of the Flora of Philadelphia and Vicinity*.[200]

The third American woman to receive her doctoral degree in botany at Zurich was Harriet Randolph (1856-1927),[201] who both studied and taught at Bryn Mawr College. After completing her Bachelor's at Bryn Mawr (1889), Randolph was a fellow in biology at Bryn Mawr for one year. She then spent the next two years at the Polytechnical School and at the University of Zurich. In 1892 she completed her doctoral thesis on "The Regeneration of the Tail in Lumbriculus."[202] Randolph then began a twenty-two-year career at Bryn Mawr as a demonstrator and reader in botany. She retired in 1914 to resume graduate studies at the University of California (1915) and Columbia University (1917-1918).[203] In 1906 she published an article for the Torrey Botanical Club on "The Influence of Moisture upon the Formation of Roots by Cuttings of Ivy." In 1908 she published an article in the *Biological Bulletin* on "The Spermatogenesis of the Earwig Anisolabis Maritima."

Julia Warner Snow (1863-1927),[204] the fourth American woman to complete her doctoral degree, was associated with Smith College, where she taught for many years but did no research.[205] In her records at Zurich, she wrote that she remained in La Salle, Illinois until she entered the Hungerford Collegiate Institute at Adams, New York, at the age of sixteen. After completing her studies there, she returned to live with her parents. Then in 1884 she began her studies at Cornell University. Snow earned her Bachelor's (1888) and Master's (1889) from Cornell. She taught botany for one year at the Hardy Preparatory School in Eau Claire, Wisconsin, and for one year at Coates College for Women in Terre Haute, Indiana. Snow was awarded an ACA European Fellowship, which she used to study in Zurich for the 1891/92 academic year. She then received a WEA fellowship, which she used to continue her studies in Zurich a second year.[206]

In Zurich, Snow did her research in botany with Dodel and Karl Schröter (1855-1939).[207] She did additional coursework with the zoologist Arnold Lang (1855-1914), the chemist Abeljanz and the biologist Charles Ernest Overton (1865-1933).[208] Her dissertation was on "The Conductive Tissue of the mono-cotyledonous plants."[209] After completing her doctoral degree at Zurich in 1893, Snow held a variety of teaching positions. From 1894 to 1896 she taught at the American College for Girls at Constantinople (Istanbul) and apparently did some coursework at the University of Basel. The following year she held a fellowship at the University of Michigan, where she taught botany from 1898 to 1900. She was appointed head of the Biology Department at Rockford College for the following year. She settled down in the botany department at Smith College, where she taught from 1901 until 1927. Snow was known for her great adventures. In the 1890s she traveled alone from Constantinople (Istanbul) to Russia. She circled the world twice, spending a lot of time in China and India. She also worked for several years on the biological survey of Lake Erie with the U.S. Fish Commission and published several articles on algae.[210]

The most extensive doctoral file exists for the fifth woman in this group of Zurich doctorates, Grace Emily Cooley (1857-1916), of East Hartford, Connecticut. Cooley is known today for her discovery of a new species of buttercup in Alaska in 1891, which was later named for her, Ranunculus cooleyae. After graduating from high school in 1875, Cooley taught for several years. In 1883 Cooley began to work as an instructor in botany at Wellesley, where she eventually earned her Bachelor's in 1885. While working, Cooley continued her graduate studies. She took a course in experimental plant physiology at McGill University in Montreal and earned her Master's from Brown University in 1893. When Cooley took a leave from Wellesley in 1894 to study in Zurich, she, like Gregory, Keller and Snow before her, was drawn to the botany laboratory of Dodel.[211]

Cooley gives a detailed account of her coursework at Zurich, which is helpful, as the records remaining for the other women contain little more than the names of their professors. Cooley's coursework gives us some idea of what was required for these women in their doctoral studies. With Dodel, Cooley did work in botany and plant physiology. With Overton, she studied cell biology and microchemistry. She took plant-geography with Schröter. Her coursework with Lang was in zoology and included morphology, physiology, anatomy and zootomical microscopy. In addition to these courses, she did work in entomology, organic chemistry and geology. She completed her dissertation "On the reserve cellulose of the seeds of Liliaceae and of some related orders" in 1895.[212] After returning from Zurich, Cooley continued to work at Wellesley until 1904. She died on January 27, 1916.[213]

Most of the women studying botany at German-speaking universities did not earn their doctorates. Some, like Alice Mills of Wellesley, traveled to Europe to take courses in water colors for the botanical department. Others simply took courses to further their education and improve their teaching. Martha Mann Magoun, who both studied and taught at Wellesley, studied botany in Zurich in 1887. Magoun later taught biology at MIT and Colorado College. While at Colorado College, she identified a new species of moss from the Rocky

Mountains. Asa Grey of the Harvard Botanical Department later named this species after Magoun.[214] Another botanist, Wellesley professor Susan Hallowell, spent her sabbatical year, 1887 to 1888, in Germany studying in the plant physiology laboratory of Leopold Kny at the University of Berlin, and visiting botanical gardens and laboratories in Dresden, Leipzig, Nuremberg and Munich.[215]

But there is also the unusual case of Janet Russell Perkins (1853-1933) of LaFayette, Indiana. She studied for eight semesters at Berlin (1895-1899), before finally transferring to Heidelberg, where she earned her doctoral degree in botany in 1900 with her thesis "A Monograph of the Family *Mollinedia*" (Eine Monographie der Gattung *Mollinedia*).[216] Before studying in Europe, she had completed her Bachelor's at the University of Wisconsin (1872). Apparently, after completing her degree in Heidelberg, Perkins returned to Berlin, where she worked at the Royal Botanic Museum in Dahlem. She published numerous articles in both German and English on tropical plants.[217]

GEOGRAPHY

This section focuses on the work of two women, Ellen Churchill Semple (1863-1932) and Dixie Lee Bryant, who were pioneers in the field of geography in the United States. Semple has been described as belonging to "the small but distinguished group whose pioneer work established geography on a firm and lasting foundation in this country."[218] Bryant became the first woman to earn a doctoral degree at the University of Erlangen, when she graduated in 1904.

Germany played a leadership role in the newly emerging field of geography at the end of the nineteenth century. By 1899 there were thirty universities and technical colleges where geography was taught as a discipline separate from geology. At Berlin, leading scholars in the field included Karl Ritter, Heinrich Kiepert and Ferdinand von Richthofen. At Leipzig, there was Friedrich Ratzel (1844-1904).[219]

Ellen Churchill Semple has been credited with introducing the method of cultural geography to the United States. She was introduced to the field by Ratzel during three semesters of study (1891/92) at the University of Leipzig. Ratzel was at that time the foremost cultural geographer. Before coming to Leipzig, Semple had majored in history. She had completed a Bachelor's (1882) and a Master's (1891) at Vassar College. During her studies she came across the work of Ratzel. Later, during the summer of 1891, while traveling abroad with her mother, she met another American who had studied with Ratzel and who hardily recommended going to Leipzig to study with him.[220] Semple did indeed go to Leipzig rather than return home.

The universities of Saxony still did not allow women to matriculate or earn degrees. With Ratzel's permission, however, Semple was allowed to attend his lectures and seminar. Semple returned to Leipzig a second time in 1895 to continue her work with Ratzel. Shortly thereafter, in 1897, the first of her numerous articles and books was published.

Semple contributed to the acceptance of cultural geography as a science through her publications and teaching. Her first teaching position was as a visiting lecturer at the newly formed department of geography at the University of Chicago in 1906. For the next eighteen years, Semple returned to Chicago to teach every other year. In the summers of 1912 and 1914, she was invited to lecture at Oxford University. Returning from Oxford the second time, Semple taught for a year at Wellesley. She taught the summer of 1916 at the University of Colorado and the summer of 1918 at Columbia University. In 1921, when Clark University established its School of Geography, Semple was appointed professor of anthropogeography. She kept this position until her death. At Clark, Semple worked primarily with graduate students. During her tenure there, she continued to lecture as a guest professor at other universities, including the University of Chicago, the University of Michigan, the University of Kentucky and UCLA. Wallace W. Atwood, who brought Semple to Clark, believed that she had inspired the entire team of geographers hired after her. In her praise, he wrote:

> She has retained this leadership, as well as the leadership of the profession in America, if not of the world, by virtue of her indefatigable research, her eminent standard of integrity and thoroness [sic] in investigation, her genius for clear, forceful expression, and her inspiring and invigorating personality....Most of the geographers who are guiding the future of their profession in American today have been her students; or if they have not had this privilege they have been closely enough associated with her to have been inspired and guided by her enthusiasm and advice.[221]

Semple's most significant publications were her early article, "The Anglo-Saxons of the Kentucky Mountains" (1901) and her three books, *American History and Its Geographic Conditions* (1903), *Influences of Geographic Environment* (1911) and *The Geography of the Mediterranean Region* (1931). Semple was a charter member of the Association of American Geographers and received several prestigious awards, including the Cullom Geographical Medal of the American Geographical Society (1914) and the Helen Culver Gold Medal of the Geographic Society of Chicago (1932).[222]

Dixie Lee Bryant broke barriers in both the United States and Germany. In 1897 Bryant and four other women became the first women to attend the University of North Carolina at Chapel Hill. At that time women were still barred from lower-level undergraduate courses, but the trustees and president of the university had voted to allow women into upper-level undergraduate courses and graduate programs. Although women had been allowed to attend courses at the summer normal school, this was the first time in 102 years that women were admitted as regular students to the University of North Carolina at Chapel Hill.[223] Before enrolling at Chapel Hill, Bryant had completed an undergraduate degree at MIT and taught courses for the summer normal school at Chapel Hill. After graduating from Chapel Hill, Bryant studied geography at the University of Erlangen. On July 30, 1904, she completed her doctoral degree with a thesis on "Studies on the Petrography of Spitsbergen" (Beiträge zur Petrographie Spitzbergens).[224]

GEOLOGY

In her essay on Canadian women geologists, Marianne Gosztonyi Ainley writes that although Canadian women began working for the Geological Survey (established 1842) in the early 1880s, most of these women worked as librarians, clerks, assistants or photographers and not as scientists. Only one woman, Alice Wilson (1881-1964), held a scientific position before World War II. The first woman to graduate from a Canadian institute with a degree in geology, Grace

Anna Stewart (1893-1970), ended up having to work in the United States at Ohio State University to find an academic position in higher education.[225]

As in Canada, American women found positions with the U.S. Geological Survey (established 1879), but to become a professional scientist, a woman needed to have an advanced degree. Women had contributed to the field of geology throughout the nineteenth century as amateur collectors of fossils and minerals. But as geology, like other scientific fields, was increasingly institutionalized and professionalized in the late nineteenth century, women had to do graduate work in geology or be satisfied with lower-level positions in their field. Unlike other scientific fields such as biology and chemistry, however, geology remained marginal in women's higher education. According to Rossiter, although large numbers of women in the nineteenth century attended popular lectures on geology, there was no market for geological books geared towards women. In most colleges, geology remained an elective. The programs for women that existed produced few graduates who became professionals in the field.[226]

Two classic examples of women who were active in the field but never made the leap to higher education are Erminnie A. Platt Smith (1836-1886) and Mary Hegeler Carus (1861-1936). Both women are remarkable for having studied at the prestigious Freiberg School of Mines in Saxony. They may have been the only two women to enroll at that school as students in the nineteenth century.

The Freiberg School of Mines had a rigorous and comprehensive curriculum, especially for those hoping to complete a degree. The school also had provisions for those students who were not working towards a degree and wanted to specialize in one area. Half of each course was made up of laboratory work, which included, for example, work with collections, in the mines and in the smelters. When Smith attended the school sometime between the mid-1860s and 1875, it would have been at the height of the first wave of American students to attend the school. From its beginning in 1765, the small mining school had such a reputation of excellence that it attracted foreign students and competed with larger institutions. Most Americans, however, did not arrive until the second half of the nineteenth century. Enrollments of Americans started to climb after 1854 and had already fallen significantly before the outbreak of World War I.[227] A famous memoir of an American, Frederick Gleason Corning, who studied in Freiberg right after Smith, emphasizes how Americans and other foreigners were welcomed at the school.[228] In the memoir, published in 1920, Corning notes the unique contribution Freiberg made to American science at a time when American schools did not yet have the same high standards. By 1920 there was no longer an advantage for American engineers to study abroad. American schools had matched or surpassed the standards of the German schools. Further, American schools were better prepared to train students for mining practices specific to America. But for a time, Freiberg had offered the "rounded out" curriculum and high standards American schools could not match.[229]

Smith's interest in geology was awakened at an early age by her father Joseph Platt, a farmer, deacon and rock collector. From 1850 to 1853 Smith attended the Troy Female Seminary established by Emma Willard. In 1855 she married Simeon H. Smith. As Smith raised four children, she continued to educate herself and pursue her interest in geology. While the family was in Germany for four years, Smith took advantage of the opportunity to study crystallography at Strasbourg, and German language and literature at Heidelberg. The seriousness of her efforts is further demonstrated in that she completed a two-year course in mineralogy at Freiberg. There is a delightful account of Smith descending hundreds of feet into a mine in the Harz Mountains in a bucket.[230]

After returning from Freiberg, Smith made a name for herself by delivering a series of popular lectures and publishing several papers on minerals.[231] Smith had one of the finest cabinets of fossils, shells and gems in the country:

> The drawing-rooms each side of the entrance, and running the
> entire length of the house, had their walls lined with cabinets
> filled with geographical and mineral specimens, fossil fishes,
> petrifactions, rare pieces of spar, arsenic, and silver ore; tour-
> maline, malachite, lapis lazuli, rhodenite, and some unequalled
> examples of agate and precious gems, beside curious treasures
> from the animal and vegetable kingdoms.[232]

Among the treasures of these cabinets was a piece of amber containing a small lizard. Smith was fascinated by amber and wrote an entire paper on its history and composition.[233] Smith remained an active lecturer and researcher for the rest of her life. In 1876 she founded the Aesthetic Society, "a group of women who met monthly to read and discuss papers on science, literature and art."[234] She directed the science programs for Sorosis, a New York City women's club, for four years. Smith became the first woman to be named a Fellow of the New York Academy of Sciences; she was also named a Fellow of the AAAS and the London Scientific Society. In 1888 an award was established in her name at Vassar for the best student research paper on mineralogy or geology. For the last six years of her life, Smith shifted her research to ethnography and focused on the Iroquois. Her contributions in that field included the compilation of an Iroquois dictionary and a collection of Iroquois myths. She also trained Native American ethnologists to continue with similar research. Her work in this field was partially financed and published by the Smithsonian Institution's Bureau of American Ethnology.[235]

The connections with Freiberg were more direct for Mary Hegeler Carus. Her father, Edward Hegeler from Bremen, studied at Freiberg and married Camilla Weisbach, the daughter of one of his professors. With a fellow student from Freiberg, Edward came to the United States and built a zinc plant in La Salle, Illinois. Mary began working in her father's plant when she was sixteen. She then studied mathematics and chemistry at the University of Michigan, where she earned her Bachelor's in 1882. Mary traveled to Freiberg, where she took courses in metallurgy. In Freiberg, she also worked in the laboratory of her uncle, the renowned chemist Clemens Winkler (1838-1904). In 1886, while Mary was still working with Winkler, he discovered the element Germanium (Ge).[236] After extensive training in Freiberg, Mary returned to La Salle to continue working in her father's plant. Shortly thereafter, her father hired the German mathematician Dr. Paul Carus to tutor his children. Carus was also to help translate and write for the *Open Court*, a journal founded by Edward in 1887. Mary and Paul Carus soon married. The rest of her career was devoted to running the zinc plant and serving as an editor and adviser to mathematical publications in her control, including the *Carus Mathematical Monographs*, the *Monist* and the *Open Court*.

In contrast to Smith and Hegeler Carus, Florence Bascom (1862-1945) offers a example of a woman who did compete successfully with men in the increasingly professionalized field of geology and who emerged as a leading researcher and educator in geology at the end of the nineteenth century. Bascom would train most of America's women geologists of the early twentieth century in her classes and laboratories at Bryn Mawr College.

Bascom grew up in a privileged household as the daughter of Emma Curtiss Bascom, an artist and feminist, and John Bascom, the president of the University of Wisconsin and later of Williams College. She received her Bachelor's (1884) and her Master's (1887) from Wisconsin. She then taught at a college in Illinois for two years before enrolling at The Johns Hopkins University in 1889. In 1893 Bascom became the first woman to earn a Ph.D. from Hopkins and the second woman to earn a Ph.D. in geology in the United States.[237] Rossiter speculates as to why the administration made an exception for Bascom and granted her the degree, where it had denied the same privilege to Christine Ladd-Franklin.[238] Factors in Bascom's favor may have been the connections of her father, the excellence of her work and the support of her advisor. It also probably helped that she had the support of M. Carey Thomas, who was raising money for the new Hopkins Medical School.

After earning her Ph.D. Bascom taught for two years at Ohio State University as an assistant to Edward Orton (1829-1899), a family friend. Orton, who served as a professor of geology and president at both Antioch College and Ohio State, appears to have played a critical role in encouraging women in the field of geology. The two programs that produced the largest number of women graduates who later became geologists were at Bryn Mawr and Ohio State.[239] Bascom started the program at Bryn Mawr after leaving Ohio State. In addition to encouraging Bascom, Orton also took women students, including Mignon Talbot who would later teach at Mount Holyoke, on field trips. The geology department at Ohio State would remain relatively welcoming to women even after Orton's death. It was here that the Canadian Grace Anna Stewart was able to find a position in higher education.

In 1895 Bascom left Ohio State to begin her career as a professor of geology at Bryn Mawr College. The following year she became the first woman scientist hired to work for the U.S. Geological Survey. Throughout the rest of her teaching career, Bascom would struggle to devote enough time to her work for the Geological Survey, her own research and to building and maintaining the geology department. Geology departments were not the strength of any women's college at that time and Bascom had to create her own library, collections and laboratories at Bryn Mawr. Her efforts were rewarded by the success of so many of her students.

Throughout her career, Bascom continued to do research with leaders in the emerging fields of crystallography and metamorphism. As an undergraduate at the University of Wisconsin, she had studied with Charles Van Hise and Roland Irving. At Hopkins, she worked with George Huntington Williams. In 1906 she traveled to Heidelberg to study optical crystallography with Victor Goldschmidt (1853-1933), one of the founders of modern crystallography. In Heidelberg, Bascom was able to study the latest techniques in this emerging field. She would later spread Goldschmidt's methods throughout the United States and Europe. Her efforts would bring long-term benefits to the field. Her student Ida Ogilvie (1874-1963) would later teach Elizabeth A. Wood, who wrote what was long the standard textbook for optical crystallography, *Crystals and Light*.[240] Other famous students of Bascom included Julia Gardner (1882-1960) and Eleanora Bliss Knopf (1883-1974).[241]

An extensive correspondence between Bascom and Goldschmidt exists documenting their rich professional and personal exchange. Bascom's contact with Goldschmidt proved very productive for her. Goldschmidt introduced her to new laboratory techniques and equipment. She became an early advocate of his methods of using the two-circle goniometer, a simple yet effective device for measuring the faces of crystals.[242] Through the years, Goldschmidt kept her informed about his research and sent her lab specimens, plates of crystal forms and copies of his publications, all of which she incorporated into her own teaching and research. Bascom, in turn, helped Goldschmidt by assisting with his 1911 lecture tour in the United States. She sent her most promising students to work in his laboratory. After a stint in Heidelberg, these students themselves helped to spread Goldschmidt's methods.

A classic example of such an exchange is the case of the crystallographer Mary Porter, who started out as a student with Bascom at Bryn Mawr. In January 1914, Bascom asked Goldschmidt to accept Porter in his laboratory. She described Porter as having significant "gaps in her education" but "an unusual aptitude for crystal measurement."[243] Bascom hoped that after a period of study with Goldschmidt, Porter would be allowed to teach at Bryn Mawr even without a doctoral degree. With the start of World War I, Porter's plans changed. She left Goldschmidt's laboratory to work in Geneva and at Oxford. She remained, however, an advocate of his methods. In a letter to Goldschmidt from January 1917, which was returned from Germany undelivered, Bascom wrote of Porter's work in support of Goldschmidt's methods:

> It is a delight to me to know that she [Porter] is convincing the Oxford mineralogists of the value of the 2-circle goniometer. If the goniometer (the first!) is once installed, it will end in the teaching of the Goldschmidt methods. Miss Porter is going to measure one of Dr. Sutton's compounds with the 2-circle goniometer and place the result side by side with his in order to confute Dr. Sutton's charge that the 2-circle goniometer is inaccurate (He has not used the instrument)! [244]

Bascom corresponded with Goldschmidt throughout World War I and continued to encourage her students to study with him. In March 1915, one of her students received the Bryn Mawr European Fellowship. Bascom hoped that student would be able to use the fellowship to study in Heidelberg as soon as the war was over. Four years after the end of the war, Bascom was delighted to find Goldschmidt's laboratory once again "alive with young crystallographers from many countries."[245]

Chapter Five
Women in the Social Sciences and Psychology

In 1868, the beginning of the period of this study, psychology and the social sciences, including economics, sociology, political science and anthropology, were not clearly defined, independent disciplines in North America. As Dorothy Ross writes in her essay on the development of the social sciences in the United States, the above five subjects were generally treated as part of broader discussions of history, morals, philosophy, and natural history.[1] With the expansion of universities in the 1870s and 1880s, there was a period of transition and all five subjects eventually became separate disciplines. Graduate programs and professional journals were formed for all of the subjects except sociology in the 1880s. Sociology would follow in the 1890s. Although each of the five disciplines had a separate national professional association by 1905, it was not until after World War I that psychology and the social sciences diverged completely from the humanistic disciplines, including history and philosophy.[2] In this chapter, an awareness of the overlap within the social sciences and psychology and the influence of the humanistic disciplines is important for understanding the courses of study and professional choices of women in these subjects.

SOCIAL SCIENCES

Much has been written about the key role the University of Chicago played in the advancement of the social sciences, in particular sociology, in the United States. Although courses in sociology had been introduced at other universities as early as 1871, it was Chicago in 1892 that became the first university to establish an entire department of sociology with a chair. Other major universities with graduate courses in sociology before 1900 included Yale, the University of Pennsylvania, the University of Michigan, Johns Hopkins, Cornell, Harvard and Columbia. Of these universities, Chicago had the most faculty appointments in sociology before 1905. Columbia became the second largest center of graduate study in the field under the leadership of President Frederick Augustus Porter Barnard, John W. Burgess and the social scientists Richmond Mayo-Smith, Franklin Giddings, William Z. Ripley and Edwin Robert Anderson Seligman.

In his posthumously published dissertation, Christopher Bernert describes the key role William Rainey Harper, president of the University of Chicago from 1891 to 1906, played in promoting sociology at the university. In addition to establishing the department and appointing Albion Small to chair the new department, he challenged Small to turn the *University Extension Magazine* into the *American Journal of Sociology*. As Bernert notes, Harper was responsible for keeping the Christian element in sociology with the large number of ministers on the Chicago faculty and for Chicago's emergence as the new capital of the Chautauqua movement.[3]

In addition to the leadership role Chicago played in sociology, the university also fostered the scholarship of women in the social sciences. Not by chance did the majority of the women mentioned in this chapter do graduate coursework in the social sciences at Chicago. In her history of women social scientists, Ellen Fitzpatrick describes the circumstances that created the supportive atmosphere for women at Chicago.

First, Harper appointed women in key leadership positions: Alice Freeman Palmer as dean of women and Marion Talbot as assistant dean of women. Fitzpatrick writes that Talbot loved presenting Harper with her annual report praising the achievements of the women students and faculty.[4] Eventually two social scientists, Sophonisba Breckenridge and Edith Abbott, would be promoted to full professors on the faculty. Abbott would also serve as dean of the Graduate School of Social Service Administration.

Second, limited financial support was available to women pursuing graduate studies. Although only a few women benefited from the fellowships, one of these allowed one of the women mentioned below, Amy Hewes, to study sociology in Germany. Fitzpatrick notes that between 1893 and 1899, there were ten fellowships awarded to female graduate students in political economy, political science and sociology.[5] Third, once a core of women students enrolled, the support network expanded to later students. Women's dormitories became centers for social activities.[6] Communities of alumnae from various colleges, Wellesley in particular, developed. Fourth, a number of wealthy Chicago women contributed money for buildings, especially for women's dormitories, and thus ensured a place for women at the university.[7] Fifth, the city of Chicago itself offered opportunities to work with labor activists and social reformers such as Jane Addams in Hull House. Last, there simply were not many opportunities for graduate study available to women in the United States when the University of Chicago opened in 1892. All these factors combined to boost enrollments of women in the social sciences at the university. According to Fitzpatrick, from 1892 until 1902 almost one-quarter of the graduate students in sociology, political economy or political science were women.[8]

While women doing graduate study at the University of Chicago were not forced to go abroad to complete a doctoral degree, a number of women who would later become prominent social activists and social scientists did choose to enhance their graduate education at Chicago with a semester or two of study abroad, in particular at the University of Berlin. In the late nineteenth and early twentieth centuries, Berlin had become a center for emerging fields of the social sciences and psychology. Professors of particular note in the social sciences were Georg Simmel (1858-1918) in sociology and economists Adolf Wagner (1835-1917), Gustav Schmoller (1838-1917) and Max Sering (1857-1939). The first records of women auditors at Berlin, which begin with the Winter Semester of 1895/96, include the names of the professors whose lectures the student attended. That Winter Semester of 1895/96, almost half, or thirty-eight, of the seventy-nine women auditing classes were from North America. Of those thirty-eight women, five listed attending lectures in the social sciences. While five women might not appear to be significant, what these women lacked in numbers they made up for in their efforts for progressive social reform. Emily Greene Balch became an international peace activist and later won the Nobel Peace Prize. Mary M. Kingsbury Simkhovitch became a leading social activist and advocate of labor reform. Ethel Puffer Howes, fought to create ways for women to combine careers with a family and became one of the first women to teach on the Harvard faculty. Anna Davis played an important role in progressive reforms in the Chicago public schools.[9] Three years later, another American woman who would emerge as a leader in prison reform, Katharine Bement Davis, came to Berlin to study political economy.

In an article from 1900, Amy Hewes (1877-1970), a graduate of Goucher (1897) then studying sociology in Berlin, compared opportunities for the study of sociology in Chicago and Berlin. Hewes was in Berlin on a foreign fellowship from Chicago, where she was doing graduate work. She praised Chicago for having a separate department of sociology. In Berlin, relevant courses were scattered throughout various departments. Hewes noted the relative ease with which women could audit lectures at Berlin. Attending seminars was the only difficulty. At that point in 1900, Hewes wrote that the matriculation of women at Berlin in the near future was "more or less confidently expected." Unfortunately, Hewes was wrong, and another eight years would pass before the Prussian universities would allow women to matriculate.[10]

The two professors Hewes praised in her article were Albion Small and Georg Simmel. She considered Simmel one of the most important sociologists of Europe, and included the names of three courses he had taught the prior semester: sociology, with particular consideration of the form of government; nineteenth-century philosophy in relationship to life problems; and ethics, with historical-philosophical excursuses. In addition to her praise of Berlin, Hewes commented in general on the benefits of studying abroad in the social sciences. One year was always too short because a student needed time to learn the language properly and adjust to the greater academic freedom. In one year, a student would barely have the time to be exposed to some of the new methods of research. Hewes appears in the Berlin auditor records for only two semesters, from Winter Semester 1899/1900 to Summer Semester 1900. But a notice in a Goucher publication from June 1900 mentions that Hewes would be continuing her sociological studies in Germany for another year. Hewes became a pioneer in the fight for minimum wage laws. After studying in Berlin, Hewes returned to the University of Chicago, where she completed her Ph.D. in 1903. After working at the Library of Congress and as an editor for a year, Hewes became a professor of applied economics and sociology at Mount Holyoke College, where she remained until her retirement in 1943. Hewes served as executive secretary of the Minimum Wage Commission of Massachusetts from 1913 to 1915. In her history of women scientists, Margaret Rossiter refers briefly to a 1919 article by Hewes, which claimed the new Carnegie pension plan for professors discriminated against women.[11] After retiring, Hewes continued to serve on state and national advisory committees on labor arbitration. In 1962 she received the

Award of Merit from the Department of Labor for her efforts "to foster, promote and develop the welfare of the wage earner in the United States."[12]

Like Hewes, most of the women mentioned studied for only a semester or two at a German-speaking university. Nevertheless, the brief stay in Europe radicalized or affirmed the progressive social outlook of these women. It exposed many of them to socialism for the first time and allowed them to engage Eastern European activists in a dialogue.

One of the first American auditors in the social sciences at the University of Berlin, Emily Greene Balch,[13] later became one of the most famous American peace activists of the early twentieth century. With Jane Addams and Alice Hamilton, she attended the International Congress of Women in The Hague in April 1915, along with about forty-seven other American women, and published an account of her experiences there. At that time, Addams was the President of the International Congress of Women and the Women's Peace Party of America. Hamilton was a physician and public health inspector for the U.S. Department of Labor. Balch was a professor of economics and sociology at Wellesley. The optimistic goal of the conference convening in the thick of war was to prepare for a permanent peace. The two key parts of the platform were "(a) That international disputes should be settled by pacific means; (b) that the Parliamentary franchise should be extended to women."[14] At the conference, Balch was inspired by "a passionate human sympathy" that united even the women from warring countries and that was "not inconsistent with patriotism, but transcending it."[15]

Unfortunately, Balch's peace activism eventually cost her the teaching position at Wellesley that she had held since 1896. In her history of Wellesley, Patricia Palmieri gives a moving account of Balch's dismissal from the campus for speaking out against the war. Despite widespread protest from the faculty, the trustees voted not to reappoint Balch in the spring of 1919. Although she was confronted with economic hardships, Balch was not defeated. She continued her work in the international arena for peace and women's rights. She became a Quaker and a member of the Women's International League for Peace and Freedom (WILPF), an organization in which she held several important offices. She endorsed a number of efforts to use sanctions or other political or economic measures to prevent war. In 1946 she was awarded the Nobel Peace Prize for her work with WILPF.

Balch began her studies at Bryn Mawr in 1886, one year after the college had opened. She took courses in economics, modern languages, the classics and philosophy. After graduating in 1889 she became the first recipient of the Bryn Mawr European Fellowship, which she used to study economics at the Sorbonne.[16] After returning from Paris, Balch sought out practical experience in social reform. She worked at the Boston Children's Aid Society and in 1892 studied at Felix Adler's Summer School of Applied Ethics, where she first met Katharine Coman, Vida Scudder and Jane Addams.[17] In December 1892 Balch helped found Denison House, a center for education and social relief, in Boston. In her biography of Balch, Mercedes M. Randall writes that at Denison House Balch first gained experience of the labor movement and the realities of the labor struggle.[18] Randall captures some of the idealism of the labor movement in a quote from Balch. Balch wrote that the leaders of the movement she was working with in the early 1890s:

> understood trade unionism not as a struggle for material advantages for a limited class of people but in the same sense in

which I understood my teaching at Wellesley College, as a part
of a wide-spread and many-sided effort for juster and more humane social relations everywhere. There was a great deal of
idealism in the trade union movement of the time as we saw
it, and it has been one of the sad experiences of my life that it
has done so relatively little for the weakest and most unskilled
laborers.[19]

In the early 1890s, however, Balch was far from disillusioned. She was inspired
by the social activism of those working through Denison House. The list of
those with whom Balch worked is long, but it includes Mary Kingsbury, with
whom Balch later studied at the University of Chicago and with whom she traveled to Berlin.

Eventually, Balch determined to become a college teacher to have more influence on women students. She studied economics and sociology at the Harvard
Annex (Radcliffe) and at the University of Chicago before traveling to Berlin in
1895. Balch later described herself as always having embraced the Austrian
school of economics with its theory of marginal values.[20] But at both the Harvard Annex and the University of Chicago, she worked with professors who sub-
scribed to the opposing German camp, mockingly known as the *Kathedersozialisten*. These economic reformers rejected socialism but advocated greater state
intervention to ameliorate growing social problems associated with industrialization and urbanization. Balch chose to study economics and sociology at the
University of Berlin, where some of her professors, particularly Gustav
Schmoller, a leading *Kathedersozialist*, were responsible for the suppression of
Austrian economic theory at Berlin. In her later recollections, Balch rejected the
teachings of Schmoller and his colleagues. She wrote that she was startled to
realize how much of what later became a fundamental part of Nazi policies already existed in the teachings of these German economists. The state in Germany did not function even in the 1890s as "an instrument to do for the public
what the people will," but rather it was an independent, self-perpetuating body of
civil servants.[21] At the time she was studying in Berlin, however, Balch considered Schmoller an exceptional scholar and a good teacher.[22]

Professors and other students at the University of Berlin exposed Balch to
concepts of socialism that opposed the teachings of the *Kathedersozialisten*. She
was particularly inspired by hearing Wilhelm Liebknecht speak at a mass meeting. Outside of the university at gatherings of students interested in socialism,
Balch heard lectures by professors on unemployment. Other students spoke on
socialism or agricultural conditions. In Berlin, Balch also came into contact
with German and Polish women working on issues of women's education and
employment. On her way home from Berlin in July 1896, Balch stopped in
London to attend what would turn out to be the last International Socialist
Workers' and Trade Union Congress. There, Balch was exposed to some of the
most influential labor and socialist leaders of the time. Balch sailed back to
America on the same ship as her friend Katharine Coman, who was then the
only teacher for economics at Wellesley College. Coman offered Balch a part-
time position in economics at Wellesley, which Balch accepted. Balch remained
at Wellesley for over twenty years, where she taught courses on socialism,
Marxism and the economic role of women.

In her history of Wellesley, Patricia Palmieri provides a startling and inspiring account of Balch as a teacher. For Balch, economic and social theory was always linked to real social conditions:

> In all of her courses Emily Balch emphasized fieldwork. She took field trips to immigrant neighborhoods in Boston's North End, to factories, and to prisons. The college once received letters from parents protesting that she was taking their daughters to investigate brothels! Besides her involvement in Denison House Settlement, she became a cofounder and president of the Boston Women's Trade Union League (1902), supporting striking workers and speaking out against class exploitation. This activism infused her courses with a contagious enthusiasm.[23]

While at Wellesley, Balch continued her travels to Europe and especially to Eastern Europe to study social and economic conditions. A 1905 edition of the *Wellesley College News* mentions her concern for Moravian Slavs who had migrated to the United States as well as her interest in socialist agitation in Austria and Russia. In 1910 she published perhaps her most important work, *Our Slavic Fellow Citizens*, which was a study of immigrants to the United States from Eastern and Southern Europe. A review of her book that appeared in the *Bryn Mawr Alumnae Quarterly* in 1911 described Balch as one of Bryn Mawr's most distinguished alumnae and gave an interesting account of the work that led up to the book:

> For some time before 1905 she had been specially interested in work among the foreign immigrants, and in that year she spent many months in Austria-Hungary studying the Slavic populations in their own home. This investigation was supplemented by a year devoted to Slavic colonies in the United States, ranging from New York to Colorado and from the Upper Peninsula of Michigan to Galveston. One autumn was given to residence in the family of a Bohemian workingman in New York City.[24]

During her brief stay in Germany during 1895 and 1896, Balch developed a closer friendship with another American, Mary Kingsbury, with whom Balch had previously worked at Denison House. Kingsbury was born on September 8, 1867, in Chestnut Hill, Massachusetts. She received her Bachelor's from Boston University in 1890. Like Balch, Kingsbury also studied economics and sociology at the Harvard Annex (Radcliffe) and at the University of Chicago before coming to Berlin. Kingsbury came to Berlin on a European Fellowship of the Women's Educational and Industrial Union, which had been founded by Mary Morton Kimball Kehew (1859-1918), one of the founders of Denison House. In part, the friendship between Kingsbury and Balch was simply their sharing the excitement of life in Berlin. They took walks together and went to the opera. But it was also a chance for both women to discuss philosophy and social and economic theories. Both studied political economy and philosophy at Berlin. They took courses together in economics with Gustav Schmoller and Adolf Wagner. They attended lectures by Georg Simmel in sociology and by Friedrich Paulsen in philosophy.

Kingsbury was impressed by foreign students attending the lectures of Adolf Wagner in political economy. There were students from Russia, Poland, Bulgaria, Italy, England, Japan and America. Her classmates included the Polish labor activist Sonya Daszynska as well as Bertrand Russell and his first wife, the American Alice Pearsall Smith, who was a cousin of M. Carey Thomas, and Helen Whitall Thomas Flexner.[25] Among the students in Wagner's lectures, there was also a young Russian, Vladimir Simkhovitch, whom Kingsbury married in 1899. In Berlin, Simkhovitch and two friends organized an economics club for discussing labor issues. From her own account, Kingsbury spent time in Berlin educating herself about socialism. She attended meetings by activists and was offended by the military presence at all public meetings that was there to prevent any criticism of the monarchy.[26]

On her way home from Berlin, Kingsbury went with Balch to the last International Socialist Workers' and Trade Union Congress in London. The next year Kingsbury studied sociology at Columbia with Seligman, Giddings, Clark and James Harvey Robinson. Simkhovitch, who followed Kingsbury to America in 1898 and continued his studies at Cornell, became a professor of political science at Columbia University, where he remained for his entire career.

In September 1897 Kingsbury began her social work with the College Settlement House in the Lower East Side of New York City. There, Kingsbury worked closely with the Jewish laboring class. She became an advocate for housing reform and tenants' rights and took time to study Yiddish.

The following year Kingsbury became the chief resident at another settlement, the Unitarian Friendly Aid House. Several factors contributed to Kingsbury's discontent in this new position. She was discouraged from political activism and experimenting with new theories of social reform. The settlement did not emphasize cooperation with the local residents as had been the case at the College Settlement and focused too much on the moral improvement of the local population.[27]

In 1901 Kingsbury left the Friendly Aid House and, along with Felix Adler, Carl Schurz, Bishop Henry C. Potter, Eugene Philbin, Jacob Riis and Robert Fulton Cutting, helped found Greenwich House, a settlement run more closely in accord with her own principles and values. In 1929 Greenwich House became officially associated with Columbia University. One of the most devoted patrons of Greenwich House was Anna Woerishoffer, who in 1907 had established the Bryn Mawr Anna Ottendorfer Memorial Research Fellowship in Teutonic Philology in honor of her mother.

Throughout most of her career, Kingsbury worked to improve public housing. From 1931 to 1943 she was the president of the Public Housing Conference, which lobbied for a permanent federal housing program. In 1934 she was appointed the vice chair of the New York City Housing Authority. Even after retiring as the director of Greenwich House in 1946, Kingsbury continued to work for the Housing Authority.[28]

From 1898 to 1917 Kingsbury also served on the executive board of the National Consumers League. The League worked to educate consumers so that they would purchase only products that had been manufactured and sold under proper working conditions.[29] Through her work with the League, Kingsbury came into contact with Florence Kelley, one of the earliest activists against child labor and for protective labor legislation for women and children.

Although Florence Kelley (1859-1932) studied at Zurich and not at Berlin, it seems appropriate to include her at this point because her career corresponds so closely to those of Balch and Kingsbury. Kelley was born in Philadelphia. Her father, William Darrah Kelley, was a judge and member of Congress. Her mother, Caroline Bartram Kelley, had been adopted by Isaac Pugh when her parents died. Isaac's sister Sarah Pugh, a Quaker reformer and abolitionist, also shared Caroline's childhood home. Kelley was impressed by her "great-aunt" Sarah's refusal to use cotton and sugar, the products of slave labor.[30] Before studying in Europe, Kelley had received private instruction and earned an undergraduate degree from Cornell (1882). Years later, in an article for *The Survey*, a journal for social workers, Kelley wrote of her excitement about finally being able to attend college:

> Entering college was for me an almost sacramental experience. Two long years I had lived for it, since that lonely morning when I found in an otherwise empty waste-basket in my father's study, Cornell's offer of equal opportunities to women. Cornell was the first eastern university to make this glorious offer. Careful inquiry soon revealed that there was no school in Philadelphia equipped to fit a girl thoroughly for college. It was my grotesque experience to be prepared by tutors and governesses not college bred - to enter the freshman class in 1876.[31]

After graduating from Cornell, Kelley studied law at the University of Zurich, starting the Winter Semester of 1883. Her decision to study at Zurich was made after an encounter in Avignon with M. Carey Thomas, whom Kelley had known from Cornell. Thomas had just received her doctoral degree *summa cum laude* from Zurich after being denied a doctoral degree at Leipzig.[32] At Zurich, Kelley was inspired by the work of socialists she encountered. She wrote of her mind as "tinder" awaiting the match of socialism. The philosophy of socialism helped her to make sense of the suffering she had seen among newly freed slaves and child laborers. Now in Zurich, "among students from many lands, was the philosophy of Socialism, its assurance flooding the minds of youth and the wage-earners with hope that, within the inevitable development of modern industry, was the coming solution."[33] In Zurich, Kelley's thesis on workers' protection was well received, and Kelley spent the rest of her life as a labor activist.[34]

At Zurich, Kelley met her future husband, a Russian-Polish Jewish medical student and socialist, Lazare Wischnewetsky, whom she married in 1884. That same year, she translated Friedrich Engels's 1845 work *Die Lage der arbeitenden Klasse in England* (The Condition of the Working Class in England) into English. In Zurich, Kelley came into contact with members of the socialist press who had been driven out of Germany. She wrote of her first experience in Zurich at a meeting for socialists, where she had to grasp the sides of her chair to keep from trembling with excitement as Eduard Bernstein (1850-1932), the exiled editor of the organ of the German Socialist Party, gave a speech.[35]

In 1886 Kelley returned to the United States with Wischnewetsky and their three children. They lived in New York City until 1891. During their first year in New York they became active in the local Socialist Labor party. But in 1887 they were both temporarily expelled from the party, possibly for being too outspoken. That same year Kelley published a short article, "The Need of Theoretical Preparation for Philanthropic Work," which applied Marx's theory of surplus-value from *Das Kapital*. In this essay, Kelley praised *Das Kapital*, claiming that "[s]he who has mastered this work thoroughly finds a wholly new standpoint from which to judge the society of today, with its good and its evils."[36]

While in New York Kelley translated further works by Marx and Engels. She even began a correspondence with Engels that lasted until his death. In 1910 she helped to edit and complete a book on twentieth-century socialism by Edmond Kelly, who had taught political science at Columbia University. Chapters in that book have particularly delightful titles, such as "Capitalism is Stupid" or " Capitalism is Disorderly."[37]

Eventually Kelley and her husband became estranged. According to Kelley's biographer, Kathryn Kish Sklar, the period in New York marked Kelley's movement away from the more male-dominated world of the Socialist Labor Party to the more female-dominated world of women's reform organizations.[38] In 1891 Kelley moved with her three children to Illinois, where she obtained a divorce and became a resident at Hull House in Chicago. Her children and mother lived in an apartment nearby. At Hull House she continued to speak and write about socialism, protective labor legislation for women and children, and compulsory school laws. It was at Hull House that Alice Hamilton first encountered Kelley. Hamilton gives a lively description in her autobiography of the stern but inspiring Kelley:

> Mrs. Kelley was one of the most vivid personalities I have ever met. She used to make me think of two verses in the Old Testament: the one in Job about the war horse who scents the battle from afar and says among the trumpets, "Ha, ha"; and the one where the Psalmist says, "The zeal of thine house hath eaten me up." It was impossible for the most sluggish to be with her and not catch fire. A little group of us residents used to wait for her return from the Crerar Library, where she was in charge evenings, and bribe her with hot chocolate to talk to us. We had to be careful; foolish questions, half-baked opinions, sentimental attitudes, met with no mercy at her hands. We loved to hear her and the Scotch lawyer, Andrew Alexander Bruce, discuss the cases they had had under the Altgeld administration.[39]

Kelley worked at the John Crerar Library during the evenings to help support her family and remained at Hull House until 1899.

In 1892, shortly after beginning her work at Hull House, Kelley was hired by the Illinois Bureau of Labor Statistics to investigate sweatshops in the garment industry. She also helped to conduct a survey of city slums for the Federal Commissioner of Labor. Kelley's efforts played a key role in the Illinois legislature's passage of the 1893 factory act "limiting hours of work for women, prohibiting child labor, and controlling tenement sweatshops."[40] During this period, Kelley also took evening classes at Northwestern University Law School, where she earned her law degree in 1894.

In the late 1890s Kelley became active in the newly formed National Consumers League. She served as the general secretary and gave lectures explaining the purpose of the League. Kelley would eventually organize Consumers Leagues in twenty states. In 1905 Kelley published one of her most important works, *Some Ethical Gains through Legislation*, which described her program for protecting women workers and eliminating child labor. She argued for wage and hour laws. Largely through her efforts nine states had adopted some form of minimum-wage legislation by 1913.[41]

Kelley's work continued to cover a wide range of critical social issues. In 1902 she and Lillian Wald helped to establish the New York Child Labor Committee. In 1904 she helped organize the National Child Labor Committee. In 1909, she helped organize the National Association for the Advancement of Colored People. From 1911 on she was active in socialist organizations, joining the Socialist Party of America in 1912. She served as president of the socialist League for Industrial Democracy from 1918 to 1920. In 1919 she became one of the founding members of WILPF and was an active supporter of women's suffrage.

In May 1919 Kelley was able to attend the second International Conference of Women in Zurich along with Emily Greene Balch, Alice Hamilton, Jane Addams and Lillian Wald, among others. Although many of the women at the conference had suffered for their pacifist beliefs, and although the Versailles Treaty, published the week of the conference, was denounced by the women at the conference, Kelley was thrilled to be in the company of such inspiring women and to return to the town where she had studied over thirty years before. Of her experiences at the conference, she wrote:

> It was unbelievably wonderful. There were twenty-five English women sitting with the Germans in front, and the Irish at one side, alike engrossed in the common effort....The English leaders amazed every one by emphasizing at every opportunity that they were all Socialists....Never have I seen so generous a spirit in any group of human beings....The public meetings were in the aula of the University of Zurich where I was a student thirty-five years ago. The audiences were tremendous. Jane Addams was at her very best.[42]

In her biographical essay, Louise C. Wade writes that Kelley became disheartened in the 1920s when the Supreme Court struck down measures against child labor and for a minimum wage for women. Kelley was branded for her association with socialists and her work with Engels. Wade quotes a U.S. senator from 1926 who described a child labor amendment as part of the "'Engels-Kelley program...derived straight from the fundamental communist manifesto of 1848.'"[43] Kelley died on February 17, 1932, after suffering from anemia for several months.

Like Florence Kelley, Emily Greene Balch and Mary Kingsbury, the great social scientist and prison reformer, Katharine Bement Davis, was also active in the Settlement movement. Like Kelley, Balch and Kingsbury, Davis studied at both the University of Chicago and Berlin. Davis was born in Buffalo, New York, in 1860. After graduating from the Rochester Free Academy, Davis taught science at the high school in Dunkirk, New York, for ten years. She saved her money and studied at night until at the age of thirty she could afford to enroll at Vassar College. After graduating from Vassar, Davis returned to teaching at the Brooklyn Heights Seminary for Girls. During this period, Davis took a graduate course in food chemistry at Columbia University.

Ellen Fitzpatrick, in her study of women social scientists, describes how the work Davis did in food chemistry at Columbia led to her appointment as director of an exhibit at the Chicago World's Columbian Exhibition in 1893. The exhibit included a model home that showed how to eat a healthy diet on the limited income of most workers. The exhibit won Davis the position as head resident at the College Settlement in Philadelphia, where she remained until 1897. In Philadelphia, Davis worked closely with poor African Americans and Russian Jews. She created model apartments to demonstrate how to lead a healthy lifestyle with a limited income. She organized reading classes and neighborhood clubs and taught English.[44]

In 1897 Davis left Philadelphia to begin graduate studies in political economy at the University of Chicago. Her mentor at Chicago was Thorstein Veblen, who attempted to explain economic trends and developments by placing them in a social and historical context.[45] Davis was influenced by Veblen's early work in the economics of agriculture. Together with Veblen, she examined economic and social problems faced by American farmers. Eventually, Davis would write her doctoral thesis about related problems faced by agricultural workers in Bohemia.

Davis traveled to Europe to study on a fellowship from the New England Women's Educational Association. She attended courses at universities in Berlin and Vienna. Of her time in Berlin, she wrote that she gained a lot of weight and saw the emperor every day:

> I felt that I knew Emperor William very well, for when I was a student in Berlin, a four o'clock seminar took me to the University several times a week, and always it seemed I reached Unter der Linden [sic] just as the Emperor returned from his afternoon horseback ride in the Thiergarten[sic]. He went accompanied by only two or three of his gentlemen-in-waiting. I stood on the edge of the sidewalk and waved at him anything I happened to have in my hand. He always saluted very politely and I daresay said to himself, "Another crazy American."[46]

Her extensive study on Czech farm workers, "The Modern Condition of Agricultural Labor in Bohemia," was published in 1900 in the *Journal of Political Economy*. In her essay, Davis was critical of child labor, inhuman working conditions and wage inequity between male and female workers.[47] According to Fitzpatrick, Davis's research was revolutionary for using the combination of personal observation, public records, account books, government statistics and interviews with workers and estate owners as sources. She moved away from abstract social theories and laws of political economy to empirical research. She focused on social, economic and political factors rather than on hereditary ones in seeking the cause of social ills, especially in her work on the Czech immigrant population in the United States.

In 1900 Davis completed her doctoral degree at Chicago *cum laude*. Her career immediately took Davis away from the university, where there were few opportunities for women. Even the University of Chicago, which welcomed women in its graduate programs, was reluctant to hire women as faculty members.[48] Davis took a position as superintendent of the Reformatory for Women in Bedford Hills, New York, where she remained until 1913. As superintendent, Davis sought to apply social scientific research to finding new methods of reforming female criminals. Her work with these women was informed by her earlier research at Chicago and in Berlin and Vienna with Czech workers and immigrants. She believed that Czech workers and immigrants and the women in the reformatory were not criminals by nature. Any criminal or vicious behavior was due to lack of education and training.[49]

With the support of John D. Rockefeller, Jr., Davis managed to establish the short-lived female-run Laboratory of Social Hygiene at Bedford Hills to conduct social scientific research that would lead to more appropriate reforms. Rockefeller was impressed not only by Davis's work and person, but also by her having done graduate work at Chicago and in Germany. Although the laboratory failed to gain the necessary state support and closed down, Rockefeller remained an advocate for Davis's work in prison reform and social scientific research.[50]

Elizabeth Dabney Langhorne Lewis,[51] another graduate student from the University of Chicago who studied at Berlin, became a socialist, women's rights activist and labor reformer. Lewis was the only one of the women in this chapter who earned her doctoral degree in the social sciences while at Berlin. When she successfully defended her thesis on March 15, 1907, Lewis became the sixth American woman to earn a doctoral degree at the University of Berlin.

Before studying in Berlin, Lewis studied at Randolph-Macon Woman's College in Lynchburg, Virginia, and completed her Bachelor's in Greek and Mathematics at Bryn Mawr in 1901. After completing her degree, Lewis began graduate studies in political science and economics. She attended the University of Chicago in 1903, where she studied sociology with Veblen. Lewis returned to Bryn Mawr for the 1904/05 academic year and then continued her work in Berlin.

Lewis began auditing courses at Berlin during the Winter Semester of 1904/05. Early in her stay at Berlin, she made contact with other women students, including Germans. An article in a 1904 issue of the progressive women's journal, *Frauen-Rundschau*, mentions a gathering of students at which Lewis and two other American students, a Miss [Flora] Heinz and a Miss Allan [Helen Allen or Florence Allen] spoke.[52] While "Miss Allan," who had attended the University of Cleveland (Case Western Reserve University), talked about literary work done at American colleges, and "Miss Heinz," who had attended Wellesley, talked about the life of women at American colleges, Lewis gave the evening a more serious tone by discussing the Settlement movement associated with universities and efforts to educate the poor.[53]

During the Summer Semester of 1906, Lewis left Berlin, but returned that fall for the Winter Semester of 1906/07 to complete her degree. In Berlin she studied sociology with Simmel and Ernst von Halle, and economics with Wagner, Schmoller and Sering. She also completed courses in her minors of art history and philosophy with Max Dessoir and Carl Stumpf, among others. With Wagner and Schmoller as her advisors, Lewis wrote her thesis on the cotton industry in the American South ("Ein Beitrag zur Entwicklung der Baumwollindustrie in den nordamerikanischen Südstaaten"). The thesis, written in a sophisticated German, deals with poverty in the South and barriers to industrialization. Lewis deals openly with issues of racism, sexism and class conflicts. She also examines the social and economic structures in the South that encouraged child labor. In the curriculum vitae in Lewis's doctoral file, she gave special thanks to Wagner and Schmoller for their encouragement. She also thanked Ernst von Halle and one of her professors at the University of Chicago, J. Lawrence Laughlin, head of the Department of Political Economy.[54]

After returning from Berlin, Lewis worked as a special agent investigating conditions of employment for women and children for the U.S. Department of Labor for three years. In 1910 Lewis married Dexter Otey, a manager in a manufacturing company in Lynchburg, Virginia. She had one child, a daughter Elizabeth, born in 1911, who graduated from Radcliffe. After marrying Otey, Lewis focused her attention on women's suffrage. A 1973 issue of the *Bryn Mawr Alumnae Bulletin* has a photo of Lewis and her mother picketing for women's suffrage in 1917. Reflecting on those times at the age of ninety-two, Lewis says, "'Mother was perfectly charming about it, but I'm afraid my intentions were more bellicose.'"[55] Lewis was a member of the Women's Suffrage League of Virginia and of the National Woman's Party. She took an active part in the campaign for suffrage, giving speeches and "doing what came to hand."

During World War I, she was a member of the Virginia Council of Defense. In the 1920s and early 1930s Lewis ran for various offices in Virginia as a socialist and "was not surprised to lose." In 1923 she returned to Bryn Mawr to tutor in economics. She took a leadership role in the American Association of University Women, serving as president of its chapter in Lynchburg from 1927 to 1929 and in all of Virginia from 1929 to 1931.

After her husband died in 1933, Lewis moved to Washington, DC and returned to government work for the new Social Security Administration. She worked as a social science analyst for a monograph on voluntary disability insurance for the Bureau of Research and Statistics. She was a code advisor for the Labor Advisory Board and wrote articles on the employment of women and wage differentials. During this same period, she organized and directed a women's center which offered employment opportunities for unemployed African American and white women, as well as day care. She later held positions as a research economist for the Foreign Economic Administration and the State Department until she retired in 1948. Lewis published several articles on labor issues, such as child labor legislation, women and children in Southern industry, and disability insurance. She died on February 28, 1974.[56]

Several years after Lewis completed her degree at Berlin, another Chicago graduate in economics, Anna Pritchett Youngman, came to Berlin to study. Youngman had an illustrious and varied career as an economics professor and editorial writer for the *Washington Post*. She was born in Lexington, Kentucky, in 1883. After attending the public school there, she enrolled at the University of Chicago, where she completed both her Bachelor's (1904) and her Ph.D. (1908). After completing her doctoral degree, Youngman took a position as an instructor in economics at Wellesley College. In 1914 she was promoted to associate professor. During her stay at Wellesley, Youngman took time off to study economics at Berlin for the Winter Semester of 1911/12. At Berlin and later at the University of Frankfurt/Main, she concentrated on taxation and banking.

In 1919 Youngman took a leave of absence from Wellesley to work as an economist for the Federal Reserve Board. Youngman then resigned from Wellesley to continue her work with the Federal Reserve Board. From 1924 to 1933 she held a position as an editorial writer for the *Journal of Commerce* in New York City. She left that position to become an editorial writer for the *Washington Post*, where she remained until her retirement in 1952. At the *Post*, she wrote columns on financial and business topics. After retiring, Youngman continued to write for the *Journal of Commerce*. She died on February 16, 1974, in Silver Spring, Maryland.[57]

Although this section has focused on women who studied at the University of Berlin, there were other destinations for women in the social sciences. Ellen

Deborah Ellis, a graduate student in economics and politics at Bryn Mawr, used a fellowship to study at the University of Leipzig for the 1902/03 academic year. Another Bryn Mawr graduate student in economics and politics, Marion Parris, used her European Research Fellowship to study for the 1907/08 academic year at the University of Vienna. Beatrice Julia Whiteside from Olean, New York, studied political science at Munich for the Summer Semester of 1914 and then transferred to Zurich to study law beginning that Winter Semester.

It is difficult to gain an accurate and broad view of the extent of North American women's work in this area at German-speaking universities. For example, Ellis studied at Leipzig, but the records for auditors for the years 1890 through 1903 are missing. Her trip to Leipzig is recorded in the alumnae records of Bryn Mawr.[58] Of the few records that do exist for American women who studied at Leipzig between 1878 and 1914, none of the records that list an area of study mention the social sciences. That does not mean, however, that Ellis was the only North American woman in that whole period who ever did work in the social sciences at Leipzig. Her case simply points out the difficulty of dealing with such varied historical records.

Records from other universities also seem to confirm that almost all of the women who studied in the social sciences went to Berlin. For example, between 1897 and 1914, only one woman, Beatrice Julia Whiteside, appears to have majored in the social sciences at Munich. At Zurich, between 1872 and 1915, only two American women appear to have majored in the social sciences or law, Florence Kelley and Beatrice Julia Whiteside mentioned above. The records of auditors and matriculated students at Göttingen between 1895 and 1915 list only one American woman, Clara Hannah Kerr with a Ph.D. in history from Cornell (1895), who did coursework in the social sciences (Winter Semester 1897/98). The records at Heidelberg and Freiburg for the period of this study are incomplete and rarely list the area studied; from the records that exist in Vienna, one would hardly think that an American woman had ever set foot there.

This section on women in the social sciences would not be complete, however, without mentioning Katharine Susan Anthony,[59] who studied in Germany but does not appear in the matriculation records of any German-speaking university. She studied in Heidelberg and Freiburg for the 1901/02 academic year. Anthony was part of the group of women in this section who did graduate work at the University of Chicago. It was her story, along with that of Alice and Edith Hamilton, that inspired much of this research.

Anthony's interest in the European women's movement grew after she studied in Germany. At the beginning of World War I, Anthony published two works that have been invaluable sources to modern feminist scholars: *Mothers Who Must Earn* (1914) and *Feminism in Germany and Scandinavia* (1915). Anthony's goals in publishing these works at such a period seem to correspond with those of Balch, Addams and Hamilton as they traveled to the Netherlands in 1915 to attend the International Congress of Women. Her goals were to inspire international cooperation and understanding among women, and to further international efforts for women's and children's rights in the face of the nationalist fever of war.

After returning from Germany, Anthony enrolled at the University of Chicago and lived for a period of time in New York City. After publishing her first two political works, Anthony devoted the rest of her career to writing biographies of famous women, including Margaret Fuller, Catherine the Great, Queen

Elizabeth I, Marie Antoinette, Louisa May Alcott, Mary Lamb, Dolly Madison and Susan B. Anthony [no relation].

PHILOSOPHY/PEDAGOGY/PSYCHOLOGY

During the historical period of this study, from the end of the Civil War to the beginning of World War I, there was considerable overlap among the fields of philosophy, psychology and pedagogy. Although our current understanding of those fields would require examining developments in each area separately, such a separation would be arbitrary when describing the work of both students and faculty in these fields during the period of this study. Typically, women who studied psychology at German-speaking universities also took courses in philosophy. Sometimes a woman worked in both areas simultaneously, and sometimes she alternated between the two. Some notable women included in this study, Mary Whiton Calkins, Eleanor Gamble and Christine Ladd-Franklin, had successful careers that embraced both fields.

Philosophy and new theories from psychology also guided and were incorporated into pedagogical practices by progressive teachers challenging old teaching methods. Certain teachers' colleges, like Oswego in New York (SUNY Oswego) played an important role in spreading theories of pedagogy from Europe throughout North America. The Sage School of Philosophy, established at Cornell University in 1890, temporarily included the Department for the Science and Art of Teaching and thus offered courses in philosophy, pedagogy and psychology. The school even included a laboratory for psychological research, which had been imported from Germany, and soon became a renowned center for graduate studies and research.[60]

Just as the field of sociology was separating itself from economics and political science during the period of this study, psychology was slowly emerging as a science separate from philosophy. "Physiological psychology" and "mental philosophy" began to diverge in the 1870s with the beginning of work in the field of experimental psychology.[61] Many of the leaders in this field at German-speaking universities, such as Wundt and Georg Elias Müller, are listed in catalogues only as members of a philosophy department.

Germany became an important center for the newly emerging field of experimental psychology. North American men and women traveled to Germany to work in the psychological laboratories there. Even after the early 1890s, when opportunities for women to pursue graduate studies in psychology were available in the United States, women continued to travel to Germany to conduct research.[62]

Despite the overlap of these three fields, women in this section have been divided into two groups. The first includes women whose research focused primarily on philosophy and pedagogy; the second those whose research was mainly in experimental psychology.

The background of the women in the first group makes apparent the important role played by the Sage School of Philosophy at Cornell University. In the mid-1880s, Henry W. Sage wanted to improve the study of philosophy at Cornell. He created and endowed a new Department of Ethics and Philosophy. In 1886 he appointed the Canadian scholar Jacob Gould Schurman, who would later become president of Cornell, to lead this new department.[63] Schurman was an extremely popular and dynamic teacher. His History of Ethics class was well attended, and the department flourished.[64] In the fall of 1890 Sage established an entire school for philosophy, the Sage School of Philosophy. Several of the women in philosophy mentioned below benefited from Sage's vision and generosity, and from Schurman's excellence in teaching. Schurman, like many of the teachers and students of Cornell, had studied abroad. He had earned degrees from the University of London and a doctorate from the University of Edinburgh and had studied in Berlin. It is not surprising that the women who studied philosophy at Cornell were encouraged in their graduate studies and efforts to study abroad.[65]

In addition to Cornell, the University of Jena also played an important role in the study of philosophy and pedagogy. The university had a long tradition of liberalism and intellectual freedom. After 1815 and the revolution of 1848, several liberal professors who had lost positions elsewhere were able to find refuge at Jena. While professors at Jena had extremely low salaries in comparison with other even smaller German universities, the faculty did enjoy precious academic freedom. In his autobiography, Nobel laureate and philosophy professor Rudolf Eucken (1846-1926) praised the intellectual freedom and appreciation of individual differences that reigned in Jena.[66] Jena was the center of Herbartianism, a school of pedagogy based upon the teachings of the renowned pedagogue Johann Friedrich Herbart (1776-1841). Six of the philosophy students mentioned below, Margaret Keiver Smith, Mary Elizabeth Laing, Grace Neal Dolson, Rowena Morse, Lucinde Pearl Boggs and Edith Corrinne Stephenson, studied in Jena. Although it would not be until 1904 that a woman was permitted to earn a doctoral degree at Jena and not until 1907 that women could matriculate at the university, certain faculty members were advocates of women's study. These faculty members included Eucken, who was particularly supportive of the efforts of the first two American women who applied to earn doctoral degrees at Jena, Lucinde Pearl Boggs and Rowena Morse.

The first North American woman to complete a doctoral degree in philosophy at the University of Zurich was a Canadian, Janet Donalda MacFee[67] from Montreal. MacFee earned her degree in 1895 with a thesis on "Berkeleys New Theory of Perception and its Further Development in the English Association-School and in the Modern School of Empiricism in Germany" (Berkeleys neue Theorie des Sehens und ihre Weiterentwicklung in der englischen Associations-Schule und in der modernen empiristischen Schule in Deutschland).[68] Her major, philosophy, included the history of philosophy and psychology. Her minors were pedagogy and English Literature. MacFee did her undergraduate work at McGill University in philosophy with Professor Rev. J. Clark Murray. After completing her Bachelor's in 1888, she did graduate work at Cornell University in philosophy with Schurman. Her studies were interrupted for two years by illness. Then in 1891 she continued her studies in experimental psychology at the University of Leipzig under Professors Wundt, Max Heinze and Oswald Külpe for three semesters. Apparently MacFee, like M. Carey Thomas and so many other women, was unable to complete her degree at Leipzig, for in the spring of 1893 she transferred to Zurich, where she studied philosophy and pedagogy with Richard Avenarius, Theodor Vetter and O. Hunziker.[69] After earning her degree from Zurich, MacFee settled in New York City with her sister, Anna Maria MacFee, a physician. Together they established the Misses MacFee School.[70]

One year after MacFee, Julia Ellen Bulkley completed her dissertation in philosophy on "The Influence of Pestalozzi on Herbart" (Der Einfluss Pestalozzis auf Herbart).[71] Bulkley's interest in Herbart's pedagogical teachings would be shared by Margaret Keiver Smith, the next North American to earn her doctoral degree from Zurich in this field. According to her doctoral file, Bulkley was born in 1850 in Danbury, Connecticut. At the age of seventeen, she graduated from Fort Edward Collegiate Institute in New York. Two years later she got her teaching certification in Connecticut. In 1890 she studied the history of pedagogy and teaching methods at CUNY. From 1892 to 1895 she studied in Zurich, where she took courses, just as MacFee had done, with Avenarius, Hunziker and Vetter. At Zurich, her major was the history of philosophy and psychology. Her minors were pedagogy, teaching methods and English literature. [72]

In 1893 the American, Mary Mills Patrick (1850-1940), came to Zurich to study philosophy at the age of forty-three. But she left Zurich for Bern, where she completed her doctoral degree in 1897 with a thesis on Greek philosophy, "Sextus Empiricus and Greek Scepticism." Before coming to Europe, Patrick had studied at Lyons Collegiate Institute in Lyons, Iowa. She had served for years as a teacher at a mission school in the Ottoman Empire and as both teacher and principal at the American High School for Girls outside of Istanbul. She played a key role in turning the high school into a college, the American College for Girls at Constantinople (Istanbul),[73] and became its first president. After earning her degree at the University of Bern, Patrick returned to the American College for Girls and remained there until her retirement in 1924. Patrick was a skilled linguist and mastered ancient and modern Armenian, ancient and modern Greek, Turkish, French and German. She continued to spend summers studying abroad and returned to Germany to study philosophy in Berlin in 1901. Patrick received honorary doctoral degrees from Smith College and Columbia University. She published two scholarly works, *Sappho and the Island of Lesbos* (1912) and *The Greek Skeptics* (1929).[74]

In 1899, four years after MacFee, another Canadian, Margaret Keiver Smith (1856-1934),[75] earned her degree in philosophy and psychology from Zurich with a thesis that focused on her minor of English Literature: "Milton and Drama: His Views and His Work" (Milton und das Drama – seine Ansichten und sein Werk). Her other minor at Zurich was the history of pedagogy. From 1880 to 1883 she had studied at the Normal School in Oswego, New York (SUNY Oswego), where she majored in pedagogy and psychology. Keiver Smith then studied philosophy at Cornell University for two years. During the summer of 1885 she traveled to Jena, where she studied philosophy and the pedagogy of Herbart for three semesters.[76]

In 1887 Keiver Smith returned to Oswego as the "Teacher of Exact Philosophy as founded by Herbart."[77] From 1887 to 1895 she taught psychology and pedagogy at Oswego and played a leading role among the faculty in popularizing Herbart's teaching philosophy. The U.S. Commissioner of Education requested that she translate Herbart's work for use in the United States. In the fall of 1896 she began auditing courses at the University of Göttingen in psychology, philosophy, physics, history and English. At Göttingen, Keiver Smith was not allowed to participate in any seminars and could not audit courses in pedagogy. This may explain why she left Göttingen after three semesters and enrolled at Zurich for the Summer Semester of 1898. In 1901 Keiver Smith was appointed professor and director of psychology and geography at the State Normal School at New Paltz, New York (SUNY New Paltz). Her diverse research interests included the psychology of rhythm and work, reaction time as a measure of physical condition and the value of Latin as a normal school subject. Keiver Smith continued to publish articles on psychology in both English and German.[78]

Keiver Smith was not the only advocate of Herbartianism at Oswego. Her colleague Mary Elizabeth Laing[79] of New Hebron, New York, also went to Jena to study Herbart's theories. Laing had earned a degree from Oswego and a Bachelor's from Cornell before studying abroad at Zurich, Jena and Göttingen. Laing was an advocate of the Kindergarten Movement and organized the Froebel Academy in Brooklyn in 1884, where she became the first principal. She began studying philosophy at the University of Zurich during the Winter Semester of 1894. Records indicate that she remained in Zurich for one semester. She is then listed among the female auditors for the first semester such records were kept at the University of Göttingen, the Winter Semester of 1895/96. In Göttingen she studied philosophy and pedagogy for two semesters. At Oswego, Laing became head of the department of psychology and child study. Like Keiver Smith, Laing became one of the first North American educators to apply new psychological research to pedagogical problems.[80]

Another colleague from Oswego who embraced Herbartianism, Ida B. Earhart[81] of Worthington, Pennsylvania, came to Göttingen to study philosophy, psychology and history the Winter Semester of 1896/97 after graduating from Oswego in 1895. She studied in Göttingen for two semesters. Earhart had attended high school in Pittsburgh and later enrolled at the Normal School in St. Cloud, Minnesota. In her history of Oswego, Dorothy Rogers notes that Earhart continued to embrace Herbartianism long after newer theories of pedagogy were replacing such earlier philosophies. As late as 1915, Earhart published a book, *Types of Teaching*, based upon Herbart's methods.[82]

The American Grace Neal Dolson (1874-1961) came to Germany in 1897 to do graduate work in philosophy after having earned her Bachelor's from Cornell University in 1896. Like MacFee, Keiver Smith and Laing, she had studied at Cornell before coming to Germany. In Germany she studied at both Leipzig and Jena (1897-1898) on ACA and WEA fellowships, but returned home without a doctoral degree. For the 1898/99 academic year, Dolson was the recipient of the Sage Scholar of Philosophy from Cornell University, which may explain why she decided to return home to America to complete her degree rather than attempting to earn her degree in Zurich. After completing her doctoral degree with a thesis on Friedrich Nietzsche at Cornell in 1899, Dolson taught philosophy and psychology at Wells College from 1900 to 1911. She then taught philosophy at Smith College from 1911 to 1915. In 1915 Dolson resigned to enter the Community of St. Mary's on the Mountain in Sewanee, Tennessee. In 1929 she became the superintendent of a children's hospital associated with her order. Eventually Dolson became assistant superior of St. Mary's Convent in Peekskill, New York.[83]

The Germanist, Birgit Eckardt, investigated the case of Lucinde Pearl Boggs (1873-1931) of Hayes, Illinois, who in 1900 attempted to become the first woman to earn a doctoral degree at Jena. Boggs came to Jena with a Bachelor's from the University of Illinois (1894) and three years of experience as a school administrator and teacher for Greek and Latin. Boggs chose as her thesis topic "Interest and its Application in Pedagogy" (Das Interesse und seine Anwendung in der Pedagogik). The philosophy professor Rudolf Eucken and the majority of the faculty in philosophy supported Boggs' efforts, but one professor, Berthold

Delbrück, was not satisfied with the subject areas Boggs had chosen for her examination. Delbrück was not opposed to women studying at the university, but he argued that any male student would have been rejected under the same conditions. Delbrück found it particularly important that caution and strict standards be applied to the first doctoral examination for a woman at Jena. The trustee of the university supported Delbrück rather than Eucken, despite permission from the government to allow Boggs to proceed with the examination if the subject areas were changed. The trustee was especially irritated that a group of professors had encouraged Boggs to try to break the barrier for women doctoral candidates at Jena. The trustee's decision did not slow Boggs down. Instead of completing her work at Jena, she transferred to the University of Halle, where she earned her doctoral degree in philosophy the following year with minors in modern art history and zoology.

The final title of her thesis was "John Dewey's Theory of Interest and its Application in Pedagogy." In her thesis, Boggs took her position in the debate between advocates of Herbart and his theory of interest and those supporting formal discipline and the training of the will. After returning from Halle, Boggs had a successful career in teaching and school administration. She served for one year as principal of the Primary Training Department of the State Normal School in Ellensburg, Washington. She published a series of articles on "interest" in the *Journal of Philosophy* and an article on "The Physical Accomplishments of Feeling" in *Psychological Review*. The 1906/07 academic year, Boggs taught psychology and education at Western College for Women in Oxford, Ohio. In 1910 she served as the Illinois State delegate to the World's Congress on Home Education in Brussels. That same year, she began a two-year stint as director of normal training at the Methodist Episcopal Mission schools in Central China. In her lifetime, Boggs published a number of articles in both the United States and China on topics ranging from home education to Chinese womanhood.[84]

In 1904 Rowena Morse[85] became the first woman to earn a doctoral degree at the University of Jena. Morse took her degree in philosophy with minors in geology and art history. Her thesis was "On the Contradiction in the Concept of Truth in Locke's Teachings on Knowledge" (Über den Widerspruch im Wahrheitsbegriff in Lockes Erkenntnislehre).[86] Before coming to Jena, Morse had studied at Berlin, where the same thesis on Locke was rejected. Morse was encouraged to complete a doctoral degree by Eucken, who in 1900 had supported the efforts of Lucinde Pearl Boggs to earn a doctoral degree at Jena. Morse resubmitted her thesis from Berlin, this time with success. Morse had come to Europe with a Bachelor's in psychology from the University of Iowa. She taught high school in Omaha before beginning her graduate studies at the University of Chicago in 1899. In 1901 Morse came to Germany to continue her studies.[87] After completing her degree at Jena, Morse began an exciting career as both a faculty member in the philosophy department of the University of Chicago and as a Unitarian minister.[88] In 1906 Morse was ordained in Geneva, Illinois.[89] In 1912, at the age of forty-one, Morse married Newton Mann, who was thirty-five years older. Mann had been her minister in Omaha and inspired her to prepare for the ministry.[90] Morse was also influenced in her choice of a career by her exposure to a group of liberal women ministers in rural Iowa during her childhood and adolescence, although she would later deny the significance of this portion of her life.[91]

In 1911 Morse took over as the minister at the Third Unitarian Church on Chicago's West Side and was loved by her congregation. Eventually, however, the flight from the city to the suburbs diminished her congregation to such a degree that her position was threatened. Despite efforts by congregation members to retain her as their minister by forming a central Unitarian church downtown, the American Unitarian Association (AUA) in Boston did not offer the financial backing to support Morse's ministry. Morse continued to preach at a hall near the University of Chicago for several more years, but she never received the support from the AUA necessary to find a new parish. Finally, in the mid-1920s, when Morse was in her mid-fifties, she was forced into retirement.[92]

Edith Corrinne Stephenson used her ACA European Fellowship to study philosophy at the University of Jena for the 1911/12 academic year. Before her stay in Germany, Stephenson had completed her Bachelor's (1909) at Ottawa University in Ottawa, Kansas. Like almost all of the other scholars in philosophy mentioned thus far, she also studied at Cornell University, where she was a graduate scholar in the Sage School of Philosophy from 1909 to 1911. Stephenson later married the philosopher Radoslav A. Tsanoff and worked as his secretary at Rice University and also wrote some works of fiction.[93]

One Canadian and one American woman earned doctoral degrees in philosophy at the University of Heidelberg. The Canadian Helena Adell Snyder (Dickinson) (1875-1957) of Port Elmsley, Ontario, completed her thesis in 1902 on "Thoreau's Philosophy of Life, with Special Consideration of the Influence of Ohindoo Philosophy." Snyder later published a book on art history, *German Masters of Art* (1914). Jennie Giehl (1880-?) of Rome, New York, completed her Bachelor's (1902) at Vassar and her Master's (1908) at Columbia University before studying at Heidelberg. Giehl completed her doctoral degree in 1911 under the direction of the Germanist von Waldberg with a thesis on "Johann Heinrich Schlegel–His Life and His Works" (Johann Heinrich Schlegel–Sein Leben und seine Werke).[94]

Of the seven American women who earned doctoral degrees in the humanities or social sciences at the University of Berlin before World War I, the only one to earn a degree in philosophy was Florence Mary Fitch[95] of Stratford, Connecticut. Before coming to Berlin, Fitch had completed her Bachelor's at Oberlin (1897) and worked as a high school teacher in Buffalo for three years. In 1900 Fitch went to Germany, where she studied one summer at the University of Munich and five semesters at the University of Berlin (Winter Semester 1900/01 through Summer Semester 1903). For the 1902/03 academic year, Fitch was recipient of the ACA's European Fellowship. In Berlin, she attended lectures in philosophy and psychology with Carl Stumpf, Max Dessoir (1867-1947) and Friedrich Paulsen; in sociology with Georg Simmel; in theology with Otto Pfleiderer (1839-1908), Hermann Gunkel (1862-1932) and Adolf von Harnack (1851-1930); and in history with Hans Delbrück (1848-1929). In 1903 Fitch earned her doctoral degree *cum laude* from the University of Berlin. Her thesis was on "Hedonism in the Works of Lotze and Fechner" (Der Hedonismus bei Lotze und Fechner). Rudolph Hermann Lotze and Gustav Theodor Fechner had been leading philosophers and psychologists of their day; Fechner was one of the earliest experimental psychologists. After returning from Germany, Fitch taught philosophy and biblical literature at Oberlin as well as serving at that college as the dean of women from 1904 to 1920. She published two articles, "What are our social standards?" (1915) and "Principles of social conduct" (1917). Fitch was very active in church work and supported missionary societies.[96]

The same year that Fitch earned her doctoral degree in philosophy at the University of Berlin, Ettie Stettheimer of Rochester, New York, one of the very few Jewish-American women to attend German-speaking universities, earned her doctoral degree from the University of Freiburg in philosophy with minors in economics and medieval history. Stettheimer was one of three American women who earned their doctoral degrees at the University of Freiburg between 1895 and 1903. During her studies in Germany, Stettheimer alternated semesters between Freiburg and the University of Berlin. In Freiburg, she studied with the philosopher Heinrich Rickert. She completed her degree at Freiburg in March 1903, with a thesis examining the philosophy of William James, "Freedom of Judgment as the Foundation of the Justification of Religious Belief with Special Consideration of the Teaching of James" (Die Urteilsfreiheit als Grundlage der Rechtfertigung des religiösen Glaubens mit besonderer Berücksichtigung der Lehre von James).[97] Stettheimer was born into a wealthy German-Jewish family on July 31, 1875, the daughter of Joseph S. and Rosetta Stettheimer. Joseph Stettheimer very early deserted his wife and five children, but the family seems to have flourished without him. Ettie was particularly close to two of her sisters, Florine, who became an artist, and Carrie, who designed and built one of the most famous dollhouses in the world.[98] Ettie attended private schools in Berlin and Stuttgart as well as in New York. In 1896 she earned her Bachelor's from Barnard College and began her graduate studies at Columbia University. She completed her Master's in psychology at Columbia in 1898 and then traveled to Germany to work on her doctoral degree.

Stettheimer, a women's rights activist, attended rallies for women's suffrage. She also published novels under the pseudonym Henrie Waste (an anagram of her full name, Henrietta Walter Stettheimer).[99] Her novels include *Philosophy* (1917), a fictionalized account of her life in Freiburg, and *Love Days* (1923).

This section on women who focused on philosophy and pedagogy ends with the case of Laura Emilie Mau (1878-?), who was still trying to complete her doctorate at Leipzig in 1915. Mau, a native of Young America, Minnesota (Norwood Young America), already had several degrees and extensive teaching experience before coming to Leipzig. In 1897 she graduated from the State Normal School in Mankato, Minnesota. She then taught first grade for the next ten years. Mau left teaching to study at the State Teachers College of Colorado, where she received her Bachelor's of Pedagogy in 1908. Mau taught for a year in Spokane, Washington, before traveling east to study at Columbia University, where she earned a Bachelor of Science and a Bachelor in Education (1910) as well as a Master's (1912). She spent the 1911/12 academic year at the University of Chicago, where she continued her studies in biology and science education. The following year she worked as a supervisor at the Georgia Normal and Industrial College in Milledgeville. Mau then returned to Columbia for an additional year of study before making her way to Leipzig. Mau had almost finished her thesis before she left for Germany. Her topic was a comparison of the interest shown by children in kindergarten and sixth, seventh and eighth grades in certain science materials. In Leipzig she was given access to a kindergarten, where she continued her research. Mau received help with her dissertation from Max Brahn and Eduard Spranger. Unfortunately, despite what would have seemed like ample preparation on Mau's part, her thesis was rejected for lacking individual analysis of the material. Thus, no North American woman included in this study was able to complete a doctoral degree at Leipzig.[100]

In experimental psychology, Leipzig played a key role. It was here in 1875 that Wilhelm Wundt (1832-1920) established the first institute for experimental psychology. Although his laboratory was originally set up for demonstrations, within four years it became a true research laboratory for conducting experiments. His work and that of his students used experiments in physiology to answer questions about perception and knowledge. One of his students, Oswald Külpe (1863-1915), who also studied with G. E. Müller at Göttingen, would later establish important laboratories in Würzburg, Bonn and Munich. Leipzig was also home to Gustav Theodor Fechner (1801-1887), who began his career at the university teaching physics. Fechner soon branched out to teach philosophy, aesthetics and psychophysics. He conducted experiments examining the physiology of perception and aesthetic theory.

Laboratories similar to the one in Leipzig were soon established in Göttingen (1887) and Breslau (1888), as well as in Bonn and Freiburg. Although Berlin was the largest university, its first laboratories, run by Hermann Ebbinghaus (1850-1909), most famous for his memory research, were poorly equipped in comparison to those at Leipzig. In Freiburg, Hugo Münsterberg (1862-1916) funded his highly successful laboratory out of his own resources. In the early 1890s Munich still had no laboratory for experimental psychology. One of its professors, Carl Stumpf (1848-1936), the musicologist who would later become a popular lecturer at Berlin, still managed to conduct experiments examining the relation between sound and psychology. Göttingen was the home of Georg Elias Müller,[101] a leader in the field of experimental psychology, who became an important mentor to a number of North American women. He came to Göttingen to do his doctoral studies with the philosopher Rudolph Hermann Lotze (1817-1881). After Lotze's death, Müller assumed his position at Göttingen and worked to separate psychology from philosophy by making it a true science of experimentation. His major contributions to the field of psychology were in psychophysics, learning and vision.[102]

Women studying experimental psychology were not concentrated at one university. Julia Gulliver studied at Leipzig with Wilhelm Wundt. Ethel Puffer Howes studied for one semester at Berlin with Carl Stumpf before transferring to Freiburg to work with the experimental psychologist Hugo Münsterberg, a former student of Wundt's. At Berlin, records show only five North American women majoring in psychology up to 1914. Theodors Lipps (1851-1914) drew other women to Munich, but only two of the seventy-four North American women auditors and matriculated students at Munich between 1895 and 1914 majored in psychology.[103]

Women went to universities to work with specific researchers. For example, Kate Gordon and Helen Dodd Cook went to Würzburg to study with Oswald Külpe.[104] Kate Gordon had earned both her Bachelor's (1900) and her Ph.D. (1903) from the University of Chicago, before traveling to Würzburg on an ACA European Fellowship. In Germany Gordon presented a paper before the German Psychological Association. In 1905 she published an article in German on "The Memory Process for Affectively Determined Impressions" (Über das Gedächtnis für affectiv bestimmte Eindrücke). Gordon returned from Germany to teach at Mount Holyoke (1904-1906), the Teachers College of Columbia (1906-

1907), Bryn Mawr (1912-1916), the Carnegie Institute of Technology (1916-1921) and UCLA (1921-1948). While teaching, Gordon continued to conduct research on memory, attention, vision, aesthetics and mental testing of children.[105] Gordon served as a psychologist for the children's department of the California State Board of Control (1918-1919) and was a member of numerous professional organizations, including the AAAS, Psychological Association, Philosophical Association, German Society for Experimental Psychology and Western Psychological Association. Gordon had a long publication record with articles placed in the major organs of her field.[106] Despite such a record of accomplishment, it is likely that Gordon would never have been promoted to full professor at UCLA, if unusual circumstances had not required that she be promoted to serve temporarily as chair of her department. Gordon married Ernest Carroll Moore, who played a key role in the founding of UCLA.[107]

Gordon's career as a researcher and teacher stands in contrast with the more traditional path chosen by Helen Dodd Cook (1883-1954) of Montclair, New Jersey, who also studied with Külpe and was one of three American women to earn a doctoral degree at Würzburg before 1915. Before coming to Würzburg, Cook had earned her Bachelor's (1905) and Master's (1907) in psychology at Wellesley College. Cook completed her thesis, "The Tactile Estimation of Filled-out and Empty Spaces" (Die taktile Schätzung von ausgefüllten und leeren Strecken) under Külpe's supervision on February 8, 1910. Cook taught psychology on the Wellesley faculty from 1909 to 1913. In 1916 she married a minister, Harold G. Vincent, and spent the rest of her career raising three children, teaching Sunday school and serving in various clubs.[108]

At Leipzig, Julia Henrietta Gulliver (1856-1940) studied with Wundt in 1892/93. Gulliver translated the first part of Wundt's *Ethics*. Before studying in Leipzig, Gulliver had earned her Bachelor's (1879) and her Ph.D. (1888) from Smith College. She had taught philosophy and been the head of the Department of Philosophy and Biblical Literature at the Rockford Female Seminary (Rockford College) in Rockford, Illinois for two years. Even after being appointed president of the college in 1902, Gulliver continued to teach and remained at Rockford for the rest of her career. She was made an *Officier d'Académie* by the French government in 1908. In 1910 she received an honorary degree from Smith College.[109]

Göttingen, where the great experimental psychologist Georg Elias Müller had his laboratory, emerged as the most important center for psychology for North American women. The auditor records of the University of Göttingen between 1895 and 1914 include the names of eight North American women who studied psychology there, six of them for at least two and up to five semesters. One of these women, Lillien J. Martin, became an important researcher in the field of psychophysics. Another, Eleanor Acheson McCulloch Gamble, taught psychology for thirty-five years at Wellesley.

But the story of North American women in psychology at Göttingen actually begins with another famous researcher, Christine Ladd-Franklin (1847-1930), who had unsuccessfully attempted to earn her degree at Göttingen in 1891, three years before Lillien J. Martin arrived there. After earning her Bachelor's in mathematics at Vassar in 1869, Ladd-Franklin taught science for nine years in secondary schools while continuing to publish a number of articles on mathematics. Ladd-Franklin's articles impressed the British mathematician James J. Sylvester (1814-1897), who had been appointed the first mathematics professor at The Johns Hopkins University in 1876. When Ladd-Franklin applied to Hopkins in 1878, the university was still closed to women. With the support of Sylvester and Fabian Franklin, a mathematics instructor, an exception was made for Ladd-Franklin. For the next three years, she was awarded a mathematics fellowship based upon the excellence of her work.[110] In 1878, Ladd-Franklin was allowed to pursue graduate studies in mathematics at Johns Hopkins as a special student. Care was taken, however, that her case should not be seen as a precedent for allowing women to enroll at the university. After completing her doctoral studies, she was denied a degree in 1882. Even without the degree, Ladd-Franklin enjoyed an active career as both a teacher and researcher, but she never abandoned her efforts to claim the degree that was rightfully hers and to smooth the way for other women following in her footsteps.[111]

In Göttingen, Ladd-Franklin hoped to earn the doctoral degree denied her at Hopkins. Both Georg Elias Müller and the mathematician Felix Klein argued with the administration on her behalf, but with no success.[112] In Göttingen, Ladd-Franklin worked with Müller on his vision experiments in which he, like Hermann von Helmholtz and other researchers, tried to develop a theory for color vision. Supposedly, Ladd-Franklin was not able to attend Müller's classes, so he repeated his lectures just for her. Ladd-Franklin eventually left Göttingen for Berlin, where she continued her research with Helmholtz and attended lectures by Koenig. In a relatively short period of time, she was able to develop her own theory of color vision that attempted to incorporate elements of the theories of both Müller and Helmholtz. In 1892, after having been in Germany for one year, she presented this theory at the International Congress of Psychology in London.[113]

After returning from Germany, Ladd-Franklin dedicated herself to establishing fellowships for American women to pursue graduate studies abroad. As noted in the section on mathematics in Chapter Four, Ladd-Franklin played a key role in the establishment of a European Fellowship for graduate studies by the ACA, and in 1889, became chair of the first Committee on Fellowships of the ACA. She gave Mary Winston, then a graduate student at the University of Chicago, $500 of her own money so that Winston might be able to study mathematics at Göttingen in 1893.

Ladd-Franklin also continued her work on color theory. A collection of her work on this topic was published in 1929, *Colour and Colour Theories*. Moreover, she was active in the fields of both philosophy and psychology. She was an associate editor for logic and philosophy for three volumes of the *Dictionary of Philosophy and Psychology*, which appeared between 1901 and 1905. She taught psychology and logic at Hopkins from 1904 to 1909. When she moved with her husband to New York City the following year, she continued her teaching career as a lecturer on psychology and logic at Columbia University. She was active in both the American Philosophical Association and the American Psychological Association.[114]

Three years after Ladd-Franklin came to Göttingen, another American woman, Lillien J. Martin (1851-1943),[115] was drawn to the experimental laboratory of Georg Elias Müller. As a young girl, Martin studied mathematics, surveying and psychology. Her family could not afford a college education for her, so at age sixteen she began teaching at an Episcopal school for girls in Racine, Wisconsin. She then taught at other schools for girls in Omaha, Nebraska, and Chicago. During her years of teaching, Martin developed an interest in pedagogy and applied psychology. After nine years of teaching, she had saved enough money to be able to study at Vassar, where she focused on chemistry and physics and completed her Bachelor's in 1880. While at Vassar, Martin worked as an assistant to the librarian, Mary Jordan. Jordan's brother, David Starr Jordan, would be instrumental in getting Martin her next job as a chemistry and physics teacher at Indianapolis High School. He later offered her a position at Stanford University and played an active part in seeing that Martin was promoted there. At the high school in Indianapolis, Martin had the girls studying physics for the first time. She created her own physics and chemistry laboratories. She spent two summers studying and teaching botany, physics and chemistry at the University of Iowa. Martin was so devoted to improving her teaching methods that after reading a book by William James, she traveled to Harvard to discuss his methods with him. In 1889 she moved to San Francisco, where she became head of the science department and vice-principal of a girls' high school.

While teaching in San Francisco, Martin began reading the works of Wilhelm Wundt in experimental psychology and the writings of the French psychologist Théodule Armand Ribot. Through the years she developed a desire to return to the university to study psychology. She chose Germany, which led in the field of experimental psychology at that time. Of the German universities she chose Göttingen, which was small and had Georg Elias Müller as the chair of psychology. After her mother died in 1891 and her father the following year, Martin was free from familial obligations that had limited her travels. In 1894 Martin quit her job and used all her savings to study for four years in Göttingen and Bonn. During those four years, Martin also traveled in Europe and worked for ten months in a psychiatric clinic in Switzerland, where she studied and practiced hypnosis.[116]

While in Göttingen and Bonn, Martin completed all the requirements for her doctoral degree, but it would not be until August 1913, through the efforts of Oswald Külpe, one of her teachers, and the philosophy professor, Adolf Dyroff, another advocate of women in higher education, that the University of Bonn would award her an honorary doctoral degree. In Göttingen, Martin worked with Müller in psychophysics. In 1899 she and Müller co-authored one of the classic studies in psychophysics, *Zur Analyse der Unterschiedsempfindlichkeit*. This was a study of the psychophysics of lifted weights. Martin continued to publish primarily in German throughout her career, and returned to Germany several times to pursue further studies in experimental psychology in Bonn (1908 and 1912) as well as at the laboratories of Oswald Külpe in Würzburg (1907) and Munich (1914).

After returning from Göttingen in 1899, Martin was appointed assistant professor at Stanford University, where she was promoted to full professor in 1911 and taught until she was forced to retire in 1916. From the beginning of her appointment, Martin was expected to use the training she had received in Germany to plan and set up psychology laboratories.[117] Martin continued to benefit from the training she had received in Göttingen in experimental psychology. In 1905 she published a study called "Experimental Prospecting in the Field of the Comic," which appeared as the lead article in the *American Journal of Psychology*.[118] Miriam Allen DeFord praises that article in her biography of Martin, noting that Martin was finally "able to employ the methods she had mastered in Göttingen, and, at last, with laboratory subjects who could speak English!"[119]

Martin continued to study the work of German psychologists. In 1906 she published an article on the work of one of the first Germans in experimental psychology, Gustav Theodor Fechner. Martin had conducted numerous experiments to test and modify Fechner's work in aesthetic theory. Martin was interested in why individuals preferred certain forms and shapes. In 1909 Martin published an article for the *Zeitschrift für Psychologie* about a condition in which sensations are aroused indirectly, for example, from a smell or visual cues. In 1914 she published another German article on the relation between imagery and thought.[120]

In 1915 Martin became the first woman at Stanford to serve as chair of a department. That same year she became vice-president of the AAAS and chair of the section for anthropology and psychology.[121] She was a member of the American Psychological Association, the California Society of Mental Hygiene, and the German Kongress für experimentelle Psychologie. After retiring in 1916, the inexhaustible Martin began yet another career in private practice and at two hospital clinics. She developed an interest in the field of gerontology and in 1929 established one of the first counseling centers for the elderly.[122] For five years Martin also ran a farm to give employment to elderly men.[123] Martin continued to publish, lecture and travel until her death in 1943.[124]

Of the other women who studied psychology at Göttingen, two, Margaret Keiver Smith and Ida B. Earhart, have already been mentioned as leading advocates of the educational principles of Herbartianism at the Normal School at Oswego, New York. Three of the other women were students from Stanford. The last of this group of women from Göttingen, Eleanor Gamble, had a long and successful career teaching philosophy and psychology at Wellesley.

Eleanor Acheson McCulloch Gamble[125] (1868-1933) had already completed her Bachelor's at Wellesley (1889) and her Ph.D. in psychology at Cornell (1898)[126] and had been teaching at Wellesley for eight years before she went to Göttingen in 1906. Her research interests were the processes of memorization and the exhaustion of the sense of smell, and her work received attention in the broader scientific community.[127] Gamble was appointed to the philosophy department at Wellesley in 1898, the same year her famous colleague, Mary Whiton Calkins, became a full professor. Calkins had founded the first psychology laboratory at Wellesley, but she was eager to allow Gamble to take over supervision of the laboratory so that she could concentrate on philosophy. As Patricia Palmieri writes in her history of Wellesley, Calkins considered Gamble a "superior experimentalist." Gamble remained at Wellesley for thirty-five years. According to Palmieri, although Gamble and Calkins had several joint publications, Gamble was content to live in the shadow of her more renowned colleague.[128] Gamble edited the second volume of *Wellesley College Studies in Psychology*.[129] Gamble, herself, remained a supportive colleague to younger faculty members, such as Lucy Wilson, who recalled Gamble's help when she first came to Wellesley.

The university with the next largest number of women studying in psychology was the University of Berlin. Of the five North American women who studied psychology there, three contributed the most to the field: Theodate Louise Smith, Mary Whiton Calkins, and Ethel Puffer Howes. Ethel Puffer Howes and Mary Whiton Calkins, both of whom were colleagues of Gamble at Wellesley, became renowned scholars and teachers in their field. Theodate Louise Smith collaborated with G. Stanley Hall on important works on child psychology.

Theodate Smith[130] earned her Bachelor's (1882) from Smith. While working on her Master's degree for the next two years, she taught high school in Gardiner, Maine. After completing her Master's at Smith (1884), she continued to teach at the Brooklyn Heights Seminary in New York City and at Mount Vernon Seminary in Washington, DC. She entered the doctoral program at Yale in 1893, but spent the 1895/96 academic year studying at Clark University. In 1896 she earned her Ph.D. from Yale. Her mentor at Yale was E. W. Scripture, who had received his doctoral degree from Leipzig and was interested in experimental psychology and pedagogy. Smith's own doctoral research was on the relationship between motor activity and memory.[131]   After completing her Ph.D., Smith returned to Mount Vernon and took courses at the Catholic University in DC. In 1902 Smith devoted herself more intensively to research. From 1902 to 1909 she was a research assistant to G. Stanley Hall, then president of Clark University. Her research during those years was funded in part by a Carnegie grant and an Estabrook grant. In 1905 Smith used part of an Estabrook grant to study psychology in Berlin. After returning from Berlin, she edited a collaborative work by Hall and several of his students, *Aspects of Child Life and Education*, which was published in 1907.[132]   In 1909 she became a lecturer and librarian at the Children's Institute of Clark University. Smith became an important advocate of Maria Montessori's pedagogical methods in the United States. Smith died suddenly from diabetes in 1914.[133]

Although Smith became an important assistant to Hall, she was never promoted to a full professorship. Her peers, Gamble and Calkins, who obtained positions at women's colleges, fared better. Palmieri's history of Wellesley provides an invaluable complex and appealing portrait of Mary Whiton Calkins. Calkins had a long, illustrious career at Wellesley, where she taught Greek, then philosophy and psychology for forty-two years. Calkins was born on March 30, 1863, in Hartford, Connecticut, and completed her Bachelor's at Smith College in 1885. After graduating from Smith, she spent a year at home. The following year, during a trip to Europe with her family, she encountered Abby Leach, a professor of Greek at Vassar, who encouraged Calkins to go with her to Greece and study the language. Calkins ended up staying in Europe for sixteen months and returned to a teaching position in Greek at Wellesley that had been arranged for her by her father. Three years later, in 1890, one of her colleagues in philosophy, Mary Case, encouraged Calkins to do graduate work in philosophy and psychology. Eventually Calkins took up the challenge and considered studying in Germany, but was discouraged by friends and colleagues. Mary Case found that opportunities for study in the United States were just as good as those in Germany. A female friend wrote from Germany writing of the bad treatment of women students. Calkins may have received permission to study with Wundt in Leipzig, but ultimately she decided to pursue graduate studies at Clark University and Harvard University, although women could not officially enroll at either institute at that time.[134]   Calkins was highly respected at Harvard by her teachers, who included Josiah Royce, William James and Hugo Münsterberg. Without exception, all of them recommended her for a doctoral degree. The administration of Harvard, however, refused to grant her the degree, although she had completed the requirements. Thus, although Calkins was never officially awarded a degree from Harvard, she completed her doctorate there in 1891.[135] Calkins then returned to Wellesley to teach philosophy and psychology. While at Wellesley, Calkins explored opportunities for further study. Edmund C.

Sanford, her mentor at Clark University, encouraged her to earn a degree in Germany. He believed such a degree would bring her more prestige than an American one.[136] But just when Calkins was considering traveling to Freiburg to study with Hugo Münsterberg, Münsterberg came to Harvard as a visiting professor. From 1892 to 1895 Calkins continued to work at the psychology laboratory at Harvard with Münsterberg.

Calkins made important contributions to the field of psychology. It was Calkins who invented the paired-associate technique for studying memory.[137] Moreover, Calkins established the first psychology laboratory at a women's college at Wellesley in 1891. Palmieri provides a description of the laboratory's humble beginnings, its successes, and Calkins's perseverance:

> It began in a one-room attic with two hundred dollars' worth of equipment. Calkins almost single-handedly taught all of the psychology offerings and directed the laboratory until 1898, when she was joined by Eleanor McCulloch Gamble. By that time, the laboratory had expanded to five attic rooms and had "moderately good equipment for beginners and a few good pieces for advanced investigations." A steady stream of publications flowed from this laboratory. Most of the studies appearing between 1893 and 1916 were the work of undergraduates supervised by Calkins and, later, Gamble. Fifteen Master's' degrees were awarded to women who had worked in experimental psychology. During this period, Calkins herself also published numerous studies on color theory, time, space, and children's dreams.[138]

Both Calkins and Gamble had successful careers at Wellesley before they traveled to Germany to study psychology. Calkins finally made it to Berlin for the Summer Semester of 1902 and may have studied in Leipzig for a period of time. Gamble studied in Göttingen for an entire year, from the Winter Semester of 1906/07 through the Summer Semester of 1907. For them, the stay in Germany meant an opportunity to familiarize themselves with new theories and a commitment to research. It meant a chance to share this knowledge with students and to advance the graduate program in psychology at Wellesley.

For Ethel Puffer Howes[139] the stay in Germany meant something different. Puffer Howes studied in Berlin and Freiburg before completing her doctoral degree and establishing a teaching career. She completed her Bachelor's at Smith College in 1891, taught English and Latin for one year at Keene High School in New Hampshire and then became a mathematics instructor at Smith. She came to Germany the Winter Semester of 1895/96, where she studied with psychologist and musicologist Carl Stumpf at the University of Berlin for one semester. According to Palmieri, Puffer Howes was never content at Berlin. She felt uncomfortable in lectures, where she was the only woman at times, and she never found a professor who would mentor her. There was too much noise for her to sleep at night and the food was terrible.[140] Through a chance encounter with a Canadian doing postgraduate work, Puffer Howes received an introduction to Hugo Münsterberg in Freiburg. In a letter to her mother, Puffer Howes described how she used her intellect and wit to overcome the initial reluctance of Münsterberg to accept her as a student in his private laboratory at the University of Freiburg.[141]

Puffer Howes worked for three semesters with Münsterberg in Freiburg. She also took courses on aesthetic theory from Heinrich Rickert, the philosophy professor who mentored Ettie Stettheimer.[142] At Freiburg, she met other Americans but was the only woman in her classes. She worked long hours both attending Münsterberg's lectures and conducting experiments on aesthetic theory under his supervision. Münsterberg was so impressed by her research, that he encouraged her to apply for an ACA fellowship. Puffer Howes won the fellowship and returned to the United States to study at Radcliffe for the 1897/98 academic year.[143] At Radcliffe, she continued her work with Münsterberg, who had accepted a permanent position in the Harvard department of psychology in 1897. From 1898 to 1908 Puffer Howes taught as an instructor in the Radcliffe Psychology Laboratory under Münsterberg, who considered Puffer Howes "his most brilliant and most thorough disciple."[144]

While enrolled at Radcliffe, Puffer Howes completed all the requirements for a Ph.D. at Harvard in 1898. Puffer Howes wrote her thesis on "Studies in Symmetry," an early work in a series of studies on aesthetic theory. She would later publish her most famous work on aesthetic theory, *The Psychology of Beauty* (1905), while teaching at Wellesley. Puffer Howes had to wait until 1902, when Radcliffe finally began to grant doctoral degrees, to receive her Ph.D. Mary Whiton Calkins was also offered a doctoral degree at the same time, but she refused it, determined to wait instead for Harvard to grant her the degree she had earned there. Calkins never received that degree.

After completing her degree at Radcliffe in 1898, Puffer Howes held several positions, some of them simultaneously. She worked at the Radcliffe Psychology Laboratory until 1908. From 1901 to 1906 she was an instructor in philosophy at Wellesley, where she was promoted to an associate professor of aesthetics in 1906. From 1904 to 1907 Puffer Howes also worked as an instructor in psychology at Simmons College. She remained at Wellesley until 1908, when she married Benjamin Howes. She immediately found herself without any teaching prospects and little time for research.[145]

Puffer Howes remained active in the suffrage movement and in World War I helped to organize the Women's Land Army, which sent women and girls to work on farms in place of the men who were away fighting. She reemerged in the late 1920s with important work on resolving conflicts faced by women combining a career with a family. To this end, she helped to create and became the director of the Institute for the Coordination of Women's Interests at Smith College in 1925.[146] The institute was financed by a grant from the Laura Spelman Rockefeller Fund. Unfortunately, the practical, applied nature of research at the institute was not considered appropriate for a liberal arts college by some faculty, and after three years the grant was not renewed.[147]

In a 1929 article on the progress of the women's movement, Puffer Howes argued that advances in higher education for women were not enough. It was not enough to train women, if marriage continued to mean the surrender of a woman's career. The goal was for women no longer to have to choose between a career and love. Any social solutions that denied the full range of women's intellectual and emotional needs would continue to cause women suffering. She wrote:

> It is as futile to deny that the present social framework does
> not allow the natural and necessary development of woman's
> affectional life, along with the natural continuous development

and exercise of her individual powers. The man demands of
life that he have love, home, fatherhood and the special work
which his particular brain combination fits. Shall the woman
demand less?[148]

Puffer Howes supported having more day care centers available for children of
working mothers. She especially advocated cooperative day care centers, where
mothers would take turns taking care of each other's children. But Puffer Howes
had very modest goals for mothers of children under ten. A mother, who planned
to return someday to a career outside of the home, could only hope to grab one
or two free hours a day, during which she would have to read professional maga-
zines and "an occasional book" so as not to lose the intellectual thread of her
field. Significantly, Puffer Howes made no mention of the father's role in helping the mother to balance career and family.[149]

It seems appropriate to conclude this section on experimental psychology
with a passage from an obituary for Lillien J. Martin that captures the remarkable impact of German universities on the work of leading women in this field:

In the days when [Martin] started off for Göttingen, women
psychologists were very few indeed. Mrs. Ladd-Franklin's
color theory had been published in 1892. In the same year that
Miss Martin began her work with Müller, Margaret Floy
Washburn was completing her doctorate with Titchener, then
fresh from Wundt's laboratory, and writing a dissertation in
German on the influence of visual associations on the space
perceptions of the skin. Calkins' article on the attributes of
sensation appeared in the same year as the *Analyse* of Martin
and Müller. Trained in the traditional school, Martin and Ladd-
Franklin at Göttingen and Berlin, Calkins at Leipzig and
Washburn in the Leipzig atmosphere at Cornell, these women
had in common the pioneering spirit that seeks new horizons,
perseveres in the face of obstacles, and creates new frontiers.[150]

Chapter Six
Women in the Fine Arts

During the nineteenth century, North American women musicians, composers and artists studying and performing in German-speaking countries rarely enrolled at a university. While early auditor records at the University of Berlin include about a dozen North American women who studied music or music history between 1895 and 1915, most women seeking instruction in art or music took private lessons or studied at private academies or conservatories. Women were excluded from the state-sponsored art academies for most of the nineteenth century, although women did gain access to the state-financed conservatories during that period. Still, when the harpist, pianist and composer Constance Faunt Le Roy[1] traveled to German-speaking countries to further her musical training in the mid-nineteenth century, her only options were to take private lessons or enroll in a private conservatory. Until women were officially allowed to enroll at the public institutions, admission to state-financed academies and conservatories was granted only as a favor or exception. Moreover, it was not necessarily in the financial interests of instructors at those institutions to admit women, as many profited from giving private lessons or setting up private schools for women outside of the state-financed academies and conservatories.[2]

For those women studying instrumental music, Berlin was by far the most popular destination, whereas those studying voice could also be found in Vienna, Hamburg, Dresden, Munich, Stuttgart and Frankfurt am Main – that is, wherever there was an opera company that offered an opportunity for training and performing. For those women studying painting, Munich was the primary destination, although some went to Dusseldorf, Dresden or Leipzig.[3] Dusseldorf lost its draw for male and female North American artists after the 1860s. Dresden continued to attract a few painters, such as Candace Thurber Wheeler (1827-1923)[4] and Adelaide Johnson (1859-1955), even after Munich came to dominate as the center of the German art world in the 1870s. Berlin attracted most of the sculptors, and Dresden the very few who studied photography. While Berlin became a major international center of the music world during the nineteenth century, Munich was never a rival for Paris, London or Rome in the art world. Nevertheless, the studios and galleries of Munich attracted a large number of North American women artists, who gained some renown in their field.

Women in art and music studied abroad for reasons they shared with women in other fields. They needed the polish gained from a period of study in Europe for membership among the professional elite. Unfortunately, even with experience in Europe, few women artists and musicians were able to become part of the networks established among male artists and musicians during their European stay. Therefore, a stay in Europe rarely translated into the same career successes as it did for male artists and musicians.[5] Moreover, for some of these women, the stay in Europe did not teach them any techniques that they could not have learned back home. Still, at least for a number of the more famous musicians, the time in Europe provided invaluable opportunities to perform and exposed them to techniques and cultural institutions that would not have been available to them elsewhere.

This chapter has been divided into three parts, to include women in art, instrumental music and vocal music. Each section contains a description of the educational opportunities available to women as well as accounts of the experiences of representative women in each field.

ART AND ART HISTORY

North American women had a number of excellent art schools available to them in the nineteenth century. Art schools specifically designed to train women for careers in the decorative and industrial arts included the Philadelphia School of Design for Women (1844), the Cooper Union Free Art School in New York City (1854) and the Pratt Institute in Brooklyn (1877). The Art Students League, founded in 1875, was established in part to provide equal opportunities for female and male art students. By 1868 women were finally allowed to attend the life classes at the Pennsylvania Academy of Fine Arts. Three years later women were admitted to the life classes at the National Academy of Design in New York City.[6]

In Canada, private schools for women with art instruction opened as early as the 1820s. The first public Canadian school, The Ontario School of Art, opened in 1876 and admitted women. Several important private art academies were founded by women in the late nineteenth century, including the Associated Art School in Toronto (1886), the Victoria School of Art and Design in Halifax (1887) and the Montreal School of Art and Applied Design (1891).[7]

Despite such opportunities in North America, a period of study in Europe was an essential part of a complete art education, if a woman artist hoped to compete with men at the most prestigious exhibitions and become a part of the professional elite. There are many biographical and autobiographical accounts of North American women who flourished in the studios and artist colonies of Europe. One of the most famous practical guides of the time for women art students traveling to Europe was Amy Nieriker's *Studying Art Abroad, and How to do it Cheaply* (1879). But, as Nieriker's guide and biographical sources make clear, for most North American women studying art in the nineteenth century, German-speaking countries were far less of a draw than Italy, France or England.

While Germany could not compete with the popularity of Rome, Paris or London,[8] it did have its own highly developed centers of art. From the 1840s through the 1860s, Dusseldorf drew students from Europe and North America. The Dusseldorf School allowed no drawing from the nude. The most popular compositions were elaborate historical or religious scenes painted with great detail. One American artist who studied at Dusseldorf and enjoyed a brief period of recognition was Imogene Robinson Morrell (?-1908) of Attleboro, Massachusetts.

Robinson began studying art at the age of sixteen and taught art at the Lasell Seminary in Auburndale, Massachusetts, in the 1850s. In 1856 Robinson traveled to Dusseldorf, where she studied with Adolf Schroedter (1805-1875) and Wilhelm Camphausen (1818-1885), who became the imperial court painter.[9] Robinson returned to the United States where she became known for her historical and patriotic paintings. With one of her former students, Elizabeth Gardner (1837-1922), Robinson started a School of Design in Worcester, Massachusetts. In 1864 Robinson and Gardner traveled to France, where they both eventually launched successful careers. Robinson won numerous medals at exhibitions. Gardner also gained recognition and eventually married the painter William Bouguereau.

In the mid-1870s Robinson returned to the United States where she received the highest praise for her work. The following is an excerpt from a review of her paintings in an 1876 issue of *The Boston Journal* :

> They are spoken of in terms of the highest admiration by artists and art-critics, both at home and abroad. They are the result of long years of study and labor, under the first masters in France and Germany, and show great genius, inspired by patriotic enthusiasm....The composition is strictly original in all its details: each figure and every animal was painted from a living model, after the strictest rules of genuine art.[10]

That year, Robinson won medals at the Mechanics Fair in Boston and the Philadelphia Centennial Exposition, but her career took a turn for the worse shortly thereafter. After the death of her husband in 1879, Robinson tried to start another art school in Washington, DC, but was unsuccessful. She managed to sell only one of her paintings to the federal government for the Capitol building. In 1886 a fire destroyed two hundred of her paintings. She was later saved from a life of destitution by her old friend Elizabeth Gardner.[11]

The style of the Dusseldorf School that influenced Robinson and others was later criticized for being too stilted and unrealistic. In her critique of the school, Josephine Duveneck wrote:

> The Art School was under the domination of the Düsseldorf theatre where German historic plays were performed in a romantic manner. Students were encouraged to portray historical and religious subjects, using peasants as models, but dressing them up in elaborate and unrealistic costumes. Painting took on the nature of theatrical tableaux. The colors were hard and mechanical and the style meticulous and highly detailed.[12]

While this style dominated through the 1860s, the opening of the first international art exhibit in Germany in 1869 in the new Glass Palace (Glaspalast) in Munich shifted the focus of the art world to the south. Munich emerged as the new center of art in Germany. Men from around the world were attracted to the Munich Academy of Fine Arts (Akademie der Bildenden Künste). Karl von Piloty (1826-1886), who took over as director of the academy after the death of Wilhelm von Kaulbach (1804-1874), played an influential role in the new Munich School as did Wilhelm Diez (1839-1907), the professor of the life class, and the painter Wilhelm Leibl (1844-1900). Famous American artists who studied at the academy and set up studios in Munich at that time included Frank Duveneck and William Chase.

Munich was also home to an array of museums, including the Alte Pinakothek and Neue Pinakothek. The Glyptothek, a museum dedicated to classical sculpture, was established between 1816 and 1830, and the Bavarian National Museum was opened in 1853. These museums as well as the Schack Gallerie and other permanent exhibitions offered rich opportunities for women studying art history at the university. Many of the courses were conducted at museums.

Throughout the nineteenth century and into the 1930s, when Jewish scholars were forced into exile, German-speaking universities were centers for the study of art history. As early as 1813, the University of Göttingen had established full professorships for the discipline. Other leading centers of instruction in the field were Basel, Berlin and Munich. During the course of the nineteenth century, three leading scholars – the German philosopher Georg Wilhelm Friedrich Hegel (1770-1831), the Austrian art historian Alois Riegl (1858-1905) and the Swiss art historian Heinrich Wölfflin (1864-1945) – helped to define principles and a methodology for art history that still influence the discipline today.[13]

The auditor records for women at the University of Munich show a large number of students enrolled in art history classes. Of the sixty-two North American women who audited courses at Munich before 1915, about a third did coursework in art history. The following is a representative profile of four women who came to Munich to study art history immediately after finishing their undergraduate degrees.

The Winter Semester of 1900/01 saw the arrival of four neighbors from Holyoke, Massachusetts: Marjorie B. Hemingway, Clara E. Heywood, Edith M. Ramage and Alice E. Whiting. All four women lived within a few blocks of each other in Holyoke. The daughter of one of the women later described her mother around 1900 as "the darling of a gay social set in the New England city where she lived."[14] After graduating from college in 1900, the four traveled to Munich where they studied with the famous art historian Berthold Riehl.

Alice Whiting was the oldest of five children of H. Amelia Whiting from New Hampshire and Edward Whiting, a coal merchant from Massachusetts. She was born in October 1877, and earned her Bachelor's from Wellesley in 1900. Whiting was twenty-two, when she traveled to Munich.[15]

Marjorie Hemingway was the oldest of three children of Alice Hemingway from New Hampshire and Charles S. Hemingway, an accountant from Connecticut. Hemingway was born in July 1878, and was twenty-two when she went to Munich to study. Like Whiting, she had also graduated from Wellesley in 1900. Hemingway, like Heywood, would meet her future husband during her stay in Munich. The Wellesley alumnae notes from 1902 mention how Hemingway met her future husband, Friedrich Otto von Pfister, head of the largest grain house in Munich, at a reception while she was studying at the University of Munich. Hemingway married Pfister in 1902 and moved to Germany.[16]

Edith Ramage was the oldest of five children of Adelaide E. Risley Ramage from Connecticut and James Ramage, a paper manufacturer from Scotland. Edith was born in November 1877, and was twenty-two when she left for Munich. She graduated from Smith in 1900. According to the Smith College archives, Ramage studied primarily languages and literature at Smith. She took courses in Anglo-Saxon, English literature, French, German, Italian, Latin, logic, psychology, political economy, rhetoric, elocution, the Bible and chemistry. Ramage married in 1906 and died in 1918, most likely due to complications surrounding childbirth.[17]

The last of the four neighbors, Clara Heywood, was the older of two children of Isabelle Cady Heywood from Connecticut and Francis C. Heywood, an accountant and paper manufacturer from Massachusetts. Clara was born in August 1878, and would have just turned twenty-two when the four women left for Munich. Like Ramage, she graduated from Smith in 1900, where she took courses in languages, literature and the natural sciences. She also did coursework in Anglo-Saxon, English literature, French, German, Latin, elocution, rhetoric, psychology, political economy, history, the Bible, botany, geology and minerology, hygiene and physiology. Munich was the turning point in Heywood's life. It was there that she met Charles Scott, an American minister, whom she married. Together Heywood and Scott served as missionaries in China and the Philippines.[18]

Like the auditor records at Munich, the records at Berlin show similar high enrollments in art history. Between 1895 and 1912, sixty-six North American women are listed as auditing courses in that subject. Early Leipzig auditor records rarely list which subject students studied, but at least one student, Elizabeth H. Denio, studied art history there between 1883 and 1885. Denio was unsuccessful in her attempts to earn a doctoral degree at either Leipzig or Berlin, and eventually completed her doctorate at Heidelberg (1898). Heidelberg could not compete with Munich, Berlin or Leipzig as a center for art, but it did have more liberal policies towards women seeking graduate degrees. Denio was one of three North American women to complete a doctoral degree in art history at Heidelberg before 1915. The other two women were Neena Hamilton (1901) and Henrietta Tromanhauser (1912).

Elizabeth H. Denio (1844-1922) from Albion, New York, received her doctoral degree in October 1898.[19] Her thesis was on "The Life and Works of Nicolas Poussin" (Nicolas Poussins Leben und Werke). Denio had a varied career, much of it associated with the University of Leipzig and Wellesley College. Denio graduated from Mount Holyoke in 1866. Ten years later she became part of the Wellesley faculty, where she remained for the next twenty years as a professor of German and Art History. In 1883 Denio took a leave of absence from Wellesley to study for two years in Germany. She first went to the University of Berlin, where she found that "the number of ladies in attendance was large, and that the greater proportion could not be called young..."[20] Denio eventually settled down at the University of Leipzig for her coursework. Like M. Carey Thomas, she would eventually leave Leipzig without a degree, but her impressions of Leipzig were entirely positive. Although no new women were to be accepted beyond the women who were already there in 1879, Denio received special permission from four professors to attend their lectures. Denio returned to Leipzig several times during the following years and at one point in 1886 was able to attend lectures by ten different professors. During her first stay in Leipzig, from 1883 to 1885, Denio did coursework in both German philology and art history. She focused on Gothic and Middle High German under the direction of Zarncke, the same professor of philology who had been the favorite teacher of M. Carey Thomas. Denio also attended lectures by the famous art historian Anton Springer.

In a letter for the Wellesley College newsletter from June 1884, Denio listed the courses she was attending and described her daily routine and typical lectures. Her weekly schedule consisted of seventeen lectures in which she was the only woman in the lecture halls. She mentioned the dreaded "shuffle" for late students that Eva Channing had warned M. Carey Thomas about. Most interesting, however, is her description of the different professors' lecture styles. Certain professors read from their notes for the entire hour, but the best professors rarely read from the manuscript before them:

> Another professor, an elegant speaker, holds in his hands a few slips of paper, which he from time to time consults, mere outlines of his lecture.
>
> A third professor is the most eloquent lecturer I have ever heard. His manuscript lies on the raised desk before him; but it is rarely used; he is complete master of his subject, is an authority in his domain, and has so much to impart and knows so well how to give instruction that the hour is all too short.[21]

Denio used her studies in Leipzig to create several new courses at Wellesley, including Gothic, early Germanic languages, a critical study of the *Niebelungen-lied* and a new course in art history.

An 1889 issue of the Wellesley College newsletter contains a letter from a recent Wellesley graduate who was traveling with Denio and other students to Leipzig and Dresden. Despite the student's sentimental and superficial description, she manages to convey Denio's deep love of Leipzig and her appreciation of what she had been allowed to experience there as a student. It also contains an interesting American perspective of the great chemist, Justus Liebig:

> Our visit to Leipsic [sic] was filled with flowers. Roses accompanied the warm welcome with which we were greeted and the regret of departure was sweetened by their perfume. It was here that we made our début into German society and got a glimpse of the home life. The week was a delightful change from our usual round – from art galleries and museums to cathedrals, racking our brains trying to remember the history of the period and of the ancient objects before us. Miss Denio had impatiently anticipated this visit to her beloved University town, the professors so kind to her and the open-hearted, sincere Germans to whom she is ardently devoted....First on our program was a visit to a celebrated surgeon, where we amused ourselves while awaiting his arrival by viewing the family portraits on the wall; that of the handsome Baron Liebig of the "Extract of Beef" fame interesting us the most. On our way to make another call on a dear German lady, Miss Denio stopped to talk with a little, white-haired old man, wearing an old fashioned white stock around the neck, and introduced him as Professor Delitzsen [Delitzsch].[22] When we heard that he was the greatest living Hebrew scholar, we were filled with chagrin to think that we had not been more impressed by his appearance.[23]

Denio's career at Wellesley was cut short in 1896 when she was fired as part of a purge of senior faculty by the new college president, Julia Irvine, in an attempt to modernize the curriculum and campus life. In her history of Wellesley, Palmieri searches to find positive results from Irvine's rather brutal methods of ousting senior faculty. Among the positive changes were those in pedagogy. Denio is described as having taught her art history courses by rote memorization. Her replacement introduced laboratory methods.[24]

Fortunately, new opportunities opened up for Denio after she was cast out of that "Adamless Eden." She returned to Germany and finally earned her doctoral degree at the University of Heidelberg in 1898. Before studying at Heidelberg, Denio traveled to Berlin once more, to see whether or not she might be able to earn her degree there. At first she had high hopes. She took courses in art history and philosophy and had the support of the art historian Frye. An 1897 article in the Wellesley College newsletter speculated that Denio was "very likely to be the first woman to secure a degree from the University of Berlin."[25] But Denio was not that fortunate and did indeed need to transfer to Heidelberg to complete her studies. Four years after completing her degree, she was appointed a professor of Art History at the University of Rochester, where she taught until 1917. Ten years after her exile from Wellesley, Denio returned for a reception in her honor attended by more than fifty of her old friends. Denio continued to travel abroad, taking leave time to do research in Paris and Egypt. She served as an art guide for several international expositions and later returned to the topic of her doctoral thesis to publish a biography of Nicolas Poussin. She was also one of the directors of the Memorial Art Gallery in Rochester until her death.

One of the most interesting art history students was Neena Hamilton. Hamilton was born in 1868 in Hamilton, Ohio.[26] Before coming to Germany, Hamilton had studied at the teachers' college in Elmira, New York, and received a Master's from Hanover College in Indiana. In Europe, Hamilton studied at Berlin, Halle, Munich and Heidelberg, as well as in Paris. In Berlin, Hamilton audited courses in art history, German philology, and literature (WS 1896/97). Hamilton later audited courses at the University of Munich (WS 1898/99) with Adolf Furtwängler (1853-1907) in archaeology as well as in art history, philosophy and religion. A 1902 article in *The Nation* refers to Hamilton's long struggle with the German authorities to complete her doctoral degree. Apparently Hamilton was forced to leave Munich and completed her degree, like Denio before her, at Heidelberg.[27] The article praised her doctoral thesis, which had just been published in Strasbourg as *Die Darstellung der Anbetung der heiligen drei Könige in der toskanischen Malerei von Giotto bis Lionardo* (The Representation of the Adoration of the Three Kings in Tuscan Painting from Giotto to Leonardo) (1901). Her work was praised for using a single subject to give "penetrating insight into the whole aim and entire significance of Tuscan art."[28] The reviewer only regretted that this great work was written in German and thus was less accessible to an American audience. Hamilton married Hans Pringsheim in Toronto, Canada, in 1903. She continued to give lectures and publish on art history.

The least information is available about the third woman to earn her doctoral degree from Heidelberg in art history, the Canadian Henrietta Josephine Tromanhauser. Tromanhauser was born in Toronto in October 1865. Her father was a civil engineer. Tromanhauser completed her Bachelor's at the University of Chicago (1901). She then went to work as the principal in the training department of the State Normal School in Whatcom, Washington, before going to Germany to audit courses in pedagogy at the University of Berlin for the Winter Semester 1905/06. The following semester Tromanhauser studied at Heidelberg.

Tromanhauser returned to the United States, where she taught in Bellingham, Washington. Tromanhauser studied at Heidelberg for a total of six semesters before earning her doctoral degree in January 1912. Her thesis, "Women in the Art of Giotto" (Die Frau in der Kunst Giottos), like that of Neena Hamilton, focused on Italian art. The 1913 alumni directory for the University of Chicago still lists Tromanhauser as teaching in Bellingham, Washington. But the 1919 directory lists her as a teacher at the State College in Brookings, South Dakota.[29]

Although many women came to Germany to study art history, many others hoped to become artists. Although women were barred from the Munich Academy of Fine Arts, they had access to the Munich Women's Art Academy (Damenakademie des Münchner Künstlerinnenvereins), established in 1882. In 1868 a similar academy had been established in Berlin.[30] For those women seeking to become artists, the Women's Art Academy offered them a chance to teach and put on exhibitions.[31] In addition, summer courses outside of Munich at the Neu-Dachauto School also allowed women "to study from the nude and to concentrate on landscape painting."[32] Outside of these opportunities, women sought to further their education in the many private studios that filled the city. Munich had a thriving colony of artists. By 1886 there were close to a thousand artists living in the city. Ten years later, supposedly 4,000 painters had studios.[33] If the state-financed academy was closed to women, they could still seek private instruction with teachers from the academy.

The Munich studios most frequented by the women in this study were those of Wilhelm von Kaulbach, Fritz von Uhde, Frank Duveneck, Carl Marr, Felix Eisengräber, Moritz Heymann, Heinrich Knirr, Clyde Cook, Samuel Richards and Georg Jacobides. In addition, a number of women attended the Hofmann School for Modern Art in Munich, directed by the artist Hans Hofmann from 1915 until 1932. The period of operation of this school, however, lies outside of the scope of this study, and most North American students did not come to the Hofmann school until after World War I.

Kaulbach directed the Munich Academy of Fine Arts from 1849 until 1874. His most famous female private student was the British artist Anna Mary Howitt, who published a journal about her life as an art student in Munich from 1850 to 1851. Howitt described Kaulbach as having an "intellect, and dramatic power and poetry" superior to any other artist of the time.[34] Although Howitt received very little actual instruction from Kaulbach, she was able to witness the creation of his designs for the frescoes of the Neue Pinakothek. Biographical dictionaries of women artists also include the name of the painter Caroline Ransom (1838-1910) among Kaulbach's students.[35]

Helen Burt, a graduate of the Troy Female Seminary and the Cooper Union, taught art in the Charlottesville Academy and Peck's Military School (Greenwich, Connecticut) and opened her own studio in New York City before traveling to Europe to study art in 1872. Burt studied in Florence, Paris and Munich. In Munich she worked with Karl von Piloty, Kaulbach's successor and Rosthal. After returning from Europe, Burt again opened a studio in New York City, where she gave lessons and painted. She was best known for her portraits and paintings of animals. Burt received an award at the Centennial Exhibition (1876), and first prizes for her animal paintings at the New York State Fair and in Canada. Burt became a successful illustrator and writer. She published one book, *Perspective Drawing from the Object*. Burt was active in art associations:

one of the first members of the Ladies' Art Association of New York, a member of the New York State Drawing Teachers Association and the New York Public Educational Association.[36]

The painter Lilla Cabot Perry (1848-1933) studied with Fritz von Uhde (1848-1911) in 1888. Uhde is best known for being a leader in the Naturalist movement in Munich and one of the founders of the Munich Secession. He worked in Munich from 1880 until his death. It was Uhde who told Perry about the new artists' colony flourishing around Monet in Giverny.[37] With her entire family, Perry spent the next nine summers in Giverny, where she received no actual instruction but some informal advice from Monet as a friend on her painting.[38]

Other studios in Munich open to women included that of the German-American artist Carl von Marr (1858-1936), who was raised in Milwaukee but spent almost his entire professional career in Germany as a painter and professor. Belle Emerson, a Wellesley student, remained in Munich from 1887 to 1889 to work in his studio. The impressionist painter Felix Eisengräber (1874-1940), most famous for his landscape paintings, also opened his studio to women. The painter and etcher Winifred Bosworth (1885-?) worked with Eisengräber in Munich after having studied at the Art Institute of Chicago, the Boston Museum Fine Arts School of Art and the New York Art Students League.[39]

Several male artists stand out for their particularly significant contributions to the education of women artists. The first, Frank Duveneck (1848-1919), was an American artist and teacher from Cincinnati, who had set up a successful studio outside of Munich in Polling. In 1879 the painter Elizabeth Otis Lyman Boott (1846-1888) traveled to Munich to study with Duveneck. In 1881 the painter Helen Mary Knowlton (1832-1918) also came to Munich to study with Duveneck.[40]

Boott first came into contact with Duveneck's work at an exhibit at the Boston Art Club and later visited his studio while he was working in Venice. She was drawn by the "genius of ugliness" that seemed to possess him.[41] In 1879 Boott traveled from her adopted home in Italy to Munich to see whether she might study with Duveneck or in another studio. The artist Wilhelm Diez gave lessons to women, but they were a low priority for him. His advice to Boott was to "take a studio outside and get the help of a professor or take a studio with others."[42] Boott finally found real support in the circle of artists around Duveneck. There William Chase encouraged her to stay in Munich, because the "artistic atmosphere is so great. There are six thousand artists there and there is much mutual friendly criticism and interest."[43] Eager for an exchange of new ideas after years of working in isolation in Italy, Boott set up a studio and began her lessons with Duveneck.

Boott wrote detailed notes and letters about the techniques used by Duveneck. She was fascinated by his realism, his need to make things "'invariably uglier than they are.'"[44] She was dismayed by what seemed an overuse of blackness and dinginess in the Munich School, but she found that Duveneck compensated for this by his use of very rich color.

With encouragement from Boott, Duveneck and his followers migrated to Florence in October 1879. There, Duveneck started a class for women. Boott encouraged her women artist friends to travel to Florence to study with Duveneck. With him as a teacher, she promised, "'you have endless freedom with ample suggestion at the same time of the best ways of working out your meaning.'"[45]   In 1886 Boott and Duveneck married. During their brief married life, both continued to paint and shared models. In a note from July 1886, Boott's father describes the couple's life together: "'Lizzie and her *sposo* are painting downstairs. We have a number of large rooms in the lower floor they use for studio purposes.'"[46]   Unfortunately, Boott's death from pneumonia in 1888 brought an abrupt end to what appears to have been a loving and harmonious relationship.

Two other artists, Heinrich Knirr (1862-1944) and Moritz Heymann (1870-?), also played a very active role in supporting art education for women. In 1888 Knirr opened a private school for painting, which became very popular. From 1898 through 1910 he also taught at the Munich Women's Art Academy.[47] Heymann settled in Munich in 1902 and became the director of the lithography course for the Women's Art Association.[48] The painter Elisabeth Telling (1882-1979) studied with Heymann.[49]   The painters Roxoli Merriam Seabury (1874-1960)[50] and Marian MacIntosh (1871-1936) both worked with Knirr. Of her time in Knirr's studio, MacIntosh wrote that she delighted in "studying one thing with an intensity impossible except in Germany."[51]

A number of better-known artists came to Munich to study as well.[52]   The Canadian painter Elizabeth Armstrong Forbes (1859-1912) studied there in the early 1880s. Katharine Sophie Dreier (1877-1952), one of the founders of the Society of Independent Artists and a close friend of Marcel Duchamp (1887-1968), studied in Munich between 1911 and 1912.   The world of Marcel Duchamp also included one of the most fascinating American women artists of the turn of the century, Florine Stettheimer (1871-1944), who spent her formative years as an artist in Stuttgart, Berlin and Munich. After World War I, Stettheimer and her two sisters formed a salon in New York City that was frequented by some of the most prominent artists of the day, including Duchamp, Gaston Lachaise and William Zorach.[53]

After moving back to New York City in the early 1890s, Stettheimer and her family continued to return to Europe every year through World War I, spending extended periods of time in Germany, France and Italy. During one of those stays, Stettheimer took art lessons with a man in Munich to whom she gave the name "Herr Apotheker F" (the pharmacist F), and who taught her how to use casein, a milk derivative, as a surface for her painting. In Munich Stettheimer also worked in the studio of Raffael Schuster-Woldan (1864-1933),[54] where she benefited from his experiments in achieving warm depths in his paintings.[55]

Although Stettheimer returned to Munich year after year to work in studios, she had little praise for the city or its community of artists. In one poem, she wrote of trying "many a new painting medium" to ward off "any tedium."[56] It was really in New York that Stettheimer came to flourish as an artist and develop her own style. What she brought from Germany, however, was the concept of integrating forms of art, media and architecture into a *Gesamtkunstwerk* typical of the entire Art Nouveau movement.[57]

In addition to the numerous painters who studied in Germany, dictionaries of women artists contain the names of a few sculptors and photographers, who also went to Germany to study. The sculptor Katherine Thayer Hobson-Kraus (1889-1982) had studied at the Art Students League in New York City. In Dresden, she studied with the sculptor Walter Sintenius (1867-1911). While living in Germany in the 1920s, Hobson-Kraus built a World War I memorial for Dresden.[58]

The sculptor Lora Woodhead Steere (1888-1984), known for her work in bronze, stone and porcelain, studied in Berlin at the studio of Albert Torff and at the private art school founded by the sculptor Albert Reimann (1874-?) in 1902. While growing up, the noted American sculptor Harriet Whitney Frishmuth (1880-1980) attended schools in both Paris and Dresden. Before coming to Berlin to study art around 1900, Frishmuth had studied in Paris with Rodin and at the Académie Colarossi. In Germany she studied art in Dresden and Berlin, where she worked with Cumo von Euchtritz. Frishmuth later gained renown, especially for her bronze sculptures of nude female figures in motion.[59] Upon returning to the United States from Berlin, Frishmuth studied at the Art Students League with Gutzon Borglum and Hermon A. MacNeil. To have a better understanding of anatomy for her work in sculpture, Frishmuth also performed dissections at the College of Physicians and Surgeons in New York City.[60]

Among the photographers, two achieved international fame: Imogen Cunningham (1883-1976) and Gertrude Käsebier (1852-1934). Käsebier, born Gertrude Stanton, studied at the Pratt Institute in Brooklyn (1889-1896) and had private lessons in photography before traveling to Europe in 1894 to study. Käsebier took both private lessons and studied at the Académie Julian in Paris before traveling to Germany, where she apprenticed with a photographic chemist. Returning from Germany, Käsebier soon opened her own studio in New York City, where she worked as a commercial photographer. Käsebier was one of the co-founders of the Women's Federation of the Photographers' Association of America.[61]

Imogen Cunningham became one of the leading photographers of the first half of the twentieth century. She studied chemistry at the University of Washington in Seattle (1903-1907) and worked in a private photography studio for two years, before she won a scholarship to study photographic chemistry at the Technical College (Technische Hochschule) in Dresden. In Dresden, she did research on various printing processes with Robert Luther (1868-1945), who had been an assistant professor for physical chemistry at the University of Leipzig, before being appointed a full professor of photochemistry at the Technical College in Dresden in 1904.[62] Through the 1920s, Luther continued to do research on the effect of oxygen present in a chlorine gas mixture on the action of light.[63]

On her way back to Seattle, Cunningham was able to meet with several photographers of note, including Gertrude Käsebier and Alfred Stieglitz. Back in Seattle, Cunningham opened her own portrait studio. Cunningham gained fame for her work in San Francisco as one of the founding members of Group f/64, whose members included Edward Weston and Ansel Adams. Group f/64 emphasized realistic photography. Later in her long career, Cunningham also taught for several years at both the California School of Fine Arts in San Francisco and at the San Francisco Art Institute. Cunningham is famous for her choice of subjects that were controversial for the time, such as a nude male in a landscape (1915) or a pregnant nude (1959). In her photographs, Cunningham was also able to express a critique of popular images of women's beauty.[64]

INSTRUMENTAL MUSIC

Opportunities for studying both instrumental and vocal music in the German-speaking countries appear to have attracted far more women than those for art. We are fortunate to have numerous accounts of famous women musicians preserved, such as the correspondence of pianists Amy Fay and Mabel Daniels, or biographical accounts of Clara Langdon Clemens and Maud Powell. In addition to these more familiar sources, there are many accounts by and about less-known musicians published as books or found in popular journals, music journals or alumni publications.[65]

Germany was particularly blessed with a number of state-financed conservatories of excellent caliber, and most large German cities had at least one school of music. Large conservatories were established in Leipzig (1843) which was home as well to the famous performance hall, the Gewandhaus, and in Dresden (1856). Cologne (1850) and Stuttgart (1856) also had large conservatories, as did Munich with its Royal Academy of Music (1867). Frankfurt am Main had both the Frankfurt School of Music (Musikschule) (1860) and the Hoch Conservatory (1878). The Conservatory of Hannover was added to the already lengthy list of renowned conservatories in 1897.

Berlin, the center of the music world in Germany during the second half of the nineteenth century, had the Royal Academy of Musical Art (1822). Only advanced students sixteen and older were accepted, and an entrance examination was required.[66] No less famous was the Berlin Singakadamie, which had been founded in 1790 by Carl Friedrich Fasch and developed to a prominent institute by Carl Friedrich Zelters. Zelters also helped to start the music seminar of the University of Berlin (1829), which later grew into the School of Musical Studies (Schule der Musikwissenschaft). There was the famous College of Music (Hochschule für Musik), which was founded in 1869. In 1868, the influential violinist Joseph Joachim took over the direction of the College for the Applied Art of Music (Hochschule für Ausübende Tonkunst). He also joined the faculty of the College of Music and served as director after the reorganization of the college in 1875.

Admission to state-financed schools was on a competitive basis. Tuition costs were kept low, and the government subsidized fees for each student. There were always more applicants than vacancies. Admission was determined solely by talent; no preference was given to Germans over foreigners. Advantages for foreigners admitted to the state-financed schools were that the fees were low and students theoretically had access to the finest teachers in the country. In reality, even after the highly selective entrance examinations, very few students were chosen to work with the best teachers. Even the most talented students might have to wait a year or two before being considered for such a privilege. Foreign students rarely could commit to such a long stay in Germany, and most graduates through the early 1900s were Germans.[67]

On the other hand, the salaries at the state-financed institutions were fairly low, so many professors supplemented their income through private lessons or even through opening their own private conservatories. One account from a conference for American music teachers in 1909 indicates that these private conservatories were said to accept all students, with the only qualification being that a student could pay and pay a lot. There was a wide range of fees for private instruction and just as much variety in the quality of instruction. In fact, many of the private teachers were Americans who had settled abroad. Ironically, some American students actually ended up studying with American teachers in Europe. In Europe, however, these American teachers could charge their American students much higher fees for the same or an even worse quality of instruction these students could have received at home.[68] But accounts from students themselves indicate that there was a selection process, and that instruction at the private conservatories and in private studios was very rigorous. One piano student, Amy Fay, even preferred the type of instruction offered at the private conservatories over that at the College of Music in Berlin.

Berlin was home to many private conservatories. In 1850, together with the pianist Theodor Kullak (1818-1882) and the music theorist Adolf Bernhard Marx (1795-1866), the music pedagogue Julius Stern (1820-1883) founded the Berlin Conservatory. Disagreements soon arose among the three, however, and Kullak left in 1855 to establish his own school, the New Academy of Music (Neue Akademie der Tonkunst), also known simply as the Kullak Academy. A teacher of note at the Kullak Academy was the pianist Moritz Moszkowski (1854-1925).[69]

After Kullak left the Berlin Conservatory and Adolf Marx retired two years later, the Berlin Conservatory was run solely by Julius Stern and became known at the Stern Conservatory. Teachers of note at the Stern Conservatory were the pianists Martin Krause (1853-1918), Ernst Jedliczka (1855-1904) and Edwin Fischer (1886-1960), a former student of Krause's.

Carl Tausig (1841-1871), a former student of Liszt, opened a piano conservatory, the School of Advanced Piano Studies (Schule des Höheren Klavierspiels) in 1865. Another former student of Liszt, the pianist Karl Klindworth (1830-1916), opened his own school for pianists in Berlin in 1884. One of the most famous teachers at the Klindworth Institute was the Russian pianist Ernst Jedliczka, a former student of Tchaikovsky and Nicolai Rubinstein, who also taught at the Stern Conservatory. In 1893 the Klindworth Institute merged with the Scharwenka Conservatory, which had been founded in 1881 by two former faculty members of the Kullak Academy, Ludwig Philipp Scharwenka and Franz Xaver Scharwenka, to become one of the most famous schools for music in Germany, the Klindworth-Scharwenka Conservatory of Music (Konservatorium der Musik Klindworth-Scharwenka). Besides the Scharwenkas and Klindworth, teachers of note at the conservatory were Eugen d'Albert and August Haupt.[70]

In Austria, the center of music was Vienna, where students could take private lessons or attend the state-financed Conservatory of the Society of the Friends of Music (1817). The conservatory offered courses in composition, counterpoint, harmony, singing, dramatic art, dramaturgy, diction, opera, acting, dancing, fencing, gymnastics, piano, organ, harp, instruments of the classical orchestra, trombone, history of music, French and Italian.[71] By far the most famous piano teacher in Vienna during this period was Theodore Leschetizky (1830-1915).

There were conservatories and schools of music in Switzerland, such as the Conservatory in Geneva (1835), the Academy of Music in Geneva (1886) and the School of Music in Bern (1815), but North American women were drawn primarily to Germany and Austria, and especially to Berlin and Vienna.

Although it is beyond the scope of this study, it would be worthwhile to compare matriculation records that remain for state and private conservatories to gain a more complete picture of the enrollment of North Americans at these institutions. Which institutes attracted the most foreigners? Did women at the more competitive state conservatories have more of a chance of launching a successful career back in North America? Included here is a sample profile of North American students taken from one of the important private conservatories outside of Berlin, the Hoch Conservatory in Frankfurt am Main. This conservatory was chosen because fairly complete matriculation records exist for the entire period covered in this study. Moreover, the conservatory attracted prominent North American musicians, such as Edward A. MacDowell, and could boast of having Clara Wieck Schumann,[72] Engelbert Humperdinck, Joseph Rubinstein and Julius Stockhausen on its faculty.[73] Wieck Schumann was certainly the star of the conservatory. Students from North and South America as well as from various European countries came to study with her. The competition to get into her classes was intense. According to the matriculation records of the conservatory, her daughters Marie and Eugenie also taught piano.[74]

From the time the conservatory opened in 1878 until 1911, a steady stream of North American women came to the Hoch Conservatory, with a total of seventy-two North American women enrolled during that period. The very first year that the conservatory opened, two American women enrolled. One studied pianoforte with Carl Faelten, the other studied piano with Clara Wieck Schumann. Piano and voice were by far the most popular subjects studied, followed by violin: thirty-one women studied piano, fourteen voice and nine violin. Five women came to study theory and one to study the cello. The total number of women enrolled in any semester between 1878 and 1911 never exceeded eleven, and ranged from 0.6 percent (in 1902/03 and 1907/08) to 7.2 percent (in 1889/90) of the total female student population at the conservatory. About one-third of the women (25) came from the state of New York. Six came from Pennsylvania, five from Missouri, five from Illinois, four from Ohio, four from Massachusetts, three from Indiana, two from South Carolina, two from Idaho, and one woman from Washington, DC and each of the following states: California, Kansas, Kentucky, Louisiana, Maine, Michigan, Texas, Vermont and Wisconsin. There were also two Canadians, one from Halifax and one from Toronto.

In addition to Clara Wieck Schumann, some of the most popular piano teachers were James Kwast, Ernst Engesser, Carl Faelten, Carl Heymann, Johanna Flügge, Marie Gödecke, Alfred Hoehn, Lina Mayer, Lazzaro Uzielli, Carl Friedberg and Anton Urspruch. Some of the most popular voice teachers were Max Fleisch, Louise-Pauline-Marie Heritte-Viardot and Marie Hanfstaengl. For violin, some of the most popular teachers were Hugo Heermann, Fritz Bassermann, Willy Hess and J. Naret-Koning. For the cello, there was Bernhard Cossmann. Popular theory and composition professors included Joachim Raff, Iwan Knorr and Bernhard Scholz.

Some have argued that North America simply did not have the same quality conservatories in the nineteenth century and that a period of study in Europe was essential for a concert artist to receive the necessary rigorous training. In her biography of the master violinist Maud Powell, who left Illinois in 1881 to study at the Leipzig Conservatory with Henry Schradieck, Karen Shaffer argues:

> The necessity of European study at that time in order for a talented musician to become a finished artist should not be underestimated. The United States did not then have music conservatories that ranked with the venerable institutions in European capitals. If Maud's talent was to be developed to its fullest extent and opportunities for a career as a solo artist were to be opened to her, European study was imperative.[75]

Yet by the time Maud Powell left for Europe, ample opportunities for instruction both privately and at conservatories were available to North Americans at home. A number of conservatories had opened in the United States following the American Civil War, including the Oberlin Conservatory of Music (1865), the Peabody Conservatory of Music (1866),[76] the New England Conservatory (1867), the Boston Conservatory (1867), the Chicago Musical College (1867), the Cincinnati Conservatory (1867), and the Philadelphia Conservatory (1877). Other music schools of the period included: the Hamilton (Ontario) Conservatory; the Beethoven Conservatory in St. Louis; the Pillsbury Conservatory in Owatonna, Minnesota; the Columbia School of Music in Chicago; and the Detroit Conservatory. In addition to these schools, there were numerous short-lived conservatories in New York City, such as the Columbia Conservatory of Music (1872), the Mason-Thomas Conservatory (1873), the Grand Conservatory of Music (1874), and the Clavier Piano School. New York City was also home to what would later become the American Institute of Applied Music. In addition to these conservatories, starting in the 1860s, students were able to take a range of music courses at universities and colleges, such as Harvard and Northwestern. The conservatories were soon filled with women who were not able to study abroad.[77] Still, European music and musicians dominated North American musical education and performance in the nineteenth century. A period of study and a debut in Europe were deemed necessary for the serious student or performer.

As late as 1904 the American pianist Olga Samaroff found it almost impossible to debut in the United States as a concert pianist, because she had not performed in Europe.[78] When she confessed to the concert manager that she had no European press notices, his advice to her was cynical and clear: "'Now, you go and give some concerts in Europe and if the reviews are good, come back and see me. It isn't what *I* think of your playing, but *what Europe thinks of it that counts.*'"[79]

Samaroff became rather cynical about Americans' insistence on the European stamp of approval before they would accept a musician. There were excellent music schools and teachers in the United States. The pilgrimage to Europe was no longer essential. Still, Americans did not trust their own judgment about young talent. Samaroff wrote: "But European prestige was so important that even after practically completing their musical studies in the United States, aspirants for a public career usually betook themselves to Europe where, after a little coaching with a famous pedagogue (sometimes only for a few months), they would make a European debut and return to this country as 'a pupil of' the foreign celebrity."[80] The debuts themselves became at times simply another expensive hurdle to be overcome on the path to a public career.[81]

Nevertheless, for advanced students ready to embark on a concert career, European cities did offer unique opportunities for study and to both perform and attend performances. Music students in Europe often had access to free or reduced-price tickets and there were plenty of concerts to attend. A 1913 article in *The Nation* noted that eight concert halls had been built in Berlin since 1903.[82] Three of them could hold an audience as large as 1,600. Around 1910 Berlin had six theaters for opera and operetta, about a dozen concert halls for voice performances and about 300 smaller gardens and restaurants which accommodated informal performances.[83]

One of the obvious reasons for choosing Germany or Austria was the presence of a particular teacher. These two countries were home to some of the most influential teachers and composers of the time. For example, Maud Powell first went to Leipzig because of the violinist Henry Schradieck, and later was convinced by Joseph Joachim to study with him in Berlin. Amy Fay moved to

Weimar to study with Liszt. Clara Clemens traveled to Vienna to study with the pianist Theodore Leschetizky. Moreover, the American teachers of these women had often studied in Germany or Austria with a particular master, and thus recommended that their own pupils do the same. For example, Amy Fay's teacher in Boston, the composer John Knowles Paine (1839-1906), had studied in Berlin from 1858 to 1861, and had toured and conducted in Germany from 1886 to 1867. It was he who recommended that Fay continue her studies in Berlin.

But Germany, in particular, also attracted students with its reputation for unusually thorough and rigorous instruction, a reputation that remained undiminished throughout the late nineteenth and early twentieth centuries. In her classic history of women in American music, Christine Ammer notes that nineteenth-century Americans considered Germany the heart of the music world, it was the "wellspring of good music." Americans believed that the best musicians and teachers were either German or had trained in Germany.[84] After only a month in Berlin in 1869, the pianist Amy Fay wrote: "I wonder that people could tell us before I came away, and really seem to believe it, 'that I could learn as well in an American conservatory as in a German one.' In comparison with the drill I am now receiving, my Boston teaching was mere play."[85] The pianist Olga Samaroff praised "the general atmosphere of hard work and the prevailing thoroughness, [that] made music study in the Berlin of those days [late 1890s] extremely valuable to all serious students."[86] The pianist and composer Mabel Daniels came to Germany in the early 1900s for "that firm foundation which German thoroughness gives one."[87]

Almost all of the North American students who went to Germany or Austria to study instrumental music studied piano or composition. A minority, like Maud Powell (1868-1920) and Geraldine Morgan (1867-1918), went to study violin. The popularity of the piano is not surprising for several reasons. The most common home instrument in the United States through the mid-nineteenth century was the piano. The piano and harp had long been considered appropriate instruments for girls and women, as these instruments allowed the musician to play in a "demure seated position." Further, knowledge of the piano was considered one of the social graces for women.[88] Girls were rarely trained on the violin, "because the awkward playing position was thought to be unladylike."[89] Maud Powell's only female role model was the great violinist Camilla Urso (1842-1902). This prejudice against women playing string, brass or woodwind instruments would gradually diminish during the second half of the nineteenth century. By the 1900s the violin had even become a fashionable instrument for women in its own right, and women violinists were fairly common as both teachers and performers.[90]

As mentioned, the most popular destination for those women studying instrumental music was Berlin. In Berlin, some of the most popular piano and composition teachers chosen by the women in this study were Theodor Kullak and Moritz Moszkowski at the Kullak Academy; Carl Tausig at his Schule des Höheren Klavierspiels; Karl Klindworth, Ernst Jedliczka, Ludwig Philipp Scharwenka and Franz Xaver Scharwenka at the Konservatorium der Musik Klindworth-Scharwenka; Martin Krause, Ernst Jedliczka, Karl Barth (1847-1922) and Edwin Fischer at the Stern Conservatory; Engelbert Humperdinck (1854-1921) at the Akademische Meisterschule; and, working in their private studios, Ferruccio Busoni, Teresa Carreño (1853-1917), Ludwig Deppe (1828-1890), Jean

Paul Ertel (1865-1933), Rudolph Ganz (1877-1972), Anton Gloetzner, Leopold Godowsky (1870-1938), Hugo Kaun (1863-1932) and Egon Petri.

In Berlin, a small number of women also studied music and music history at the university. Early auditor records, which include the names of professors whose lectures the women attended, list a number of women who attended courses by Carl Stumpf (1848-1936), who worked in the fields of musicology and psychology. Stumpf came to Berlin in 1893 and founded the Psychological Institute. He was particularly interested in examining how certain tones in music were perceived. Among the first women to audit his classes in 1895 was Ethel Puffer Howes, who had come to Germany to pursue graduate studies in aesthetic theory. Women at the university also studied with the music scholar August Kretzschmar (1848-1924), who left the university in 1909 to become director of the College of Music in Berlin.

At the Leipzig Conservatory, women studying piano and composition worked with Salomon Jadassohn (1831-1902) and Carl Reinecke (1824-1910). At the Dresden Conservatory there were the pianists, Richard Burmeister (1860-1944) and Johannes Schreyer. At the Royal Academy of Music in Munich, women studying piano and composition worked with Ludwig Thuille (1861-1907) and Bernhard Stavenhagen (1862-1914), or took private lessons in composition with Victor Gluth.

Smaller towns drew students to the studios of famous teachers. Weimar had Liszt. For a period, Baden Baden had the pianists Clara Wieck Schumann and Johannes Brahms, as well as the celebrated singer Pauline Viardot-García (1821-1910), daughter of Manuel García (1775-1832), one of the most famous singing teachers of his time.[91]

Very few of the North American women included in this study went to Vienna for instrumental music, but those who did studied with the Austrian pianist Theodor Leschetizky. Leschetizky's pupils included such celebrated pianists as Paderewski, Ossip Gabrilowitsch, Artur Schnabel, Isabelle Vengerova, as well as Fannie Bloomfield-Zeisler (1863-1927), Helen Hopekirk (1856-1945) and Clara Clemens (1874-1962).[92]

To make the experiences of women studying instrumental music more vivid, what follows is a more in-depth look at the experiences of three successful musicians: Amy Fay, Mabel Daniels and Maud Powell. All three would launch successful concert careers after their studies abroad.

One of the earliest and most informative accounts of a North American woman studying music in Germany is the published correspondence of Amy Fay, an American from Mississippi, whose letters cover the years 1869 through 1875. Fay's great-grandfather was a leading Hamburg merchant who had fled from Germany with his family when Napoleon came.[93] Fay's letters are filled with detailed accounts of famous musicians of her day, including Franz Liszt, Clara Wieck Schumann, Richard Wagner and the piano pedagogue Ludwig Deppe. But Fay became a renowned artist in her own right. As Frances Dillon writes in a brief biography, Fay was the first American concert artist to play an entire piano concerto in America. In her studios in New York, Boston and Chicago, she taught many famous students, including the composer John Alden Carpenter (1876-1951). It was she who helped spread Deppe's teaching method in America, and it was her correspondence that inspired generations of Americans to study music abroad.[94]

Fay was encouraged to study abroad by one of her teachers, the American composer John Knowles Paine, who had studied in Berlin from 1858 to 1861 with the German organist Karl August Haupt (1810-1891), and other teachers. After returning from Berlin, Paine became the first professor of music at Harvard and worked as an organist at Appleton Chapel in Cambridge, Massachusetts. Paine would continue to teach at Harvard until his death. From 1866 to 1867, two years before Fay left for Germany, Paine toured and conducted in Germany. When Fay left for Germany in 1869, her goals were to refine her musical taste and to improve her technique.[95] Of the conservatories in Germany, Fay wrote that the one in Stuttgart, with teachers such as the pianist Siegmund Lebert (1821-1884), was then considered to be the best. Lebert had been one of the founders of the conservatory in 1856. She wrote of the conservatories of that time: "[T]hey have at least six lessons a week, two solo, two in reading at sight, and two in composition. Then there are often lectures held on musical subjects by some of the Professors, or by some one who is engaged for that purpose."[96]

Fay began her own studies in Berlin, where she first took instruction at Carl Tausig's School of Advanced Piano Studies. When Fay arrived in Berlin, the College of Music had just been founded. She found that the instruction there focused too much on string instruments and that its piano teachers were not on a par with those at smaller, private conservatories run by master pianists.[97] Fay enrolled at two of these smaller conservatories, each one led by a famous concert artist (Tausig and Kullak) and several colleagues. Such conservatories were not necessarily long-lived, but did attract students from around the world.

Fay's daily schedule at the conservatories consisted of six hours of practice in addition to classroom instruction in technique, sight-reading, duet-playing and music theory. Before traveling to Germany, Fay had received some instruction in German, but her knowledge of German proved inadequate for the classroom. In Berlin, for example, she hardly understood a word of her harmony professor, the great music theorist and composer Carl Friedrich Weitzmann (1808-1880). The moment of reckoning came when Weitzmann made her stand up in front of the class and work with him at the blackboard until she understood what he was saying.

Fay was eventually disappointed by some of her teachers, especially Tausig, who had no qualms about suddenly dropping all their students and closing their conservatory.[98] She was dismayed at the professional and social segregation of women and men she encountered in Germany. She shocked German women by espousing a system of coeducation and praised "the New England principle of teaching daughters to be independent and to look out for themselves from the first."[99] She formed close friendships with several of the male musicians at the conservatory and benefited from their greater musical experience. According to Fay, although women and men were separated in class, both were held to the same high standards of achievement. In general, Fay assessed musicians by their skills and not by their sex. She ranked Clara Wieck as an interpreter above Tausig and Rubenstein. But the sight of Alicia Hund, the first female conductor she had encountered, struck her as singularly unbecoming: "Somehow, a woman doesn't look well with a baton in her hand directing a body of men."[100]

In her letters, Fay was discouraging to all but the most serious students about the benefits of studying abroad. Some conservatories were crowded, and it was difficult to gain admission. An American student had to expect to spend at least a year in preparation before being allowed to take lessons with a first-class master. The best American students had to contend with teachers who believed that Americans had no real talent. In addition, Fay saw no purpose in coming to Europe, if a student was not appreciative of European culture.[101] She delighted in the cultural opportunities available to her in Europe, such as the museums and concerts. At the numerous concerts she attended, she heard, among others, Clara Wieck, Hans von Bülow, Carl Tausig, and Anton Rubenstein on the piano, and Joseph Joachim on the violin.[102]

In Berlin Fay found an established community of American residents and music students. Her description of her social life included numerous engagements with wealthy, prominent American families. She was full of praise for the Americans and described the typical American man as having "a hearty contempt for titles and a great respect for women."[103]

After Berlin, Fay moved to Weimar to take lessons with Liszt. She found herself in the company of other Americans, women and men, who had come to Weimar for the same purpose. She mentioned in particular a Miss [Cecilia] Gaul of Baltimore,[104] who had studied with Lebert at the Stuttgart Conservatory before coming to Weimar around 1871 to study with Liszt. Fay considered Gaul extremely gifted.[105]

Liszt did not separate female and male students, and his classes were at times attended by "directors of conservatories, composers, artists, aristocrats."[106] Fay's descriptions of Liszt are quite famous. He was the "monarch" and could change from the most amiable man into a dreadful one. He took no payment for lessons. Students entered his rooms and placed their music on the table, so that he could see what a student wanted to play. He then chose students to play for him. Fay was enthralled by him and recorded even his tiniest acts of genius. She described his teaching as a spiritual process: "He presents an *idea* to you, and it takes fast hold of your mind and sticks there."[107] His criticism was also tempered by humor and affection, as apparent in her description of one lesson: "One day when I was playing, I made too much movement with my hand in a rotatory sort of passage where it was difficult to avoid it. 'Keep your hand still, Fräulein,' said Liszt; *'don't make omelette.'*"[108]

After her lessons with Liszt, Fay returned to Berlin where she soon gave up her studies with Kullak, because he forced too rigid a style on her. Kullak had Fay study Czerny's *Schule des Virtuosen* for an entire year. While Fay admitted that such technical training was indispensable, she found it tedious beyond endurance. She began to take instruction with Ludwig Deppe. It was Deppe's method of teaching that she adopted when she returned as a performer and teacher to America. The last segment of the correspondence contains detailed accounts of her lessons with Deppe and the specifics of his technique. Fay refers to other Americans, female and male, who studied with Deppe and brought his method of teaching back to America.

Before leaving Germany, Fay was able to realize her dream of giving a public concert. Her French teacher's brother, the director of the Philharmonic Society in Frankfurt an der Oder, arranged her concert debut in May 1875. The published correspondence ends with a cautionary note from Fay's brother from 1880. In it, he adds that Fay would not advise any American woman to study abroad without careful consideration. Moreover, he notes, the need for studying abroad was less urgent, as many fine teachers, including those educated abroad, were now teaching the finest technique in America:

Piano teaching has developed immensely in America since the
date of the first of the foregoing letters [1869], and not only
such celebrities as Dr. William Mason, Mr. Wm. H.
Sherwood, and Mrs. Rivé King, but various other brilliant or
exquisite pianists in this country are as able to train pupils for
the technical demands of the concert-room as any masters that
are to be found abroad. American teachers best understand the
American temperament, and therefore are by far the best for
American pupils until they have got beyond the pupil stage.[109]

Germany, the "real home of music," was only for the highest level of training,
not simply for technique but rather for learning "musical insight and conception,
wider and deeper musical comprehension, and 'concert style.'"[110]

The correspondence of the Boston composer Mabel Wheeler Daniels (1878-
1971) about her stay in Germany from September 1902 to July 1903 forms a
perfect counterpart to that of Amy Fay. The correspondence was published as
An American Girl in Munich: Impressions of a Music Student in 1905.[111] The
autobiographical correspondence combines a love story and a lighthearted commentary on the adventures of Daniels with some enlightening descriptions of a
music student's everyday life.

Daniels was born in Swampscott, Massachusetts. Before studying in Munich, she had graduated with a Bachelor's from Radcliffe in 1900 and had studied
with the composer George Whitefield Chadwick in Boston at the New England
Conservatory.

Daniels's correspondence consists of letters from Munich and other travel
destinations in Germany to her friend Cecilia back home in Boston. It is possible that the great popularity enjoyed by Amy Fay's correspondence influenced
Daniels's choice of narrative structure for her tale. Certainly, the reviewer of her
work for *The Nation* compared Daniels's book to Fay's, although with a less
than favorable judgment. Daniels was moving in lesser spheres, with stars of
less brilliance than Liszt:

The reader must not expect anything resembling Amy Fay's
"Music Study in Germany," of which about twenty editions
have been printed, and which has a great deal of interest to re-
late about Liszt and other prominent musicians of his day.
The stars in the present German galaxy are fewer and smaller,
yet Miss Daniels found some very good men from whom to
learn the various branches of music, including two whose fame
is international – Thuille and Stavenhagen; and those who
have heard her compositions aver that she made good use of
her opportunities.[112]

The correspondence begins in 1902 as Daniels and her mother search for an
apartment to rent in Munich. Much to their dismay, they found that "a music
student was regarded as an incubus, and shunned accordingly."[113] No landlord
wanted the sound of a music student practicing to irritate the neighbors or drive
away other lodgers. But within a short period of time, she and her mother had
not only found a place to live, but had also rented a piano. Daniels then met
with the Austrian composer and pianist Ludwig Thuille, who was at that time a
professor at the Royal Academy of Music in Munich. After reading Daniels's
letter of introduction from Chadwick, Thuille readily agreed to allow Daniels to

study composition with him. In Boston Daniels had studied with John Knowles Paine, the same professor who had encouraged Amy Fay to study in Germany.

Daniels was fortunate to be able to enroll at the Royal Academy, where, she noted, "five years ago women were not allowed to study counterpoint....In fact, anything more advanced than elementary harmony was debarred."[114]   She also noted that among the forty professors of the conservatory there were only two women, both of whom became her teachers. At the conservatory, Daniels convinced one of her professors, the pianist, conductor and composer Bernhard Stavenhagen, to allow her to attend his score-reading class, although there had never been a woman in that class before. She gives an account of her first day in that class, that recalls the stunned reactions faced by the first women walking into lecture halls and laboratories of the German universities in other fields:

> I will acknowledge that I felt rather strange at the first meeting
> of the score-reading class, when, on entering the room with the
> score of Haydn's symphonies under my arm, I encountered the
> astonished gaze of thirty pairs of masculine eyes. You could
> have heard a pin drop, the place was so still, as I walked by the
> different groups and took a seat near the window. Then a low
> whispering started among the students.[115]

She was called upon to play before that very first class. She heard one of the men stifle a laugh and was determined to show these men that she was quite competent. She played without a mistake, and from that time on, the men in the class treated her with the utmost courtesy.

In very little time, Daniels established a study routine. She spent the mornings studying and the afternoons taking lessons. In addition to composition and score reading, she participated in the chorus, and studied singing and piano with the two women professors at the conservatory.

In Munich Daniels soon came into contact with other American women who were there to study music. From her account, it appears that hundreds of American women passed through Germany at that time hoping to launch successful careers as opera singers. She described many of the singers as misguided, but had only praise for the American pianists she encountered in Munich. The skills of the American pianists were also recognized by the Germans, for at the end of Daniels's year in Germany, two of the ten medals of excellence at the conservatory were presented to American women, one of whom is named, a Miss Bartholomay from Buffalo. At her lodgings, Daniels met two other women, Louise and Edith from New York, who were studying piano with one of Leschetizky's students, Frau Langenhan-Hirzel. She also met a Miss B. from California, who was studying piano at the conservatory with Martin Krause, a professor who, like Stavenhagen, was known for allowing foreign students to study with him.   In her piano classes, Daniels met another American, a Miss P. from Philadelphia, who was studying to be an opera singer. Miss P. encouraged Daniels to improve her German pronunciation by taking lessons with the acting coach at the opera house. Daniels eventually did take lessons, despite the acting coach's habit of humiliating foreign students in front of the class.

Along with the other graduating students, Daniels had to take her exams before returning to America. She described in detail her oral exam in the history of music, which she passed despite lapsing into a rather primitive German:

> All the pupils filed in together and sat in a single row on the
> platform. Before us was the formidable mass of professors

with folded arms. Just in front of them was Stavenhagen behind a table and two other men who wrote down what we said.
Before the director was a box full of paper slips on which were
written the questions. When a pupil's name was called, he
went to the box, drew three questions, and declaimed his answers to the joint audience of pupils and teachers. As I have
told you, whenever I am nervous my German becomes affected
in a peculiar fashion. I find myself forgetting words with remarkable rapidity and I insist on employing the English order
of expression, which, to a Münchener, is nothing less than a
mild form of madness. However, I managed to get through by
not allowing the amused faces of the onlookers to trouble me,
and although I discovered afterwards that I had called "The
Damnation of Faust" an oratorio and had mixed my genders in
the most ludicrous fashion, I was successfully "passed."[116]

After graduating, Daniels returned to the United States to continue her work
as a composer. Back in Boston Daniels became director of the Radcliffe Glee
Club (1911-1913) and then head of the music department at Simmons College
(1913-1918). Daniels received two honorary degrees, a Master's from Tufts in
1933 and a doctoral degree from Boston University in 1939. Daniels achieved
modest fame as a composer. In 1908 her first work for a full orchestra, *In the
Greenwood*, was performed by the Boston "Pops."[117] Daniels found encouragement throughout her studies and career from her friends, who included some of
the leading North American women composers of the early twentieth century,
Amy Marcy Cheney Beach (1867-1944), Margaret Ruthven Lang (1867-1972)
and the Canadian Gena Branscombe (1881-1977).

The portrait of Daniels would not be complete without an account of her
"petulance," tucked away in the preface to the seventh edition of *Baker's Biographical Dictionary of Musicians*, which reveals just as much about the petti-
ness of the editor as it does about Daniels:

Mabel Daniels, the Boston composer, once included in a piece
a C-sharp against C, explaining that she "had to use a disso-
nance," since she was living in the same town with me. She
petulantly accused me of being "no gentleman" in putting her
down as born in 1878 rather than 1879, her own chosen year.
She was born in November 1878, just a few weeks away from
1879, so why should I not accept the later year, she pleaded.
Poor Mabel! She lived a full life until well into her tenth decade, dying in 1971.[118]

Although pianists dominate the list of women instrumentalists, this section
would be incomplete without mentioning the remarkable work of the influential
American violinist Maud Powell, who inspired such masters of the violin as
Yehudi Menuhin. Maud Powell was born on August 22, 1867, in Peru, Illinois. At the age of seven Powell began taking private lessons on the violin.
Her first instructor was a German immigrant, G. W. Fickensher, the head of the
district music department. At about the same time as Maud began violin lessons, she attended a concert by Camilla Urso, a rare female violin virtuoso, in a
nearby opera house. Powell claimed that Urso inspired her for the rest of her
life.[119] Later, Powell would realize the full burden she carried, as she attempted,
like Urso, to pursue a concert career as a woman violinist. Shortly before her

death, Powell wrote about the strong prejudice against "women fiddlers"[120] that she had confronted her entire career. Early in her career, she adopted what she saw as a "masculine manner" in her playing to counter such prejudice. Eventually, however, Powell became secure enough to play, as she thought, "with no further thought of sex or sex distinctions."[121] Significantly, while arguing that sex was of secondary importance in music, Powell continued to identify with women violinists. When speaking of violin students in general, Powell frequently used the feminine pronoun in the third person. A typical bit of advice follows: "Moreover, should the student go to Europe for further study *she* will certainly command greater respect and attention than *she* would were *she* a 'slave to her notes [emphasis added].'"[122] In her advice to young musicians, she wrote: "Long before a *girl* of the right caliber has completed her studies, *she* should have received the baptism of her vocation – the words 'fame' and 'greatness' should have disappeared, to be replaced by truth and art [emphasis added]."[123] Despite the exceptional opportunities Powell received early in life, she remained aware of the struggles faced by other women violinists. She thought of herself as a pioneer and realized the significance of her success for other women.

Powell very early showed signs of an exceptional talent and quickly outgrew her first teacher. Fickensher recommended that she continue her studies with William Lewis, a British violinist who had received early training in London and who supported himself through his company, which sold sheet music and musical instruments.[124] Powell also received training in music theory from Edwin A. Stein, a German organist and conductor from Dresden. After four years, both Lewis and Stein recommended that Powell continue her studies in Europe with Henry Schradieck (1846-1918) at the Leipzig Conservatory.[125] Thus, in 1881, at the age of thirteen, Maud left for Leipzig accompanied by her mother.

After an initial audition for Schradieck in his home, Powell had to pass the official entrance examinations for the conservatory. She was tested on her performance, sight-reading and theory. Powell was immediately ranked among the most advanced students, and quickly adjusted to life both at the conservatory and in Leipzig. She gained fluency in German and became acquainted with other American students at the conservatory. One in particular, Geraldine Morgan, who had come from New York to study with Schradieck, would become a close friend.[126] A close bond also formed between Powell and Schradieck. Schradieck's greatest talent as a teacher seems to have been his ability to inspire his students to think both critically and sensitively about the music they were playing. He was also extremely demanding about tone and expression as well as technique.[127] In Leipzig, Powell also benefited from the chance to play in ensembles and to observe a variety of musicians at the numerous concerts offered about town. She later claimed that Germany had instilled in her a "reverence for art" and had given her "the best musical foundation...breadth and virility of style, earnestness of intention and truth of sentiment."[128]

After working with Powell for two semesters, Schradieck urged her to continue her education in Paris. There, Powell was admitted to the Paris Conservatory, where she studied with the French violinist Charles Dancla (1817-1907). Dancla was so taken with Powell's talents, that he gave her free, private lessons outside of the conservatory. Comparing her time in Paris to that in Germany, Powell wrote that Dancla "always put the purely musical before the purely virtuoso side of playing....he taught me to become an artist, just as I had learned in

Germany to become a musician."[129] In France Powell expanded her repertoire of Austrian and German composers to include French and Belgian literature.

But six months later Powell and her mother were on the road again, this time to London, after being advised by the Belgian violinist Hubert Léonard (1819-1890) to spend a year giving concerts. England was seen as the best testing ground because of the conservative tastes of British audiences. After almost a year of giving successful concerts, Powell was well-connected enough to gain the opportunity to play for Joseph Joachim, the Hungarian violinist and director of the College of Music in Berlin, who was then playing in London. Joachim immediately recognized the greatness of Powell's talent, and managed to persuade her and her mother to come to Berlin.

Women had gained admittance to the state-financed Berlin conservatory fairly quickly, that is, by the mid-1870s, within six years of its opening. Powell's own class with Joachim had more women than men, with a ratio of nine to five. Powell spent 1884 through 1885 in Berlin working with Joachim, who was one of the most gifted musicians of his time. From the very beginning, Powell was given unusual privileges at the conservatory. At Joachim's request, she was allowed to audition before all the other women violinists and was admitted to the conservatory immediately, with no further private instruction required. She was not required to attend the usual six months of preparatory classes. In addition, she was given the rare honor of attending Joachim's master classes without having to wait the usual year or two.[130]

Powell's descriptions of what she gained from Joachim are similar to those of her lessons with Schradieck. The most valuable things seem to be intangibles, that is, improving her methods of interpretation and her insights into composition. Joachim did not, however, explain technical aspects of playing to his students. Thus, although Joachim constantly emphasized the importance of bowing, Powell attributed her greatest skills in this area to her work with Dancla and her own determination.[131] Further, her powers of memorization, which stood her in good stead in Joachim's classes, had been developed early in childhood. Powell's experiences, like those of Amy Fay and Mabel Daniels, confirm that such musical training was most beneficial for advanced students, who had highly developed technical skills and some skill at interpreting music for themselves. A student had to be skilled enough to benefit from the strengths of a teacher while still being able to recognize and compensate for the teacher's weaknesses. A student had to understand the style of the teacher, while developing a unique style of her or his own. Powell thought "eight years of uninterrupted work" with teachers was sufficient. A student should then attempt to develop her or his own critical judgment.[132]

After studying with Joachim in Berlin, Powell returned to the United States to launch a highly successful concert career. She formed her own string quartet. Powell made numerous and highly acclaimed concert tours of Europe, returning to Leipzig and Berlin. Powell eventually married H. Godfrey Turner, the British manager of John Philip Sousa's band. Powell had met Turner while touring with Sousa. Like a number of other prominent women musicians of her time, such as the pianist Julie Rivé-King (1854-1937) and the violinist Geraldine Morgan, she continued her concert career even after marriage. Turner supported her career, and the couple chose not to have children so that Powell would have the necessary freedom to pursue her art. Performing and touring up until the very end of her life, Powell died on January 8, 1920, at the age of fifty-two from heart failure.

VOCAL MUSIC

While the composer Mabel Wheeler Daniels was studying at the Royal Academy of Music in Munich during the early 1900s, she was distressed by the number of American women she encountered there who had traveled to Germany hoping to make it big in the opera. Their eyes were blinded by the fame of Geraldine Farrar (1882-1967),[133] an American who had managed to achieve great success at the Berlin Royal Opera. They hardly seemed to realize that such success was rare and predicated on the failure of hundreds of others. Daniels wrote:

> When one studies singing merely for the love of it, it is all very well, but it would make your heart sick to see the number of American girls over here who are half-starving themselves in order to study for the grand opera stage. One sadly wonders how many of them will ever "arrive," but when an argument is raised or a doubt expressed as to their ultimate success, they immediately cite the case of Geraldine Farrar, the American who is at present singing leading roles at the Berlin opera house. The brilliancy of her success blinds their eyes to hundreds of utter failures, to countless half-way successes and to the untold drudgery which lies along the road.[134]

Certainly, Daniels was correct in observing that few North American singers achieved the fame of Geraldine Farrar. Nevertheless, a surprising number of singers did manage to launch successful careers on the German and Austrian operatic stages. Their names have faded with time, but at the end of the nineteenth century and beginning of the twentieth a number of them enjoyed great success. Even before Farrar joined the Berlin Opera in 1901, the soprano Minnie (Amalia Mignon) Hauk (1851-1929) and the mezzo-soprano Edyth Walker (1867-1950) had successful careers with opera companies in both Berlin and Vienna. Contemporaries of Farrar, who achieved fame in German opera companies outside of Berlin, include the sopranos Florence Easton (1882-1955) in Hamburg, Maude Fay (1879-1964) in Munich, Estelle Liebling (1880-1970) in Dresden and Stuttgart, Minnie Saltzmann-Stevens (1874-1950) in Bayreuth and Marcia Van Dresser (1877-1937) in Dessau and Frankfurt am Main.

A *New York Times* article from 1914 mentions another lesser star since lost to history, "a Southern girl, Miss Phadrig Agon, who was to sing Brunhilde at the Theater des Westens in Berlin."[135] A 1915 article commenting on Farrar's pro-Germanism during World War I mentions Maude Fay, who had moved to Dresden around 1900 and who was the chief lyric-dramatic soprano at the Munich Opera from the time of her debut in 1906 through 1916. Maude Fay was compared very favorably to Farrar: "She is as great an artist and as handsome a woman as Farrar, by the way – and as highly charged with electricity! She has been an idol in Munich from the first and has sung all over Europe..."[136] Maude Fay returned to the United States in 1916 to sing with the Metropolitan Opera and the Chicago Opera, but she never achieved Farrar's enduring fame.[137]

Of course, there were also the "half-starving" American girls Daniels pitied, those who kept hoping to get a big break and make it into a German or Austrian opera company. There are accounts of women singing at public occasions hoping that their talent would be recognized. Betty Scott from Wellesley was in

Berlin studying voice, when she was asked to sing at a memorial service there for President McKinley in 1901 before a "vast assemblage of noted men and women."[138] There are accounts of women whose talents were never recognized and who were exploited by teachers. Olga Samaroff's autobiography includes a moving tale of a young girl from Iowa, who "had fallen into the hands of a charlatan singing teacher whose demands soon exhausted her resources. He then induced her to remain in Paris as his mistress rather than confess her plight to her people at home."[139]

When Geraldine Farrar came to Germany to study, she went to Berlin to take private lessons with the Italian baritone, Francesco Graziani (1828-1901). In this sense, Farrar's path was typical for other North American women singers. Most had private instruction. Those who enrolled at a conservatory, like Edyth Walker who studied with the Hungarian soprano Aglaja Orgeni (1841-1926) at the Dresden Conservatory, were the exceptions. Farrar took private lessons in Germany with Graziani and the German soprano Lilli Lehmann (1848-1929), most famous for her Wagnerian roles. Two other teachers, whose names appear repeatedly in the biographies of the women included in this study, were the German singer Mathilde Marchesi de Castrone (1821-1913) and the celebrated French mezzo-soprano Pauline Viardot-García (1821-1910). Marchesi taught at the Vienna Conservatory (1854-1861 and 1869-1878) as well as in Cologne and Paris. Her students included the soprano Emma Nevada (1859-1940) and the contralto Antoinette Sterling (1850-1904). Viardot-García taught in Baden-Baden and at the Paris Conservatory. Her students included the contralto Annie Louise Cary (1841-1921) as well as Antoinette Sterling.

But it appears that many North American women did not travel to Germany or Austria to study. Instead, they went there to perform or to become a member of an opera company. Minnie Hauk had lessons in the German language during her two seasons with the Vienna Royal Opera and in Berlin, where she arrived in 1875 to sing for several seasons with the Berlin Royal Opera, supposedly the first American appointed a Royal Prussian Chamber-singer (Königliche Preussische Kammersängerin).[140]

A basic challenge faced by all of the women, who became or who hoped to become part of a German or Austrian opera company, was that they had to learn German to sing the repertoire. Minnie Hauk was so excited the first time she was invited to sign a contract with the Vienna Royal Opera, that she never considered the fact that only German was sung and that she did not know any German.[141] Hauk ended up having to break that first contract. When she finally returned to Vienna, she came in the middle of the opera season and had to learn her part in German in one week. Apparently, Hauk was a great success in the role of Gretchen in *Faust*, but she made one mistake in her German that had Vienna laughing at her expense. As Hauk tells the story:

> When Faust, on meeting Gretchen in the market place of Nuremberg, offers his arm to her, she replies in confusion:
>
> > *Bin weder Fräulein, weder schön,*
> > *Kann unbegleitet nach Hause geh'n.*
>
> Then she walks quickly off towards the back of the stage. In doing so, I heard the intense stillness broken by general tittering, followed by wild applause. Of course, I did not realize the cause of this hilarity, for I had sung the phrase to the best of my ability, and was somewhat disconcerted. Arriving behind

the scenes, I was told that instead of *"unbegleitet,"* which means "unaccompanied," I had inadvertently pronounced that word so that it sounded like *"unbekleidet,"* meaning "undressed."[142]

Hauk enjoyed continued popularity in Vienna and soon became the highest paid singer at the Royal Opera.

Geraldine Farrar was in a similar position as Hauk when she was offered a contract with the Berlin Royal Opera. At a reception in Berlin, Farrar came to the attention of Count von Hochberg, the intendant of the Berlin Royal Opera. Hochberg encouraged Farrar to audition for the Royal Opera, and she was eventually offered a three-year contract. She immediately began to study German and within two years was performing throughout Europe in French, Italian and German.

As to be expected, North American singers performing in German included Wagnerian roles in their repertoire and helped to popularize Wagner's music in North America. The contralto Annie Louise Cary, who had studied in Baden-Baden with Viardot-García, became the first American woman to sing a Wagnerian role in the United States when she sang the part of Ortrud in *Lohengrin* in 1877.[143] In the early 1880s Minnie Hauk included Wagner's music in many of her American concerts in an attempt to popularize Wagner in the United States. Some of America's most famous opera stars of the time, including Emma Eames (1865-1952) and Lillian Nordica (1857-1914), gained renown for their performances of Wagnerian operas. Nordica, for example, sang the role of Elsa for the first performance of *Lohengrin* in Bayreuth. Farrar considered the role of Elisabeth in Wagner's *Tannhäuser* one of her favorites. Lesser stars such as Mme. Charles Cahier (1870-1951), Maude Fay, Rita Fornia-Labey (1878-1922), Louise Homer (1871-1947), Minnie Saltzmann-Stevens, Edyth Walker and Florence Wickham (1880-1962) also became known for their Wagnerian roles. This popularization of Wagner could be considered one of the greatest gifts these women gave to North American audiences.

During Farrar's successful career in Germany and even in the years immediately thereafter, the teacher who influenced her the most was the famous German singer Lilli Lehmann (1848-1929). From 1903 through 1906, Farrar studied with Lehmann two or three hours every day. In 1906, while still enjoying great popularity in Europe, Farrar returned to the United States to continue her career at the Metropolitan Opera Company, where she would be a lead soprano for the next sixteen years. Even after moving back to the United States, Farrar returned to Germany every summer until World War I to continue her lessons with Lehmann. From 1915 to 1920, Farrar also enjoyed a successful career in Hollywood as a star in fourteen silent films. In her later years, Farrar became a trustee of the New England Conservatory of Music in Boston. She died on March 11, 1967, of pneumonia.

By the time World War I began, Farrar had already transplanted her career back to American soil. Yet she, along with other American singers who had enjoyed successful careers in Germany, remained loyal to Germany at the beginning of the war. The American popular press published interviews and letters from Farrar and Maude Fay in support of Germany. Maude Fay remained in Munich until 1916, and wrote in an interview with the *New York Times* in September 1915, that Germany had "enriched [her] ideals and belief in humanity." She was very happy to remain in Germany to experience "the realness of these wonderful Germans."[144]   The realities of war, however, soon interrupted the careers even of such ardent supporters of Germany as Maude Fay, and forced most North Americans lingering abroad to return home.

Conclusion

This book recalls that era when German-speaking universities and research facilities offered North American women unique academic and professional opportunities at a critical period of transition, when most North American graduate or medical schools were closed to women. Until the stories of so many women are interwoven, it is almost impossible to see the power and combined influence that these North American students of German-speaking universities had. The collective importance of these women had been lost in histories that focused on the experiences of men at German-speaking universities or on higher education for women in North America. Yet their accomplishments helped to break barriers to women's education at German universities. They proved to German professors that the excellence of German universities and German research did not require the exclusion of women. Back in North America, they used knowledge gained in Europe and the prestige associated with their European studies to establish new research and educational opportunities for women. Their experiences at German-speaking universities gave them the confidence to create undergraduate and graduate programs that could compete with similar programs for males. M. Carey Thomas, the second president of Bryn Mawr College, helped make it possible for women to engage in the highest level of graduate research.

Their work in medicine at the University of Zurich, and at clinics and hospitals in Germany and Austria, gave these women the skills necessary to open medical colleges, infirmaries and practices for women and children in North America. Their ranks included some of the first women physicians, such as Rebecca Lee Dorsey, the first woman to open a medical practice in Los Angeles. In the sciences and mathematics, they helped to create some of the first graduate programs for women.

Among these women were leaders in the emerging fields of the social sciences. Their ranks included some of the most dedicated fighters for early labor legislation protecting the rights of women and children, and for social welfare programs for immigrants and the poor. Several of these women embraced socialism as an antidote to the exploitation of workers. They joined the international women's movement in its battle for women's suffrage and world peace. Included in this group was the winner of the Nobel Peace Prize, Emily Greene Balch.

This book has been an attempt to do justice to the accomplishments not only of such prominent women but also of the efforts of hundreds of lesser-known North American women who studied abroad. Their experiences and the significance of their efforts differed from those of North American men who studied abroad at German-speaking universities. Their experiences also differed from those of European women struggling to gain admittance to these universities. In Europe, these North American women acted as the entering wedge for all women; they were the exceptions that eventually became the rule. In North America, they were the ones who realized how important it was to create a system of financial support for women's research, so that women could compete with men in higher education in disciplines that were becoming increasingly more professionalized.

Just as the story of these women began in Zurich, the first German-speaking university to allow women to matriculate, it ends in Zurich with a collection of essays published by a collective of feminist researchers. In 1988 these researchers began their study by asking, who still remembered that in 1867 Zurich became the first German-speaking university to allow women to earn a degree? Who still knew the names or accomplishments of those first women students? The 120 years of women's education were something to celebrate but they were a cause not only for joy. Over a century later, women at Swiss universities were still struggling for fair representation among the faculty. The struggles and accomplishments of nineteenth-century women pioneers in higher education had been forgotten.[1] Twenty-five years later the record of these pioneers is richer, fleshed out with the work of scores of researchers in Europe and North America. There is much reason to hope that the story of these pioneers will not be lost again. The examples of courage, brilliance and solidarity recorded here are still enough to inspire those traveling into this new century.

Notes

INTRODUCTION

1. Marjorie Housepian Dobkin, ed., *The Making of a Feminist: Early Journals and Letters of M. Carey Thomas* (Kent, OH: Kent State University Press, 1979) 262. Matriculation records for the medical school of the University of Zurich show that the American Emma Culberston [sic] of New Albany enrolled as a medical student at the university in 1882 (Staatsarchiv des Kantons Zürich, Matriculation Nr. 06461). Culbertson was born on December 2, 1854, in New Albany, Indiana. Before coming to Zurich, she had completed her Bachelor's (1877) and her Master's (1881) at Vassar. In 1881 she completed her medical degree at the Woman's Medical College of Pennsylvania. Culbertson was supposedly the first woman elected to the American Academy of Medicine. Culbertson returned from Zurich to work as a surgeon at the New England Hospital for Women and Children in Boston. See: John William Leonard, *Woman's Who's Who of America 1914-1915* (Detroit, MI: Gale Research Company, 1976) 220.

2. Dobkin, ed., *The Making of a Feminist* 234.

3. Dobkin, ed., *The Making of a Feminist* 234.

4. Dobkin, ed., *The Making of a Feminist* 265.

5. Other women's colleges had graduate programs but not a graduate school. For example, women were doing graduate work at Smith College as early as the 1881/82 academic year.

6. Only 598 of the original 1,266 database records include prior studies.

7. The following fifty-one women from the **University of Chicago** studied at German-speaking universities (with the year of graduation from the University of Chicago given in parentheses when possible): Ida C. Allen (1894); Amelia D. Alpiner; Anna Lavinia van Benschofen (Master's); Charlotte Bird (1894); Anne Lucy Bosworth (Master's 1893); Caroline M. Breyfogle (1894); Edith Clawson (1901); Theka Cole; Katharine Bement Davis (Ph.D. 1900); Flora Adams, nee Dodson; Thekla Doniat (1901); Lillian Dudley (1900); Julia F. Peet, nee Dumke (1898); Dorothea Duncan; Rose Falconer (1904); Sara Feichenfeld; Ida B. Fleischer; Jessie S. Gardner; Alice M. Gray (1903); Katharina Griffith; Clara M. Hitchcock (1897); Alma Towne, nee Ihrig; Stella Johns (1904); Dr. Jessie Louise Jones (Ph.D. 1897); Fay Kellermann (Master's 1899); Angeline Loesch (1898); Helen A. Merrill; Dr. Geneva Miesener

(Ph.D. 1903); Georgia Mills; Ina A. Milroy; M. Rowena Morse; Anna Helene Palmié; Loveen Pattee; Sarah Patterson (1904, Master's 1907); Dr. Janet Russell Perkins; Caroline L. Ransom (Master's 1900, Ph.D. 1905); Charlotta Reichmann (1899); Luanna Robertson; Lydia Schmidt (1901); Blanche Simmons; Adelaide Smith; Nettie Spencer (1899); Helen Bradford Thompson (Ph.D. 1900); Henrietta Tromanhauser (1900); Rebecca Turner; Anna Louise Wangeman (1907); Maria Waples (1901); Helen Whitehead (1904); Lucy A. Winston; Mary Frances Winston (Newson); Evelyn M. Lovejoy, nee Wood.

The following thirteen additional **University of Chicago** alumnae included in this study did not have prior studies listed or were not part of the original database: Katharine Susan Anthony (1905); Emily Greene Balch (1895); Edna Carter (graduate studies, 1898); Fanny Cook Gates (postgraduate studies, 1910); Kate Gordon (1900, Ph.D. 1903); Anna Johnson (Pell Wheeler) (Ph.D. 1910); Amy Hewes (Ph.D. 1903); May Lansfield Keller; Mary Kingsbury; Elizabeth Dabney Langhorne Lewis; Maude Menten (Ph.D. 1916); Julia B. Platt; Anna Pritchett Youngman (1904, Ph.D. 1908).

8. The following twenty-nine women from **Bryn Mawr** studied at German-speaking universities (with the year of graduation from Bryn Mawr given in parentheses when possible): Emily Greene Balch (1889); Dr. Helen Bartlett (Ph.D., 1896); Helene Billmeyer (1902); Jeanette Eva Carter; Alice Carter; Ida Prescott Clough; Isabel Frances Dodd; Helen Emerson; Clara E. Farr; Susan Braley Franklin (1889, Ph.D. 1895); Ellen Giles; Elizabeth Dabney Langhorne Lewis (1901); Grace Perley Locke; Helen J. McKeen; Kate Niles Morse; Emilie Norton-Martin (1894); Marion Edwards Park; Elizabeth Mary Perkins; Virginia Ragsdale (1896); Amy Cordoba Ransome, nee Rock (1893); Helen Elizabeth Schaeffer (Huff) (Master's 1905); Emily Shields; Helen Winifred Moulton, nee Shute; Caroline T. Stewart; Lydia L. Tilley; Helen Tredway; Florence C. Vickers; Winifred Warren (Wilson); Mary Frances Winston (Newson).

The following nineteen additional **Bryn Mawr** alumnae included in this study did not have prior studies listed or were not part of the original database: Alice Middleton Boring (1904); Margaret E. Brusstar (1903); Bertha May Clark; Elizabeth Deborah Ellis; Fanny Cook Gates; Ruth Gentry (Ph.D. 1896); Edith Hamilton (1895); Esther Harmon (Ph.D.); Mary Inda Hussey (Ph.D. 1906); Elizabeth R. Laird (Ph.D. 1901); Marion Parris; Florence Peebles (Ph.D. 1900); Julia B. Platt; Harriet Randolph (1889); Adah Blanche Roe (Ph.D. 1914); Lillian Vaughan Sampson (1891); Nettie Maria Stevens (Ph.D. 1903); Hope Traver (Ph.D. 1907); Anna Sophie Weusthoff.

9. The following thirty-nine women from **Wellesley** studied at German-speaking universities (with the year of graduation from Wellesley given in parentheses when possible): Mabel M. Adams; Clara Blattner; Fannie B. Bliss; Anne Lucy Bosworth (1890); Mary Brotherton (1897); Clara Brown; Ellen Burrell; Mariana Cogswell (1890); Maud A. Dodge; Georgia Etchison; Clara E. Farr; Caroline Fitz-Randolph; Maud M. French; Leah Friend (1903); Eleanor Acheson McCulloch Gamble (1889); Maude Gilchrist; Florence E. Hastings (1897); Josephine Wright, nee Hayward (1898); Flora Heinz (1904); Mary Hewett (1899); Flora E. Hidden (1890); Frances Libby; Anne Louise Lord; Sarah Louise Magone (1890); Oriola Martin (1898); Winona Martin (1898); Helen A. Merrill (1886); Mary W. Montgomery (1896); Hester Nichols; Frances E. Pinkham (1893); Ethel Putney (1902); Adelia Randall (1895); Frida Raynal (1897); Charlotte F. Roberts (1880); Katharine Schoepperle; Adelaide Smith (1893); Bertha Trebein (1897); Mary L. Wheeler; Lewanna Wilkins.

The following nine additional **Wellesley** alumnae included in this study did not have prior studies listed or were not part of the original database: Mary Taylor Blauvelt (1889); Grace Emily Cooley (1885); Rebecca Lee Dorsey (1881); Marjorie

B. Hemingway (1900); Alice Leonard (1881); Alice Hanson Luce (1883); Martha
Mann Magoun; Alice E. Whiting (1900); Carolyn Wilson (1910).

    10. The following thirty-four women from **Smith** studied at German-speaking
universities (with the year of graduation from Smith given in parentheses when possible): Mary Dean Adams (1899); Mary Eleanor Barrons; Daisy Luana Blaisdell
(1888); Grace D. Chester (Master's); Ellen Parmalee Cook (1893); Sarah Josephine
Cook (1900); Mary Dewey; Alice P. Goodwin; Mary Chapman Hardy (1885); Harriet
Eleanor Holden (1893); Margaret Holman (1902); Ella Hurtt; Dorothea Katzschmar
(1899); Ruth Alida Ramsey, nee Lusk (1901); Kristine Mann (1895); Sara Brayton
Marsh (1895); Frances Osgood (1898); Beatrice Pickett (1900); Georgia Washir Pope
(1896); Emma Ernestine Porter (1897); Mary H. Poud (1904); Mary E. Raymond;
Carrie Anna Babson, nee Richardson (1896); Helen Lois Russell (1907); Eloise Bent-
ley Santee (1899); Helen Winifred Moulton, nee Shute (1887); Mary Appleton Shute
(1887); Alice Skilton; Theodate Smith (1882); Elisabeth Southworth (1904); Nettie
Strobhar (1907); Bertha Alice Tildsley, nee Watters (1894); Maude Lucy White
(1899); Grace Whiting (1897).

    The following eleven additional **Smith** alumnae included in this study did not
have prior studies listed or were not part of the original database: Mary Whiton
Calkins (1885); Ethel Craighead; Clara E. Heywood (1900); Anne Louise Leonard;
Ethel Puffer (Howes) (1891); Edith M. Ramage (1900); Theodate Smith (Master's,
1884); Harriet Snell (1882); Alice Walton (1887); Cora May Williams (1883); Ruth
Goulding Wood (1898).

    11. The following thirty-one women from the **University of Michigan** studied
at German-speaking universities (with the year of graduation from the University of
Michigan given in parentheses when possible): Arletta Abott; Dora Bennett;
Winifred Bogle (1900); Mary E. B. Markley, nee Buttler; Dr. Sarah E. Conner; Leon-
ore Crowell (1904); Lucy C. Davis; Rachel Ella Dawson; Dr. Lydia M. Dewitt; Annie
Dunster (1895); Louise Fitz-Randolph-Gay; Ida B. Fleischer; Emilie Flintermann
(1898); Caroline De Greene; Maria R. Guppy; Nellie Hamilton (Master's 1904);
Esther Harmon (1906); Irma Heath; Ellen Hinsdale (Master's 1893); Mary F. Leach;
Lucila Matchett (1902); Minnie Mateva; Eleanor Oliver (1902); Luella Read (1903);
Margery Rosing (1904); Rush Scott; Jennie Belle Sherzer (1893); Edith van Slyke
(1903); Caroline T. Stewart (Master's 1895); Mary Esther Trueblood (Master's
1896); Grete B. Young (1899).

    The following four additional **University of Michigan** alumnae included in this
study did not have prior studies listed or were not part of the original database:
Mary Hegeler Carus (1882); Ruth Gentry (1890); Alice Hamilton (MD 1893);
Gertrude Sunderland Safford.

    12. The following twenty-one women from **Cornell University** studied at Ger-
man-speaking universities (with the year of graduation from Cornell given in paren-
theses when possible): Harriet Ballon (1895); Martha Barrett; Anna Lavinia van
Benschofen (Ph.D. 1908); Mary Burton (1903); Sarah M. Gallahn; Eleanor Acheson
McCulloch Gamble (Ph.D. 1898); Eloise Harding (1900); Mary Elizabeth Highet;
Winnfred Jewell; Fay Kellermann (Master's 1899); Clara H. Kerr; Helen Knox;
Gertrude Kunze (1901); Dr. Anne Louise MacKinnon (Ph.D. 1894); Maud Manfred
(1900); M. Rowena Morse; Anne Helene Palmié; Clara E. Schonton; Effie June Scott;
Janet Collier, nee Sheldon (1894); Grace Fleming Sweringen (1893).

    The following eleven additional **Cornell University** alumnae included in this
study did not have prior studies listed or were not part of the original database:
Grace Neal Dolson (1896, Ph.D. 1899); Florence Kelley (1882); Mary Elizabeth
Laing; Janet Donalda MacFee; Frances Mitchell; Pauline Orr; Margaret Keiver Smith;
Julia Warner Snow (1888, Master's 1889); Edith Corrinne Stephenson; Martha Carey
Thomas (1877); Alice Walton (Ph.D. 1892).

13. The following twenty women from **Vassar** studied at German-speaking universities (with the year of graduation from Vassar given in parentheses when possible): Helen Abbott; Gertrud Barnard (1892); Laura F. Beach; Ada Bristel (1904); Lucy Burns (1902); Lula P. Burr; Katharine Bement Davis; Lucretia Eddy (1898); Helen Foster (1901); Florence W. Howe; Lillien J. Martin (1880); Jessie Hyde Mathews; Harriet Milinowski, nee Ransom (1878); Mary Holmes Morgan; Marie Reimer; Anna G. Richey; Agnes Hayes, nee Stone (1898); Elisabeth Upton; Mabel Waller (1900); Norma Waterburg (1904).

The following eight additional **Vassar** alumnae included in this study did not have prior studies listed or were not part of the original database: Emma Brill; Edna Carter (1894); Annie Galbraith; Christine Ladd-Franklin (1869); Jennie Giehl (1902); Eugenie M. Morenus (1904, Master's 1905); Ellen Churchill Semple (1882, Master's 1891); Hope Traver (1896).

14. The following twenty-three women from **Harvard/Radcliffe** studied at German-speaking universities (with the year of graduation from Harvard/Radcliffe given in parentheses when possible): Grace C. Alden; Alice Arnold; Selia M. Bingham; Mabel Hodder, nee Boomer (Master's 1893); Mary Cady (Master's 1905); Mary Whiton Calkins; Grace D. Chester; Ida Prescott Clough (1896; 1899); Emily Helen Dutton; Myra Ellis; L. Annie Griffin; Mabel Hammond (1906); Rachel Hibbard (Master's 1903); Anna Johnson (Pell Wheeler); Mary M. Kingsbury; Ethel Lyons (1907); Grace Harriet Macurdy; Mary Elizabeth Perley; Anna Pushee; Annie L. Ransom; Dr. Eleanor Rowland (Ph.D. 1905); Katharine Schoepperle; Jeanette Wilson.

The following additional five **Harvard/Radcliffe** alumnae included in this study did not have prior studies listed or were not part of the original database: Emily Greene Balch; Carrie Matilda Derrick; Rachel Lloyd; Pauline Orr; Julia B. Platt.

15. The following twenty-one women from **Mount Holyoke** studied at German-speaking universities (with the year of graduation from Mount Holyoke given in parentheses when possible): Florence L. Adams; Grace Bacon (1901); Frances Davidson; Elizabeth H. Denio (1866); Elisabeth Dunning; Emily Helen Dutton; Julia Blau, nee Ellsworth; Gertrude Gaylord (1900); Mary Alling Hall; Marion Tyler Herrick (1895); Nellie Louise Hill; Marcia A. Keith; Mary F. Leach; Kate Niles Morse; Elizabeth Oakford; Louise F. Randolph; Caroline L. Ransom; Gertrude Sherman (1902); Alice P. Stevens; Charlotta David, nee Tenney (1894); Irma Wieand (1901).

16. The following ten women from **Columbia/** studied at German-speaking universities (with the year of graduation from Columbia/Barnard given in parentheses when possible): Harriet Brackett; Katharine Bement Davis; Alisa van Dyke; Franciska Miller; Annina Periam (Danton) (Master's 1901, Ph.D. 1905); Alice Seligsberg; Adelaide Smith; Ettie Stettheimer (1896, Master's 1898); Jennie R. White; Else Peacock, nee Wortmann.

The following nine additional **Columbia/Barnard** alumnae included in this study did not have prior studies listed or were not part of the original database: Ethel Browne (Harvey) (Ph.D. 1913); Ethel Craighead; Jennie Giehl (Master's, 1908); Mary Jane Hogue; Mary Kingsbury; Laura Emilie Mau (1910, Master's 1912); Eugenie M. Morenus; Pauline Orr (Master's); Harriet Randolph.

17. The following twelve women from **Goucher** studied at German-speaking universities (with the year of graduation from Goucher given in parentheses when possible): Eva Louise Barr (1896); Bertha May Clark (1900); Waunda Hartshorn (1898); Amy Hewes (1897); May Lansfield Keller (1898); Mabel H. Kennedy; Virginia Wadlow Kennedy (1896); Jessie Loeffler (1899); Annina Periam (Danton) (1898); Belle C. Shaw; Johnetta Van Meter (1894); Anna Sophie Weusthoff (1906).

The following six additional **Goucher** alumnae included in this study did not have prior studies listed or were not part of the original database: Ethel Browne

(Harvey) (1906); Mary Jane Hogue (1905); Florence Peebles (1895); Margaret Adaline Reed (Lewis) (1901); Adah Blanche Roe (1909); Helen Walker (1900).

18. The following sixteen women from **Stanford** studied at German-speaking universities (with the year of graduation from Stanford given in parentheses when possible): Ruth Brown (1904); Margaret Deming; Klara Eberhard (1897); Laura Emery (1899); Louise Gerich; Edith Hill (1903); Adele Meyer; Emma Rendtorff, nee Meyer (1898); Mary Montague Powers; Janette Rossiter (1896); Dorothea Heinemann, nee Roth (1900); Sara M. Spalsbury; Laura Steffens; Lottie Steffens; Mary C. Webster; Helen Younger.

One additional **Stanford** alumna included in this study, Nettie Maria Stevens (1899, Master's 1900), did not have prior studies listed or was not part of the original database.

19. The following fifteen women from **Oberlin** studied at German-speaking universities (with the year of graduation from Oberlin given in parentheses when possible): Ida C. Allen; Harriet Brackett; Anna M. Crisman (1903); Alien Daniels (1899); Alta-Grace Ellis (1902); Florence Mary Fitch (1897); Faith Fraser (1903); Georgia W. Willard, nee Johnson; Ruth Kemmer (1908?); Dr. Margaret Eliza Maltby (1882, Master's); Jennette E. Marsh; Hattie Peck (1891); Harriet Sawyer, nee Price (1894); Caroline Weiss; Helen Martin, nee White (1897).

The following two **Oberlin Conservatory of Music** alumnae included in this study did not have prior studies listed or were not part of the original database: Mary Lucinda Regal; Gail Hamilton Ridgway.

20. The following fifteen women from the **University of Wisconsin** studied at German-speaking universities (with the year of graduation from the University of Wisconsin given in parentheses when possible): Mildred Averill (1897); Caroline M. Breyfogle; Esther Cary; Alma Towne, nee Ihrig; Emma Jaeck; Nellie Noyes (1894); Lenore O'Connor; Dr. Janet Russell Perkins (1872); Frances Roddis; Mary D. Rodmann; Julia Ruebhausen (1899); Susan A. Sterling; Martha E. Torgerson; Margerethe Urdahl; Mary Frances Winston (Newson) (1889).

The following two additional **University of Wisconsin** alumnae included in this study did not have prior studies listed or were not part of the original database: Florence Bascom (1884, Master's 1887); Adolphine B. Ernst (1901, Master's 1907).

21. The following thirteen women from **Boston University** studied at German-speaking universities (with the year of graduation from Boston University given in parentheses when possible): Sally Clough (1903); Linda French (1902); Helene Harrington; Katharina Hodgdon; Mary M. Kingsbury (1890); Jessie Hyde Mathews; Gertrud Merril (1901); Marion Nickerson (1903); Alice Quirin (1902); Harriet S. Sawyer; Helene C. Seidensticker; Florence D. Shepherd; Winifred Warren (Wilson) (1891).

The following three additional **Boston University** alumnae included in this study did not have prior studies listed or were not part of the original database: Eva Channing (1877); Mabel Daniels; Rebecca Lee Dorsey.

22. The following eleven women from the **University of California** (Berkeley) studied at German-speaking universities (with the year of graduation from the University of California given in parentheses when possible): Emelyn Margolis, nee Aronson; Dr. R. Leona Ash; Georgia Etchison; Dr. Grace Feder; Fidelia Jewett; Else Mehlmann; Lucy H. Priber; Anita Putzker; Dr. Frances Greene, nee Rosenberg; Gertrud Simmons; Jennie R. White (1893).

The following two additional **University of California** alumnae included in this study did not have prior studies listed or were not part of the original database: Elizabeth A. Herrmann (1902); Harriet Randolph.

23. The following twelve women from **Swarthmore** studied at German-speaking universities (with the year of graduation from Swarthmore given in parentheses when

possible): Ellen Williams Battin, Caroline F. Comly; Jeanette Curtis (1907); Mary Gray Leiper; Elizabeth B. Miller; Clara P. Newport (1903); Edna H. Richards; Winifred Rogers; Amelia Skillin; Alice Tabor (1902); Zaida E. Udell; Maude Watters (1902).

24. The following eleven women from **Syracuse University** studied at German-speaking universities (with the year of graduation from Syracuse given in parentheses when possible): Minnie Beebe; Corinth Cook; Adelaide L. Dicklow (Master's 1891); Cora M. Dodson; Jeanette F. Graham; Janet Harris (1901); Sarah Cobb, nee Karson; Sonia Oldham; Lydia Marie Thomsen; Delight Williams; Anne Grace Wirt (1884, Master's 1887).

One additional alumna of **Syracuse University** included in this study did not have prior studies listed or was not part of the original database: Jane Marie Bancroft (Robinson) (1877, Ph.D. 1884).

25. The following eleven women from the **University of Toronto** studied at German-speaking universities (with the year of graduation from the University of Toronto given in parentheses when possible): Janthe Constantinides (Master's 1902); Georgina Cowan (1896); Mary Emerson, nee Fife (1898); Caroline Goad (1899); Mina Hutton; Mary Johnston; Elizabeth Rebecca Laird (1896); Mabel K. Mason; Florence Neelands; Agnes Rebecca Libby, nee Phillips; Louise L. Ryckman.

26. The following nine women from the **University of Kansas** studied at German-speaking universities (with the year of graduation from the University of Kansas given in parentheses when possible): Carrie O. Anderson; Dollie Hortense Brookover (1901); Mary Davis; Lillian Dudley; Dr. Annie Louise MacKinnon (1889, Master's 1891); Kate L. Riggs; Caroline T. Stewart (1892); Elizabeth Titt, nee Warren (1897); Esther Wilson (1901).

The following additional alumna of the **University of Kansas**, Virginia Eviline Spencer (1891), did not have prior studies listed or was not part of the original database.

CHAPTER ONE: STUDYING ABROAD

1. For a recent study including contributions by most of the major researchers in this area, see: Henry Geitz, Jürgen Heideking and Jurgen Herbst, eds., *German Influences on Education in the United States to 1917* (New York: Cambridge University Press, 1995).

2. James C. Albisetti, "German Influence on the Higher Education of American Women, 1865-1914," *German Influences on Education in the United States to 1917*, eds. Henry Geitz, Jürgen Heideking and Jurgen Herbst (New York: Cambridge University Press, 1995). American historian Penny Smith Eifrig has been doing research on the role of German universities in American higher education for women. Her incomplete (as of March 2002) dissertation from the Freie Universität Berlin is titled "Amerikanische Frauen und deutsche Universitäten 1865-1915: 50 Jahre akademischer Austausch und die Entwicklung der Graduate Studies für Frauen. Eine Kollektivbiographie der Fakultät und Studentenschaft von Bryn Mawr, Smith, Vassar und Wellesley Colleges."

3. Margaret W. Rossiter, *Women Scientists in America: Struggles and Strategies to 1940* (Baltimore, MD: The Johns Hopkins University Press, 1982) 29.

4. Albisetti, "German Influence on the Higher Education of American Women, 1865-1914," 234.

5. Dorothy Gies McGuigan, *A dangerous experiment. 100 years of women at the University of Michigan* (Ann Arbor, MI: Center for Continuing Education of Women, 1970) 18.

6. Albisetti, "German Influence on the Higher Education of American Women, 1865-1914," 234.

7. Albisetti, "German Influence on the Higher Education of American Women, 1865-1914," 235.

8. Charlotte Williams Conable, *Women at Cornell: The Myth of Equal Education* (Ithaca, NY: Cornell University Press, 1977) 52-53.

9. Conable, *Women at Cornell* 68.

10. A sum of $354,000 was raised by the Women's Medical School Fund, which was organized in May 1890. One of the key organizers and donors was Mary E. Garrett, who established the Bryn Mawr Preparatory School in Baltimore, Maryland. Garrett also provided the necessary financial backing for M. Carey Thomas's bid to become president of Bryn Mawr College. See: Kathleen Waters Sander, "Trailblazer for women doctors," *The Baltimore Sun* March 4, 2001.

11. Albisetti, "German Influence," 237.

12. Patricia Albjerg Graham, "Expansion and Exclusion: A History of Women in American Higher Education," *Signs* Summer 1978: 764.

13. Graham, "Expansion and Exclusion," 764.

14. Although women were officially allowed to enroll at Cornell from the very beginning, a number of conditions made it almost impossible for women to actually do so. The first woman student, Jennie Spencer, arrived in 1870 and left shortly thereafter because of inadequate housing on campus. See: Conable, *Women at Cornell* 65-66.

15. Conable, *Women at Cornell* 25.

16. The admission of women to the University of Michigan was a particularly important triumph, as it was at the time "the largest university in the country and had by far the greatest prestige of any college west of New England." See: McGuigan, *A dangerous experiment* 30.

17. Annie Nathan Meyer, *Woman's work in America* (New York: Henry Holt and Co., 1891) 424-37.

18. Isabel Maddison and Bryn Mawr College and Graduate Club, *Handbook of British, continental and Canadian universities, with special mention of the courses open to women,* 2nd ed. (New York: Macmillan Company, 1899).

19. For a discussion of professionalization in the sciences during the nineteenth century and the exclusion of women, see: Rossiter, *Women Scientists in America: Struggles and Strategies to 1940* 73-99. For a discussion of professionalization in the nineteenth century art world and the effect on women, see: Kirsten N. Swinth, "Painting Professionals: Women Artists and the Development of a Professional Ideal in American Art, 1870-1920," Diss, Yale University, 1995, 1-24.

20. Margaret W. Rossiter, "Doctorates for American Women, 1868-1907," *History of Education Quarterly* Summer (1982): 159-60.

21. Rossiter, "Doctorates," 162; Walter Crosby Eells, "Earned Doctorates for Women in the Nineteenth Century," *American Association of University Professors Bulletin* 42 (1956).

22. Rossiter, "Doctorates," 164.

23. Rossiter, "Doctorates," 174.

24. Rossiter, "Doctorates," 172.

25. For an excellent comparison of American and German graduate programs in mathematics, see: Della Dumbaugh Fenster and Karen Hunger Parshall, "A Profile of the American Mathematical Research Community: 1891-1906," *The History of Modern Mathematics*, eds. Eberhard Knobloch and David E. Rowe, vol. 3 (San Diego, CA: Academic Press, 1994).

26. Rossiter, *Women Scientists in America: Struggles and Strategies to 1940* 39-40.

27. Only one American woman studied at the University of Tübingen before 1915. Janet MacLure from New York audited classes in 1906. For a complete list of the 191 American men who studied at Tübingen between 1829 and 1915, see: Volker Schäfer, Uwe Jens Wandel and Irmela Klöden, *USA – Universität Tübingen. Die Amerika-Beziehungen der schwäbischen Landesuniversität im Kaleidoskop. Eine Ausstellung...aus Anlass des 200. Jahrestages der amerikanischen Unabhängigkeit,* Werkschriften des Universitätsarchiv Tübingen. Reihe 2, vol. 7 (Tübingen: Universitätsarchiv Tübingen, 1976). For a thorough study of women students at Tübingen, see: Edith Glaser, *Hindernisse, Umwege, Sackgassen: Die Anfänge des Frauenstudiums in Tübingen (1904-1934)* (Weinheim: Deutscher Studien Verlag, 1992).

28. According to existing archival records, only a handful of North Americans attended the University of Vienna as either auditors or matriculated students during the period covered in this study. No North American woman earned a doctoral degree there before 1915 and there were only four auditors. The first auditor, Hannah E. Klappholz-Wood from Bonham, Texas, arrived for the Winter Semester 1903/04 and took courses in philology, English, philosophy and art history. In 1905 Klappholz left Vienna to continue her studies at Zurich. In 1905 Ida von Götz from Pennsylvania audited classes in pedagogy, German history and algebra. The next auditor, Florence Margaret Brooks from Cleveland, Ohio, came for the Winter Semester of 1906/07 and studied mathematics and philosophy. She had previously attended Western Reserve University in Cleveland (Case Western Reserve University). The fourth auditor was Dr. Erla Hittle Rodakiewick from Richmond, Indiana, who had earned a doctoral degree from Heidelberg in December 1900. The topic of her dissertation was "The History of the Old English Prepositions 'mid' and 'wid' with Consideration of their two-sided Relationship"(Zur Geschichte der altenglischen Präpositionen 'mid' und 'wid' mit Berücksichtigung ihrer beiderseitigen Beziehungen). Her thesis appeared in 1901 in *Anglistische Forschungen,* Issue 2. Although Hittle received her dissertation from Heidelberg, there are no records that she ever audited or enrolled in courses there. At Vienna, she took classes in English literature and philology. See: Universitätsarchiv Heidelberg, Promotionskartei der philosophischen Fakultät; and Universitätsarchiv Wien, (1) Frauenstudium Promotionsregister, 1897-1914/15, (2) Nationale, Philosophische Fakultät, 1897-1914/15, (3) Nationale, Medizinische Fakultät, 1897-1914/15.

29. According to the matriculation records at the German part of Charles University in Prague, no North American women studied there through 1915. This information was provided by Jana Ratajova of Charles University. The matriculation records of the University of Breslau include the name of only one North American woman, Mary Violette (Violet) Dover, through 1915, although Leonard, *Woman's Who's Who of America 1914-1915* mentions one other Canadian, Bella Marcuse McIntosh, who supposedly studied at Breslau during the 1900/01 academic year. Both Marcuse and Dover were graduates of the chemistry department at McGill University.

30. The following is a list of the pre-World War I German states and the semester in which women were first allowed to matriculate at universities in that state. The list also includes the cities with universities in that state: Baden (Freiburg and Heidelberg) in Summer Semester 1900; Bavaria (Erlangen, Munich and Würzburg) in Winter Semester 1903/04; Württemberg (Tübingen) in Summer Semester 1904; Saxony (Leipzig) in Summer Semester 1906; Saxony-Weimar (Jena) in Summer Semester 1907; Prussia (Berlin, Bonn, Breslau, Göttingen, Greifswald, Kiel, Königsberg, Marburg and Münster) in Winter Semester 1908/09; Hessen (Gießen) in Winter Semester 1908/09; Alsace-Lorraine (Strasbourg) in Winter Semester 1908/09; Mecklenburg-Schwerin (Rostock) in Winter Semester 1909/10. Margret Lemberg, ed., *Es begann vor hundert Jahren. Die ersten Frauen an der Universität Marburg und die Studen-*

tinnenvereinigungen bis zur Gleichschaltung im Jahre 1934. Catalog of exhibition. 21 Jan-23 Feb 1997. Universitätsbibliothek Marburg (Marburg: Universitätsbibliothek Marburg, 1997) 45-47.

31. Kenneth M. Ludmerer, *Learning to heal: the development of American medical education* (New York: Basic Books, 1985); W. F. Bynum, *Science and the practice of medicine in the nineteenth century,* Cambridge history of science (New York: Cambridge University Press, 1994).

32. Jane B. Sherzer, "Women at the German Universities," *The Nation* 58 (1894): 116.

33. Frances Mitchell Froelicher, "Post-Graduate Work in a German University," *Kalends (Goucher)* February 1896: 114.

34. Froelicher, "Post-Graduate Work," 112.

35. Froelicher, "Post-Graduate Work," 114.

36. Waunda Hartshorn, "A Student in Freiburg," *Kalends (Goucher)* March 1901: 205. Waunda Hartshorn had earned her Bachelor's at Goucher College (1898) before traveling to Germany. She later married Alexander Petrunkevitch, an expert on arachnids who taught at Yale. Alumnae Biographical Files, Waunda Hartshorn, 1898, Goucher College Archives, Baltimore, Maryland.

37. Hartshorn, "A Student in Freiburg," 206.

38. Hartshorn, "A Student in Freiburg," 206.

39. Hartshorn, "A Student in Freiburg," 207.

40. Hartshorn, "A Student in Freiburg," 206.

41. Henrie (Ettie Stettheimer) Waste, *Philosophy: An Autobiographical Fragment* (New York: Longmans, Green and Co., 1917) 20.

42. For further details of the case of Ray Beveridge from New York, see: Laetitia Boehm, "Von den Anfängen des akademischen Frauenstudiums in Deutschland. Zugleich ein Kapitel aus der Geschichte der Ludwig-Maximilians-Universität München," *Historisches Jahrbuch* 77 (1958): 314.

43. Anna Maude Bowen, "A Woman Student's Experience in German Universities," *The Nation* 65 (1897): 262.

44. G. T. F., "Pioneer Women Students in Germany," *The Nation* 64 (1897).

45. Mabel Dunbar, "Das Deutsche Fräulein," *Scarlet and Black (Grinnell)* March 14, 1906.

46. Franziska Rogger, *Der Doktorhut im Besenschrank; das abenteuerliche Leben der ersten Studentinnen am Beispiel der Universität Bern* (Bern: eFeF Verlag, 1999) 9.

47. Brackets in original. "Johnetta" is Johnetta Van Meter, who was studying in Europe like May Lansfield Keller on a Goucher Alumnae Fellowship. Pauline Turnbull, *May Lansfield Keller: Life and Letters, 1877-1964* (Verona, VA: McClure Press, 1975) 124. Ethel Puffer Howes also writes in her letters home about taking a risk and attending courses without official permission to do so. See: Elizabeth Scarborough and Laurel Furumoto, *Untold Lives: The First Generation of American Women Psychologists* (New York: Columbia University Press, 1987) 77.

48. Birgit Eckardt, "Zwei Amerikanerinnen in Jena – Lucinde Pearl Boggs und Rowena Morse," *Entwurf und Wirklichkeit. Frauen in Jena 1900-1933,* eds. Gisela Horn and Birgitt Hellmann (Rudolstadt and Jena: Hainverlag, 2001) 236-37.

49. Universitätsarchiv Heidelberg, Promotionskartei der philosophischen Fakultät.

50. Eckardt, "Zwei Amerikanerinnen," 238.

51. Alice Hamilton, *Exploring the dangerous trades: the autobiography of Alice Hamilton, M.D.* (Boston: Northeastern University Press, 1985) 45-46. A similar quote is found in: Alice Hamilton, "Edith and Alice Hamilton: Students in Germany," *The Atlantic Monthly* March 1965: 131.

52. Renate Tobies, "Zum Beginn des mathematischen Frauenstudiums in Preußen," *Gesch. Naturwissenschaftler, Techniker und Mediziner* 28.2 (1992): 152-53. The World's Columbian Exhibition in Chicago in 1893 had a Women's Pavilion that contained an exhibit on women's education. This proved to be an important exhibit for informing Europeans about educational opportunities in the United States and, in particular, about the level of education available at the women's colleges. For example, Albisetti mentions Hermann Osthoff, a professor at Heidelberg, who was impressed by the accomplishments of women students during his visit to the Columbian Exhibition. James C. Albisetti, *Schooling German Girls and Women* (Princeton, NJ: Princeton University Press, 1988) 226. Professors were also impressed by the college graduates they encountered at European universities and many willingly made exceptions to allow these women to earn graduate degrees. Numerous biographical sketches included throughout this text contain such examples.

53. Mary Caroline Crawford, *The College Girl of America and the Institutions Which Make Her What She Is*, 4 ed. (Boston: Colonial Press C. H. Simonds Co., 1915) 246.

54. Albisetti, *Schooling German Girls and Women* 225; Hans Krabusch, "Die Vorgeschichte des Frauenstudiums an der Universität Heidelberg," *Ruperto-Carola* 19 (1956): 137-38.

55. Renate Tobies, "'Aller Männerkultur zum Trotz': Frauen erwerben den Doktortitel in Mathematik," *Barrieren und Karrieren. Die Anfänge des Frauenstudiums in Deutschland. Dokumentationsband der Konferenz "100 Jahre Frauen in der Wissenschaft" im Februar 1997 an der Universität Bremen*, eds. Elisabeth Dickmann and Eva Schöck-Quinteros, vol. 5, Schriftenreihe des Hedwig-Hintze-Instituts Bremen (Berlin: trafo verlag dr. wolfgang weist, 2000) 235.

56. Albisetti, *Schooling German Girls and Women* 226.

57. Krabusch, "Die Vorgeschichte des Frauenstudiums," 138-39.

58. Albisetti, *Schooling German Girls and Women* 225-26.

59. "Editorial," *Wellesley Magazine* December 1895: 151-52.

60. Maddison and Club, *Handbook* 64-65.

61. Rossiter, *Women Scientists in America: Struggles and Strategies to 1940* 43; *The Nation* 66 (1898): 303-04.

62. Bowen, "A Woman Student's Experience," 9.

63. "Education for Women in Germany," *The Nation* 75 (1902): 108.

64. "Women's Uphill Fight in Germany," *New York Times* June 5, 1904: 4.

65. R. W., "Professor Munsterberg's Lecture," *Wellesley College News* May 16, 1906: 2.

66. "Fifty Years of Vassar," *The Nation* 101 (1915): 487.

67. Krabusch, "Die Vorgeschichte des Frauenstudiums," 138; Albisetti, *Schooling German Girls and Women* 242; Lemberg, ed., *Es begann vor hundert Jahren* 6-8.

68. Paul Schmidt, "Vorgeschichte und Anfänge des Frauenstudiums in Bonn," *Bonn und das Rheinland. Beiträge zur Geschichte und Kultur einer Region*, eds. Manfred van Rey and Norbert Schloßmacher (Bonn: 1992) 557.

69. Else Forrer-Gutknecht, *Das Frauenstudium an den Schweizer Hochschulen* (Zurich: Rascher and CIE, 1928) 41-42; Ute Gerhard, *Unerhört. Die Geschichte der deutschen Frauenbewegung* (Reinbek bei Hamburg: Rowohlt, 1990) 161; Franziska Tiburtius, *Weibliches Schaffen und Wirken: Erinnerungen einer Achtzigjährigen* (Berlin: C. A. Schwetschke & Sohn, 1929).

70. For more on Käthe Windscheid, see: Boehm, "Von den Anfängen," 312; Albisetti, *Schooling German Girls and Women* 226; *The Nation* 69 (1899): 94. For further information on Hildegard Ziegler, see: Antje Dertinger, "Abends fuhr man im Boot auf der Saale," *Mitteldeutsche Zeitung* April 2, 1993; Projektgruppe des Cour-

age, *Frauenleben – Frauenalltag – gestern und heute. Hallenserinnen – Biographische Skizzen Teil II* (Halle: Courage e.V., 1995) 23-24. For more on Clara Immerwahr, see the excellent biography: Gerit von Leitner, *Der Fall Clara Immerwahr. Leben für eine humane Wissenschaft* (Munich: C. H. Beck, 1994).

It is beyond the scope of this study to discuss all the accomplishments of German women in their efforts to gain access to German universities. There is an extensive and growing body of literature on the topic. A brief list of recommended works follows: Albisetti, *Schooling German Girls and Women;* Albisetti, "German Influence."; Boehm, "Von den Anfängen."; Hadumod Bußmann, ed., *Stieftöchter der Alma Mater? 90 Jahre Frauenstudium in Bayern - am Beispiel der Universität München. Katalog zur Ausstellung 1993/94* (Munich: 1993); Ilse Costas, "Der Beginn des Frauenstudiums an der Universität Göttingen. Die Wissenschaft, das 'Wesen der Frau' und erste Schritte zur Öffnung männerdominierter Karrieren," *Göttingen ohne Gänseliesel. Texte und Bilder zur Stadtgeschichte*, eds. Kornelia Duwe, Carola Gottschalk and Marianne Koerner, 2nd ed. (Gudensberg-Gleichen: Wartberg Verlag, 1989); Elisabeth Dickmann and Eva Schöck-Quinteros, eds., *Barrieren und Karrieren. Die Anfänge des Frauenstudiums in Deutschland. Dokumentationsband der Konferenz "100 Jahre Frauen in der Wissenschaft" im Februar 1997 an der Universität Bremen*, vol. 5 (Berlin: trafo verlag dr. wolfgang weist, 2000); Renate Drucker, "Zur Vorgeschichte des Frauenstudiums an der Universität Leipzig. Aktenbericht," *Vom Mittelalter zur Neuzeit*, ed. Hellmut Kretzschmar, Forschungen zur Mittelalterlichen Geschichte 1 (Berlin: Rütten and Loening, 1956); Irene Franken, *"Ja, das Studium der Weiber ist schwer!" Studentinnen und Dozentinnen an der Kölner Universität bis 1933* (Cologne: Frauenbeauftragte der Universität zu Köln, Kölner Frauengeschichtsverein, Universitäts-und Stadtbibliothek Köln, 1995); Glaser, *Hindernisse;* Heike Hessenauer, *Etappen des Frauenstudiums an der Universität Würzburg (1869-1939)*, Quellen und Beiträge zur Geschichte der Universität Würzburg, ed. Peter Baumgart, vol. 4 (Neustadt an der Aisch: Verlag Degener & Co., 1998); Heike Hessenauer, "Studentinnen vor 1939 – Eine Fallstudie zur Entwicklung des Frauenstudiums," *Barrieren und Karrieren. Die Anfänge des Frauenstudiums in Deutschland. Dokumentationsband der Konferenz "100 Jahre Frauen in der Wissenschaft" im Februar 1997 an der Universität Bremen*, eds. Elisabeth Dickmann and Eva Schöck-Quinteros, vol. 5, Schriftenreihe des Hedwig-Hintze-Instituts Bremen (Berlin: trafo verlag dr. wolfgang weist, 2000); Gisela Horn, ed., *90 Jahre Frauenstudium an der Universität Jena*, vol. 2 (Rudolstadt: Hainverlag, 1999); Gisela Horn and Birgitt Hellmann, eds., *Entwurf und Wirklichkeit. Frauen in Jena 1900-1933* (Rudolstadt and Jena: Hainverlag, 2001); Elke Kleinau and Claudia Opitz, eds., *Geschichte der Mädchen-und Frauenbildung. Vom Vormärz bis zur Gegenwart*, vol. 2 (Frankfurt/Main and New York: Campus Verlag, 1996); Krabusch, "Die Vorgeschichte des Frauenstudiums."; Heidi Lauterer-Pirner and Margret Schepers-S.-W., "Studentin in Heidelberg," *Auch eine Geschichte der Universität Heidelberg*, eds. Karin Buselmeier, Dietrich Harth and Christian Jansen (Mannheim: Edition Quadrat, 1985); Lemberg, ed., *Es begann vor hundert Jahren;* Antke Luhn, "Geschichte des Frauenstudiums an der Medizinischen Fakultät der Universität Göttingen," University of Göttingen, 1972; E. Th. Nauck, *Das Frauenstudium an der Universität Freiburg i. Br.* (Freiburg i. Br.: Verlag Eberhard Albert Universitätsbuchhandlung, 1953); Anne Schlüter, *Pionierinnen - Feministinnen - Karrierefrauen? Zur Geschichte des Frauenstudiums in Deutschland*, Frauen in Geschichte und Gesellschaft, vol. 22 (Pfaffenweiler: Centaurus, 1992); Schmidt, "Vorgeschichte."; Tobies, "Zum Beginn."

For more on the efforts of the first women to study at the universities of Austria, see: Waltraud Heindl and Marina Tichy, *"Durch Erkenntnis zu Freiheit und Glück..." Frauen an der Universität Wien (ab 1897)*, Schriftenreihe des Universitätsarchivs

Universität Wien, eds. Günther Hamann, Kurt Mühlberger and Franz Skacel, vol. 5 (Vienna: WUV-Universitätsverlag, 1990).

For more on the first students at the Swiss universities, see: Katharina Belser, Gabi Einsele, Rachel Gratzfeld, et al., eds., *Ebenso neu als kühn: 120 Jahre Frauenstudium an der Universität Zürich.* (Zurich: eFeF Verlag, 1988); Ricarda Huch, *Frühling in der Schweiz. Jugenderinnerungen.*, 4th ed. (Zurich: Atlantis-Verlag, 1938); Daniela Neumann, *Studentinnen aus dem Russischen Reich in der Schweiz (1867-1914)*, Die Schweiz und der Osten Europas, ed. Carsten Goehrke, vol. 1 (Zurich: Hans Rohr, 1987); Rogger, *Der Doktorhut;* Hanny Rohner, *Die ersten 30 Jahre des medizinischen Frauenstudiums an der Universität Zürich, 1867-1897* (Zurich: Juris Druck, 1972); Johanna Siebel, *Das Leben von Frau Dr. Marie Heim-Vögtlin der ersten Schweizer Ärztin, 1845-1916* (Leipzig: Rascher and CIE. A.G., 1928); Verena Stadler-Labhart, *Rosa Luxemburg an der Universität Zürich (1889-1897)* (Zurich: Verlag Hans Rohr, 1978); Tiburtius, *Weibliches Schaffen.*

71. Drucker, "Zur Vorgeschichte," 280; Albisetti, *Schooling German Girls and Women* 122-23; Ann Hibner Koblitz, "Science, Women, and the Russian Intelligentsia. The Generation of the 1860s," *Isis* 79 (1988): 217-18.

72. Koblitz, "Science, Women, and the Russian Intelligentsia," 215-16.

73. Nauck, *Das Frauenstudium* 62.

74. Alfred Wendehorst, *Geschichte der Friedrich-Alexander-Universität Erlangen-Nürnberg 1743-1993* (Munich: 1993) 141.

75. Eckardt, "Zwei Amerikanerinnen," 237-38.

76. Judy Green and Jeanne Laduke, "Contributors to American Mathematics: An Overview and Selection," *Women of science: righting the record*, eds. G. Kass-Simon, Patricia Farnes and Deborah Nash (Bloomington: Indiana University Press, 1990) 127.

77. Koblitz, "Science, Women, and the Russian Intelligentsia," 214.

78. Koblitz, "Science, Women, and the Russian Intelligentsia," 217-18.

79. Flora Bridges, "Coeducation in Swiss Universities," *The Popular Science Monthly* 38 (1890-91): 528.

80. Neumann, *Studentinnen* 16-17.

81. Neumann, *Studentinnen* 18.

82. Anja Burchardt, "'Schwestern reicht die Hand zum Bunde'? – Zum Verhältnis zwischen russischen und deutschen Medizinstudentinnen in den Anfängen des Frauenstudiums (1865-1914)," *Barrieren und Karrieren. Die Anfänge des Frauenstudiums in Deutschland. Dokumentationsband der Konferenz "100 Jahre Frauen in der Wissenschaft" im Februar 1997 an der Universität Bremen*, eds. Elisabeth Dickmann and Eva Schöck-Quinteros, vol. 5, Schriftenreihe des Hedwig-Hintze-Instituts Bremen (Berlin: trafo verlag dr. wolfgang weist, 2000) 296.

83. Burchardt, "Schwestern," 293.

84. Neumann, *Studentinnen* 43-45.

85. Neumann, *Studentinnen* 12-13; Albisetti, *Schooling German Girls and Women* 126-28; Forrer-Gutknecht, *Das Frauenstudium* 27-29, 303-10; Phebe A. Hanaford, *Daughters of America; or, Women of the Century* (Boston: B. B. Russell, 1882) 722.

86. Forrer-Gutknecht, *Das Frauenstudium* 304; Koblitz, "Science, Women, and the Russian Intelligentsia," 220; Burchardt, "Schwestern," 294; Albisetti, *Schooling German Girls and Women* 127.

87. Thomas N. Bonner, *To the ends of the earth: women's search for education in medicine* (Cambridge, MA: Harvard University Press, 1992) 46.

88. Leonard, *Woman's Who's Who* 359; Cynthia Grant Tucker, *Prophetic Sisterhood. Liberal Women Ministers of the Frontier, 1880-1930* (Boston: Beacon Press, 1990) 25.

89. Hanaford, *Daughters of America* 722.

90. Jack Wertheimer, "The 'Ausländerfrage' at Institutions of Higher Learning: A Controversy Over Russian-Jewish Students in Imperial Germany," *Leo Baeck Institute Yearbook* 27 (1982): 204-07.

91. Forrer-Gutknecht, *Das Frauenstudium* 25, 288-89.

92. Tiburtius, *Weibliches Schaffen* 128-29.

93. Albisetti, *Schooling German Girls and Women* 244-46; Burchardt, "Schwestern," 297-99.

94. Dobkin, ed., *The Making of a Feminist* 207.

95. Drucker, "Zur Vorgeschichte," 280-81.

96. Drucker, "Zur Vorgeschichte," 285-86.

97. Drucker, "Zur Vorgeschichte," 286.

98. Drucker, "Zur Vorgeschichte," 286.

99. Rogger, *Der Doktorhut* 16-17.

100. Universitätsarchiv Göttingen, Untitled document from October 1908 signed by the Prussian Matriculation Commission (Preussische Immatrikulations-Kommission).

101. Before 1915 there were no North American women auditors or matriculated students at the Technical Colleges in Darmstadt and Karlsruhe. Documented in letters from the archives of the Universität Karlsruhe (June 10, 1997) and the Technische Hochschule Darmstadt (June 9, 1997). In 1907 German women were allowed to matriculate at the Technical College of Karlsruhe, but foreign women were excluded. This was perhaps an attempt to limit the enrollment of Russian women. See: *The Nation* 85 (1907): 350. The *Woman's Who's Who of America 1914-1915* lists one woman, Ethel Craighead, a history teacher and graduate of Smith College and Columbia University, who studied at the Technical College in Dresden sometime in the early 1900s. See: Leonard, *Woman's Who's Who* 213.

102. Karl Remme, *Das Studium der Ausländer und die Bewertung der ausländischen Zeugnisse* (Berlin: 1932) 4-5.

103. "Foreign Students in Berlin," *New York Times* October 9, 1901: 1.

104. *The Nation* 84 (1907): 467.

105. Wertheimer, "The "Ausländerfrage"," 204.

106. Wertheimer, "The "Ausländerfrage"," 201.

107. Wertheimer, "The "Ausländerfrage"," 204.

108. Remme, *Das Studium der Ausländer* 4-5.

109. "Foreign Students in Prussia," *New York Times* February 27, 1898: 19.

110. "German Campaign to Exclude Aliens," *New York Times* November 22, 1908: 4.

111. Roy Temple House, "Foreigners in German Universities," *The Nation* 96 (1913): 230.

112. Jeffrey Allan Johnson, *The Kaiser's Chemists: Science and Modernization in Imperial Germany* (Chapel Hill: University of North Carolina Press, 1990) 17-19.

113. Wertheimer, "The "Ausländerfrage"," 202-03.

114. Only six of the 658 records were for Catholic women. It is remarkable that the percentages for North Americans correspond closely to those for German women at German universities. Protestants are overrepresented and Catholic women are underrepresented. Albisetti gives two reasons for the general underrepresentation of Catholic German women in higher education during this period: (1) Catholic areas were slower to open schools to prepare girls for the college entrance examination (*Abitur*); and (2) the schools for these girls did less to encourage girls to pursue a higher education and career. See: Albisetti, *Schooling German Girls and Women* 217 and 90. Catholic men were also underrepresented in college preparatory schools

and at the universities. A contemporary commentator provides two reasons for the lower proportion of Catholics at these institutions: (1) Catholic clergy are celibate and thus do not produce offspring who might inherit their "taste for learning"; and (2) religious and political leaders of the Catholic party were supposedly "constantly denouncing scientific schools and universities as hotbeds of irreligion," thus discouraging devout Catholics from attending such institutions. See: *The Nation* 62 (1896): 456.

115. Neumann, *Studentinnen* 51.

116. Neumann, *Studentinnen* 82.

117. Albisetti, *Schooling German Girls and Women* 290.

118. Burchardt, "Schwestern," 293.

119. Neumann, *Studentinnen* 81; Wertheimer, "The "Ausländerfrage"," 190.

120. Koblitz, "Science, Women, and the Russian Intelligentsia," 226.

121. Neumann, *Studentinnen* 77; Wertheimer, "The "Ausländerfrage"," 187.

122. "The crowding of Russian students," *The Nation* 85 (1907). For more on anti-Semitism in policies of the University of Leipzig and other German universities, see: Drucker, "Zur Vorgeschichte," 286-89.

123. Florence Kelley and Kathryn Kish Sklar, *Notes of sixty years: the autobiography of Florence Kelley; with an early essay by the author on the need of theoretical preparation for philanthropic work*, First person series; no. 1 (Chicago: Published for the Illinois Labor History Society by the C.H. Kerr Pub. Co., 1986) 70.

124. Bonner, *To the ends of the earth* 45; Rogger, *Der Doktorhut* 23.

125. Wertheimer, "The "Ausländerfrage"," 192-93.

126. Wertheimer, "The "Ausländerfrage"," 194.

127. Wertheimer, "The "Ausländerfrage"," 199.

128. Rossiter, *Women Scientists in America: Struggles and Strategies to 1940* 43.

129. Christine Ladd-Franklin, "Endowed Professorships for Women," *Journal of the Association of Collegiate Alumnae* Ser.3.9 (1904): 55.

130. *The Nation* 85 (1907): 33.

131. Charles W. Super, "German Degrees," *The Nation* 98 (1914): 9.

132. Super, "German Degrees," 9.

133. Super, "German Degrees," 9.

134. Super, "German Degrees," 9.

135. Hamilton, *Exploring the dangerous trades* 44; Hamilton, "Edith and Alice Hamilton," 130.

136. Bowen, "A Woman Student's Experience," 9.

137. Sherzer, "Women at the German Universities," 117.

138. "In Memoriam. Mary Whiton Calkins, 1863-1930," Class of 1885. Smith College Archives, Northampton, Massachusetts.

139. For more on the history of these fellowships, see: Margaret E. Maltby, *History of the Fellowships Awarded by the American Association of University Women 1888-1929* (Washington, DC: AAUW, 1929) 3-11; Marion Talbot and Lois Kimball Mathews Rosenberry, *The History of the American Association of University Women, 1881-1931* (Boston: Houghton Mifflin, 1931) 143-72; Lilian Welsh, *Reminiscences of thirty years in Baltimore* (Baltimore, MD: The Norman Remington Co., 1925) 21-25.

140. Before 1922 the fellows were called ACA European Fellows. From 1922 on they were called AAUW European Fellows. Maltby, *History of the Fellowships;* "The Sarah Berliner Research Fellowship for Women," *Wellesley College News* 12.12 (1911): 1.

141. Ladd-Franklin, "Endowed Professorships for Women," 56-57.

142. For more on professional opportunities for these first Ph.D.s at the women's colleges, see: Rossiter, *Women Scientists in America: Struggles and Strategies to 1940* 1-28; Patricia Ann Palmieri, *In Adamless Eden: the community of women faculty at Wellesley* (New Haven, CT: Yale University Press, 1995) 35-54.

143. "News Notes," *Wellesley College News* February 18, 1915: 7.

CHAPTER TWO: WOMEN IN MEDICINE

1. Regina Markell Morantz-Sanchez, *Sympathy and science: women physicians in American medicine* (New York: Oxford University Press, 1985) 245.

2. Morantz-Sanchez, *Sympathy and science* 31-32.

3. Thomas N. Bonner, "Medical Women Abroad: A New Dimension of Women's Push for Opportunity in Medicine, 1850-1914," *Bull. Hist. Med.* 62 (1988): 60-61.

4. Mary Putnam-Jacobi, "Woman in Medicine," *Woman's Work in America*, ed. Annie Nathan Meyer (New York: Henry Holt and Co., 1891) 145.

5. Putnam-Jacobi, "Woman in Medicine," 146.

6. "Women as Doctors," *New York Times* November 8, 1874: 6.

7. Putnam-Jacobi, "Woman in Medicine," 157-58.

8. Welsh, *Reminiscences* 4.

9. Putnam-Jacobi, "Woman in Medicine," 190.

10. Emily Dunning Barringer, *Bowery to Bellevue; the story of New York's first woman ambulance surgeon*, 1st ed. (New York: Norton, 1950) 76-79.

11. Welsh, *Reminiscences* 37.

12. "News from the Campus," *Bryn Mawr Alumnae Quarterly* 1912: 35.

13. Welsh, *Reminiscences* 32.

14. Morantz-Sanchez, *Sympathy and science* 236.

15. Ludmerer, *Learning to heal* 29-38.

16. Morantz-Sanchez, *Sympathy and science* 92.

17. Morantz-Sanchez, *Sympathy and science* 244.

18. Morantz-Sanchez, *Sympathy and science* 93.

19. Morantz-Sanchez, *Sympathy and science* 93.

20. Morantz-Sanchez, *Sympathy and science* 100-01.

21. Putnam-Jacobi, "Woman in Medicine," 198-99.

22. Welsh, *Reminiscences* 22-23.

23. Morantz-Sanchez, *Sympathy and science* 102.

24. Morantz-Sanchez, *Sympathy and science* 107.

25. Alumnae Biographical Files, Rebecca Lee Dorsey, 1881, Wellesley College Archives.

26. Doris Stump, "Zugelassen und ausgegrenzt," *Ebenso neu als kühn: 120 Jahre Frauenstudium an der Universität Zürich.*, eds. Katharina Belser, Gabi Einsele, Rachel Gratzfeld, et al. (Zurich: eFeF Verlag, 1988) 17.

27. Angela Graf-Nold, "Weiblichkeit in Wissenschaft und Wissenschaftspolitik," *Ebenso neu als kühn: 120 Jahre Frauenstudium an der Universität Zürich.*, eds. Katharina Belser, Gabi Einsele, Rachel Gratzfeld, et al. (Zurich: eFeF Verlag, 1988) 29-30.

28. Graf-Nold, "Weiblichkeit in Wissenschaft," 30.

29. Thomas N. Bonner, "Pioneering in Women's Medical Education in the Swiss Universities, 1864-1914," *30th International Congress of the History of Medicine* (Düsseldorf: Organisationskomitee des XXX. Internationalen Kongresses für Geschichte der Medizin Düsseldorf, 1986) 1169.

30. Bonner, "Pioneering," 1169.

31. Bonner, "Pioneering," 1170. For more on the first women studying medicine at Zurich, see: Rohner, *Die ersten 30 Jahre*.

32. Thomas N. Bonner, *American doctors and German universities; a chapter in international intellectual relations, 1870-1914* (Lincoln: University of Nebraska Press, 1963) 69.

33. Susan Dimock, *Memoir of Susan Dimock* (Boston: 1875) 16-17.

34. A discussion of the complex factors that brought Russian students to Swiss universities and the hostility these students encountered is included in Chapter One.

35. Forrer-Gutknecht, *Das Frauenstudium* 288-89.

36. *Verzeichnis zürischer Universitätsschriften 1833-1897* (Zurich: Verlag der Kantonsbibliothek, 1904) Nr. 496.

37. *Verzeichnis zürischer Universitätsschriften 1833-1897*, Nr. 577.

38. *Verzeichnis zürischer Universitätsschriften 1833-1897*, Nr. 578.

39. *Verzeichnis zürischer Universitätsschriften 1833-1897*, Nr. 580.

40. *Verzeichnis zürischer Universitätsschriften 1833-1897*, Nr. 612.

41. *Verzeichnis zürischer Universitätsschriften 1833-1897*, Nr. 724.

42. *Verzeichnis zürischer Universitätsschriften 1833-1897*, Nr. 741.

43. Caroline E. Furness, "Mary W. Whitney," *Popular Astronomy* December 1922: 603.

44. Furness, "Mary W. Whitney," 607. For more on Mary Whitney's career, see: Caroline E. Furness, "Mary W. Whitney," *Popular Astronomy* January 1923: 25-35; Bessie Zaban Jones and Lyle Gifford Boyd, *The Harvard Observatory: The First Four Directorships, 1839-1919* (Cambridge, MA: Belknap Press of Harvard University Press, 1971) 414-16. For more on women in astronomy during the period of this study, see: Margaret W. Rossiter, "'Women's Work' in Science, 1880-1910," *Isis* 71 (1980): 383-87; Rossiter, *Women Scientists in America: Struggles and Strategies to 1940* 53-57; Jones and Boyd, *The Harvard Observatory* 383-417.

45. Staatsarchiv des Kantons Zürich, Universitätsmatrikel, UU24a1-5. Leonard, *Woman's Who's Who* 762.

46. Welsh, *Reminiscences* 39.

47. Janet Brock Koudelka, "Mary Sherwood," *Notable American women, 1607-1950; a biographical dictionary*, eds. Edward T. James, Janet Wilson James, Paul S. Boyer, et al., vol. 3 (Cambridge, MA: Belknap Press of Harvard University Press, 1971) 283.

48. "Women's Medical College – New Graduates," *New York Times* March 26, 1873: 5.

49. The gynecologist Winckel was a strong supporter of women in higher education. From 1873 through the end of the nineteenth century, he employed at least forty women physicians in his clinics in Munich and Dresden. Most of these women had been trained at Zurich. When asked about his experience working with women in his Dresden clinic for twenty years, he responded: "First of all, concerning the intellectual capability of these assistants, I would like to say that I was only dealing with a select group of women. Even the most delicate among them was able to complete difficult operations successfully." ("Was die geistige Befähigung dieser Assistentinnen betrifft, so muss ich zunächst bemerken, dass ich es nur mit einem auserlesenen Material zu tun hatte....Auch die zartesten unter ihnen waren imstande, schwierige Operationen glücklich zu Ende zu führen"). See: Forrer-Gutknecht, *Das Frauenstudium* 32; Boehm, "Von den Anfängen," 311-12.

50. Tiburtius, *Weibliches Schaffen* 167.

51. Welsh, *Reminiscences* 34.

52. Elizabeth Cushier, "Autobiography of Elizabeth Cushier," *Medical Women of America*, ed. Kate Campbell Hurd-Mead (New York: Froben, 1933) 89.

53. "The Woman's Medical College," *New York Times* February 28, 1870: 4.

54. In addition to the women mentioned in this chapter, the *Woman's Who's Who of America, 1914-1915* includes the names of twenty-one other North American

women doing postgraduate medical studies in Vienna: Grace W. Cahoon, Julia W. Carpenter, Margaret V. Clark, Octavia G. Ritchie England, Lilian Farrar, Melinda C. Knapheide Germann, Mabel Stevens Haynes Heissig, Rhoda G. Hendrick, Mary Chandler Lowell, Louise Hutcheson Manson, Mary Gilrutin McEwen, Ida Noyes McIntire, Eliza Johnson Merrick, Mary D. Reckly, Stella Quinby Root, Mary Dunning Rose, Isabella T. Smart, Hannah O. Staufft, Gertrude Mitchell Streeper, Alfreda Bosworth Withington and Elva Annis Wright. See: Leonard, *Woman's Who's Who*.

55. Anna M. Fullerton and Carl Breus, "Women Students in Vienna," *Medical Times* October 4, 1884: 35.

56. Irene Bandhauer-Schöffmann, "Frauenbewegung und Studentinnen. Zum Engagement der österreichischen Frauenvereine für das Frauenstudium," *Durch Erkenntnis zu Freiheit und Glück...: Frauen an der Universität Wien (ab 1897)*, eds. Waltraud Heindl and Marina Tichy, Schriftenreihe des Universitätsarchivs Universität Wien 5 (Vienna: WUV-Universitätsverlag, 1990) 75.

57. Maddison and Club, *Handbook* 8-9.

58. Bonner, *American doctors and German universities* 75.

59. Bynum, *Science* 133.

60. Bynum, *Science* 53.

61. Fullerton and Breus, "Women Students in Vienna," 35.

62. Fullerton and Breus, "Women Students in Vienna," 35.

63. Fullerton and Breus, "Women Students in Vienna," 36.

64. Alumnae Biographical Files, Rebecca Lee Dorsey, 1881, Wellesley College Archives. Cecilia Rasmussen, "A Medical Pioneer's Many Firsts," *Los Angeles Times* February 3, 1997: 3.

65. Rosalie Slaughter Morton, *A woman surgeon; the life and work of Rosalie Slaughter Morton* (New York: Frederick A. Stokes, 1937) 62.

66. Morton, *A woman surgeon* 66.

67. Le Roy H. Fisher, "Mary Jane Safford," *Notable American women, 1607-1950; a biographical dictionary*, eds. Edward T. James, Janet Wilson James, Paul S. Boyer, et al., vol. 3 (Cambridge, MA: Bellknap of Harvard University Press, 1971) 221.

68. Leonard, *Woman's Who's Who* 83.

69. Barbara J. Bloemink, *The life and art of Florine Stettheimer* (New Haven, CT: Yale University Press, 1995) 4.

70. Leonard, *Woman's Who's Who* 850.

71. Gove was born on July 6, 1867 in Whitefield, New Hampshire. There is an extensive archive for Gove located at the University of North Carolina at Greensboro Archives. Leonard, *Woman's Who's Who* 336.

72. For more on Lovejoy, see: Esther Pohl Lovejoy, *Women Doctors of the World* (New York: Macmillan, 1957); Elizabeth H. Thomson, "Esther Pohl Lovejoy," *Notable American Women, The Modern Period*, eds. Barbara Sicherman, Carol Hurd Green, Ilene Kantrov, et al. (Cambridge, MA: Belknap Press of Harvard University Press, 1980); Leonard, *Woman's Who's Who* 503.

73. Geoffrey Marks and William K. Beatty, *Women in white* (New York: Scribner, 1972) 139-40.

74. Universitätsarchiv Wien, Microfilm No. 553, Med. 28.1, Prüfungsprotokollen für Hebammen, 30.7.1872 – 22.3.1890.

75. For more on Broomall, see: Mary McKibbin-Harper, "Anna E. Broomall, M.D. [1847-1931]," *Medical Review of Reviews* March 1933: 132-39; Patricia Spain Ward, "Anna Elizabeth Broomall," *Notable American Women 1607-1950*, eds. Edward T. James, Janet Wilson James, Paul S. Boyer, et al., vol. 1 (Cambridge, MA: Belknap Press of Harvard University Press, 1971) 246-47.

76. Morantz-Sanchez, *Sympathy and science* 78-79.

77. Morantz-Sanchez, *Sympathy and science* 169.
78. McKibbin-Harper, "Anna E. Broomall," 134.
79. McKibbin-Harper, "Anna E. Broomall," 134.
80. Leonard, *Woman's Who's Who* 312.
81. Leonard, *Woman's Who's Who* 312.
82 William K. Beatty, "Lucy Waite: surgeon and free thinker," *Proceedings of the Institute of Medicine, Chicago* 45 (1992): 53.
83 Beatty, "Lucy Waite," 54-57.
84. Beatty, "Lucy Waite," 53.
85. McKibbin-Harper, "Anna E. Broomall," 136-37.
86. Humboldt-Universität zu Berlin. Universitätsarchiv: The women with medical degrees were (semesters attended indicated after name) Grace Feder (WS 1896/97-SS 1897, auditor); R. Leona Ash (WS 1900/01-SS 1901, auditor); Mary A. Harriss (WS 1900/01-SS 1901, auditor); Sarah E. Conner (WS 1901/02, auditor); Nancy Bechtol (WS 1903/04, auditor); Mrs. Keith Davenport (WS 1904/05, auditor); Eleanor Parry (WS 1904/05 and WS 1906/07, auditor); Maude Nobbe (SS 1905, auditor); Lydia M. DeWitt (WS 1905/06, auditor); Lillian Delger Powers (SS 1906-SS 1907, auditor; WS 1907/08-SS 1912, matriculated); Cora Lattin, nee Billings (WS 1906/07, auditor); Florence Manion, nee Sharp (WS 1906/07, auditor); and Rose Bebb (SS 1910, matriculated).
The other eight women studying medicine were Clara Israel (WS 1900/01-WS 1901/02, auditor); Evelyn Witmer (SS 1905, auditor); Marie Layman (WS 1908, matriculated); Caroline McGill (WS 1909/10, matriculated); Ethel Peirce (SS 1910-WS 1911/12, matriculated); Hilda Lück (WS 1910/11-WS 1911/12, matriculated); Adeline Emma Gurd (WS 1911/12, matriculated); and Mabel Stevens Heissig, nee Haynes (SS 1913, matriculated).
The *Women's Who's Who of America 1914-1915* includes the name of another physician, Clara Marie Davis, from Lansing, Michigan, who did volunteer work at the Children's Asylum (Kinderasylum) in Berlin during the summer of 1911. See: Leonard, *Woman's Who's Who* 231. Other physicians listed who supposedly studied or did clinical work in Berlin were Margaret Vaupel Clark, Margaret Abigail Cleaves, Hannah M. Graham, Mary Gilruth McEwen, Ida Noyes McIntire, Rosalie Slaughter Morton, Alice Phelps Goodwin Schirmer and Elva Annis Wright. To this list, should be added the renowned microbiologist and physician Gladys Rowena Henry Dick. See: Lewis P. Rubin, "Gladys Rowena Henry Dick," *Notable American Women: The Modern Period*, eds. Barbara Sicherman, Carol Hurd Green, Ilene Kantrov, et al. (Cambridge, MA: Belknap Press of Harvard University Press, 1980) 191-92.
87. Lillian Delger Powers (1910). Humboldt-Universität zu Berlin, Universitätsarchiv, Promotionen, Philosoph. Facultät, Littr.P, Nr.4, Vol.270, 479, S.597-605.
88. Bonner, *American doctors and German universities* 39.
89. Hanna Rion, *The Truth About Twilight Sleep* (New York: McBride, Nast and Co., 1915).
90. For more on Alice Hamilton's student life at Michigan and her subsequent career, see: McGuigan, *A dangerous experiment* 89-94.
91. Barbara Sicherman and Alice Hamilton, *Alice Hamilton, a life in letters* (Cambridge, MA: Harvard University Press, 1984) 90.
92. Hamilton, "Edith and Alice Hamilton," 130.
93. Boehm, "Von den Anfängen," 317.
94. Boehm, "Von den Anfängen," 318.
95. Hamilton, *Exploring the dangerous trades* 46; Hamilton, "Edith and Alice Hamilton," 130.
96. Lapham was born in 1860 in Northville, Michigan. See: Leonard, *Woman's Who's Who* 475.

97. Universitätsarchiv München, *Amtliche Verzeichnisse des Personals der Lehrer, Beamten und Studierenden an der königlich bayerischen Ludwig-Maximilians-Universität zu München.* The three women were Marie Layman (SS 1905-WS 1907/08; SS 1909-SS 1910; also at Heidelberg SS 1908 and Berlin WS 1908/09); Elsie Lennox (SS 1908-WS 1910/11); Bliss Dayton (SS 1912).

98. Hamilton, "Edith and Alice Hamilton," 130; Sicherman and Hamilton, *Alice Hamilton* 90.

99. Hamilton, *Exploring the dangerous trades* 47; Rossiter, *Women Scientists in America: Struggles and Strategies to 1940* 332, no. 39. In 1938 Tilly Edinger, a German Jew, fled from Germany and spent the rest of her professional career at the Harvard Museum of Comparative Zoology. See: Patricia Joan Siegel and Kay Thomas Finley, *Women in the Scientific Search: An American Bio-bibliography, 1724-1979* (Metuchen, NJ: Scarecrow Press, 1985) 182.

100. Hamilton, *Exploring the dangerous trades* 44.

101. Hamilton, *Exploring the dangerous trades* 47; Hamilton, "Edith and Alice Hamilton," 130-31.

102. Brenda Richardson, "Dr. Claribel and Miss Etta," *Dr Claribel & Miss Etta: the Cone Collection of the Baltimore Museum of Art,* eds. Brenda Richardson, William C. Ameringer and Baltimore Museum of Art (Baltimore, MD: Baltimore Museum of Art, 1985) 52.

103. Barbara Pollack, *The Collectors: Dr. Claribel and Miss Etta Cone* (Indianapolis, IN: Bobbs-Merrill, 1962) 107.

104. Cone Archives, Baltimore Museum of Art, Claribel and Etta Cone Letters, 1898-1949. Letter from Claribel Cone to Etta Cone, December 2, 1906, Frankfurt. Richardson, "Dr. Claribel and Miss Etta," 80.

105. Cone Archives, Baltimore Museum of Art, Claribel and Etta Cone Letters, 1898-1949. Letter from Claribel Cone to Etta Cone, July 7, 1910, Munich. Richardson, "Dr. Claribel and Miss Etta," 80.

106. Pollack, *The Collectors* 107.

107. Another Baltimore physician, Lilian Welsh, had the highest praise for Cone's medical abilities. She wrote: "[I]n 1892 the Women's Medical College of Baltimore was the only medical school in Maryland admitting women. How well this small school, in spite of its lack of money and its poor equipment, did its work is evidenced by the fact that in 1890 two of its graduates were appointed as internes in the Philadelphia Hospital (Blockley) after a competitive examination which would have been glad to disqualify them, if possible, on two counts, first because they were women, and second because they were neither residents of the State of Pennsylvania nor had they received their medical training in Philadelphia. These two, Dr. Claribel Cone and Dr. Flora Pollack, are worthy representatives of the character of the work of this school, which very properly went out of existence with the changed conditions of modern medical education." Welsh, *Reminiscences* 37.

108. Richardson, "Dr. Claribel and Miss Etta," 52.

109. In 2001 an entire new wing of the Baltimore Museum of Art was dedicated to the Cone Collection.

110. Richardson, "Dr. Claribel and Miss Etta," 70-71; Adelyn D. Breeskin, "Claribel Cone," *Notable American women, 1607-1950; a biographical dictionary,* eds. Edward T. James, Janet Wilson James, Paul S. Boyer, et al., vol. 1 (Cambridge, MA: Belknap Press of Harvard University Press, 1971) 371-73.

111. Universitätsarchiv Heidelberg, Promotionskartei der Naturwiss.-Mathem. Fakultät. Ida Hyde completed her doctoral degree on February 20, 1896.

112. Ida Hyde, "Before Women Were Human Beings: Adventures of an American Fellow in German Universities of the '90s," *Journal of the American Association of University Women* 31 (1938): 226-36.

113. Hyde, "Before Women Were Human Beings," 229.
114. Hyde, "Before Women Were Human Beings," 232.
115. Universitätsarchiv Heidelberg, Promotionskartei der Naturwiss.-Mathem. Fakultät.
116. Morantz-Sanchez, *Sympathy and science* 70.
117. "Ida H. Hyde, Pioneer," *Journal of the American Association of University Women*. Fall (1945): 42.
118. Maltby, *History of the Fellowships* 14-15; "Ida Henrietta Hyde," *School and Society* 62 (1945): 154.

CHAPTER THREE: WOMEN IN THE HUMANITIES

1. Universitätsarchiv Berne, Diss. phil. hist. 1894 [18].
2. Minnie Adell Mason was born on August 30,1865 in Pavillion, New York, near Rochester and later moved to Geneseo. Syracuse University Archives.
3. Staatsarchiv des Kantons Zürich, U109e.5 (1900).
4. Syracuse University Archives. Leonard, *Woman's Who's Who* 90.
5. Staatsarchiv des Kantons Zürich, Universitätsmatrikel, UU24a1-5. A. W. Fairbanks, ed., *Emma Willard and her Pupils or Fifty Years of Troy Female Seminary 1822-1872* (New York: Mrs. Russell Sage, 1898) 646-47; Leonard, *Woman's Who's Who* 695; Rossiter, "Doctorates," 162.
6. Staatsarchiv des Kantons Zürich. Universitätsmatrikel, UU24a1-5.
7. Albisetti, *Schooling German Girls and Women* 200 and 28.
8. Mercedes M. Randall, *Improper Bostonian: Emily Greene Balch* (New York: Twayne, 1964) 317.
9. Jörg Nagler, "From Culture to *Kultur*. Changing American Perceptions of Imperial Germany, 1870-1914," *Transatlantic Images and Perceptions: Germany and America Since 1776*, eds. David E. Barclay and Elisabeth Glaser-Schmidt (Cambridge, England: Cambridge University Press, 1997) 142.
10. In 1875 a Polish student earned a Ph.D. in classical philology. In 1878 an Austrian student earned a Ph.D. in English literary history. See: Hans R. Guggisberg, "Eine Amerikanerin in Zürich: die Doktorpromotion der Martha Carey Thomas aus Baltimore (1882)," *Zurich Taschenbuch* (Zurich: Buchdruckerei an der Sihl AG, 1982) 174.
11. For more on the life and accomplishments of Magill, see: Glenn C. Altschuler, *Better Than Second Best: Love and Work in the Life of Helen Magill* (Urbana: University of Illinois Press, 1990); Eells, "Earned Doctorates," 645.
12. Guggisberg, "Eine Amerikanerin in Zürich," 165.
13. Marita Baumgarten, *Professoren und Universitäten im 19. Jahrhundert*, Kritische Studien zur Geschichtswissenschaft, vol. 121 (Göttingen: Vandenhoeck & Ruprecht, 1997) 216.
14. All existing records for women auditors and matriculated students are on microfilm: Universitätsarchiv Leipzig, Hörerscheine, GA X M 1-8, Matrikelbücher, Rektor M55-M67, Film Nr. 680-683.
15. Universitätsarchiv Leipzig, Hörerscheine, WS 1873/74-WS 1889/90, SS 1903-WS 1914/15. Matrikelbücher, SS 1906-WS 1914/15. For more on the complex relationship between Thomas and Gwinn, see Helen Lefkowitz Horowitz's excellent biography of Thomas: Helen Lefkowitz Horowitz, *The Power and Passion of M. Carey Thomas* (New York: Alfred A. Knopf, 1994).
16. For references to Channing see: Altschuler, *Better Than Second Best.*
17. Boston University Archives, 1877 Boston University Records, Eva Channing, 1877.
18. "University Education of Women," *New York Times* January 19, 1891: 5.

19. Harriet Parker was born on March 3, 1857, in Grinnell, Iowa. Leonard, *Woman's Who's Who* 157.

20. Dobkin, ed., *The Making of a Feminist* 205.

21. Dobkin, ed., *The Making of a Feminist* 198.

22. Dobkin, ed., *The Making of a Feminist* 232.

23. Dobkin, ed., *The Making of a Feminist* 204-05.

24. Dobkin, ed., *The Making of a Feminist* 187.

25. Guggisberg, "Eine Amerikanerin in Zürich," 165.

26. Dobkin, ed., *The Making of a Feminist* 206.

27. "The Contributors' Club," *The Atlantic Monthly* 44 (1879): 791.

28. "The Contributors' Club," 790.

29. Dobkin, ed., *The Making of a Feminist* 207.

30. Gwinn did not attempt to earn a degree at Zurich. In 1888 she completed her doctoral degree in English at Bryn Mawr. For more on Gwinn and her subsequent career, see: Horowitz, *The Power and Passion*.

31. Staatsarchiv des Kantons Zürich, U109e.2 (1882). *Verzeichnis zürischer Universitätsschriften 1833-1897*, Nr. 1267.

32. Staatsarchiv des Kantons Zürich, U109e.2 (1882). Guggisberg, "Eine Amerikanerin in Zürich," 173; Dobkin, ed., *The Making of a Feminist* 262-63.

33. Dobkin, ed., *The Making of a Feminist* 278.

34. Dobkin, ed., *The Making of a Feminist* 281.

35. Dell Richards, *Superstars: twelve lesbians who changed the world* (New York: Carroll & Graf, 1993) 165-66.

36. M. Carey Thomas, "President Thomas's Address," *Bryn Mawr Alumnae Quarterly* January 1908: 46-47.

37. M. Carey Thomas, "The President's Address," *Bryn Mawr Alumnae Quarterly* November 1910: 189-90.

38. Universitätsarchiv Heidelberg. Alice Luce earned her doctoral degree on April 24, 1897.

39. Frances H. Mitchell was born on March 26, 1854, to Anna C. Jackson and businessman Charles W. Mitchell, in Philadelphia. Staatsarchiv des Kantons Zürich, U109e.2 (1887).

40. Staatsarchiv des Kantons Zürich, U109e.2 (1887). *Verzeichnis zürischer Universitätsschriften 1833-1897*, Nr. 1396.

41. There is an interesting account about how Mitchell came to study at Cornell. "[Mitchell] happened to visit her brother, a Cornell student, at a time when entrance examinations were being given. She suddenly resolved to take them just to see if she could pass, although, if she had desired to go to Cornell she could have entered on certificate. Being a zealous scholar, she easily passed the examinations. She then decided to enter Cornell." Anna Heubeck Knipp and Thaddeus P. Thomas, *The History of Goucher College* (Baltimore, MD: Goucher College, 1938) 305.

42. Mitchell and Froelicher had three sons, all of whom became leaders in the field of education: Charles Mitchell Froelicher, Hans Froehlicher Jr. and Francis M. Froelicher.

43. Frances Mitchell Froelicher, "Germanic Philology at Zürich," *Kalends (Goucher)* April 1896: 171.

44. Froelicher, "Post-Graduate Work," 114.

45. Froelicher, "Germanic Philology," 172.

46. Mary Noyes Colvin was born in 1850. Staatsarchiv des Kantons Zürich, Universitätsmatrikel, UU24a1-5.

47. *Verzeichnis zürischer Universitätsschriften 1833-1897*, Nr. 1412.

48. Staatsarchiv des Kantons Zürich, U109e.2 (1888).

49. Helen L. Webster was born in 1853.

50. *Verzeichnis zürischer Universitätsschriften 1833-1897*, Nr. 1457.
51. Staatsarchiv des Kantons Zürich, U109e.3 (1889/90).
52. Palmieri, *In Adamless Eden* 47.
53. Palmieri, *In Adamless Eden* 47.
54. Palmieri, *In Adamless Eden* 39.
55. Helen L. Webster, "University Education for Women in Germany," *Wellesley Magazine* March 1895: 294.
56. Anne Louise Leonard was born on May 2,1862, the daughter of Granville Hall Leonard, a businessman in Easthampton, Massachusetts.
57. *Verzeichnis zürischer Universitätsschriften 1833-1897*, Nr. 1475.
58. Staatsarchiv des Kantons Zürich, U109e.3 (1890).
59. Cornelia Hartwell, "Four Moons Abroad. Amid the Mountains," *Courant (Wellesley)* March 1, 1889: 2-3.
60. Emma A. Yarnell was born in 1846.
61. Staatsarchiv des Kantons Zürich, U109e.4 (1896). Universitätsmatrikel, UU24a1-5.
62. Sarah May Thomas was born in Green Bay, Wisconsin, in 1858 and traveled with her mother, Jane E. Thomas, to Zurich.
63. Staatsarchiv des Kantons Zürich, U109e.4 (1897).
64. *Verzeichnis zürischer Universitätsschriften 1833-1897*, Nr. 1675.
65. Virginia Eviline Spencer was born in Lawrence, Kansas, in 1864. Staatsarchiv des Kantons Zürich, Universitätsmatrikel, UU24a1-5.
66. Staatsarchiv des Kantons Zürich, U109e.5 (1899).
67. Mary Vance Young was born on May 22, 1866, in Washington, Pennsylvania.
68. Staatsarchiv des Kantons Zürich, U109e.5 (1900). Universitätsmatrikel, UU24a1-5. See also: Leonard, *Woman's Who's Who* 913.
69. For more information on these professors and other faculty members, see: Dagmar Drüll, *Heidelberger Gelehrtenlexikon 1803-1932* (Berlin: Springer-Verlag, 1986).
70. Biographical Files, Alice Luce, 1883, Wellesley College Archives. Universitätsarchiv Heidelberg, Promotionskartei der philosophischen Fakultät.
71. Universitätsarchiv Heidelberg, Promotionskartei der philosophischen Fakultät.
72. Clune was born on August 12, 1870, in Warkworth, Ontario. See: Leonard, *Woman's Who's Who* 152.
73. Universitätsarchiv Heidelberg, Promotionskartei der philosophischen Fakultät. Ellen Clune completed her doctoral degree on January 9, 1899.
74. In Berlin, Clune studied English and German philology for one semester (WS 1895/96). The auditor records for that period in Leipzig no longer exist, so there is no record of her stay there.
75. Universitätsarchiv Heidelberg, Promotionskartei der philosophischen Fakultät. Universitätsarchiv Wien, Nationale, Philosophische Fakultät, 1897-1914/15.
76. Universitätsarchiv Heidelberg, Promotionskartei der philosophischen Fakultät.
77. For more on Cather's passionate attachment to Pound during their student days, see: Sharon O'Brien, *Willa Cather: The Emerging Voice* (New York: Oxford University Press, 1987) 129-31; James Woodress, *Willa Cather: A Literary Life* (Lincoln: University of Nebraska Press, 1987) 84-87.
78. O'Brien, *Willa Cather* 129.
79. O'Brien, *Willa Cather* 129.
80. Keller was born on September 28, 1877, in Baltimore, Maryland.
81. Turnbull, *May Lansfield Keller* 124.

82. Turnbull, *May Lansfield Keller* 167-68.
83. Turnbull, *May Lansfield Keller* 210.
84. Turnbull, *May Lansfield Keller* 195.
85. Turnbull, *May Lansfield Keller* 31.
86. Universitätsarchiv Heidelberg, Promotionskartei der philosophischen Fakultät.
87. Universitätsarchiv Heidelberg, Promotionskartei der philosophischen Fakultät.
88. Ellen Clarinda Hinsdale was born on May 10, 1864, the daughter of Mary Turner Hinsdale and Professor Burke A. Hinsdale. Universitätsarchiv Göttingen, Promotionsakten, Phil. Fak. I. Vol. 182c.
89. Universitätsarchiv Göttingen, Promotionsakten, Phil. Fak. I. Vol. 182c. Hinsdale's doctoral file includes a detailed letter from Moriz Heyne in support of her doctoral thesis.
90. *Wellesley Magazine* March 1897: 335-36.
91. Ida Hakemeyer, "Ellen Hinsdale promovierte in Göttingen vor 58 Jahren," *Mädchenbildung und Frauenschaffen* January 1956: 43-44; A. B., "An American Woman at the German Universities," *The Nation* 64 (1897): 223-24.
92. Bowen, "A Woman Student's Experience," 9. Bowen completed her Ph.D. in 1897 at Cornell. See: Eells, "Earned Doctorates," 650.
93. Maltby, *History of the Fellowships* 14.
94. Maltby, *History of the Fellowships* 43.
95. Humboldt-Universität zu Berlin, Universitätsarchiv, Promotionen, Philosoph. Facultät, Littr.P, Nr.4, Vol.153, 362, S.128-171.
96. Maltby, *History of the Fellowships* 18.
97. Humboldt-Universität zu Berlin, Universitätsarchiv, Promotionen, Philosoph. Facultät, Littr.P, Nr.4, Vol.158, 367, S.434-460.
98. "Alumnae Notes," *Wellesley College News* April 24, 1907: 7.
99. Alumnae Biographical Files, Mary Montgomery Borglum, 1896, Wellesley College Archives. Leonard, *Woman's Who's Who* 115.
100. Humboldt-Universität zu Berlin, Universitätsarchiv, Promotionen, Philosoph. Facultät, Littr.P, Nr.4, Vol.167, 376, S.196-230. Leonard, *Woman's Who's Who* 742; Olive Flower, *The History of Oxford College for Women, 1830-1928*, Miami University Books, vol. 2 (Hamilton, OH: The Miami University Alumni Association, 1949) 75-92, 140-48.
101. Flower, *The History of Oxford College* 143.
102. Flower, *The History of Oxford College* 144.
103. Flower, *The History of Oxford College* 145.
104. Flower, *The History of Oxford College* 90-92.
105. Flower, *The History of Oxford College* 147.
106. "Women's Uphill Fight in Germany," 4.
107. Grace Fleming Sweringen was born on January 13, 1866.
108. Leonard, *Woman's Who's Who* 798.
109. Eva Johnston's father was a minister in Ashland, Missouri. Humboldt-Universität zu Berlin, Universitätsarchiv, Gasthörerverzeichnisse (WS 1899/00; WS 1900/01; SS 1902).
110. University Archives, University of Missouri-Columbia; Humboldt-Universität zu Berlin, Universitätsarchiv, Gasthörerverzeichnisse (WS 1899/00; WS 1900/01; SS 1902); Universitätsarchiv Göttingen, Verzeichnisse der Studierenden von Ostern 1911 bis Ostern 1914, WS 1911/12 and SS 1912; Leonard, *Woman's Who's Who* 437.

111. Edith's letters from Germany were destroyed in a flood in 1938. See: Doris Fielding Reid, *Edith Hamilton: An Intimate Portrait* (New York: W. W. Norton, 1967) 34.

112. Richards, *Superstars* 145.

113. Boehm, "Von den Anfängen," 317-18.

114. Hamilton, "Edith and Alice Hamilton," 130; Reid, *Edith Hamilton* 36.

115. Hamilton, *Exploring the dangerous trades* 44-45; Hamilton, "Edith and Alice Hamilton," 131; Boehm, "Von den Anfängen," 317-18.

116. Reid, *Edith Hamilton* 37.

117. Reid, *Edith Hamilton* 37.

118. Universitätsarchiv München, Gasthörerverzeichnis, SS 1899.

119. Hamilton, "Edith and Alice Hamilton," 132.

120. Universitätsarchiv München, Gasthörerverzeichnis, SS 1899.

121. Sicherman and Hamilton, *Alice Hamilton* 141.

122. "Alumnae Notes [1897]," *Fortnightly Philistine (Bryn Mawr)* December 22, 1899: 15.

123. "Alumnae Notes," *The Fortnightly Philistine (Bryn Mawr)* December 22, 1899: 15; *The Fortnightly Philistine (Bryn Mawr)* November 9, 1900: 13.

124. Richards, *Superstars* 136; Hamilton, *Exploring the dangerous trades* 78.

125. Richards, *Superstars* 136.

126. Warren was born in 1870 in Cambridge, Massachusetts, the daughter of William Fairfield and Harriet Cornelia (Merrick) Warren.

127. Boehm, "Von den Anfängen," 320; Leonard, *Woman's Who's Who* 893; Eells, "Earned Doctorates," 649. Humboldt-Universität zu Berlin, Universitätsarchiv, Gasthörerverzeichnisse (SS 1897; WS 1909/10).

128. Universitätsarchiv München, Gasthörerverzeichnis, SS 1903 and WS 1903/04.

129. Belle Wright to Mr. and Mrs. Don Webb, May 22, 1961, Town of Springport Records, Cayuga, New York.

130. 1900 U.S. Census. That I know anything more about Wright is due to the generosity of a local historian, J. Berry, of the town of Springport, New York. Berry sent me a copy of a letter Wright wrote in 1961 to a couple residing in Wright's childhood home in Union Springs. Wright lived from the time she was eight until she was fifteen in Union Springs with an uncle and aunt, Luther Austin and Emily E. Wales. Her letter to the current residents of her former home in Union Springs is a touching one. After so many years, Wright still remembered certain trees, especially a hickory and two peach trees, and the garden with day lilies and roses. She mentioned that most of the people who knew her then had since died. But with the hope of reaching out to someone from her past, she enclosed a photo of herself as a college-age woman with the letter.

131. Frieda Patrick Davison, the former Director of Library Services at MUW, emphasized the importance of Orr's role at the university.

132. Mississippi University for Women Archives, Columbus, Mississippi. Thomas E. Kelly, *Who's Who in Mississippi* (Jackson, Mississippi: Tucker Printing House, 1914) 78; "Miss Orr, 93, is Grateful at Newest MSCW Tribute," *The Commercial Appeal* October 21, 1954.

133. Mississippi University for Women Archives, Columbus, Mississippi. "Miss Orr, 93, is Grateful at Newest MSCW Tribute."

134. Mississippi University for Women Archives, Columbus, Mississippi. "Miss Orr, 93, is Grateful at Newest MSCW Tribute."

135. Bridget Smith Pieschel and Stephen Robert Pieschel, *Loyal daughters: one hundred years at Mississippi University for Women, 1884-1984* (Jackson: University Press of Mississippi, 1984) 5-6.

136. Pieschel and Pieschel, *Loyal daughters* 19.

137. Pieschel and Pieschel, *Loyal daughters* 133.

138. "State College for Women Loses a Valuable Instructor," *The Commercial Appeal* May 18, 1913.

139. 1900 U.S. Census. Mississippi University for Women Archives, Columbus, Mississippi. "Miriam Pasley," *Mississippi State College Alumnae Quarterly* (1926).

140. Faculty Biographical Files, Hope Traver, Mills College Archives, Oakland, California.

141. Rosalind Amelia Keep, *Fourscore and Ten Years: A History of Mills College* (Oakland, CA: Mills College, 1946) 159.

142. Faculty Biographical Files, Hope Traver, Mills College Archives, Oakland, California. Hope Traver, *Bulletin of the Class of 1896. Vassar College* (1919).

143. Faculty Biographical Files, Hope Traver, Mills College Archives, Oakland, California. Hope Traver, "The Institute of International Education," *Mills Quarterly* 4 (1921): 27.

144. Faculty Biographical Files, Hope Traver, Mills College Archives, Oakland, California. Mills College Catalogue, 1910-1911. Alumnae Biographical Files, Hope Traver, Bryn Mawr College Archives. Helen Funnell, "In Remembrance," *Mills Quarterly* (1963): 47; "Hope Traver," *Decennial Bulletin of the Class of 1896. Vassar College* (1906): 9; "Hope Traver," *Bulletin of the Class of 1896. Vassar College* (1911): 15; "Hope Traver," *Vassar College Alumnae Directory* (1939): 76; "Hope Traver," *Vassar '96. Fiftieth Reunion, 1896-1946* (1946): 28-29; Keep, *Fourscore and ten years* 111, 159.

145. Frances Fincke Hand, Edna Shearer, Eunice M. Schenk, et al., "The Academic Committee's Report on the Bryn Mawr Graduate School," *Bryn Mawr Alumnae Bulletin* 7.1 (1927): 7-9.

146. Helen Thomas Flexner, "Bryn Mawr: A Characterization," *Bryn Mawr Alumnae Quarterly* January 1908: 15.

147. Alumnae Biographical Files, Johnetta Van Meter, 1894, Goucher College Archives, Baltimore, Maryland. "Johnetta Van Meter," *Goucher Kalends* March 1909: 8.

148. Alumnae Biographical Files, May Lansfield Keller, 1898, Goucher College Archives, Baltimore, Maryland. "May L. Keller," *Goucher Kalends* March 1909: 20; "Faculty Notes," *Goucher Kalends* May 1912: 261; "Commencement," *Goucher Kalends* June 1914: 283.

149. "Annina Periam," *Goucher Kalends* March 1909: 21.

150. Alumnae Biographical Files, Annina Periam, 1898, Goucher College Archives, Baltimore, Maryland. Agnes Murray Boland, "1898, Annina Periam Danton," *Goucher Quarterly* Winter (1954).

151. "Fellowships," *Bryn Mawr Alumnae Quarterly* April 1909: 9.

152. Weusthoff was born on March 24, 1884, in Dayton, Ohio. Her father was a physician.

153. "Anna Sophie Weusthoff," *Bulletin Goucher College* 2.2 (1914-1915): 52.

154. Alumnae Biographical Files, Anna Sophie Weusthoff, 1906, Goucher College Archives, Baltimore, Maryland.

155. Harmon was born on September 18, 1876, in Toledo, Ohio. Her father was a lawyer.

156. "Fellowships," 9.

157. "Reunion of Class of 1909," *Goucher Kalends* June 1914: 290; "Adah Blanche Roe," *Bulletin Goucher College* 2.2 (1914-1915): 61.

158. Alumnae Biographical Files, Adah Blanche Roe, 1909, Goucher College Archives, Baltimore, Maryland.

159. Maltby, *History of the Fellowships* 27.
160. Maltby, *History of the Fellowships* 21.
161. Maltby, *History of the Fellowships* 37; Eells, "Earned Doctorates," 649.
162. Maltby, *History of the Fellowships* 56.

CHAPTER FOUR: WOMEN IN MATHEMATICS AND SCIENCE

1. Albisetti, "German Influence," 242-43.
2. Krabusch, "Die Vorgeschichte des Frauenstudiums," 136.
3. Green and Laduke, "Contributors to American Mathematics," 127.
4. Green and Laduke, "Contributors to American Mathematics," 119. These 216 women made up 14.3 percent of all American Ph.D.s in mathematics at that time.
5. According to the archival records at the University of Göttingen, the following Ph.D.s studied for some period at that university: Annie MacKinnon Fitch, Mary Frances Winston (Newson), Anne Lucy Bosworth (Focke), Emilie Norton-Martin, Ruth Goulding Wood, Helen Abbot Merrill, Virginia Ragsdale, Clara Eliza Smith, Anna Lavinia van Benschofen and Anna Johnson Pell Wheeler. Other influential mathematicians of the time who studied at Göttingen include Mary Esther Trueblood (Paine), Helen Schaeffer Huff and Eugenie M. Morenus. See: Universitätsarchiv Göttingen, Sek. XA555a-f. Judy Green, "American Women In Mathematics – The First Ph.D.'s," *Association for Women in Mathematics Newsletter* 8 (1978): 13.
6. Bosworth defended her thesis in 1899 but did not receive her degree until 1900. See: Della Dumbaugh Fenster and Karen Hunger Parshall, "Women in the American Mathematical Research Community: 1891-1906," *The History of Modern Mathematics*, eds. Eberhard Knobloch and David E. Rowe, vol. 3 (San Diego, CA: Academic Press, 1994) 235.
7. Siegel and Finley, *Women in the Scientific Search* 218-19; Tobies, ""Aller Männerkultur zum Trotz"," 247-49.
8. Engelbert L. Schucking, "Jordan, Pauli, Politics, Brecht, and a Variable Gravitational Constant," *Physics Today* (1999): 28-29.
9. Simon Singh, *Fermat's Enigma* (New York: Anchor Books, 1997) 109.
10. Costas, "Der Beginn des Frauenstudiums," 190; Patricia Rothman, "Genius, Gender and Culture: Women Mathematicians of the Nineteenth Century," *Interdisciplinary Science Reviews* 13.1 (1988): 64-72.
11. The American Margaret Maltby received her doctoral degree in physics. The British student Grace Emily Chisholm received her doctoral degree in mathematics.
12. Baumgarten, *Professoren und Universitäten* 189.
13. Renate Tobies and Fritz König, *Felix Klein*, Biographien hervorragender Naturwissenschaftler, Techniker und Mediziner, vol. 50 (Leipzig: Teubner, 1981) 61.
14. Tobies, "Zum Beginn," 152.
15. Rossiter, *Women Scientists in America: Struggles and Strategies to 1940* 96-98.
16. After the conference in Chicago, Klein gave a series of lectures at Northwestern. The lectures were so successful, Klein returned to the United States in 1895 and gave another series of lectures at Princeton, where he was offered a position. Klein declined the offer and a similar one from Yale the following year. See: Tobies and König, *Felix Klein* 61-62.
17. Tobies, "Zum Beginn," 153; Tobies and König, *Felix Klein* 62.
18. Grace Chisholm worked as a mathematician with her husband William Henry Young. See: Else Høyrup, *Women of Science, Technology, and Medicine: A Bibliography*, Skriftserie fra Roskilde Universitetsbibliothek, vol. 15 (Roskilde, Denmark: Roskilde University Library, 1987) 106; Tobies, "Zum Beginn," 164.

19. Rossiter, *Women Scientists in America: Struggles and Strategies to 1940* 40.

20. Rossiter, *Women Scientists in America: Struggles and Strategies to 1940* 41.

21. Rossiter, *Women Scientists in America: Struggles and Strategies to 1940* 38-40; Talbot and Rosenberry, *The History* 147. For more on Ladd-Franklin's research and career, see Chapter Five.

22. Konrad H. Jarausch, "American Students in Germany, 1815-1914: The Structure of German and U.S. Matriculants at Göttingen University," *German Influence on Education in the United States to 1917*, eds. Henry Geitz, Jürgen Heideking and Jurgen Herbst (New York: Cambridge University Press, 1995) 196.

23. Margarette Muller, "Some Groans and Warnings from Abroad," *Wellesley Magazine* April 1895: 372.

24. After returning from a year in Göttingen and Berlin, Kennedy did further graduate work in English literature at Yale, where she studied from 1900-02 and from 1907-08. Kennedy taught English at the University of Southern California (1899-1900) and was head of the English department at Rockford College (1902-07). In 1907 she taught as an instructor in English Literature at Mount Holyoke for one year, before returning to Yale for another year of study. After teaching for a year at Mary Baldwin Seminary in Staunton, Virginia, she served as head of a private secondary school in Clarksburg, West Virginia, for six years. For the next four years, she served as associate head of a private school, which she had helped to found, in South Hadley, Massachusetts. In 1920 Kennedy took a position teaching English at Hollins College, where she remained for seven years. From 1930 until her retirement, Kennedy taught English at Indiana University in Bloomington. See: Alumnae Biographical Files, Virginia Wadlow Kennedy, 1896, Goucher College Archives, Baltimore, Maryland. "Alumnae Notes," *Kalends (Goucher)* November 1899: 55; "Alumnae Notes," *Kalends (Goucher)* March 1911: 189.

25. Jarausch, "American Students in Germany," 201 and 09.

26. Virginia Kennedy, "Alumnae Letters," *Kalends (Goucher)* January 1897: 97.

27. Winston was born in Forreston, Illinois on August 7, 1869. She was the daughter of Carolyn (Mumford) Winston and the physician Thomas Winston.

28. Universitätsarchiv Göttingen, Promotionsakten, Phil. Fak. I, Vol. 182c.

29. Green and Laduke, "Contributors to American Mathematics," 140.

30. Patricia C. Kenschaft, "Women in Mathematics around 1900," *Signs* Summer 1982: 908; Siegel and Finley, *Women in the Scientific Search* 211; Fenster and Parshall, "Women in the American Mathematical Research Community," 242-43.

31. Fenster and Parshall, "A Profile," 206.

32. Fenster and Parshall, "Women in the American Mathematical Research Community," 237-38.

33. Universitätsarchiv Göttingen, Promotionsakten, Phil. Fak. I, Vol. 182c.

34. Fenster and Parshall, "Women in the American Mathematical Research Community," 238.

35. Maltby, *History of the Fellowships* 16; Green and Laduke, "Contributors to American Mathematics," 129; Green, "American Women In Mathematics," 14.

36. Green and Laduke, "Contributors to American Mathematics," 127.

37. Universitätsarchiv Göttingen, Sek. XA555a. Fenster and Parshall, "Women in the American Mathematical Research Community," 235.

38. Letter from MacKinnon to Felix Klein, dated July 1894. Cited in: Fenster and Parshall, "Women in the American Mathematical Research Community," 238-39.

39. Tobies, "Zum Beginn," 160.

40. Maltby, *History of the Fellowships* 15-16; Green, "American Women In Mathematics," 13.

41. Miriam Allen De Ford, *Psychologist unretired; the life pattern of Lillien J. Martin* (Stanford, CA: Stanford University Press, 1948) 44.

42. Martin tutored her friend so that Jewett could enroll at the University of California at Berkeley, where she earned her Bachelor's degree in art and architecture in 1906. Jewett's studies at Berkeley changed the focus of her teaching. She began teaching an art course and became active in the art community. Jewett was always concerned with helping minorities and the disadvantaged. After World War I, she spent her evenings teaching English at the local Chinese Independent Baptist Church. She also helped to found schools for African-Americans in Louisiana and Mississippi.

43. Palmieri, *In Adamless Eden* 78.

44. Universitätsarchiv Göttingen, Sek. XA555a.

45. Siegel and Finley, *Women in the Scientific Search* 217; Green, "American Women In Mathematics," 13; Leonard, *Woman's Who's Who* 543.

46. Shelby L. Eaton, *Women in Mathematics in the United States: 1866-1900*, 1997, World Wide Web Document, Available: http://www.faculty.washington.edu/marykirk/herstory/seaton.htm, June 16, 2000; Leonard, *Woman's Who's Who* 669; Green, "American Women In Mathematics," 13; "Collegiana: Resident Fellows for the Year 1901-02," *The Lantern (Bryn Mawr)* June 1902: 93.

47. Tobies, ""Aller Männerkultur zum Trotz"," 247-48; Green, "American Women In Mathematics," 13.

48. Leonard, *Woman's Who's Who* 633.

49. Universitätsarchiv Göttingen, Sek. XA555a. Siegel and Finley, *Women in the Scientific Search* 214; Leonard, *Woman's Who's Who* 619.

50. Universitätsarchiv Göttingen, Sek. XA555a. Leonard, *Woman's Who's Who* 753-54.

51. Green, "American Women In Mathematics," 13; Leonard, *Woman's Who's Who* 833.

52. Universitätsarchiv Göttingen, Sek. XA555a. Siegel and Finley, *Women in the Scientific Search* 218; Leonard, *Woman's Who's Who* 825.

53. Helen Abbot Merrill was born on March 30, 1864.

54. Green, "American Women In Mathematics," 13; Siegel and Finley, *Women in the Scientific Search* 214-15; "Helen A. Merrill of Wellesley, 85," *New York Times* May 3, 1949: 25; Leonard, *Woman's Who's Who* 557.

55. Green, "American Women In Mathematics," 13; Siegel and Finley, *Women in the Scientific Search* 214. Universitätsarchiv Göttingen, Verzeichnisse der Studierenden von Ostern 1911 bis Ostern 1914, WS 1911/12 and SS 1912.

56. Universitätsarchiv Göttingen, Sek. XA555a and XA555d.

57. Schaeffer Huff was born on December 31, 1883, in Pennsylvania. Her father, Nathan Schaeffer of Lancaster, was the Superintendent of Public Instruction in Pennsylvania. See: "In Memoriam," *Bryn Mawr Alumnae Quarterly* January 1913: 210.

58. Universitätsarchiv Göttingen, Sek. XA555d. "News from the Faculty and Staff," *Bryn Mawr Alumnae Quarterly* November 1911: 128; "In Memoriam," 210.

59. Universitätsarchiv Göttingen, Sek. XA555d.

60. John C. Oxtoby, "Anna Pell Wheeler," *Bryn Mawr Alumnae Bulletin* Summer 1966: 22.

61. Anna Johnson, "Alumnae Notes," *Wellesley College News* March 6, 1907: 8.

62. Ruth Stauffer McKee, "Anna Pell Wheeler," *Bryn Mawr Alumnae Bulletin* Summer 1966: 23.

63. Oxtoby, "Anna Pell Wheeler," 22.

64. Green and Laduke, "Contributors to American Mathematics," 131; Green, "American Women In Mathematics," 13-14.

65. Ruth Goulding Wood was born on January 29, 1875, in Pawtucket, Rhode Island.

66. Siegel and Finley, *Women in the Scientific Search* 218-19; Leonard, *Woman's Who's Who* 900; Fenster and Parshall, "Women in the American Mathematical Research Community," 248.

67. Universitätsarchiv Göttingen, Verzeichnisse der Studierenden von Ostern 1911 bis Ostern 1914. "Here and There with the Alumnae," *Bryn Mawr Alumnae Quarterly* June 1913: 51.

68. Maltby, *History of the Fellowships* 58. Universitätsarchiv Göttingen, Sek. XA555f.

69. Webster, "University Education," 293.

70. Baumgarten, *Professoren und Universitäten* 149.

71. Baumgarten, *Professoren und Universitäten* 149; Fenster and Parshall, "A Profile," 202.

72. Ruth Gentry, "A Winter in Berlin," *The Lantern (Bryn Mawr)* June 1892: 45.

73. Krabusch, "Die Vorgeschichte des Frauenstudiums," 137.

74. Gentry, "A Winter in Berlin," 46.

75. Maltby, *History of the Fellowships* 13; Green, "American Women In Mathematics," 13; Eells, "Earned Doctorates," 649; Fenster and Parshall, "Women in the American Mathematical Research Community," 245.

76. Gustav Beuermann, Margrit Hische, Ulrich Hunger, et al., eds., *250 Jahre Georg-August-Universität Göttingen. Ausstellung im Auditorium. Göttingen. May 19-July 12, 1987* (Göttingen: Georg-August-Universität, 1987) 82-98.

77. Maltby was born on December 10, 1860, in Bristolville, Ohio, to Lydia Jane (Brockway) Maltby and the landowner Edmund Maltby. See: Universitätsarchiv Göttingen, Promotionsakten, Phil. Fak. I, Vol.181c.

78. "Editorial," 151-52.

79. Universitätsarchiv Göttingen, Promotionsakten, Phil. Fak. I, Vol.181c.

80. Maltby, *History of the Fellowships* 16; "Dr. M. E. Maltby, Long at Barnard," *New York Times* May 5, 1944: 19; Siegel and Finley, *Women in the Scientific Search* 286.

81. Rossiter, *Women Scientists in America: Struggles and Strategies to 1940* 26-27.

82. Sarah F. Whiting, "The Experiences of a Woman Physicist," *Wellesley College News* January 9, 1913: 5.

83. Whiting, "The Experiences of a Woman Physicist," 5.

84. Sarah F. Whiting, "Heidelberg," *Courant (Wellesley)* February 22, 1889: 3.

85. Whiting, "The Experiences of a Woman Physicist," 5.

86. Siegel and Finley, *Women in the Scientific Search* 289.

87. Maltby, *History of the Fellowships* 71-72.

88. Regula Schnurrenberger, "Ein Überblick," *Ebenso neu als kühn: 120 Jahre Frauenstudium an der Universität Zürich.*, eds. Katharina Belser, Gabi Einsele, Rachel Gratzfeld, et al. (Zurich: eFeF Verlag, 1988) 208-11.

89. Marelene F. Rayner-Canham and Geoffrey W. Rayner-Canham, *A Devotion to Their Science: Pioneer Women of Radioactivity* (Montreal: McGill-Queen's University Press, 1997) 139-40.

90. Maltby, *History of the Fellowships* 17-18; Siegel and Finley, *Women in the Scientific Search* 289; Rossiter, "'Women's Work' in Science," 397; Rayner-Canham and Rayner-Canham, *A Devotion to Their Science* 138-44.

91. Welsh, *Reminiscences* 26.

92. Universitätsarchiv Göttingen, Sek. XA555a and XA555d; Alumnae Biographical Files, Bertha May Clark, 1900, Goucher College Archives, Baltimore, Maryland.

93. Hessenauer, *Etappen des Frauenstudiums* 175.

94. Hessenauer, "Studentinnen vor 1939," 320-21. Hessenauer, *Etappen des Frauenstudiums* 174.

95. Maltby, *History of the Fellowships* 67-71.

96. G. Kass-Simon, "Biology Is Destiny," *Women of science: righting the record*, eds. G. Kass-Simon, Patricia Farnes and Deborah Nash (Bloomington: Indiana University Press, 1990) 215.

97. Kass-Simon, "Biology Is Destiny," 215.

98. Margaret R. Wright, "Marcella O'Grady Boveri (1863-1950): Her Three Careers in Biology," *Isis* 88 (1997): 638.

99. Wright, "Marcella O'Grady Boveri," 634.

100. Hessenauer, *Etappen des Frauenstudiums* 44. The biologist, Helen Dean King (1869-1955), did not study at a German-speaking university and is not included here, although her background at Vassar (Bachelor's 1892) and Bryn Mawr (Ph.D. 1899) corresponds closely to that of the biologists discussed here. She became known for her role in breeding the Wistar rat for research. Siegel and Finley, *Women in the Scientific Search* 358.

101. Wright, "Marcella O'Grady Boveri," 629.

102. Wright, "Marcella O'Grady Boveri," 632.

103. Universitätsarchiv Freiburg, B 42/1267, D 29/6-2289. Nauck, *Das Frauenstudium* 62.

104. Wright, "Marcella O'Grady Boveri," 635.

105. Louise S. Horton, Elizabeth H. Underhill and Eleanor D. Deal, *Piermont, New Hampshire, 1764-1947* (Bradford, VT: Green Mountain Press, n. d.) 111-12 and 70.

106. Hessenauer, *Etappen des Frauenstudiums* 44.

107. Hessenauer, *Etappen des Frauenstudiums* 24-25.

108. In 1895, one year before O'Grady's arrival, Röntgen discovered X-rays. He would win a Nobel Prize in physics for his work in 1901.

109. Hessenauer, *Etappen des Frauenstudiums* 130.; Wright, "Marcella O'Grady Boveri," 641.

110. Margret Boveri, *Verzweigungen. Eine Autobiographie*, ed. Uwe Johnson (Munich and Zurich: R. Piper and Co., 1977) 10. [translation by the author]. Original quote: Während meine Mutter zur ersten Generation der studierenden Frauen in Amerika gehörte, die alle Zeit und alles Denken der Wissenschaft widmeten, war Edna mehr ein college girl der Jahrhundertwende, weniger einseitig im Bestreben, den Männern geistig Ebenbürtigkeit zu beweisen; sie trieb Sport, war überhaupt für Spiele und Lustbarkeiten zu haben – das ging meiner Mutter ab.

111. Wright, "Marcella O'Grady Boveri," 644.

112. Theodor Boveri, *The Origin of Malignant Tumors*, trans. Marcella Boveri (Baltimore, MD: Williams and Wilkins, 1929).

113. Born in 1861 in Cavendish, Vermont, to the family of a carpenter, Stevens did not receive a higher education until she was in her thirties.

114. Stephen G. Brush, "Nettie M. Stevens and the Discovery of Sex Determination by Chromosomes," *Isis* 69 (1978): 167-69.

115. Kass-Simon, "Biology Is Destiny," 226.

116. M., "In Memoriam: Nettie Maria Stevens," *Bryn Mawr Alumnae Quarterly* June 1912: 124-25.

117. Maltby, *History of the Fellowships* 42.

118. Brush, "Nettie M. Stevens," 164.

119. Maltby, *History of the Fellowships* 41-42.

120. Eells, "Earned Doctorates," 649.

121. Siegel and Finley, *Women in the Scientific Search* 361.

122. Leonard, *Woman's Who's Who* 429.

123. "Dr. Peebles Gets Honorary Degree From Goucher College," *Pasadena Star News* June 25, 1954.

124. Alumnae Biographical Files, Florence Peebles, 1895, Goucher College Archives, Baltimore, Maryland. Mary Jane Hogue, "The Contributions of Goucher Women to the Biological Sciences," *Goucher Alumnae Quarterly* Summer 1951: 14-15; Maltby, *History of the Fellowships* 50-51; "Dr. Peebles Gets Honorary Degree From Goucher College."

125. Kass-Simon, "Biology Is Destiny," 220.

126. Wright, "Marcella O'Grady Boveri," 641; "Alumnae Notes," *Kalends (Goucher)* November 1909: 44; Hessenauer, *Etappen des Frauenstudiums* 175.

127. Mary Jane Hogue and Theodor Boveri, "Über die Möglichkeit, Ascaris-Eier zur Teilung in zwei gleichwertige Blastomeren zu veranlassen," *Sitz.-Ber. Phys.-Med. Ges. Würzburg* (1909).

128. "Dr. Mary Jane Hogue, Anatomist, was 78," *New York Times* September 13, 1962: 37. Alumnae Biographical Files, Mary Jane Hogue, 1905, Goucher College Archives, Baltimore, Maryland. Hogue is also mentioned in Leonard, *Woman's Who's Who* 396.

129. Boring was born on February 22, 1883, in Philadelphia.

130. Alice Middleton Boring, "A Small Chromosome in *Ascaris megalocephala*," *Archiv für Zellforschung* 4 (1909); Alice Middleton Boring, "On the Effects of Different Temperatures on the Size of the Nuclei in the Embryo of *Ascaris megalocephala*, with Remarks on the Size-Relation of the Nuclei in Univalens and Bivalens," *Arch. Entwick.-Mech.* 28 (1909): 118-26.

131. Wright, "Marcella O'Grady Boveri," 641.

132. Leonard, *Woman's Who's Who* 115.

133. *Woman's Who's Who of America, 1914-1915* has Platt earning her doctoral degree in 1895. Doctoral records from the university archives at Freiburg give the 1898 date. Universitätsarchiv Freiburg, B 42/1363, D 29/7-2539. Nauck, *Das Frauenstudium* 62.

134. Platt was the daughter of Ellen Loomis Barlow and the lawyer George King Platt. She was born on September 14, 1857, in San Francisco and was baptized in the Unitarian Church. At some point, her family relocated to Burlington, Vermont.

135. Universitätsarchiv Freiburg, B 42/1363, D 29/7-2539. For more on Platt, see: Boehm, "Von den Anfängen," 319-20.

136. Leonard, *Woman's Who's Who* 576.

137. "Graduate Scholarships," *Bryn Mawr Alumnae Quarterly* June 1911: 78; *The Lantern (Bryn Mawr)* 1895: 99.

138. Siegel and Finley, *Women in the Scientific Search* 237.

139. Siegel and Finley, *Women in the Scientific Search* 237; Hogue, "The Contributions of Goucher Women," 15-16.

140. Maltby, *History of the Fellowships;* "Alumnae Notes," *Goucher Kalends* 25 (1914): 223.

141. Alumnae Biographical Files, Ethel Browne Harvey, 1906, Goucher College Archives, Baltimore, Maryland.. Siegel and Finley, *Women in the Scientific Search* 364; Hogue, "The Contributions of Goucher Women," 16-17. Browne Harvey went on to become an important researcher in zoology, publishing *The American Arbacia and Other Sea Urchins* (1956) as well as numerous papers. She completed her Ph.D. at Columbia University (1913) and received an honorary degree from Goucher in 1956. Some have argued that she did not receive all the recognition she deserved.

For an excellent article about Browne Harvey's work, see: Howard M. Lenhoff, "Ethel Browne, Hans Spemann, and the Discovery of the Organizer Phenomenon," *Biological Bulletin* 181 (1991): 72-80.

142. Palmieri, *In Adamless Eden* 82.

143. Palmieri, *In Adamless Eden* 173-74.

144. Palmieri, *In Adamless Eden* 47-48.

145. Staatsarchiv des Kantons Zürich, Universitätsmatrikel, UU24a1-5.

146. Palmieri, *In Adamless Eden* 175.

147. "Mary A. Willcox of Wellesley, 97," *New York Times* June 7, 1953: 84.

148. "The American Women's Table. Zoological Station at Naples. 1914-1915," *Wellesley College News* November 19, 1914: 7.

149. "College Notes," *Wellesley College News* October 21, 1903: 3.

150. Palmieri, *In Adamless Eden* 175.

151. Palmieri, *In Adamless Eden* 119, 133.

152. Emma Perry Carr, "One Hundred Years of Science at Mount Holyoke College," *Mount Holyoke Alumnae Quarterly* 20 (1936): 135-38.

153. Rossiter, *Women Scientists in America: Struggles and Strategies to 1940* 36.

154. Rossiter, *Women Scientists in America: Struggles and Strategies to 1940* 35, 37.

155. For more on the influence of Liebig on American chemists, see: Margaret W. Rossiter, *The Emergence of Agricultural Science: Justus Liebig and the Americans, 1840-1880* (New Haven, CT: Yale University Press, 1975); John W. Servos, *Physical Chemistry from Ostwald to Pauling: The Making of a Science in America* (Princeton, NJ: Princeton University Press, 1990). For an excellent article on the growing synthetic fuel industry of the early twentieth century, see: Anthony N. Stranges, "Friedrich Bergius and the Rise of the German Synthetic Fuel Industry," *Isis* 75 (1984): 643-67.

156. For more on the history of the study of chemistry and chemical research in Germany during the period of this study, see: Johnson, *The Kaiser's Chemists;* David Cahan, "Helmholtz and the Civilizing Power of Science," *Hermann von Helmholtz and the Foundations of Nineteenth-Century Science*, ed. David Cahan, vol. 12, California Studies in the History of Science (Berkeley: University of California Press, 1993) 559-601; Baumgarten, *Professoren und Universitäten;* Leitner, *Der Fall Clara Immerwahr.*

157. Helen Cecilia De Silver Abbott Michael, *Studies in Plant and Organic Chemistry and Literary Papers* (Cambridge, MA: Riverside Press, 1907).

158. Michael, *Studies in Plant and Organic Chemistry* 38.

159. Michael, *Studies in Plant and Organic Chemistry* 46.

160. Michael, *Studies in Plant and Organic Chemistry* 54.

161. The "Miss Gregory" mentioned here is Emily L. Gregory, who is discussed further in the section on Botany. Michael, *Studies in Plant and Organic Chemistry* 59.

162. Michael, *Studies in Plant and Organic Chemistry* 66.

163. "Our Outlook," *Courant (Wellesley)* December 14, 1888: 3.

164. Ann T. Tarbell and D. Stanley Tarbell, "Helen Abbott Michael: Pioneer in Plant Chemistry," *Journal of Chemical Education* 59.7 (1982): 549.

165. Michael, *Studies in Plant and Organic Chemistry* 101.

166. Tarbell and Tarbell, "Helen Abbott Michael," 549.

167. *Verzeichnis zürischer Universitätsschriften 1833-1897*, Nr. 1377.

168. Staatsarchiv des Kantons Zürich, U110e.3 (1886).

169. Jane A. Miller, "Women in Chemistry," *Women of science: righting the record*, eds. G. Kass-Simon, Patricia Farnes and Deborah Nash (Bloomington: Indiana University Press, 1990) 314.

170. Robert E. Knoll, *Prairie University: A History of the University of Nebraska* (Lincoln: University of Nebraska Press, 1995) 19.

171. Knoll, *Prairie University* 21.

172. Knoll, *Prairie University* 23.; Ann T. Tarbell and D. Stanley Tarbell, "Dr. Rachel Lloyd (1839-1900): American Chemist," *Journal of Chemical Education* 59.9 (1982): 744.

173. Miller, "Women in Chemistry," 315.

174. Rossiter, *Women Scientists in America: Struggles and Strategies to 1940* 78.

175. "Als Professorin der Chemie," *Dokumente der Frauen* 5 (1901): 161.

176. Humboldt-Universität zu Berlin, Universitätsarchiv, Hörerlisten, WS 1899/00. Palmieri, *In Adamless Eden* 85, 175-76; Ellen L. Burrell, "Charlotte Fitch Roberts," *The Wellesley Alumnae Quarterly* January, 1918; "Alumnae Notes," *The Wellesley College News* March 21, 1906: 6.

177. Palmieri, *In Adamless Eden* 176. Chemistry laboratories were a regular part of the curriculum from the time Mount Holyoke opened in 1837. From 1897 to 1907, Dr. Nellie E. Goldthwaite continued the tradition of excellence in the Mount Holyoke chemistry department. See: Carr, "One Hundred Years."

178. Biographical Files, Helen S. French, Wellesley College Archives.

179. Milroy was born in Detroit on December 4, 1869. Her father was a landowner.

180. Humboldt-Universität zu Berlin, Universitätsarchiv, Promotionen, Philosoph. Facultät, Littr.P, Nr.4, Vol.179, 388, S.606-641.

181. Miller, "Women in Chemistry," 323.

182. Miller, "Women in Chemistry," 333.

183. Miller, "Women in Chemistry," 323.

184. Mary Violet Dover, "Experiments with Diphenylcyclohexenone," *American Chemical Journal* 37 (1907): 385-92.

185. Universitätsarchiv Wroclaw, Philosophische Fakultät Acta, Doctor Promotionen 1907/08, vol.4. F208, p.25-35.

186. Biographical Dictionary 1937, Mount Holyoke College Archives, South Hadley, Massachusetts. Herman Schlundt Papers, 1913-1941 (C15), Western Historical Manuscript Collection, University of Missouri-Columbia.

187. Rossiter, *Women Scientists in America: Struggles and Strategies to 1940* 3.

188. Rossiter, *Women Scientists in America: Struggles and Strategies to 1940* 61.

189. Rossiter, *Women Scientists in America: Struggles and Strategies to 1940* 61.

190. Marianne Gosztonyi Ainley, "Last in the Field? Canadian Women Natural Scientists, 1815-1965," *Despite the odds: essays on Canadian women and science*, ed. Marianne Gosztonyi Ainley (Buffalo, NY: Véhicule Press, 1990) 29.

191. Ainley, "Last in the Field?" 36.

192. Margaret Gillett, "Carrie Derick (1862-1941) and the Chair of Botany at McGill," *Despite the odds: essays on Canadian women and science*, ed. Marianne Gosztonyi Ainley (Buffalo, NY: Véhicule Press, 1990) 76-77.

193. Gillett, "Carrie Derick," 77.

194. "Aus wissenschaftlichen Berufsständen," *Zürcher Wochen-Chronik* 1908: 141.

195. Staatsarchiv des Kantons Zürich, U110e.3 (1886). *Verzeichnis zürischer Universitätsschriften 1833-1897*, Nr. 1363.

196. Rossiter, *Women Scientists in America: Struggles and Strategies to 1940* 17.

197. Rossiter, *Women Scientists in America: Struggles and Strategies to 1940* 83.

198. Ida Augusta Keller was born in Darmstadt on July 1, 1866, while her American parents were temporarily living in Germany. In 1872 Keller's family returned to Philadelphia. See: Staatsarchiv des Kantons Zürich, U110e.3 (1890).

199. Staatsarchiv des Kantons Zürich, U110e.3 (1890). *Verzeichnis zürischer Universitätsschriften 1833-1897*, Nr. 1469.

200. Siegel and Finley, *Women in the Scientific Search* 98; Leonard, *Woman's Who's Who* 448.

201. Randolph was born in Philadelphia. Leonard, *Woman's Who's Who* 671.

202. Staatsarchiv des Kantons Zürich, U 110e.4 (1892).

203. Siegel and Finley, *Women in the Scientific Search* 353.

204. Julia Warner Snow was born on August 30, 1863 in La Salle, Illinois, to E. Charlotte D. Snow and Norman G. Snow. See: Leonard, *Woman's Who's Who* 765.

205. Rossiter, *Women Scientists in America: Struggles and Strategies to 1940* 19.

206. Staatsarchiv des Kantons Zürich, U110e.4 (1893). Maltby, *History of the Fellowships* 13-14.

207. Schröter specialized in geographical adaptions of plants and published numerous articles and books on the subject. H. Tribolet, *Historisch-Biographisches Lexikon der Schweiz*, vol. 6 (Neuenburg: Administration des Historisch-Biographischen Lexikons der Schweiz, 1931) 245. Staatsarchiv des Kantons Zürich.

208. Staatsarchiv des Kantons Zürich, U110e.4 (1893).

209. *Verzeichnis zürischer Universitätsschriften 1833-1897*, Nr. 1550.

210. Maltby, *History of the Fellowships* 13-14; Siegel and Finley, *Women in the Scientific Search* 97; "Julia W. Snow: In Memoriam," *The Smith Alumnae Quarterly* November (1927); Leonard, *Woman's Who's Who* 765.

211. Biographical Files, Grace E. Cooley, Wellesley College Archives. "Alumnae Notes," *Wellesley Magazine* May 1894: 438.

212. Staatsarchiv des Kantons Zürich, U110e.4 (1894). *Verzeichnis zürischer Universitätsschriften 1833-1897*, Nr. 1613.

213. Biographical Files, Grace E. Cooley, Wellesley College Archives.

214. Alumnae Biographical Files, Martha Mann Magoun, Wellesley College Archives.

215. "Wellesley College," *The Courant (Wellesley)* September 21, 1888: 1.

216. Universitätsarchiv Heidelberg, Promotionskartei der Naturwiss.-Mathem. Fakultät. Janet Russell Perkins completed her doctoral degree on March 9, 1900. Humboldt-Universität zu Berlin, Universitätsarchiv, Hörerlisten.

217. Leonard, *Woman's Who's Who* 640.

218. Charles C. Colby, "Ellen Churchill Semple," *Annals of the Association of American Geographers* 23 (1933): 238.

219. Baumgarten, *Professoren und Universitäten* 78; *The Nation* 69 (1899): 486-87.

220. Colby, "Ellen Churchill Semple," 231.

221. Wallace W. Atwood, "An Appreciation of Ellen Churchill Semple, 1863-1932," *The Journal of Geography* 31 (1932): 267.

222. Colby, "Ellen Churchill Semple," 237-38.

223. Gladys Hall Coates, "The Coming of Women to the University of North Carolina," *By Her Own Bootstraps*, ed. Albert Coates (Chapel Hill, NC: Albert Coates,

1975) 43-45. For more on the history of women at the University of North Carolina, see: Albert Coates, *By her bootstraps: a saga of women in North Carolina* (Chapel Hill, NC: Albert Coates, 1975); Gladys Hall Coates, *Some recollections of early days in Chapel Hill and the University* (Chapel Hill, NC: n. p., 1992).

224. Wendehorst, *Geschichte* 141. Although the geology of the island of Spitsbergen had been studied since the 1820s, it was not until 1896 that a study of the interior of the island began. In 1897, William Martin Conway published a chronicle of an expedition through part of the interior, *The First Crossing of Spitsbergen.*

225. Grace Anna Stewart earned her degree from the University of Alberta in 1918. Ainley, "Last in the Field?" 31.

226.. Margaret W. Rossiter, "Geology in Nineteenth-Century Women's Education in the United States," *Journal of Geological Education* 29 (1981): 231.

227. Frederick Gleason Corning, *A Student Reverie: An Album of Saxony Days* (New York: 1920) 25.

228. Corning's work, published two years after the conclusion of World War I, was significant for portraying Germany as a valuable friend at a time when anti-German sentiment continued to dominate. Almost forty years after it was published, Corning's work was praised for having helped to reestablish the reputation of Freiberg in the international community. In 1922 Corning was made an honorary member of the faculty senate of the Freiberg School of Mines, and in 1937 he received an honorary doctorate from the school. See: Walter Hoffmann, *Bergakademie Freiberg* (Frankfurt am Main: Wolfgang Weidlich, 1959) 98.

229. Corning, *A Student Reverie* 22.

230. Sara L. Saunders-Lee, ed., *In Memoriam. Mrs. Erminnie A. Smith* (Boston: Lee and Shepard, 1890) 19.

231. Hanaford, *Daughters of America* 269.

232. Saunders-Lee, ed., *In Memoriam. Mrs. Erminnie A. Smith* 16-17.

233. Saunders-Lee, ed., *In Memoriam. Mrs. Erminnie A. Smith* 68-84.

234. Nancy Oestreich Lurie, "Erminnie Adele Platt Smith," *Notable American Women 1607-1950*, eds. Edward T. James, Janet Wilson James, Paul S. Boyer, et al., vol. 3 (Cambridge, MA: Belknap Press of Harvard University Press, 1971) 312.

235. Lurie, "Erminnie Adele Platt Smith," 313; Siegel and Finley, *Women in the Scientific Search* 16-17.

236. David Eugene Smith, "Mary Hegeler Carus, 1861-1936," *The American Mathematical Monthly* 44.5 (1937): 280.

237. The first woman to earn a doctoral degree in geology was Mary E. Holmes, who earned her degree at the University of Michigan in 1888. Jill S. Schneiderman, "Rock Stars. A Life of Firsts: Florence Bascom," *GSA Today* (1997): 8; Rossiter, "Geology," 231.

238. Rossiter, *Women Scientists in America: Struggles and Strategies to 1940* 45.

239. Rossiter, "Geology," 231; A. C. Swinnerton, "Edward Orton, Geologist," *Science* 89 (1939): 373-78.

240. Elizabeth A. Wood, *Crystals and light; an introduction to optical crystallography* (Princeton, NJ: Published for the Commission on College Physics [by] Van Nostrand, 1964).

241. For a more complete list of Bascom's students, see: Schneiderman, "Rock Stars," 9.

242. Although Goldschmidt had a patent for his own version of the goniometer, the instrument was actually constructed in 1874 by H. Miller (1801-1880), a British scientist famous for the concept of the Miller indices for identifying crystal faces.

243. Florence Bascom to Victor Goldschmidt, January 14, 1914, Florence Bascom Papers, Sophia Smith Collection, Smith College, Northampton, Massachusetts.

244. Florence Bascom to Victor Goldschmidt, January 28, 1917, Florence Bascom Papers, Sophia Smith Collection, Smith College, Northampton, Massachusetts.

245. Florence Bascom to Victor Goldschmidt, September 4, 1922, Florence Bascom Papers, Sophia Smith Collection, Smith College, Northampton, Massachusetts.

CHAPTER FIVE: WOMEN IN THE SOCIAL SCIENCES AND PSYCHOLOGY

1. Dorothy Ross, "The Development of the Social Sciences," *The Organization of Knowledge in Modern America, 1860-1920*, eds. Alexandra Oleson and John Voss (Baltimore, MD: The Johns Hopkins University Press, 1979) 107.

2. Ross, "The Development of the Social Sciences," 108.

3. Christopher Bernert, "Die Wanderjahre: The Higher Education of American Students in German Universities, 1870 to 1914," Diss, SUNY Stony Brook, 1984, 65-66.

4. Ellen F. Fitzpatrick, *Endless Crusade: Women Social Scientists and Progressive Reform* (New York: Oxford University Press, 1990) 32.

5. Fitzpatrick, *Endless Crusade* 13.

6. Fitzpatrick, *Endless Crusade* 30.

7. Fitzpatrick, *Endless Crusade* 32-33.

8. Fitzpatrick, *Endless Crusade* 29-30.

9. Fitzpatrick, *Endless Crusade* 190.

10. Amy Hewes, "The Study of Sociology in Chicago and Berlin," *Kalends (Goucher)* April 1900: 196-99.

11. Rossiter, *Women Scientists in America: Struggles and Strategies to 1940* 198.

12. Alumnae Biographical Files, Amy Hewes, 1897, Goucher College Archives, Baltimore, Maryland. "Mt Holyoke's Amy Hewes, wage pioneer, dies at 93," *The Boston Globe (evening)* March 25, 1970; "Alumnae Notes," *Kalends (Goucher)* January 1914: 110.

13. Emily Greene Balch was born on January 8, 1867, near Boston, the daughter of Ellen Maria Noyes and the attorney Francis Vergnies Balch.

14. Jane Addams, Emily G. Balch and Alice Hamilton, *Women at the Hague: The International Congress of Women and its Results* (New York: Macmillan, 1916) 9.

15. Addams, Balch and Hamilton, *Women at the Hague* 15.

16. Barbara Miller Solomon, "Emily Greene Balch," *Notable American Women, The Modern Period*, eds. Barbara Sicherman, Carol Hurd Green, Ilene Kantrov, et al. (Cambridge, MA: Belknap Press of Harvard University Press, 1980) 42.

17. Randall, *Improper Bostonian* 82.

18. Randall, *Improper Bostonian* 83.

19. Randall, *Improper Bostonian* 83-84.

20. Randall, *Improper Bostonian* 86-87.

21. Randall, *Improper Bostonian* 90.

22. Randall, *Improper Bostonian* 92.

23. Palmieri, *In Adamless Eden* 170-71.

24. "Review of Our Slavic Fellow Citizens," *Bryn Mawr Alumnae Quarterly* April 1911: 37-38.

25. Mary Melinda Kingsbury Simkhovitch, *Neighborhood; my story of Greenwich House*, 1st ed. (New York: Norton, 1938) 51.

26. Simkhovitch, *Neighborhood* 52.

27. Carroll Smith-Rosenberg, "Mary Kingsbury Simkhovitch," *Notable American Women, The Modern Period*, eds. Barbara Sicherman, Carol Hurd Green, Ilene Kantrov, et al. (Cambridge, MA: Belknap Press of Harvard University Press, 1980) 649.

28. Smith-Rosenberg, "Mary Kingsbury Simkhovitch," 650.

29. Louise C Wade, "Florence Kelley," *Notable American Women, 1607-1950*, eds. Edward T. James, Janet Wilson James, Paul S. Boyer, et al., vol. 2 (Cambridge, MA: Belknap Press of Harvard University Press, 1971) 317.

30. Kelley and Sklar, *Notes of sixty years* 38.

31. Randall, *Improper Bostonian* 51-52.

32. Kelley and Sklar, *Notes of sixty years* 54.

33. Kelley and Sklar, *Notes of sixty years* 72.

34. Forrer-Gutknecht, *Das Frauenstudium* 49.

35. Kelley and Sklar, *Notes of sixty years* 73.

36. Kelley and Sklar, *Notes of sixty years* 103.

37. Edmond Kelly and Florence Kelley, *Twentieth Century Socialism; What it is Not; What it is; How it May Come* (New York: Longmans Green and Co., 1910).

38. Kelley and Sklar, *Notes of sixty years* 10.

39. Hamilton, *Exploring the dangerous trades* 62.

40. Wade, "Florence Kelley," 316.

41. Wade, "Florence Kelley," 318.

42. Randall, *Improper Bostonian* 264-65.

43. Wade, "Florence Kelley," 318.

44. Fitzpatrick, *Endless Crusade* 15-16.

45. Fitzpatrick, *Endless Crusade* 47.

46. Katharine Bement Davis, "Three Score Years and Ten: An Autobiographical Essay," *University of Chicago Magazine* 26.2 (1933): 59.

47. Katharine Bement Davis, "The Modern Condition of Agricultural Labor in Bohemia," *Journal of Political Economy* 8 (1900); Fitzpatrick, *Endless Crusade* 55-56.

48. Fitzpatrick, *Endless Crusade* 73.

49. Fitzpatrick, *Endless Crusade* 98.

50. Most of Davis's attempts at reform failed in the face of a limited budget, lack of state support and overcrowded facilities. Her attempts at improving conditions had included training women in nontraditional jobs, such as working in a steam laundry and doing grounds maintenance, as well as educational programs. She encouraged activities that allowed women to be outside to improve their health. Davis was also progressive for her time in believing that the causes of criminal behavior in African American and white women were the same. Therefore, she housed African American and white women together in the reformatory.

Eventually, Davis would leave Bedford Hills to become the commissioner of correction for New York City, a position she would hold until 1916. Not only was Davis the first woman to hold this position, she was the first woman to hold a cabinet-level position in that city. As commissioner, Davis got rid of the striped clothing for prisoners and enforced tighter security at the prisons. She helped to improve the food and medical care at the prisons and ended sightseeing tours at the Tombs. While Davis did manage to start a new farm school reformatory for boys on Hart's Island, she failed to win for women sentenced for misdemeanors the funding for a new facility that would keep these women separate from those accused of more severe crimes. A plan of hers for a drug treatment center on Riker's Island also failed for lack of funding. Fitzpatrick's biography of Davis includes numerous examples of her failures and shortsightedness, but also evidence of Davis's great courage. During a riot at the Blackwell Island prison, Davis risked her life to remain at the prison to negotiate with the inmates.

In addition to other measures of reform, Davis was an advocate of parole. In 1916 Davis served on the newly created New York City Parole Commission, a position she held for one year. With a change in the mayor's office, Davis lost her appointment. Most of the rest of her career, Davis worked for the Bureau of Social Hygiene, which had been formed in 1911 to support research on prostitution and was funded through the Rockefeller Foundation. Her Laboratory of Social Hygiene at Bedford Hills closed in 1918, and with that her dream of an extensive social scientific research institute led by women came to an end.

51. Elizabeth D. L. Lewis was born on October 4, 1880, in Lynchburg, Virginia. She was the daughter of Elizabeth née Langhorne and John H. Lewis, an attorney. Elizabeth Dabney Langhorne Lewis Otey (1880-1974) Collection, Jones Memorial Library, Lynchburg, Virginia. Alumnae Biographical Files, Elizabeth Dabney Langhorne Lewis, 1901, Bryn Mawr College Archives.

52. Both Helen and Florence Allen were studying history at the University of Berlin during Winter Semester 1904/05. Both women had attended the University of Cleveland before coming to Berlin.

53. E. S., "Ein geselliger Abend bei den Berliner Studentinnen," *Frauen-Rundschau* (1904): 1465.

54. Humboldt-Universität zu Berlin, Universitätsarchiv, Promotionen, Philosoph. Facultät, Littr.P, Nr.4, Vol.216, 425, S.425-459.

55. "Class Notes," *Bryn Mawr Alumnae Bulletin* Fall 1973: 26.

56. Elizabeth Dabney Langhorne Lewis Otey (1880-1974) Collection, Jones Memorial Library, Lynchburg, Virginia. Alumnae Biographical Files, Elizabeth Dabney Langhorne Lewis, 1901, Bryn Mawr College Archives. "The Alumnae," *Bryn Mawr Alumnae Quarterly* June 1908: 76; "The Alumnae ['01]," *Bryn Mawr Alumnae Quarterly* October 1908: 57; "News from the Classes," *Bryn Mawr Alumnae Quarterly* April 1913: 16.

57. Faculty Biographical File, Anna Pritchett Youngman, Wellesley College Archives. "Anna P. Youngman, Former Post Writer," *Washington Post* February 17, 1974; "President's Report (Wellesley College)," (1921): 6-7; Maltby, *History of the Fellowships* 43-44.

58. "Resident Fellows for the Year 1904-1905," *The Lantern (Bryn Mawr)* 1904: 80.

59. Katharine Susan Anthony was born on November 27, 1877, in Roseville, Arkansas, as the daughter of Susan Jane (Cathey) and Ernest Augustus Anthony. Before traveling to Germany, she studied at the Peabody College for Teachers in Nashville, Tennessee from 1895 to 1897.

60. Morris Bishop, *A History of Cornell* (Ithaca, NY: Cornell University Press, 1962) 277-78.

61. Scarborough and Furumoto, *Untold Lives* 6-8.

62. In the 1890s four American universities had doctoral programs in psychology and admitted women: the University of Chicago, Cornell, the University of Pennsylvania and Yale. See: Scarborough and Furumoto, *Untold Lives* 211, no.8.

63. Bishop, *A History of Cornell* 167.

64. Bishop, *A History of Cornell* 276.

65. Bishop, *A History of Cornell* 201.

66. In 1908 Eucken won the Nobel Prize for Literature. Baumgarten, *Professoren und Universitäten* 206-09; Rudolf Eucken, *Lebenserinnerungen. Ein Stück deutschen Lebens* (Leipzig: 1922) 122.

67. MacFee was born in St. Chrysostome, Quebec. Her parents were Colonel M. and Catharine (McNaughton) MacFee. Staatsarchiv des Kantons Zürich, U109e.4(1895). Leonard, *Woman's Who's Who* 519.

68. Staatsarchiv des Kantons Zürich, U109e.4(1895).

69. Staatsarchiv des Kantons Zürich, U109e.4(1895).

70. Leonard, *Woman's Who's Who* 519.

71. *Verzeichnis zürischer Universitätsschriften 1833-1897*, Nr. 1644.

72. Staatsarchiv des Kantons Zürich, U109e.4(1895).

73. Apparently this college offered remarkable opportunities for faculty members to complete graduate studies while teaching. The American botanist, Julia Warner Snow, also taught at this college from 1894 to 1896 while taking courses at the University of Basel. For more on Snow, see Chapter Four.

74. Roderic H. Davison, "Mary Mills Patrick," *Notable American women, 1607-1950; a biographical dictionary*, eds. Edward T. James, Janet Wilson James, Paul S. Boyer, et al., vol. 3 (Cambridge, MA: Belknap Press of Harvard University Press, 1971) 25-26. Staatsarchiv des Kantons Zürich, Matriculation Nr. 10079. Humboldt-Universität zu Berlin, Universitätsarchiv, Gasthörerverzeichnisse (SS 1901).

75. Keiver Smith was born in Amherst, Nova Scotia, on December 29, 1856, and completed her teachers' exams at Saint John, New Brunswick.

76. Staatsarchiv des Kantons Zürich, U109e.5 (1899).

77. Dorothy Rogers, *Oswego: fountainhead of teacher education; a century in the Sheldon tradition* (New York: Appleton-Century-Crofts, 1961) 12.

78. Siegel and Finley, *Women in the Scientific Search* 303-04; Leonard, *Woman's Who's Who* 761-62; Scarborough and Furumoto, *Untold Lives* 161.

79. Mary Elizabeth Laing was born on September 15, 1853 [or 1854].

80. Rogers, *Oswego* 25; Leonard, *Woman's Who's Who* 470.

81. Ida B. Earhart was born on October 26, 1864.

82. Rogers, *Oswego* 142.

83. Maltby, *History of the Fellowships* 18; Siegel and Finley, *Women in the Scientific Search* 284; Eells, "Earned Doctorates," 650.

84. Universitätsarchiv Halle, Rep.21 II Nr.173; Eckardt, "Zwei Amerikanerinnen," 236-37; Leonard, *Woman's Who's Who* 111.

85. "Minnie Belle" Rowena Morse was born on June 16, 1870, in Ithaca, New York. See: Tucker, *Prophetic Sisterhood* 34; Leonard, *Woman's Who's Who* 537.

86. Eckardt, "Zwei Amerikanerinnen," 244.

87. Eckardt, "Zwei Amerikanerinnen," 236-38.

88. Eckardt, "Zwei Amerikanerinnen," 240-41.

89. Tucker, *Prophetic Sisterhood* 225.

90. Tucker, *Prophetic Sisterhood* 76.

91. Tucker, *Prophetic Sisterhood* 34-35 and 232-33.

92. Tucker, *Prophetic Sisterhood* 226-27.

93. Maltby, *History of the Fellowships* 28.

94. Universitätsarchiv Heidelberg, Promotionskartei der philosophischen Fakultät.

95. Florence Mary Fitch was born on February 17, 1875, the younger of two daughters of Anna H. Fitch and Pastor Frank S. Fitch. 1900 U.S. Census.

96. Humboldt-Universität zu Berlin, Universitätsarchiv, Promotionen, Philosoph. Facultät, Littr.P, Nr.4, Vol.173, 384, S.75-86. Leonard, *Woman's Who's Who* 293-94; Maltby, *History of the Fellowships* 23.

97. Universitätsarchiv Freiburg, B 42/1421. Nauck, *Das Frauenstudium* 62.

98. For more on Florine and Carrie Stettheimer, see Chapter Six on Fine Arts.

99. Bloemink, *The life and art of Florine Stettheimer* 133.

100. Universitätsarchiv Leipzig, Phil. Fak. Prom., 4523, No.20.

101. Julian Jaynes, "Georg Elias Müller," *Dictionary of Scientific Biography*, vol. 9 (New York: Charles Scribner's Sons, 1974) 561-63.

102. William O. Krohn, "Facilities in Experimental Psychology at the Various German Universities," *American Journal of Psychology* 4 (1892): 585-94.

103. These women were Emily K. Schupp from Duluth, Minnesota, who studied in Munich from 1900 to 1902, and Emma Wilson Mooers, a physician, who studied psychiatry and anatomy during the Winter Semester of 1905-06. Universitätsarchiv München, Gasthörerverzeichnisse.

104. Külpe taught philosophy and psychology at Würzburg from 1894 to 1909. The British psychologist Beatrice Edgell, the first woman to earn a doctoral degree (1902) from Würzburg, went there to work with Oswald Külpe. Albisetti states that Edgell earned her degree in 1901; Harrower claims Edgell earned her doctorate in 1906. Albisetti, *Schooling German Girls and Women* 232; Molly R. Harrower, "Molly R. Harrower," *Models of Achievement: Reflections of Eminent Women in Psychology*, eds. Agnes N. O'Connell and Nancy Felipe Russo (New York: Columbia University Press, 1983) 155. For more complete information, see: Hessenauer, *Etappen des Frauenstudiums* 174.

105. Scarborough and Furumoto, *Untold Lives* 187; Maltby, *History of the Fellowships* 23.

106. Maltby, *History of the Fellowships* 23-24.

107. Scarborough and Furumoto, *Untold Lives* 187-88.

108. Alumnae Biographical Files, Helen Dodd Cook, 1905, Wellesley College Archives. Hessenauer, *Etappen des Frauenstudiums* 175.

109. Siegel and Finley, *Women in the Scientific Search* 282; Leonard, *Woman's Who's Who* 348; Rossiter, "Doctorates," 162.

110. "Dr. Ladd-Franklin, Educator, 82, Dies," *New York Times* March 6, 1930: 23.

111. Ladd-Franklin, "Endowed Professorships for Women."

112. Rossiter, *Women Scientists in America: Struggles and Strategies to 1940* 40.

113. Dorothea Jameson Hurvich, "Christine Ladd-Franklin," *Notable American Women, 1607-1950*, eds. Edward T. James, Janet Wilson James, Paul S. Boyer, et al., vol. 2 (Cambridge, MA: Belknap Press of Harvard University Press, 1971) 355; "Dr. Ladd-Franklin, Educator, 82, Dies."; Siegel and Finley, *Women in the Scientific Search* 299-300.

114. "Dr. Ladd-Franklin, Educator, 82, Dies," 23.

115. Martin was born in Olean, New York, the daughter of Lydia (Hawes) Martin and Russel Martin, a businessman. See: "Martin, Lillien Jane," *Current Biography Yearbook* (New York: H. W. Wilson Co., 1942) 575-76.

116. De Ford, *Psychologist unretired* 55.

117. De Ford, *Psychologist unretired* 58.

118. De Ford, *Psychologist unretired* 59-60.

119. De Ford, *Psychologist unretired* 59.

120. De Ford, *Psychologist unretired* 64.

121. Rossiter, *Women Scientists in America: Struggles and Strategies to 1940* 285.

122. De Ford, *Psychologist unretired* 88.

123. "Martin, Lillien Jane," 577.

124. Scarborough and Furumoto, *Untold Lives* 189-91; Siegel and Finley, *Women in the Scientific Search* 301.

125. Eleanor Acheson McCulloch Gamble was born in Cincinnati, Ohio, in 1868. Her father was a pastor.

126. Eells, "Earned Doctorates," 650.

127. Siegel and Finley, *Women in the Scientific Search* 310; Scarborough and Furumoto, *Untold Lives* 170.

128. Palmieri, *In Adamless Eden* 126. One joint publication was: Mary Whiton Calkins and Eleanor Acheson McCulloch Gamble, "The Self-Psychology of the Psychoanalysis," *The Psychological Review*.July (1930).

129. Siegel and Finley, *Women in the Scientific Search* 310.

130. Theodate Smith was born on April 11, 1859, in Hallowell, Maine, the daughter of Philomela Hall Smith and Thomas Smith, a shipowner.

131. Scarborough and Furumoto, *Untold Lives* 198.

132. G. Stanley Hall, *Aspects of child life and education*, ed. Theodate Louise Smith (Boston: Ginn and Co., 1907).

133. "Smith, Theodate Louise," *Obituary Record of Graduates of Yale University 1910-1915* (New Haven, CT: Yale University Press, 1915); Scarborough and Furumoto, *Untold Lives* 198-99.

134. Scarborough and Furumoto, *Untold Lives* 23-24.

135. Margaret W. Rossiter, "Women Scientists in America before 1920," *American Scientist* 62 (1974): 319.

136. Scarborough and Furumoto, *Untold Lives* 41.

137. Laurel Furumoto, "From 'Paired Associates' to a Psychology of Self: The Intellectual Odyssey of Mary Whiton Calkins," *Portraits of Pioneers in Psychology*, eds. Gregory A. Kimble, Michael Wertheimer and Charlotte L. White (Washington, DC and Hillsdale, NJ: American Psychological Association and Lawrence Erlbaum Associates, 1991) 70.

138. Palmieri, *In Adamless Eden* 171-72.

139. Puffer Howes was born in Framingham, Massachusetts, in 1872. "Pioneer Psychologist was Teacher in KHS," *Sentinel* (Keene, N.H.) November 2, 1950, Ethel Puffer Howes, 42. Faculty Biographical File, Smith College Archives, Northampton, Massachusetts.

140. Palmieri, *In Adamless Eden* 88; Scarborough and Furumoto, *Untold Lives* 78.

141. Furumoto, "From "Paired Associates" to a Psychology of Self," 109-10.

142. Furumoto, "From "Paired Associates" to a Psychology of Self," 110.

143. Scarborough and Furumoto, *Untold Lives* 79-80.

144. Untitled article, Ethel Puffer Howes, 42. Faculty Biographical File, Smith College Archives, Northampton, Massachusetts.

145. Maltby, *History of the Fellowships* 39.

146. For more on Puffer Howes's work at the Institute, see: C. Todd Stephenson, "Dialogue: 'Integrating the Carol Kennicotts': Ethel Puffer Howes and the Institute for the Coordination of Women's Interests," *Journal of Women's History* 4.1 (1992): 89-113.

147. Scarborough and Furumoto, *Untold Lives* 88-90; Furumoto, "From "Paired Associates" to a Psychology of Self," 115-17.

148. Ethel Puffer Howes, "The Meaning of Progress in the Woman Movement," *Annals of the American Academy of Political and Social Science* 143 (1929): 19.

149. Ethel Puffer Howes, "Accepting the Universe," *Atlantic Monthly* April 1922: 444-53.

150. Maud A. Merrill, "Lillien Jane Martin: 1851-1943," *The American Journal of Psychology* 56.3 (1943): 454.

CHAPTER SIX: WOMEN IN THE FINE ARTS

1. Christine Ammer, *Unsung: A History of Women in American Music* (Westport, CT: Greenwood Press, 1980) 163.

2. Renate Berger, "Training and Professionalism: Germany, Austria and Switzerland," *Dictionary of Women Artists*, ed. Delia Graze, vol. 1 (London and Chicago: Fitzroy Dearborn Publishers, 1997) 100; Adolf Weidig, "Observations Upon Present Musical Life in Germany," *Studies in Musical Education History and Aesthetics. Papers and Proceedings of the Music Teachers' National Association* (Northwestern University, Evanston, IL: Music Teachers' National Association, 1909) 48-50.

3. It is rare to find the name of any North American artist who studied in Leipzig. Anna Wilhelmina Grant graduated from the Troy Female Seminary in 1872 and studied art at the National Academy of Design in New York City and in Leipzig. In 1880 Grant married Edward A. Birge, a professor of zoology at the University of Wisconsin in Madison. See: Fairbanks, ed., *Emma Willard* 694.

4. Candace Wheeler, *Yesterdays In a Busy Life* (New York: Harper and Brothers, 1918) 198-99. For more on Wheeler, see: Madeleine B. Stern, *We the Women: Career Firsts of Nineteenth-Century America* (New York: Schulte, 1963) 273-303. The painter Anna Lea Merritt (1844-1930) also studied briefly in Dresden with Heinrich Hoffmann in 1867. See: Charlotte Streifer Rubinstein, *American Women Artists: from Early Indian Times to the Present* (Boston: G. K. Hall, 1982) 112.

5. Swinth, "Painting Professionals."

6. Nancy Mowll Mathews, "Training and Professionalism: North American, 19th Century, U.S.A.," *Dictionary of Women Artists*, ed. Delia Graze, vol. 1 (London and Chicago: Fitzroy Dearborn Publishers, 1997) 132-36.

7. Natalie Luckyj, "Training and Professionalism: North America, 19th Century, Canada," *Dictionary of Women Artists*, ed. Delia Graze, vol. 1 (London and Chicago: Fitzroy Dearborn Publishers, 1997) 136.

8. For accounts of nineteenth-century communities of North American women artists in Italy, France and England, see: Deborah Ellen Barker, "Painting Women: The Woman Artist in Nineteenth-Century American Fiction," Diss, Princeton University, 1991; May Alcott Nieriker, *Studying Art Abroad, and How to do it Cheaply* (Boston: Roberts Brothers, 1879); Sara Foose Parrott, "Expatriates and Professionals: The Careers in Italy of Nineteenth-Century American Women Writers and Artists," Diss, George Washington University, 1988; Swinth, "Painting Professionals."

9. Rubinstein, *American Women Artists* 56.

10. Hanaford, *Daughters of America* 283.

11. Rubinstein, *American Women Artists* 57-58.

12. Josephine W. Duveneck, *Frank Duveneck: Painter – Teacher* (San Francisco, CA: John Howell - Books, 1970) 37.

13. Vernon Hyde Minor, *Art history's history* (Englewood Cliffs, NJ: Prentice Hall, 1994) 86-87.

14. 80, Class of 1900, Heywood, Smith College Archives, Northampton, Massachusetts.

15. 1900 U.S. Census. "Alumnae Notes," *Wellesley College News* October 10, 1901: 3-4.

16. 1900 U.S. Census. "Alumnae Notes," *Wellesley College News* February 20, 1902: 1-2.

17. 1900 U.S. Census. *Smith College Alumnae Biographical Register, 1871-1935*, (Northampton, MA: Smith College, 1935) 87; *Smith Class Yearbook*, (Northampton, Massachusetts: Smith College, 1900).

18. 1900 U.S. Census. *Smith College Alumnae Biographical Register, 1871-1935*, 85; *Smith Class Yearbook*. 80, Class of 1900, Heywood, Smith College Archives, Northampton, Massachusetts.

19. Universitätsarchiv Heidelberg, Promotionskartei der philosophischen Fakultät. Elizabeth H. Denio received her doctoral degree on October 1, 1898.

20. Elizabeth H. Denio, "Letter from Germany," *Wellesley Courant* November 23, 1883: 23.

21. Elizabeth H. Denio, "Letter from Germany," *Wellesley Courant* June 20, 1884: 3.

22 Franz Delitzsch (1813-1890) was a theologian and Hebraist. He was the father of the great linguist Friedrich Delitzsch.

23. Hartwell, "Four Moons Abroad. Amid the Mountains," 3.

24. Palmieri, *In Adamless Eden* 48.

25. "Alumnae Notes," *Wellesley Magazine* October 1897: 34.

26. Her father, Edward J. Hamilton, was a professor. Her mother was Eliza (Cleland) Hamilton.

27. Universitätsarchiv Heidelberg, Promotionskartei der philosophischen Fakultät. Neena Hamilton earned her doctoral degree on September 26, 1901. Leonard, *Woman's Who's Who* 663.

28. *The Nation* 74 (1902): 253.

29. Universitätsarchiv Heidelberg, Promotionskartei der philosophischen Fakultät. Special Collections Research Center, University of Chicago Library.

30. Paula Chiarmonte, ed., *Women Artists in the United States: A Selective Bibliography and Resource Guide on the Fine and Decorative Arts, 1750-1986* (Boston: G. K. Hall, 1990) 20.

31. Berger, "Training and Professionalism," 101.

32. Berger, "Training and Professionalism," 103.

33. A. L., "Munich in Summer," *The Nation* 65 (1897): 128.

34. Anna Mary Howitt, *An art student in Munich* (Boston: Ticknor Reed and Fields, 1854) 92.

35. Jim Collins and Glenn B. Opitz, eds., *Women Artists in America: 18th Century To The Present (1790-1980)* (Poughkeepsie, NY: Apollo, 1980) n.p.

36. Fairbanks, ed., *Emma Willard* 661-62.

37. Pamela Dawson Moffat, "Lilla Cabot Perry," *Dictionary of Women Artists*, ed. Delia Graze, vol. 2 (London and Chicago: Fitzroy Dearborn Publishers, 1997) 1092-94.

38. Moffat, "Lilla Cabot Perry," 1094.

39. Collins and Opitz, eds., *Women Artists* n.p.

40. Duveneck, *Frank Duveneck* 111.

41. Duveneck, *Frank Duveneck* 76.

42. Duveneck, *Frank Duveneck* 76.

43. Duveneck, *Frank Duveneck* 76.

44. Duveneck, *Frank Duveneck* 78.

45. Duveneck, *Frank Duveneck* 80.

46. Duveneck, *Frank Duveneck* 117-18.

47. "Heinrich Knirr," *Allgemeines Lexikon der bildenden Künstler*, ed. Hans Vollmer, vol. 21 (Leipzig: E.A. Seemann, 1927) 3-4.

48. "Moritz Heymann," *Allgemeines Lexikon der bildenden Künstler*, ed. Hans Vollmer, vol. 17 (Leipzig: E.A. Seemann, 1924) 33.

49. Collins and Opitz, eds., *Women Artists* n.p.

50. Collins and Opitz, eds., *Women Artists* n.p.

51. Marian MacIntosh, "News from the Classes [1890]," *Bryn Mawr Alumnae Quarterly* January 1914: 115.

52. Of course, many lesser artists studied in Munich as well. Harriet Sophia Phillips, a painter from New York, studied at the Women's Art Academy. The sculptor Frances Norma Loring of Idaho came to Munich after studying at the Art Institute of Chicago, the Boston Museum Fine Arts School of Art, the Art Students League in New York City as well as in Paris and Geneva. Lillian Bayard Taylor Kiliani studied

etching with Jacobides. After studying at the Denver School of Fine Arts, the artist Harriett McCreary Jackson Shaw of Arkansas came to Munich to study with Samuel Richards. Eva Augusta Ford Cline Smith of Vermont came to Munich, where she studied with Clyde Cook. See: Leonard, *Woman's Who's Who*.

53. Florine Stettheimer had a close and supportive relationship with her sisters Ettie (Henrietta) and Carrie. Carrie (1869-1944) decorated one of the most famous dollhouses of the century, which is still on display in the toy collection of the Museum of the City of New York. Ettie received a doctoral degree from the University of Freiburg and became a novelist.

54. "Raffael Schuster-Woldan," *Allgemeines Lexikon der bildenden Künstler*, ed. Hans Vollmer, vol. 30 (Leipzig: E.A. Seemann, 1936) 346.

55. Bloemink, *The life and art of Florine Stettheimer* 27.

56. Bloemink, *The life and art of Florine Stettheimer* 33. This poem originally appeared in a privately printed text by Stettheimer, *Crystal Flowers* (1949).

57. Bloemink, *The life and art of Florine Stettheimer* 42.

58. Chris Petteys, *Dictionary of Women Artists: An International Dictionary of Women Artists Born Before 1900* (Boston: G.K. Hall, 1985) 341.

59. Kent Ahrens, "Harriet Whitney Frishmuth," *Dictionary of Women Artists*, ed. Delia Graze, vol. 1 (London and Chicago: Fitzroy Dearborn Publishers, 1997) 553.

60. Ahrens, "Harriet Whitney Frishmuth," 553.

61. Barbara L. Michaels, "Gertrude Käsebier," *Dictionary of Women Artists*, ed. Delia Graze, vol. 2 (London and Chicago: Fitzroy Dearborn Publishers, 1997) 762-64.

62. Josef Maria Eder, *History of Photography*, trans. Edward Epstean (New York: Dover Publications, 1978) 687.

63. Eder, *History of Photography* 777.

64. Betty Ann Brown, "Imogen Cunningham," *Dictionary of Women Artists*, ed. Delia Graze, vol. 1 (London and Chicago: Fitzroy Dearborn Publishers, 1997) 423-26.

65. The following is a brief, representative list of the many other North American women whose biographies helped to inform this study. All the women included in the following list studied piano and/or composition in Germany and Austria, and became professional musicians or composers. They are grouped according to the cities, in which they studied. The names below were taken from the following sources: Nicolas Slonimsky, *Baker's Biographical Dictionary of Musicians*, 7th ed. (New York: Schirmer Books, 1984); Ammer, *Unsung*.

Berlin: Alice Barnett (1886-1975), Marion Eugenie Bauer (1887-1955), Isabella Beaton (1870-1929), Gena Branscombe (1881-1977), Augusta Cottlow (1878-1954), Lucile Crews (1888-1972), Ruth Lynda Deyo (1884-1960), Fannie Charles Dillon (1881-1947), Helen Hood (1863-1949), Jessie Stillman Kelley (1866-1949), Mana-Zucca (Augusta Zuckermann) (1887-1981), Olga Hickenlooper Samaroff (1882-1948), Rose Laura Sutro (1870-1957), Ottilie Sutro (1872-1970) and Harriet Ware (1877-1962).

Dresden: Angela Diller (1877-1968) and Mary Howe (1882-1964)

Leipzig: Fay Foster (1886-1960), Eleanor Everest Freer (1864-1942) and Julie Rivé-King (1854-1937).

Munich: Fay Foster (1886-1960) and Margaret Ruthven Lang (1867-1972).

Vienna: Ethel Newcomb (1875-1959)

66. Albert Lavignac, *Musical education*, trans. Esther Singleton (New York: Appleton, 1903) 394.

67. Weidig, "Observations," 47.

68. Weidig, "Observations," 50.

69. Moszkowski was an extremely popular piano teacher. The following list shows the wide range of students drawn to his classes. The composer and teacher, Eleanor Smith of Illinois, one of the founders of the Hull House Music School and a graduate of the Hershey School of Music studied with Moszkowski between 1887 and 1891. Gertrude Sunderland Safford of Massachusetts, who later became a music teacher for children, studied with Moszkowski after studying at both the University of Michigan and the University of Chicago. Mary Lucinda Regal of Ohio studied with Moszkowski after graduating from the Oberlin Conservatory of Music. The pianist Mary Kimball Kutchin of Washington, DC also studied with Moszkowski. Kullak, himself, had many foreign students. His students included the composer and pianist, Cara Pratt Mason, who had studied with Liszt, Lebert and Pruckner. See: Leonard, *Woman's Who's Who.*

70. Students at the Klindworth-Scharwenka Conservatory included Mary A. Stowell, who eventually became head of the piano department at Wellesley; as well as Gertrude Foster Brown and Mary Spencer Conrade, graduates of the New England Conservatory. See: Leonard, *Woman's Who's Who.*

71. Lavignac, *Musical education* 400.

72. Clara Wieck Schumann (1819-1896) taught as the principal piano teacher at the Hoch Conservatory from 1879 to 1893. After leaving the conservatory for health reasons, she continued to give lessons at her home until shortly before her death on May 20, 1896. See: Diane Peacock Jezic, *Women Composers: The Lost Tradition Found*, ed. Elizabeth Wood, 2nd ed. (New York: The Feminist Press at CUNY, 1994) 93.

73. Jahresberichte des Dr. Hoch'schen Conservatoriums zu Frankfurt a. M., Schülerlisten (1878-1915), Stadt-und Universitätsbibliothek, Musik-und Theaterabteilung, Frankfurt am Main.

74. Jane Bowers and Judith Tick, *Women Making Music: The Western Art Tradition, 1150-1950* (Urbana: University of Illinois Press, 1987) 273.

75. Karen A. Shaffer, *Maud Powell, Pioneer American Violinist* (Ames: Iowa State University Press, 1988) 25.

76. Peabody had been scheduled to open in 1857, but its opening was delayed until after the Civil War.

77. Ammer, *Unsung* 225; Andrea Olmstead, *Juilliard: a history* (Urbana: University of Illinois Press, 1999) 8-9; Adrienne Fried Block, "Women in American Music, 1800-1918," *Women and Music: A History,* ed. Karin Pendle (Bloomington: Indiana University Press, 1991) 149.

78. Ammer, *Unsung* 63.

79. Olga Samaroff Stokowski, *An American Musician's Story* (New York: W.W. Norton & Co., 1939) 30.

80. Stokowski, *An American Musician's Story* 17-18.

81. Stokowski, *An American Musician's Story* 27-28.

82. "Music," *The Nation* 97 (1913): 318-19.

83. Roland Bauer and Erik Hühns, eds., *Berlin: 800 Jahre Geschichte in Wort und Bild* (Berlin: VEB Deutscher Verlag der Wissenschaften, 1980) 187.

84. Ammer, *Unsung* 60.

85. Amy Fay, *Music-study in Germany* (New York: Dover Publications, 1965) 24.

86. Stokowski, *An American Musician's Story* 26.

87. Mabel W. Daniels, *An American girl in Munich: impressions of a music student* (Boston: Little Brown, 1905) 49.

88. Ammer, *Unsung* 22.

89. Shaffer, *Maud Powell* 11.

90. Other violinists of note were Gail Hamilton Ridgway, a graduate of Oberlin, who went to Berlin to study with Fritz Kreisler; Nora Clench Streeton, who went to Leipzig to study with the Russian violinist Bordsky; Maidelle Cummings, who studied in Munich, and later performed under her married name as Madame de Lewandowska; and the composer Margaret Ruthven Lang, who studied violin in Munich with Drechsler and Abel. See: Leonard, *Woman's Who's Who*. Ammer, *Unsung* 21. The prejudice against women composers, however, remained. While the number of women composers increased, there was no corresponding increase in public performances of their works. Far into the twentieth century, only a few pieces by women had entered the repertoire of any major North American orchestra. See: Ammer, *Unsung* 98. Nevertheless, some composers did have their works played by major orchestras during their lifetime. Block, "Women in American Music, 1800-1918," 157-70.

91. For more on the García dynasty, see: Patricia Adkins Chiti, ed., *Songs and Duets of García, Malibran and Viardot* (Van Nuys, CA: Alfred Publishing Co., 1997) 3-9. For more on the life of Pauline Viardot, see: April Fitzlyon, *The Price of Genius: A Life of Pauline Viardot* (London: John Calder, 1964).

92. Leschetizky's students also included the following less-known musicians and teachers: Genevieve Bisbee, Emily Hutchinson Crane, Mary Kimball Kutchin, Grace Hamilton Morrey, Clare Osborne Reed, Mary A. Stowell and Mabel Chauvenet Holden Tuttle. See: Leonard, *Woman's Who's Who*.

93. Fay, *Music-study in Germany* 335.

94. Frances Dillon, introduction, *Music-Study in Germany*, by Amy Fay (New York: Dover, 1965) xii-xiv.

95. Dillon, introduction, ix.

96. Fay, *Music-study in Germany* 266.

97. Fay, *Music-study in Germany* 187.

98. Fay, *Music-study in Germany* 197.

99. Fay, *Music-study in Germany* 82.

100. Fay, *Music-study in Germany* 117.

101. Fay, *Music-study in Germany* 159.

102. Fay, *Music-study in Germany* 27.

103. Fay, *Music-study in Germany* 54.

104. Cecilia Gaul, the pianist, was a close friend of Etta Cone, the art collector and sister of Claribel Cone. Gaul and Etta Cone had become acquainted at the Peabody Institute in Baltimore, where both studied piano. Gaul made several successful tours in Europe but never played before an American audience. Her career as a performer ended when she developed a fear of performing in public. See: Pollack, *The Collectors* 131.

105. Fay, *Music-study in Germany* 211.

106. Fay, *Music-study in Germany* 232.

107. Fay, *Music-study in Germany* 223.

108. Fay, *Music-study in Germany* 223.

109. Fay, *Music-study in Germany* 351-52.

110. Fay, *Music-study in Germany* 352.

111. Daniels, *An American Girl*.

112. *The Nation* 81 (1905): 83.

113. Daniels, *An American Girl* 9.

114. Daniels, *An American Girl* 41.

115. Daniels, *An American Girl* 67-68.

116. Daniels, *An American Girl* 277-78.

117. Ammer, *Unsung* 89.

118. Slonimsky, *Baker's Biographical Dictionary of Musicians* xxxi.

119. Shaffer, *Maud Powell* 16.
120. Shaffer, *Maud Powell* 101.
121. Shaffer, *Maud Powell* 101.
122. Shaffer, *Maud Powell* 71.
123. Shaffer, *Maud Powell* 153.
124. Shaffer, *Maud Powell* 21.
125. Shaffer, *Maud Powell* 24.
126. Geraldine Morgan was born in New York City on November 15, 1868. Her father was the organist at Trinity Church. Morgan began to study violin at the age of four, taking lessons with her father and Leopold Damrosch. She studied in Berlin with Joachim for four years (1882-1886) and in Leipzig with Schradieck. Supposedly, she was the first American to win the Mendelssohn prize at the Royal Academy of Berlin (1885). In 1886 Morgan toured with Joachim. She remained in Berlin until 1890, when she returned to the United States. Morgan continued to tour and founded the Morgan String Quartet. She also taught in New York City. In 1901 Morgan married Benjamin F. Roeder. Shaffer, *Maud Powell* 29; Leonard, *Woman's Who's Who* 697.
127. Shaffer, *Maud Powell* 34.
128. Shaffer, *Maud Powell* 42.
129. Shaffer, *Maud Powell* 48.
130. Shaffer, *Maud Powell* 67.
131. Shaffer, *Maud Powell* 70.
132. Shaffer, *Maud Powell* 103.
133. Farrar was born on February 28, 1882, in Melrose near Boston. At a very early age, she was given lessons in both piano and voice. She was inspired to become a singer by the performances of opera divas such as Lillian Nordica, Emma Calvé and Nellie Melba. Farrar's parents devoted themselves to her career. They sold the family business to raise the money necessary for Farrar to study and perform in Europe. Farrar studied voice and acting for almost a year in Paris, but remained dissatisfied with the instruction she received there. On the advice of Lillian Nordica and her husband, Zoldan Dome, Farrar decided to move to Berlin to continue her studies under the guidance of the Italian singer Graziani.

Farrar's story has been well documented in her own autobiographies and a number of biographical treatments. Mabel Wagnalls's contemporary biography (1909?) includes Farrar as one of the greatest opera stars of the turn of the century along with Eames, Nordica, Marcella Sembrich, Emma Calvé, Lilli Lehmann and Nellie Melba. She was one of the fifteen "great American stars" included in DeWitt Bodeen's tribute to Hollywood (1976). She was also the subject of an extensive study by Elizabeth Nash, *Always First Class* (1981). Farrar wrote two lengthy autobiographies, *Geraldine Farrar: The Story of an American Singer* (1916) and *Such Sweet Compulsion* (1938).
134. Daniels, *An American Girl* 228.
135. "Berlin Gets Warm and Society Flees," *New York Times* June 28, 1914: 2.
136. "One Woman's Germany," *New York Times* September 2, 1915: 8.
137. Other lesser stars include the following vocalists: Jennie E. Slater, who studied in Berlin with Reinhold Herman; Lessie Southgate Simmons, who studied in Berlin with Mrs. Nicholas Kempner; Katherine A. Rood, who studied in Berlin with Felix Schmidt; Marie Parcello (Maritje V. Parcells Bixby) and Agatha Parlett Meloney, who studied in Berlin; Mary Poppleton Learned, who studied in Berlin with Mary Münchhoff; and the opera singer Alma Webster Hall Powell, who sang in Berlin as well as in Munich, Prague, Vienna, Frankfurt am Main and Breslau. At the Leipzig Conservatory, there were Florence Lee Whitman and Helene Boericke. In Dresden, the opera singer Agnes Huntington Cravath studied for three years with G.

B. Lamperti, before beginning a successful career on the opera and concert stages of Leipzig, Stuttgart and Berlin. The voice teacher Cedelia May-Cox studied in Dresden with Richter. See: Leonard, *Woman's Who's Who.*

138. "Alumnae Notes," 4.

139. Stokowski, *An American Musician's Story* 24.

140. Minnie Hauk, *Memories of a Singer*, Opera Biographies, ed. Andrew Farkas (New York: Arno Press, 1977) 124.

141. Hauk, *Memories of a Singer* 54-55.

142. Hauk, *Memories of a Singer* 70.

143. Slonimsky, *Baker's Biographical Dictionary of Musicians* 421.

144. "One Woman's Germany," 8.

CONCLUSION

1. Gabi Einsele and Rachel Gratzfeld, "Einleitung," *Ebenso neu als kühn*, eds. Katharina Belser, Gabi Einsele, Rachel Gratzfeld, et al. (Zurich: eFeF Verlag, 1988) 9.

Bibliography

BOOKS AND ARTICLES

Addams, Jane, Emily G. Balch, and Alice Hamilton. *Women at the Hague: The International Congress of Women and its Results*. New York: Macmillan, 1916.

Ahrens, Kent. "Harriet Whitney Frishmuth." *Dictionary of Women Artists*. Ed. Delia Graze. Vol. 1. London and Chicago: Fitzroy Dearborn Publishers, 1997. 553-55.

Ainley, Marianne Gosztonyi. "Last in the Field? Canadian Women Natural Scientists, 1815-1965." *Despite the odds: essays on Canadian women and science*. Ed. Marianne Gosztonyi Ainley. Buffalo, NY: Véhicule Press, 1990. 25-62.

Albisetti, James C. "German Influence on the Higher Education of American Women, 1865-1914." *German Influences on Education in the United States to 1917*. Eds. Henry Geitz, Jürgen Heideking and Jurgen Herbst. New York: Cambridge University Press, 1995. 227-44.

_____. *Schooling German Girls and Women*. Princeton, NJ: Princeton University Press, 1988.

Altschuler, Glenn C. *Better Than Second Best: Love and Work in the Life of Helen Magill*. Urbana: University of Illinois Press, 1990.

Ammer, Christine. *Unsung: A History of Women in American Music*. Westport, CT: Greenwood Press, 1980.

Atwood, Wallace W. "An Appreciation of Ellen Churchill Semple, 1863-1932." *The Journal of Geography* 31 (1932): 267-68.

B., A. "An American Woman at the German Universities." *The Nation* 64 (1897): 223-24.

Bandhauer-Schöffmann, Irene. "Frauenbewegung und Studentinnen. Zum Engagement der österreichischen Frauenvereine für das Frauenstudium." *Durch Erkenntnis zu Freiheit und Glück...: Frauen an der Universität Wien (ab 1897)*. Eds. Waltraud Heindl and Marina Tichy. Schriftenreihe des Universitätsarchivs Universität Wien 5. Vienna: WUV-Universitätsverlag, 1990. 49-78.

Barker, Deborah Ellen. "Painting Women: The Woman Artist in Nineteenth-Century American Fiction." Diss. Princeton University, 1991.

Barringer, Emily Dunning. *Bowery to Bellevue; the story of New York's first woman ambulance surgeon*. 1st ed. New York: Norton, 1950.

Bauer, Roland, and Erik Hühns, eds. *Berlin: 800 Jahre Geschichte in Wort und Bild*. Berlin: VEB Deutscher Verlag der Wissenschaften, 1980.

Baumgarten, Marita. *Professoren und Universitäten im 19. Jahrhundert*. Kritische Studien zur Geschichtswissenschaft. Vol. 121. Göttingen: Vandenhoeck & Ruprecht, 1997.

Beatty, William K. "Lucy Waite: surgeon and free thinker." *Proceedings of the Institute of Medicine, Chicago* 45 (1992): 52-58.

Belser, Katharina, Gabi Einsele, Rachel Gratzfeld, et al., eds. *Ebenso neu als kühn: 120 Jahre Frauenstudium an der Universität Zürich*. Zurich: eFeF Verlag, 1988.

Berger, Renate. "Training and Professionalism: Germany, Austria and Switzerland." *Dictionary of Women Artists*. Ed. Delia Graze. Vol. 1. London and Chicago: Fitzroy Dearborn Publishers, 1997. 98-106.

Bernert, Christopher. "Die Wanderjahre: The Higher Education of American Students in German Universities, 1870 to 1914." Diss. SUNY Stony Brook, 1984.

Beuermann, Gustav, Margrit Hische, Ulrich Hunger, et al., eds. *250 Jahre Georg-August-Universität Göttingen. Ausstellung im Auditorium. Göttingen. May 19-July 12, 1987*. Göttingen: Georg-August-Universität, 1987.

Bishop, Morris. *A History of Cornell*. Ithaca, NY: Cornell University Press, 1962.

Block, Adrienne Fried. "Women in American Music, 1800-1918." *Women and Music: A History*. Ed. Karin Pendle. Bloomington: Indiana University Press, 1991. 142-72.

Bloemink, Barbara J. *The life and art of Florine Stettheimer*. New Haven, CT: Yale University Press, 1995.

Boehm, Laetitia. "Von den Anfängen des akademischen Frauenstudiums in Deutschland. Zugleich ein Kapitel aus der Geschichte der Ludwig-Maximilians-Universität München." *Historisches Jahrbuch* 77 (1958): 298-327.

Boland, Agnes Murray. "1898, Annina Periam Danton." *Goucher Quarterly*.Winter (1954).

Bonner, Thomas N. *American doctors and German universities; a chapter in international intellectual relations, 1870-1914*. Lincoln: University of Nebraska Press, 1963.

_____. "Medical Women Abroad: A New Dimension of Women's Push for Opportunity in Medicine, 1850-1914." *Bull. Hist. Med.* 62 (1988): 58-73.

_____. "Pioneering in Women's Medical Education in the Swiss Universities, 1864-1914." *30th International Congress of the History of Medicine*. Düsseldorf: Organisationskomitee des XXX. Internationalen Kongresses für Geschichte der Medizin Düsseldorf, 1986. 1167-76.

_____. *To the ends of the earth: women's search for education in medicine*. Cambridge, MA: Harvard University Press, 1992.

Boring, Alice Middleton. "On the Effects of Different Temperatures on the Size of the Nuclei in the Embryo of *Ascaris megalocephala*, with Remarks on the Size-Relation of the Nuclei in Univalens and Bivalens." *Arch. Entwick.-Mech.* 28 (1909): 118-26.

_____. "A Small Chromosome in *Ascaris megalocephala*." *Archiv für Zellforschung* 4 (1909).

Boveri, Margret. *Verzweigungen. Eine Autobiographie*. Ed. Uwe Johnson. Munich and Zurich: R. Piper and Co., 1977.

Boveri, Theodor. *The Origin of Malignant Tumors*. Trans. Marcella Boveri. Baltimore, MD: Williams and Wilkins, 1929.

Bowen, Anna Maude. "A Woman Student's Experience in German Universities." *The Nation* 65 (1897): 9.

Bowers, Jane, and Judith Tick. *Women Making Music: The Western Art Tradition, 1150-1950*. Urbana: University of Illinois Press, 1987.

Breeskin, Adelyn D. "Claribel Cone." *Notable American women, 1607-1950; a biographical dictionary*. Eds. Edward T. James, Janet Wilson James, Paul S. Boyer, et al. Vol. 1. Cambridge, MA: Belknap Press of Harvard University Press, 1971. 371-73.

Bridges, Flora. "Coeducation in Swiss Universities." *The Popular Science Monthly* 38 (1890-91): 524-30.

Brown, Betty Ann. "Imogen Cunningham." *Dictionary of Women Artists*. Ed. Delia Graze. Vol. 1. London and Chicago: Fitzroy Dearborn Publishers, 1997. 423-26.

Brush, Stephen G. "Nettie M. Stevens and the Discovery of Sex Determination by Chromosomes." *Isis* 69 (1978): 163-72.

Burchardt, Anja. "'Schwestern reicht die Hand zum Bunde'? – Zum Verhältnis zwischen russischen und deutschen Medizinstudentinnen in den Anfängen des Frauenstudiums (1865-1914)." *Barrieren und Karrieren. Die Anfänge des Frauenstudiums in Deutschland. Dokumentationsband der Konferenz "100 Jahre Frauen in der Wissenschaft" im Februar 1997 an der Universität Bremen.* Eds. Elisabeth Dickmann and Eva Schöck-Quinteros. Vol. 5. Schriftenreihe des Hedwig-Hintze-Instituts Bremen. Berlin: trafo verlag dr. wolfgang weist, 2000. 292-301.

Burrell, Ellen L. "Charlotte Fitch Roberts." *The Wellesley Alumnae Quarterly* January, 1918: 80-81.

Bußmann, Hadumod, ed. *Stieftöchter der Alma Mater? 90 Jahre Frauenstudium in Bayern - am Beispiel der Universität München. Katalog zur Ausstellung 1993/94.* Munich, 1993.

Bynum, W. F. *Science and the practice of medicine in the nineteenth century.* Cambridge history of science. New York: Cambridge University Press, 1994.

Cahan, David. "Helmholtz and the Civilizing Power of Science." *Hermann von Helmholtz and the Foundations of Nineteenth-Century Science.* Ed. David Cahan. Vol. 12. California Studies in the History of Science. Berkeley: University of California Press, 1993. 559-601.

Calkins, Mary Whiton, and Eleanor Acheson McCulloch Gamble. "The Self-Psychology of the Psychoanalysis." *The Psychological Review.*July (1930).

Carr, Emma Perry. "One Hundred Years of Science at Mount Holyoke College." *Mount Holyoke Alumnae Quarterly.*20 (1936): 135-38.

Chiarmonte, Paula, ed. *Women Artists in the United States: A Selective Bibliography and Resource Guide on the Fine and Decorative Arts, 1750-1986.* Boston: G. K. Hall, 1990.

Chiti, Patricia Adkins, ed. *Songs and Duets of García, Malibran and Viardot.* Van Nuys, CA: Alfred Publishing Co., 1997.

Coates, Albert. *By her bootstraps: a saga of women in North Carolina.* Chapel Hill, NC: Albert Coates, 1975.

Coates, Gladys Hall. "The Coming of Women to the University of North Carolina." *By Her Own Bootstraps.* Ed. Albert Coates. Chapel Hill, NC: Albert Coates, 1975. 38-59.

———. *Some recollections of early days in Chapel Hill and the University.* Chapel Hill, NC: n. p., 1992.

Colby, Charles C. "Ellen Churchill Semple." *Annals of the Association of American Geographers* 23 (1933): 229-40.

Collins, Jim, and Glenn B. Opitz, eds. *Women Artists in America: 18th Century To The Present (1790-1980).* Poughkeepsie, NY: Apollo, 1980.

Conable, Charlotte Williams. *Women at Cornell: The Myth of Equal Education.* Ithaca, NY: Cornell University Press, 1977.

Corning, Frederick Gleason. *A Student Reverie: An Album of Saxony Days.* New York, 1920.

Costas, Ilse. "Der Beginn des Frauenstudiums an der Universität Göttingen. Die Wissenschaft, das 'Wesen der Frau' und erste Schritte zur Öffnung männerdominierter Karrieren." *Göttingen ohne Gänseliesel. Texte und Bilder zur*

Stadtgeschichte. Eds. Kornelia Duwe, Carola Gottschalk and Marianne Koerner. 2nd ed. Gudensberg-Gleichen: Wartberg Verlag, 1989. 185-93.

Courage, Projektgruppe des. *Frauenleben – Frauenalltag – gestern und heute. Hallenserinnen – Biographische Skizzen Teil II*. Halle: Courage e.V., 1995.

Crawford, Mary Caroline. *The College Girl of America and the Institutions Which Make Her What She Is*. 1904. 4 ed. Boston: Colonial Press C. H. Simonds Co., 1915.

Cushier, Elizabeth. "Autobiography of Elizabeth Cushier." *Medical Women of America*. Ed. Kate Campbell Hurd-Mead. New York: Froben, 1933. 85-95.

Daniels, Mabel W. *An American girl in Munich: impressions of a music student*. Boston: Little Brown, 1905.

Davis, Katharine Bement. "The Modern Condition of Agricultural Labor in Bohemia." *Journal of Political Economy* 8 (1900): 491-523.

_____. "Three Score Years and Ten: An Autobiographical Essay." *University of Chicago Magazine* 26.2 (1933): 58-61.

Davison, Roderic H. "Mary Mills Patrick." *Notable American women, 1607-1950; a biographical dictionary*. Eds. Edward T. James, Janet Wilson James, Paul S. Boyer, et al. Vol. 3. Cambridge, MA: Belknap Press of Harvard University Press, 1971. 25-26.

De Ford, Miriam Allen. *Psychologist unretired; the life pattern of Lillien J. Martin*. Stanford, CA: Stanford University Press, 1948.

Denio, Elizabeth H. "Letter from Germany." *Wellesley Courant* November 23, 1883: 4-5.

_____. "Letter from Germany." *Wellesley Courant* June 20, 1884: 2-3.

Dertinger, Antje. "Abends fuhr man im Boot auf der Saale." *Mitteldeutsche Zeitung* April 2, 1993.

Dickmann, Elisabeth, and Eva Schöck-Quinteros, eds. *Barrieren und Karrieren. Die Anfänge des Frauenstudiums in Deutschland. Dokumentationsband der Konferenz "100 Jahre Frauen in der Wissenschaft" im Februar 1997 an der Universität Bremen*. Vol. 5. Berlin: trafo verlag dr. wolfgang weist, 2000.

Dillon, Frances. Introduction. *Music-Study in Germany*. By Amy Fay. New York: Dover, 1965. v-xiv.

Dimock, Susan. *Memoir of Susan Dimock*. Boston, 1875.

Dobkin, Marjorie Housepian, ed. *The Making of a Feminist: Early Journals and Letters of M. Carey Thomas*. Kent, OH: Kent State University Press, 1979.

Dover, Mary Violet. "Experiments with Diphenylcyclohexenone." *American Chemical Journal* 37 (1907): 385-92.

Drucker, Renate. "Zur Vorgeschichte des Frauenstudiums an der Universität Leipzig. Aktenbericht." *Vom Mittelalter zur Neuzeit*. Ed. Hellmut Kretzschmar. Forschungen zur Mittelalterlichen Geschichte 1. Berlin: Rütten and Loening, 1956. 278-90.

Drüll, Dagmar. *Heidelberger Gelehrtenlexikon 1803-1932*. Berlin: Springer-Verlag, 1986.

Dunbar, Mabel. "Das Deutsche Fräulein." *Scarlet and Black (Grinnell)* March 14, 1906.

Duveneck, Josephine W. *Frank Duveneck: Painter – Teacher*. San Francisco, CA: John Howell - Books, 1970.

Eaton, Shelby L. *Women in Mathematics in the United States: 1866-1900*. 1997. World Wide Web Document. Available: http://www.faculty.washington.edu/marykirk/herstory/seaton.htm. June 16, 2000.

Eckardt, Birgit. "Zwei Amerikanerinnen in Jena – Lucinde Pearl Boggs und Rowena Morse." *Entwurf und Wirklichkeit. Frauen in Jena 1900-1933*. Eds. Gisela Horn and Birgitt Hellmann. Rudolstadt and Jena: Hainverlag, 2001. 235-44.

Eder, Josef Maria. *History of Photography*. 1945. Trans. Edward Epstean. New York: Dover Publications, 1978.

Eells, Walter Crosby. "Earned Doctorates for Women in the Nineteenth Century." *American Association of University Professors Bulletin* 42 (1956): 644-51.

Einsele, Gabi, and Rachel Gratzfeld. "Einleitung." *Ebenso neu als kühn.* Eds. Katharina Belser, Gabi Einsele, Rachel Gratzfeld, et al. Zurich: eFeF Verlag, 1988. 9-11.

Eucken, Rudolf. *Lebenserinnerungen. Ein Stück deutschen Lebens.* Leipzig, 1922.

F., G. T. "Pioneer Women Students in Germany." *The Nation* 64 (1897): 262.

Fairbanks, A. W., ed. *Emma Willard and her Pupils or Fifty Years of Troy Female Seminary 1822-1872.* New York: Mrs. Russell Sage, 1898.

Fay, Amy. *Music-study in Germany.* 1880. New York: Dover Publications, 1965.

Fenster, Della Dumbaugh, and Karen Hunger Parshall. "A Profile of the American Mathematical Research Community: 1891-1906." *The History of Modern Mathematics.* Eds. Eberhard Knobloch and David E. Rowe. Vol. 3. San Diego, CA: Academic Press, 1994. 178-227.

_____. "Women in the American Mathematical Research Community: 1891-1906." *The History of Modern Mathematics.* Eds. Eberhard Knobloch and David E. Rowe. Vol. 3. San Diego, CA: Academic Press, 1994. 228-61.

Fisher, Le Roy H. "Mary Jane Safford." *Notable American women, 1607-1950; a biographical dictionary.* Eds. Edward T. James, Janet Wilson James, Paul S. Boyer, et al. Vol. 3. Cambridge, MA: Bellknap of Harvard University Press, 1971. 220-22.

Fitzlyon, April. *The Price of Genius: A Life of Pauline Viardot.* London: John Calder, 1964.

Fitzpatrick, Ellen F. *Endless Crusade: Women Social Scientists and Progressive Reform.* New York: Oxford University Press, 1990.

Flexner, Helen Thomas. "Bryn Mawr: A Characterization." *Bryn Mawr Alumnae Quarterly* January 1908: 5-17.

Flower, Olive. *The History of Oxford College for Women, 1830-1928.* Miami University Books. Vol. 2. Hamilton, OH: The Miami University Alumni Association, 1949.

Forrer-Gutknecht, Else. *Das Frauenstudium an den Schweizer Hochschulen.* Zurich: Rascher and CIE, 1928.

Franken, Irene. *"Ja, das Studium der Weiber ist schwer!" Studentinnen und Dozentinnen an der Kölner Universität bis 1933.* Cologne: Frauenbeauftragte der Universität zu Köln, Kölner Frauengeschichtsverein, Universitäts-und Stadtbibliothek Köln, 1995.

Froelicher, Frances Mitchell. "Germanic Philology at Zürich." *Kalends (Goucher)* April 1896: 170-72.

_____. "Post-Graduate Work in a German University." *Kalends (Goucher)* February 1896: 112-14.

Fullerton, Anna M., and Carl Breus. "Women Students in Vienna." *Medical Times* October 4, 1884: 35-36.

Funnell, Helen. "In Remembrance." *Mills Quarterly* (1963): 47.

Furness, Caroline E. "Mary W. Whitney." *Popular Astronomy* December 1922: 597-608.

_____. "Mary W. Whitney." *Popular Astronomy* January 1923: 25-35.

Furumoto, Laurel. "From 'Paired Associates' to a Psychology of Self: The Intellectual Odyssey of Mary Whiton Calkins." *Portraits of Pioneers in Psychology.* Eds. Gregory A. Kimble, Michael Wertheimer and Charlotte L. White. Washington, DC and Hillsdale, NJ: American Psychological Association and Lawrence Erlbaum Associates, 1991. 57-72.

Geitz, Henry, Jürgen Heideking, and Jurgen Herbst, eds. *German Influences on Education in the United States to 1917.* New York: Cambridge University Press, 1995.

Gentry, Ruth. "A Winter in Berlin." *The Lantern (Bryn Mawr)* June 1892: 45-49.

Gerhard, Ute. *Unerhört. Die Geschichte der deutschen Frauenbewegung.* Reinbek bei Hamburg: Rowohlt, 1990.

Gillett, Margaret. "Carrie Derick (1862-1941) and the Chair of Botany at McGill." *Despite the odds: essays on Canadian women and science.* Ed. Marianne Gosztonyi Ainley. Buffalo, NY: Véhicule Press, 1990. 25-62.

Glaser, Edith. *Hindernisse, Umwege, Sackgassen: Die Anfänge des Frauenstudiums in Tübingen (1904-1934)*. Weinheim: Deutscher Studien Verlag, 1992.

Graf-Nold, Angela. "Weiblichkeit in Wissenschaft und Wissenschaftspolitik." *Ebenso neu als kühn: 120 Jahre Frauenstudium an der Universität Zürich*. Eds. Katharina Belser, Gabi Einsele, Rachel Gratzfeld, et al. Zurich: eFeF Verlag, 1988. 29-50.

Graham, Patricia Albjerg. "Expansion and Exclusion: A History of Women in American Higher Education." *Signs* Summer 1978: 759-73.

Green, Judy. "American Women In Mathematics – The First Ph.D.'s." *Association for Women in Mathematics Newsletter* 8 (1978): 13-15.

Green, Judy, and Jeanne Laduke. "Contributors to American Mathematics: An Overview and Selection." *Women of science: righting the record*. Eds. G. Kass-Simon, Patricia Farnes and Deborah Nash. Bloomington: Indiana University Press, 1990. 117-46.

Guggisberg, Hans R. "Eine Amerikanerin in Zürich: die Doktorpromotion der Martha Carey Thomas aus Baltimore (1882)." *Zurich Taschenbuch*. Zurich: Buchdruckerei an der Sihl AG, 1982. 163-74.

Hakemeyer, Ida. "Ellen Hinsdale promovierte in Göttingen vor 58 Jahren." *Mädchenbildung und Frauenschaffen* January 1956: 43-44.

Hall, G. Stanley. *Aspects of child life and education*. Ed. Theodate Louise Smith. Boston: Ginn and Co., 1907.

Hamilton, Alice. "Edith and Alice Hamilton: Students in Germany." *The Atlantic Monthly* March 1965: 129-32.

_____. *Exploring the dangerous trades: the autobiography of Alice Hamilton, M.D.* 1943. Boston: Northeastern University Press, 1985.

Hanaford, Phebe A. *Daughters of America; or, Women of the Century*. Boston: B. B. Russell, 1882.

Hand, Frances Fincke, Edna Shearer, Eunice M. Schenk, et al. "The Academic Committee's Report on the Bryn Mawr Graduate School." *Bryn Mawr Alumnae Bulletin* 7.1 (1927): 3-36.

Harrower, Molly R. "Molly R. Harrower." *Models of Achievement: Reflections of Eminent Women in Psychology*. Eds. Agnes N. O'Connell and Nancy Felipe Russo. New York: Columbia University Press, 1983. 154-71.

Hartshorn, Waunda. "A Student in Freiburg." *Kalends (Goucher)* March 1901: 205-07.

Hartwell, Cornelia. "Four Moons Abroad. Amid the Mountains." *Courant (Wellesley)* March 1, 1889: 2-3.

Hauk, Minnie. *Memories of a Singer*. 1925. Opera Biographies. Ed. Andrew Farkas. New York: Arno Press, 1977.

Heindl, Waltraud, and Marina Tichy. *"Durch Erkenntnis zu Freiheit und Glück..." Frauen an der Universität Wien (ab 1897)*. Schriftenreihe des Universitätsarchivs Universität Wien. Eds. Günther Hamann, Kurt Mühlberger and Franz Skacel. Vol. 5. Vienna: WUV-Universitätsverlag, 1990.

"Heinrich Knirr." *Allgemeines Lexikon der bildenden Künstler*. Ed. Hans Vollmer. Vol. 21. Leipzig: E.A. Seemann, 1927. 3-4.

Hessenauer, Heike. *Etappen des Frauenstudiums an der Universität Würzburg (1869-1939)*. Quellen und Beiträge zur Geschichte der Universität Würzburg. Ed. Peter Baumgart. Vol. 4. Neustadt an der Aisch: Verlag Degener & Co., 1998.

_____. "Studentinnen vor 1939 – Eine Fallstudie zur Entwicklung des Frauenstudiums." *Barrieren und Karrieren. Die Anfänge des Frauenstudiums in Deutschland. Dokumentationsband der Konferenz "100 Jahre Frauen in der Wissenschaft" im Februar 1997 an der Universität Bremen*. Eds. Elisabeth Dickmann and Eva Schöck-Quinteros. Vol. 5. Schriftenreihe des Hedwig-Hintze-Instituts Bremen. Berlin: trafo verlag dr. wolfgang weist, 2000. 315-27.

Hewes, Amy. "The Study of Sociology in Chicago and Berlin." *Kalends (Goucher)* April 1900: 196-99.

Hoffmann, Walter. *Bergakademie Freiberg.* Frankfurt am Main: Wolfgang Weidlich, 1959.

Hogue, Mary Jane. "The Contributions of Goucher Women to the Biological Sciences." *Goucher Alumnae Quarterly* Summer 1951: 13-22.

Hogue, Mary Jane, and Theodor Boveri. "Über die Möglichkeit, Ascaris-Eier zur Teilung in zwei gleichwertige Blastomeren zu veranlassen." *Sitz.-Ber. Phys.-Med. Ges. Würzburg* (1909).

Horn, Gisela, ed. *90 Jahre Frauenstudium an der Universität Jena.* Vol. 2. Rudolstadt: Hainverlag, 1999.

Horn, Gisela, and Birgitt Hellmann, eds. *Entwurf und Wirklichkeit. Frauen in Jena 1900-1933.* Rudolstadt and Jena: Hainverlag, 2001.

Horowitz, Helen Lefkowitz. *The Power and Passion of M. Carey Thomas.* New York: Alfred A. Knopf, 1994.

Horton, Louise S., Elizabeth H. Underhill, and Eleanor D. Deal. *Piermont, New Hampshire, 1764-1947.* Bradford, VT: Green Mountain Press, n. d.

House, Roy Temple. "Foreigners in German Universities." *The Nation* 96 (1913): 230.

Howes, Ethel Puffer. "Accepting the Universe." *Atlantic Monthly* April 1922: 444-53.

_____. "The Meaning of Progress in the Woman Movement." *Annals of the American Academy of Political and Social Science* 143 (1929): 14-20.

Howitt, Anna Mary. *An art student in Munich.* Boston: Ticknor Reed and Fields, 1854.

Høyrup, Else. *Women of Science, Technology, and Medicine: A Bibliography.* Skriftserie fra Roskilde Universitetsbibliothek. Vol. 15. Roskilde, Denmark: Roskilde University Library, 1987.

Huch, Ricarda. *Frühling in der Schweiz. Jugenderinnerungen.* 4th ed. Zurich: Atlantis-Verlag, 1938.

Hurvich, Dorothea Jameson. "Christine Ladd-Franklin." *Notable American Women, 1607-1950.* Eds. Edward T. James, Janet Wilson James, Paul S. Boyer, et al. Vol. 2. Cambridge, MA: Belknap Press of Harvard University Press, 1971. 354-56.

Hyde, Ida. "Before Women Were Human Beings: Adventures of an American Fellow in German Universities of the '90s." *Journal of the American Association of University Women* 31 (1938): 226-36.

Jarausch, Konrad H. "American Students in Germany, 1815-1914: The Structure of German and U.S. Matriculants at Göttingen University." *German Influence on Education in the United States to 1917.* Eds. Henry Geitz, Jürgen Heideking and Jurgen Herbst. New York: Cambridge University Press, 1995. 195-211.

Jaynes, Julian. "Georg Elias Müller." *Dictionary of Scientific Biography.* Vol. 9. New York: Charles Scribner's Sons, 1974. 561-63.

Jezic, Diane Peacock. *Women Composers: The Lost Tradition Found.* Ed. Elizabeth Wood. 2nd ed. New York: The Feminist Press at CUNY, 1994.

Johnson, Anna. "Alumnae Notes." *Wellesley College News* March 6, 1907: 8.

Johnson, Jeffrey Allan. *The Kaiser's Chemists: Science and Modernization in Imperial Germany.* Chapel Hill: University of North Carolina Press, 1990.

Jones, Bessie Zaban, and Lyle Gifford Boyd. *The Harvard Observatory: The First Four Directorships, 1839-1919.* Cambridge, MA: Belknap Press of Harvard University Press, 1971.

Kass-Simon, G. "Biology Is Destiny." *Women of science: righting the record.* Eds. G. Kass-Simon, Patricia Farnes and Deborah Nash. Bloomington: Indiana University Press, 1990. 215-67.

Keep, Rosalind Amelia. *Fourscore and Ten Years: A History of Mills College.* Oakland, CA: Mills College, 1946.

Kelley, Florence, and Kathryn Kish Sklar. *Notes of sixty years: the autobiography of Florence Kelley; with an early essay by the author on the need of theoretical preparation for philanthropic work*. First person series; no. 1. Chicago: Published for the Illinois Labor History Society by the C.H. Kerr Pub. Co., 1986.

Kelly, Edmond, and Florence Kelley. *Twentieth Century Socialism; What it is Not; What it is; How it May Come*. New York: Longmans Green and Co., 1910.

Kelly, Thomas E. *Who's Who in Mississippi*. Jackson, Mississippi: Tucker Printing House, 1914.

Kennedy, Virginia. "Alumnae Letters." *Kalends (Goucher)* January 1897: 97.

Kenschaft, Patricia C. "Women in Mathematics around 1900." *Signs* Summer 1982: 906-09.

Kleinau, Elke, and Claudia Opitz, eds. *Geschichte der Mädchen-und Frauenbildung. Vom Vormärz bis zur Gegenwart*. Vol. 2. Frankfurt/Main and New York: Campus Verlag, 1996.

Knipp, Anna Heubeck, and Thaddeus P. Thomas. *The History of Goucher College*. Baltimore, MD: Goucher College, 1938.

Knoll, Robert E. *Prairie University: A History of the University of Nebraska*. Lincoln: University of Nebraska Press, 1995.

Koblitz, Ann Hibner. "Science, Women, and the Russian Intelligentsia. The Generation of the 1860s." *Isis* 79 (1988): 208-26.

Koudelka, Janet Brock. "Mary Sherwood." *Notable American women, 1607-1950; a biographical dictionary*. Eds. Edward T. James, Janet Wilson James, Paul S. Boyer, et al. Vol. 3. Cambridge, MA: Belknap Press of Harvard University Press, 1971. 283-84.

Krabusch, Hans. "Die Vorgeschichte des Frauenstudiums an der Universität Heidelberg." *Ruperto-Carola* 19 (1956): 135-39.

Krohn, William O. "Facilities in Experimental Psychology at the Various German Universities." *American Journal of Psychology* 4 (1892): 585-94.

L., A. "Munich in Summer." *The Nation* 65 (1897): 127-28.

Ladd-Franklin, Christine. "Endowed Professorships for Women." *Journal of the Association of Collegiate Alumnae* Ser.3.9 (1904): 53-61.

Lauterer-Pirner, Heidi, and Margret Schepers-S.-W. "Studentin in Heidelberg." *Auch eine Geschichte der Universität Heidelberg*. Eds. Karin Buselmeier, Dietrich Harth and Christian Jansen. Mannheim: Edition Quadrat, 1985. 101-22.

Lavignac, Albert. *Musical education*. Trans. Esther Singleton. New York: Appleton, 1903.

Leitner, Gerit von. *Der Fall Clara Immerwahr. Leben für eine humane Wissenschaft*. Munich: C. H. Beck, 1994.

Lemberg, Margret, ed. *Es begann vor hundert Jahren. Die ersten Frauen an der Universität Marburg und die Studentinnenvereinigungen bis zur Gleichschaltung im Jahre 1934. Catalog of exhibition. 21 Jan-23 Feb 1997. Universitätsbibliothek Marburg*. Marburg: Universitätsbibliothek Marburg, 1997.

Lenhoff, Howard M. "Ethel Browne, Hans Spemann, and the Discovery of the Organizer Phenomenon." *Biological Bulletin* 181 (1991): 72-80.

Leonard, John William. *Woman's Who's Who of America 1914-1915*. 1914. Detroit, MI: Gale Research Company, 1976.

Lovejoy, Esther Pohl. *Women Doctors of the World*. New York: Macmillan, 1957.

Luckyj, Natalie. "Training and Professionalism: North America, 19th Century, Canada." *Dictionary of Women Artists*. Ed. Delia Graze. Vol. 1. London and Chicago: Fitzroy Dearborn Publishers, 1997. 136-37.

Ludmerer, Kenneth M. *Learning to heal: the development of American medical education*. New York: Basic Books, 1985.

Luhn, Antke. "Geschichte des Frauenstudiums an der Medizinischen Fakultät der Universität Göttingen." University of Göttingen, 1972.

Lurie, Nancy Oestreich. "Erminnie Adele Platt Smith." *Notable American Women 1607-1950*. Eds. Edward T. James, Janet Wilson James, Paul S. Boyer, et al. Vol. 3. Cambridge, MA: Belknap Press of Harvard University Press, 1971. 312-13.

M. "In Memoriam: Nettie Maria Stevens." *Bryn Mawr Alumnae Quarterly* June 1912: 124-25.

MacIntosh, Marian. "News from the Classes [1890]." *Bryn Mawr Alumnae Quarterly* January 1914: 115.

Maddison, Isabel, and Bryn Mawr College and Graduate Club. *Handbook of British, continental and Canadian universities, with special mention of the courses open to women*. 2nd ed. New York: Macmillan Company, 1899.

Maltby, Margaret E. *History of the Fellowships Awarded by the American Association of University Women 1888-1929*. Washington, DC: AAUW, 1929.

Marks, Geoffrey, and William K. Beatty. *Women in white*. New York: Scribner, 1972.

"Martin, Lillien Jane." *Current Biography Yearbook*. New York: H. W. Wilson Co., 1942. 575-77.

Mathews, Nancy Mowll. "Training and Professionalism: North American, 19th Century, U.S.A." *Dictionary of Women Artists*. Ed. Delia Graze. Vol. 1. London and Chicago: Fitzroy Dearborn Publishers, 1997. 132-36.

McGuigan, Dorothy Gies. *A dangerous experiment. 100 years of women at the University of Michigan*. Ann Arbor, MI: Center for Continuing Education of Women, 1970.

McKee, Ruth Stauffer. "Anna Pell Wheeler." *Bryn Mawr Alumnae Bulletin* Summer 1966: 22-23.

McKibbin-Harper, Mary. "Anna E. Broomall, M.D. [1847-1931]." *Medical Review of Reviews* March 1933: 132-39.

Merrill, Maud A. "Lillien Jane Martin: 1851-1943." *The American Journal of Psychology* 56.3 (1943): 453-54.

Meyer, Annie Nathan. *Woman's work in America*. New York: Henry Holt and Co., 1891.

Michael, Helen Cecilia De Silver Abbott. *Studies in Plant and Organic Chemistry and Literary Papers*. Cambridge, MA: Riverside Press, 1907.

Michaels, Barbara L. "Gertrude Käsebier." *Dictionary of Women Artists*. Ed. Delia Graze. Vol. 2. London and Chicago: Fitzroy Dearborn Publishers, 1997. 762-64.

Miller, Jane A. "Women in Chemistry." *Women of science: righting the record*. Eds. G. Kass-Simon, Patricia Farnes and Deborah Nash. Bloomington: Indiana University Press, 1990. 300-34.

Minor, Vernon Hyde. *Art history's history*. Englewood Cliffs, NJ: Prentice Hall, 1994.

Moffat, Pamela Dawson. "Lilla Cabot Perry." *Dictionary of Women Artists*. Ed. Delia Graze. Vol. 2. London and Chicago: Fitzroy Dearborn Publishers, 1997. 1092-95.

Morantz-Sanchez, Regina Markell. *Sympathy and science: women physicians in American medicine*. New York: Oxford University Press, 1985.

"Moritz Heymann." *Allgemeines Lexikon der bildenden Künstler*. Ed. Hans Vollmer. Vol. 17. Leipzig: E.A. Seemann, 1924. 33.

Morton, Rosalie Slaughter. *A woman surgeon; the life and work of Rosalie Slaughter Morton*. New York: Frederick A. Stokes, 1937.

Muller, Margarette. "Some Groans and Warnings from Abroad." *Wellesley Magazine* April 1895: 368-72.

Nagler, Jörg. "From Culture to *Kultur*. Changing American Perceptions of Imperial Germany, 1870-1914." *Transatlantic Images and Perceptions: Germany and America Since 1776*. Eds. David E. Barclay and Elisabeth Glaser-Schmidt. Cambridge, England: Cambridge University Press, 1997. 131-54.

Nauck, E. Th. *Das Frauenstudium an der Universität Freiburg i. Br.* Freiburg i. Br.: Verlag Eberhard Albert Universitätsbuchhandlung, 1953.

Neumann, Daniela. *Studentinnen aus dem Russischen Reich in der Schweiz (1867-1914).* Die Schweiz und der Osten Europas. Ed. Carsten Goehrke. Vol. 1. Zurich: Hans Rohr, 1987.

Nieriker, May Alcott. *Studying Art Abroad, and How to do it Cheaply.* Boston: Roberts Brothers, 1879.

O'Brien, Sharon. *Willa Cather: The Emerging Voice.* New York: Oxford University Press, 1987.

Olmstead, Andrea. *Juilliard: a history.* Urbana: University of Illinois Press, 1999.

Oxtoby, John C. "Anna Pell Wheeler." *Bryn Mawr Alumnae Bulletin* Summer 1966: 22.

Palmieri, Patricia Ann. *In Adamless Eden: the community of women faculty at Wellesley.* New Haven, CT: Yale University Press, 1995.

Parrott, Sara Foose. "Expatriates and Professionals: The Careers in Italy of Nineteenth-Century American Women Writers and Artists." Diss. George Washington University, 1988.

Petteys, Chris. *Dictionary of Women Artists: An International Dictionary of Women Artists Born Before 1900.* Boston: G.K. Hall, 1985.

Pieschel, Bridget Smith, and Stephen Robert Pieschel. *Loyal daughters: one hundred years at Mississippi University for Women, 1884-1984.* Jackson: University Press of Mississippi, 1984.

Pollack, Barbara. *The Collectors: Dr. Claribel and Miss Etta Cone.* Indianapolis, IN: Bobbs-Merrill, 1962.

Putnam-Jacobi, Mary. "Woman in Medicine." *Woman's Work in America.* Ed. Annie Nathan Meyer. New York: Henry Holt and Co., 1891. 139-205.

"Raffael Schuster-Woldan." *Allgemeines Lexikon der bildenden Künstler.* Ed. Hans Vollmer. Vol. 30. Leipzig: E.A. Seemann, 1936. 346.

Randall, Mercedes M. *Improper Bostonian: Emily Greene Balch.* New York: Twayne, 1964.

Rasmussen, Cecilia. "A Medical Pioneer's Many Firsts." *Los Angeles Times* February 3, 1997, sec. B: 3.

Rayner-Canham, Marelene F., and Geoffrey W. Rayner-Canham. *A Devotion to Their Science: Pioneer Women of Radioactivity.* Montreal: McGill-Queen's University Press, 1997.

Reid, Doris Fielding. *Edith Hamilton: An Intimate Portrait.* New York: W. W. Norton, 1967.

Remme, Karl. *Das Studium der Ausländer und die Bewertung der ausländischen Zeugnisse.* Berlin, 1932.

Richards, Dell. *Superstars: twelve lesbians who changed the world.* New York: Carroll & Graf, 1993.

Richardson, Brenda. "Dr. Claribel and Miss Etta." *Dr Claribel & Miss Etta: the Cone Collection of the Baltimore Museum of Art.* Eds. Brenda Richardson, William C. Ameringer and Baltimore Museum of Art. Baltimore, MD: Baltimore Museum of Art, 1985. 45-161.

Rion, Hanna. *The Truth About Twilight Sleep.* New York: McBride, Nast and Co., 1915.

Rogers, Dorothy. *Oswego: fountainhead of teacher education; a century in the Sheldon tradition.* New York: Appleton-Century-Crofts, 1961.

Rogger, Franziska. *Der Doktorhut im Besenschrank; das abenteuerliche Leben der ersten Studentinnen am Beispiel der Universität Bern.* Bern: eFeF Verlag, 1999.

Rohner, Hanny. *Die ersten 30 Jahre des medizinischen Frauenstudiums an der Universität Zürich, 1867-1897.* Zurich: Juris Druck, 1972.

Ross, Dorothy. "The Development of the Social Sciences." *The Organization of Knowledge in Modern America, 1860-1920.* Eds. Alexandra Oleson and John Voss. Baltimore, MD: The Johns Hopkins University Press, 1979. 107-38.

Rossiter, Margaret W. "Doctorates for American Women, 1868-1907." *History of Education Quarterly.*Summer (1982): 159-83.

———. *The Emergence of Agricultural Science: Justus Liebig and the Americans, 1840-1880.* New Haven, CT: Yale University Press, 1975.

———. "Geology in Nineteenth-Century Women's Education in the United States." *Journal of Geological Education* 29 (1981): 228-32.

———. "Women Scientists in America before 1920." *American Scientist* 62 (1974): 312-23.

———. *Women Scientists in America: Struggles and Strategies to 1940.* Baltimore, MD: The Johns Hopkins University Press, 1982.

———. "'Women's Work' in Science, 1880-1910." *Isis* 71 (1980): 381-98.

Rothman, Patricia. "Genius, Gender and Culture: Women Mathematicians of the Nineteenth Century." *Interdisciplinary Science Reviews* 13.1 (1988): 64-72.

Rubin, Lewis P. "Gladys Rowena Henry Dick." *Notable American Women: The Modern Period.* Eds. Barbara Sicherman, Carol Hurd Green, Ilene Kantrov, et al. Cambridge, MA: Belknap Press of Harvard University Press, 1980. 191-92.

Rubinstein, Charlotte Streifer. *American Women Artists: from Early Indian Times to the Present.* Boston: G. K. Hall, 1982.

S., E. "Ein geselliger Abend bei den Berliner Studentinnen." *Frauen-Rundschau* (1904): 1465.

Sander, Kathleen Waters. "Trailblazer for women doctors." *The Baltimore Sun* March 4, 2001, sec. C: 1 and 4.

Saunders-Lee, Sara L., ed. *In Memoriam. Mrs. Erminnie A. Smith.* Boston: Lee and Shepard, 1890.

Scarborough, Elizabeth, and Laurel Furumoto. *Untold Lives: The First Generation of American Women Psychologists.* New York: Columbia University Press, 1987.

Schäfer, Volker, Uwe Jens Wandel, and Irmela Klöden. *USA – Universität Tübingen. Die Amerika-Beziehungen der schwäbischen Landesuniversität im Kaleidoskop. Eine Ausstellung...aus Anlass des 200. Jahrestages der amerikanischen Unabhängigkeit.* Werkschriften des Universitätsarchiv Tübingen. Reihe 2. Vol. 7. Tübingen: Universitätsarchiv Tübingen, 1976.

Schlüter, Anne. *Pionierinnen - Feministinnen - Karrierefrauen? Zur Geschichte des Frauenstudiums in Deutschland.* Frauen in Geschichte und Gesellschaft. Vol. 22. Pfaffenweiler: Centaurus, 1992.

Schmidt, Paul. "Vorgeschichte und Anfänge des Frauenstudiums in Bonn." *Bonn und das Rheinland. Beiträge zur Geschichte und Kultur einer Region.* Eds. Manfred van Rey and Norbert Schloßmacher. Bonn, 1992. 545-69.

Schneiderman, Jill S. "Rock Stars. A Life of Firsts: Florence Bascom." *GSA Today* (1997): 8-9.

Schnurrenberger, Regula. "Ein Überblick." *Ebenso neu als kühn: 120 Jahre Frauenstudium an der Universität Zürich.* Eds. Katharina Belser, Gabi Einsele, Rachel Gratzfeld, et al. Zurich: eFeF Verlag, 1988. 195-211.

Schucking, Engelbert L. "Jordan, Pauli, Politics, Brecht, and a Variable Gravitational Constant." *Physics Today* (1999): 26-31.

Servos, John W. *Physical Chemistry from Ostwald to Pauling: The Making of a Science in America.* Princeton, NJ: Princeton University Press, 1990.

Shaffer, Karen A. *Maud Powell, Pioneer American Violinist.* Ames: Iowa State University Press, 1988.

Sherzer, Jane B. "Women at the German Universities." *The Nation* 58 (1894): 116-17.

Sicherman, Barbara, and Alice Hamilton. *Alice Hamilton, a life in letters.* Cambridge, MA: Harvard University Press, 1984.

Siebel, Johanna. *Das Leben von Frau Dr. Marie Heim-Vögtlin der ersten Schweizer Ärztin, 1845-1916.* Leipzig: Rascher and CIE. A.G., 1928.

Siegel, Patricia Joan, and Kay Thomas Finley. *Women in the Scientific Search: An American Bio-bibliography, 1724-1979.* Metuchen, NJ: Scarecrow Press, 1985.

Simkhovitch, Mary Melinda Kingsbury. *Neighborhood; my story of Greenwich House.* 1st ed. New York: Norton, 1938.

Singh, Simon. *Fermat's Enigma.* New York: Anchor Books, 1997.

Slonimsky, Nicolas. *Baker's Biographical Dictionary of Musicians.* 1900. 7th ed. New York: Schirmer Books, 1984.

Smith Class Yearbook. Northampton, Massachusetts: Smith College, 1900.

Smith College Alumnae Biographical Register, 1871-1935. Northampton, MA: Smith College, 1935.

Smith, David Eugene. "Mary Hegeler Carus, 1861-1936." *The American Mathematical Monthly* 44.5 (1937): 280-83.

"Smith, Theodate Louise." *Obituary Record of Graduates of Yale University 1910-1915.* New Haven, CT: Yale University Press, 1915. 712.

Smith-Rosenberg, Carroll. "Mary Kingsbury Simkhovitch." *Notable American Women, The Modern Period.* Eds. Barbara Sicherman, Carol Hurd Green, Ilene Kantrov, et al. Cambridge, MA: Belknap Press of Harvard University Press, 1980. 648-51.

Solomon, Barbara Miller. "Emily Greene Balch." *Notable American Women, The Modern Period.* Eds. Barbara Sicherman, Carol Hurd Green, Ilene Kantrov, et al. Cambridge, MA: Belknap Press of Harvard University Press, 1980. 41-45.

Stadler-Labhart, Verena. *Rosa Luxemburg an der Universität Zürich (1889-1897).* Zurich: Verlag Hans Rohr, 1978.

Stephenson, C. Todd. "Dialogue: 'Integrating the Carol Kennicotts': Ethel Puffer Howes and the Institute for the Coordination of Women's Interests." *Journal of Women's History* 4.1 (1992): 89-113.

Stern, Madeleine B. *We the Women: Career Firsts of Nineteenth-Century America.* New York: Schulte, 1963.

Stokowski, Olga Samaroff. *An American Musician's Story.* New York: W.W. Norton & Co., 1939.

Stranges, Anthony N. "Friedrich Bergius and the Rise of the German Synthetic Fuel Industry." *Isis* 75 (1984): 643-67.

Stump, Doris. "Zugelassen und ausgegrenzt." *Ebenso neu als kühn: 120 Jahre Frauenstudium an der Universität Zürich.* Eds. Katharina Belser, Gabi Einsele, Rachel Gratzfeld, et al. Zurich: eFeF Verlag, 1988. 15-28.

Super, Charles W. "German Degrees." *The Nation* 98 (1914): 9.

Swinnerton, A. C. "Edward Orton, Geologist." *Science* 89 (1939): 373-78.

Swinth, Kirsten N. "Painting Professionals: Women Artists and the Development of a Professional Ideal in American Art, 1870-1920." Diss. Yale University, 1995.

Talbot, Marion, and Lois Kimball Mathews Rosenberry. *The History of the American Association of University Women, 1881-1931.* Boston: Houghton Mifflin, 1931.

Tarbell, Ann T., and D. Stanley Tarbell. "Dr. Rachel Lloyd (1839-1900): American Chemist." *Journal of Chemical Education* 59.9 (1982): 743-44.

_____. "Helen Abbott Michael: Pioneer in Plant Chemistry." *Journal of Chemical Education* 59.7 (1982): 548-49.

Thomas, M. Carey. "President Thomas's Address." *Bryn Mawr Alumnae Quarterly* January 1908: 44-48.

_____. "The President's Address." *Bryn Mawr Alumnae Quarterly* November 1910: 178-92.

Thomson, Elizabeth H. "Esther Pohl Lovejoy." *Notable American Women, The Modern Period.* Eds. Barbara Sicherman, Carol Hurd Green, Ilene Kantrov, et al. Cambridge, MA: Belknap Press of Harvard University Press, 1980. 424-26.

Tiburtius, Franziska. *Weibliches Schaffen und Wirken: Erinnerungen einer Achtzigjährigen.* 1923. Berlin: C. A. Schwetschke & Sohn, 1929.

Tobies, Renate. "'Aller Männerkultur zum Trotz': Frauen erwerben den Doktortitel in Mathematik." *Barrieren und Karrieren. Die Anfänge des Frauenstudiums in Deutschland. Dokumentationsband der Konferenz "100 Jahre Frauen in der Wissenschaft" im Februar 1997 an der Universität Bremen.* Eds. Elisabeth Dickmann and Eva Schöck-Quinteros. Vol. 5. Schriftenreihe des Hedwig-Hintze-Instituts Bremen. Berlin: trafo verlag dr. wolfgang weist, 2000. 231-52.

———. "Zum Beginn des mathematischen Frauenstudiums in Preußen." *Gesch. Naturwissenschaftler, Techniker und Mediziner* 28.2 (1992): 151-72.

Tobies, Renate, and Fritz König. *Felix Klein.* Biographien hervorragender Naturwissenschaftler, Techniker und Mediziner. Vol. 50. Leipzig: Teubner, 1981.

Traver, Hope. *Bulletin of the Class of 1896. Vassar College* (1919): 30.

———. "The Institute of International Education." *Mills Quarterly* 4 (1921): 25-27.

Tribolet, H. *Historisch-Biographisches Lexikon der Schweiz.* Vol. 6. Neuenburg: Administration des Historisch-Biographischen Lexikons der Schweiz, 1931.

Tucker, Cynthia Grant. *Prophetic Sisterhood. Liberal Women Ministers of the Frontier, 1880-1930.* Boston: Beacon Press, 1990.

Turnbull, Pauline. *May Lansfield Keller: Life and Letters, 1877-1964.* Verona, VA: McClure Press, 1975.

Verzeichnis zürischer Universitätsschriften 1833-1897. Zurich: Verlag der Kantonsbibliothek, 1904.

W., R. "Professor Munsterberg's Lecture." *Wellesley College News* May 16, 1906: 1-2.

Wade, Louise C. "Florence Kelley." *Notable American Women, 1607-1950.* Eds. Edward T. James, Janet Wilson James, Paul S. Boyer, et al. Vol. 2. Cambridge, MA: Belknap Press of Harvard University Press, 1971. 316-19.

Ward, Patricia Spain. "Anna Elizabeth Broomall." *Notable American Women 1607-1950.* Eds. Edward T. James, Janet Wilson James, Paul S. Boyer, et al. Vol. 1. Cambridge, MA: Belknap Press of Harvard University Press, 1971. 246-47.

Waste, Henrie (Ettie Stettheimer). *Philosophy: An Autobiographical Fragment.* New York: Longmans, Green and Co., 1917.

Webster, Helen L. "University Education for Women in Germany." *Wellesley Magazine* March 1895: 292-94.

Weidig, Adolf. "Observations Upon Present Musical Life in Germany." *Studies in Musical Education History and Aesthetics. Papers and Proceedings of the Music Teachers' National Association.* Northwestern University, Evanston, IL: Music Teachers' National Association, 1909. 30-51.

Welsh, Lilian. *Reminiscences of thirty years in Baltimore.* Baltimore, MD: The Norman Remington Co., 1925.

Wendehorst, Alfred. *Geschichte der Friedrich-Alexander-Universität Erlangen-Nürnberg 1743-1993.* Munich, 1993.

Wertheimer, Jack. "The 'Ausländerfrage' at Institutions of Higher Learning: A Controversy Over Russian-Jewish Students in Imperial Germany." *Leo Baeck Institute Yearbook* 27 (1982): 187-215.

Wheeler, Candace. *Yesterdays In a Busy Life.* New York: Harper and Brothers, 1918.

Whiting, Sarah F. "The Experiences of a Woman Physicist." *Wellesley College News* January 9, 1913: 1-6.

———. "Heidelberg." *Courant (Wellesley)* February 22, 1889: 3.

Wood, Elizabeth A. *Crystals and light; an introduction to optical crystallography.* Princeton, NJ: Published for the Commission on College Physics [by] Van Nostrand, 1964.

Woodress, James. *Willa Cather: A Literary Life.* Lincoln: University of Nebraska Press, 1987.

Wright, Margaret R. "Marcella O'Grady Boveri (1863-1950): Her Three Careers in Biology." *Isis* 88 (1997): 627-52.

UNATTRIBUTED JOURNAL AND ALUMNAE ARTICLES

The Fortnightly Philistine (Bryn Mawr) November 9, 1900: 13.

The Lantern (Bryn Mawr) 1895: 99.

The Nation 62 (1896): 456.

The Nation 66 (1898): 303-04.

The Nation 69 (1899): 94.

The Nation 69 (1899): 486-87.

The Nation 84 (1907): 467.

The Nation 85 (1907): 33.

The Nation 85 (1907): 350.

Wellesley Magazine March 1897: 335-36.

"Adah Blanche Roe." *Bulletin Goucher College* 2.2 (1914-1915): 61.

"Als Professorin der Chemie." *Dokumente der Frauen* 5 (1901): 161.

"The Alumnae." *Bryn Mawr Alumnae Quarterly* June 1908: 76.

"The Alumnae ['01]." *Bryn Mawr Alumnae Quarterly* October 1908: 57.

"Alumnae Notes." *The Fortnightly Philistine (Bryn Mawr)* December 22, 1899: 15.

"Alumnae Notes [1897]." *Fortnightly Philistine (Bryn Mawr)* December 22, 1899: 15.

"Alumnae Notes." *Goucher Kalends* 25 (1914): 223.

"Alumnae Notes." *Kalends (Goucher)* November 1899: 55.

"Alumnae Notes." *Kalends (Goucher)* November 1909: 43-46.

"Alumnae Notes." *Kalends (Goucher)* March 1911: 189-91.

"Alumnae Notes." *Kalends (Goucher)* January 1914: 110-13.

"Alumnae Notes." *Wellesley College News* October 10, 1901: 3-4.

"Alumnae Notes." *Wellesley College News* February 20, 1902: 1-2.

"Alumnae Notes." *The Wellesley College News* March 21, 1906: 6.

"Alumnae Notes." *Wellesley College News* April 24, 1907: 7.

"Alumnae Notes." *Wellesley Magazine* May 1894: 438-40.

"Alumnae Notes." *Wellesley Magazine* October 1897: 34.

"The American Women's Table. Zoological Station at Naples. 1914-1915." *Wellesley College News* November 19, 1914: 7.

"Anna P. Youngman, Former Post Writer." *Washington Post* February 17, 1974.

"Anna Sophie Weusthoff." *Bulletin Goucher College* 2.2 (1914-1915): 52.

"Annina Periam." *Goucher Kalends* March 1909: 21.

"Aus wissenschaftlichen Berufsständen." *Zürcher Wochen-Chronik* 1908: 141.

"Berlin Gets Warm and Society Flees." *New York Times* June 28, 1914, sec. 3: 2.

"Class Notes." *Bryn Mawr Alumnae Bulletin* Fall 1973: 26.

"College Notes." *Wellesley College News* October 21, 1903: 3.

"Collegiana: Resident Fellows for the Year 1901-02." *The Lantern (Bryn Mawr)* June 1902: 93.

"Commencement." *Goucher Kalends* June 1914: 283.

"The Contributors' Club." *The Atlantic Monthly* 44 (1879): 788-91.

"The crowding of Russian students." *The Nation* 85 (1907): 231.

"Dr. Ladd-Franklin, Educator, 82, Dies." *New York Times* March 6, 1930: 23.

"Dr Mary Hogue, Anatomist, was 78." *New York Times* September 13, 1962: 37.

"Dr. M. E. Maltby, Long at Barnard." *New York Times* May 5, 1944: 19.

"Dr. Peebles Gets Honorary Degree From Goucher College." *Pasadena Star News* June 25, 1954.

"Editorial." *Wellesley Magazine* December 1895: 151-52.

"Education for Women in Germany." *The Nation* 75 (1902): 107-08.

"Faculty Notes." *Goucher Kalends* May 1912: 261.

"Fellowships." *Bryn Mawr Alumnae Quarterly* April 1909: 9.

"Fifty Years of Vassar." *The Nation* 101 (1915): 487.

"Foreign Students in Berlin." *New York Times* October 9, 1901: 1.

"Foreign Students in Prussia." *New York Times* February 27, 1898: 19.

"German Campaign to Exclude Aliens." *New York Times* November 22, 1908, sec. III: 4.

"Graduate Scholarships." *Bryn Mawr Alumnae Quarterly* June 1911: 78.

"Helen A. Merrill of Wellesley, 85." *New York Times* May 3, 1949: 25.

"Here and There with the Alumnae." *Bryn Mawr Alumnae Quarterly* June 1913: 51.

"Hope Traver." *Bulletin of the Class of 1896. Vassar College* (1911): 15.

"Hope Traver." *Decennial Bulletin of the Class of 1896. Vassar College* (1906): 9.

"Hope Traver." *Vassar College Alumnae Directory* (1939): 76.

"Hope Traver." *Vassar '96. Fiftieth Reunion, 1896-1946* (1946): 28-29.

"Ida H. Hyde, Pioneer." *Journal of the American Association of University Women.*Fall (1945): 42.

"Ida Henrietta Hyde." *School and Society* 62 (1945): 154.

"In Memoriam." *Bryn Mawr Alumnae Quarterly* January 1913: 210.

"Johnetta Van Meter." *Goucher Kalends* March 1909: 8.

"Julia W. Snow: In Memoriam." *The Smith Alumnae Quarterly.*November (1927): 66.

"Mary A. Willcox of Wellesley, 97." *New York Times* June 7, 1953: 84.

"May L. Keller." *Goucher Kalends* March 1909: 20.

"Miriam Pasley." *Mississippi State College Alumnae Quarterly* (1926): 5.

"Miss Orr, 93, is Grateful at Newest MSCW Tribute." *The Commercial Appeal* October 21, 1954.

"Mt Holyoke's Amy Hewes, wage pioneer, dies at 93." *The Boston Globe (evening)* March 25, 1970.

"Music." *The Nation* 97 (1913): 318-19.

"News from the Campus." *Bryn Mawr Alumnae Quarterly* 1912: 35.

"News from the Classes." *Bryn Mawr Alumnae Quarterly* April 1913: 16.

"News from the Faculty and Staff." *Bryn Mawr Alumnae Quarterly* November 1911: 128.

"News Notes." *Wellesley College News* February 18, 1915: 7.

"One Woman's Germany." *New York Times* September 2, 1915: 8.

"Our Outlook." *Courant (Wellesley)* December 14, 1888: 3.

"Pioneer Psychologist was Teacher in KHS." *Sentinel (Keene, N.H.)* November 2, 1950.

"President's Report (Wellesley College)." 1921. 6-7.

"Resident Fellows for the Year 1904-1905." *The Lantern (Bryn Mawr)* 1904: 80.

"Reunion of Class of 1909." *Goucher Kalends* June 1914: 290.

Rev. of *An American Girl in Munich. The Nation* 81 (1905): 83.

Rev. of *Die Darstellung der Anbetung der heiligen drei Könige in der toskanischen Malerei von Giotto bis Lionardo. The Nation* 74 (1902): 253.

"Review of Our Slavic Fellow Citizens." *Bryn Mawr Alumnae Quarterly* April 1911: 37-38.

"The Sarah Berliner Research Fellowship for Women." *Wellesley College News* 12.12 (1911): 1.

"State College for Women Loses a Valuable Instructor." *The Commercial Appeal* May 18, 1913.

"University Education of Women." *New York Times* January 19, 1891: 5.

"Wellesley College." *The Courant (Wellesley)* September 21, 1888: 1.

"The Woman's Medical College." *New York Times* February 28, 1870: 4.

"Women as Doctors." *New York Times* November 8, 1874: 6.

"Women's Medical College – New Graduates." *New York Times* March 26, 1873: 5.

"Women's Uphill Fight in Germany." *New York Times* June 5, 1904, sec. 3: 4.

Index

About the Author

SANDRA L. SINGER is Associate Professor of German at Alfred University.